AFRICA SHOOTS BACK

Alternative Perspectives in
Sub-Saharan Francophone African Film

AFRICA SHOOTS BACK
Alternative Perspectives in Sub-Saharan Francophone African Film

Melissa Thackway

Indiana University Press
BLOOMINGTON

James Currey
OXFORD

David Philip
CAPE TOWN

First published in 2003 in the United Kingdom by
James Currey Ltd
73 Botley Road
Oxford OX2 0BS

in North America by
Indiana University Press
601 North Morton Street
Bloomington, Indiana 47404-3797

and in South Africa by
David Philip
an imprint of New Africa Books (Pty) Ltd
99 Garfield Road
Kenilworth, Cape Town

Manufactured in Great Britain

British Library Cataloguing in Publication Data
Thackway, Melissa
    Africa shoots back : alternative perspectives in
    sub-Saharan francophone African film
    1. Motion pictures - Africa, French-speaking - History
    2. Motion pictures - Africa, Sub-Saharan - History 3. Africa,
    French-speaking - In motion pictures 4. Africa, Sub-Saharan
    - In motion pictures
    I. Title
    791.4'3'0967

ISBN 0-85255-577-6 (James Currey cloth)
ISBN 0-85255-576-8 (James Currey paper)

Library of Congress Cataloging-in-Publication Data
A catalog record for this book is available from the Library of Congress

ISBN 0-253-34349-6 (Indiana cloth)
ISBN 0-253-21642-7 (Indiana paper)

Contents

List of Photographs, Stills & Posters

Acknowledgments

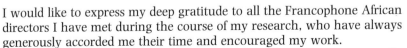

I would like to express my deep gratitude to all the Francophone African directors I have met during the course of my research, who have always generously accorded me their time and encouraged my work.

Many thanks to Annabel Thomas and Andrée Davanture at the former ATRIA offices in Paris, and to Jeanick Le Naour at the French Ministry of Foreign Affairs' Cinémathèque Afrique for their warm welcome, support, and help in gaining access to many of the Francophone African films necessary for my research.

I would also like to thank the British Academy for enabling me to travel to the Pan-African Festival of Film and Television in Ouagadougou, Burkina Faso, in 1995.

Special thanks to my PhD supervisor, Wendy Everett, for her unfailing support, patience, and invaluable comments. Thanks too to Mike Witt and Anna-Louise Milne for their advice and help, and to Philippe Gautreau for editing the French appendixes.

And finally, a very special thanks to my parents, my daughter Zélie, and my partner, Xavier, for all their support and encouragement over the years.

Introduction

Sub-Saharan Francophone African directors have produced a plethora of fascinating films ever since their countries first gained independence in the early Sixties. Many of these films have yet to receive adequate recognition in the West despite the fact that Francophone African directors have clearly appropriated a medium denied to them under colonial rule. Films from the sub-Saharan Francophone African countries, most of which are situated in West Africa, demonstrate that local filmmakers use film's representational capacities to produce a range of alternative, challenging images of the continent and its people. Individual directors have developed a variety of film styles that draw on universal film techniques as well as African narrative and artistic traditions to forge exciting new cinematic codes.

This book aims to give these films the serious critical attention they deserve. Fascinated by the continuing and often contentious cultural links between France and its former African colonies and/or French-speaking spheres of influence[1] – ties that are most clearly embodied here by the French film funding programmes set up to assist Francophone African film after decolonisation – the book will consider exactly how Francophone Africa's directors have approached a medium so 'compromised' by its Western origins and legacy of demeaning images of the continent. It will thereby consider how filmmakers have tried, in the words of the pioneering Senegalese filmmaker Ousmane Sembene, to 'see, feel, and understand [themselves] through the mirror of film'.[2]

Given the many ways in which these filmmakers' images challenge existing representations of Africa, it is vital to examine exactly how Francophone African filmmakers have chosen to represent themselves and their people through film. It is important that audiences and critics who are often unfamiliar with the rich and heterogeneous cultures found in Africa should be willing to let their own cultural norms, viewpoints and cinematic habits be challenged by the filmic practices that have emerged in Francophone Africa. These need to be treated on their own terms, hence the importance placed in this study on situating these films in their specific social, cultural and political contexts, in order to help audiences appreciate and evaluate them.

Before going any further, it is important to clarify the two potentially contentious terms already used here: 'Francophone' and 'African film'. References to 'Francophone', 'Anglophone', or 'Lusophone' Africa, which

1 Films from the Democratic Republic of the Congo (DRC, ex-Zaire) are, for example, included in this book. Whilst formerly a Belgian colony, it has always maintained the same close economic, political, and cultural ties with France as the former French colonies due to its official use of the French language. Filmmakers from the DRC thus benefit from the same French funding networks as the Francophone West African filmmakers and belong to the same pan-African filmmaking bodies.

2 Cited in Françoise Pffaf, *The Cinema of Ousmane Sembene, A Pioneer of African Film* (Westport, Connecticut: Greenwood Press, 1984), p 11.

Introduction

describe the sub-Saharan African countries in terms of their 'official' languages originally imposed by the colonial powers, have been challenged for continuing to position contemporary Africa in relation to its relatively short colonial heritage. Kenyan writer Ngugi wa Thiong'o has argued that this tendency demeans African languages and encourages Africans to identify with the former colonial powers, reinforcing neo-colonial subordination.[3] The term 'Francophone' has also been accused of oversimplifying and distorting the complex linguistic realities of the region by implying that the French language is dominant when it is in fact only fluently used by a relative minority of the population (predominantly urban and educated).

This linguistic issue is, unsurprisingly, reflected in the region's films. Although referred to as 'Francophone' African films by virtue of their directors' geographic/national descent, the majority of these works are rarely French-language films. French is frequently present in these works, however, where it often denotes a speaker's social status. French usage is also especially common in films from Côte d'Ivoire, Cameroon and the Democratic Republic of the Congo (ex-Zaire) where French remains a common mode of communication.

References to 'Francophone' Africa are more pertinent in socio-cultural terms. They reflect the real convergences in the region that arise from common linguistic ties, a shared legacy of French colonisation, and the inheritance of convergent political and economic structures and continuing (neo-colonial) ties with France. The term 'Francophone' here reflects this common socio-political heritage, rather than suggesting the primacy of France/French as a cultural reference in any form.

Secondly, certain African filmmakers have rejected the term 'African cinema' in recent years. Some directors, including the Burkinabè, Idrissa Ouedraogo, have argued that the term is often used to stigmatise works from the continent, encouraging Western viewers and critics to see them as a homogeneous entity. It is argued that this not only erases the diversity of these films and the cultures they reflect, but also imposes a restrictive (Western) vision of what African films should be like.[4]

Other filmmakers continue to defend the term 'African cinema', arguing that it reflects the specific historic, cultural and geographic context in which African filmmaking was born and continues to develop. This context is particularly significant in that it distinguishes African cinema from its American or European counterparts in many ways and can be seen as one of its defining characteristics. Another Burkinabè filmmaker, Gaston Kaboré, denies that the term necessarily negates plurality and diversity: 'Le "cinéma africain" n'est pas un terme pour uniformiser. Il évoque le contexte dans lequel évolue ce cinéma, où un continent essaye de se réapproprier son image' ['"African cinema" is not a term that aims to standardise. It evokes the context in which this cinema is evolving, in which a continent is trying to reappropriate its image'].[5]

The use of the term 'African cinema' here in no way ignores diversity

3 See Ngugi wa Thiong'o, *Decolonising the Mind: The Politics of Language in African Literature* (London & Nairobi: James Currey/Heinemann, 1986).

4 See Frédéric Richard, 'Entretien avec Idrissa Ouedraogo: Pour une alliance des différences', *Positif*, 385, Mars 1993, p 29.

5 Public meeting with Gaston Kaboré organised by the Formation Internationale Culture and the Parc de la Villette. Paris, 7 April 1997. Kwame Appiah has also addressed this question in relation to African literature. He also justifies using the term, insisting that African writers face 'a constellation of problems and projects ... not often found outside Africa: a recent colonial history, a multiplicity of diverse subnational indigenous traditions, a foreign language whose metropolitan culture has traditionally defined the 'natives' by their race as inferior ... *It is because they share this problematic that it makes sense to speak of a Nigerian writer as an African writer*'. See *In My Father's House: Africa in the Philosophy of Culture* (New York & Oxford: Oxford University Press, 1992), pp 76–77.

and plurality, but evokes the film and/or filmmaker's origin and the film's setting, and recognises the films' often shared socio-cultural pre-occupations.

Rather than duplicating existing surveys of African film, this book focuses on dominant and repeated preoccupations that emerge in sub-Saharan Francophone African films.[6] As discussions with the directors themselves reveal, the questions of representation, identity and voice constitute central preoccupations in their work, providing constants in an otherwise heterogeneous cinematic landscape. While recognising that these concerns are not exclusive to the realm of Francophone African filmmaking, the book will demonstrate that they have taken on particular significance in the specific postcolonial context in which Francophone African filmmaking has emerged and continues to evolve.

Irrespective of their individual artistic styles, motivations, or goals, Francophone African filmmakers have come up against issues that are intrinsic to film as a medium of visual representation. These have become all the more urgent in a postcolonial context in which artists and intellectuals struggle to repair the damage done by the colonial regime and its efforts to impose a completely alien culture. Like other subjugated and/or marginalized groups, Francophone African filmmakers face questions of how to represent a people hitherto denied the right to represent themselves and whose image – and by extension identities – have systematically been misrepresented in Western texts. As Francophone African filmmakers have 'come to voice' and reclaimed control of their own images and art forms, they have seized the opportunity to provide alternative representations of their disfigured selves. Film has become a means of constituting and interrogating the diverse and multiple identities by which people define themselves and their realities. It is clear that identities need to be understood here as multifarious and changing, rather than homogeneous and static, and as being defined and articulated rather than simply reflected in film – a theme developed further in Chapter 2. It is important to bear in mind that different readings by different audiences, whether Western, African, rural, urban, male or female, also influence the reception and understanding of these identities. Questions of spectatorship contribute to the construction of the filmic identities discussed, although it is beyond the range of this work to analyse that influence in depth.

As they challenge the stereotypes and the absences of Western images of Africa, filmmakers have sought to formulate more representative and empowering images and to foreground their own concerns. The Cameroonian filmmaker Jean-Marie Teno has confirmed the importance of appropriating visual representation, arguing, for example, that:

> It is ... important for people to be able to speak about themselves, so that they don't just become objects or settings ... It is important for individuals to be able to identify with people who are like them, to be able to see their reality on the screen, so that they feel that they exist, especially for people who have been colonised, because colonisation amounts to reducing the other to a non-being.[7]

6 See note on related reading (p 210).

7 Interview with the author. Paris, August 1997. The original French text of all the interviews with the author cited throughout the book can be found in the appendices.

Gaston Kaboré has also insisted that the cinema has a key role to play in helping Africans to 'dialoguer avec leur propre image, à pouvoir se voir et se projeter' ['dialogue with their own image, to be able to see and project themselves'].[8] Representation, identity and the quest to reclaim a proud and independent voice have clearly become key issues in this context. This preoccupation has been all the more reinforced by many Francophone African filmmakers' open embracing of political issues and their responsibility as artists, as shown throughout this book.

As Francophone African film has developed in such a singular and highly influential context, it is vital to define this and to consider the ways in which it has informed the agendas of, and conferred certain characteristics on these films. This contextualisation will help non-African audiences to understand and appreciate what are often culturally unfamiliar works. It will also illustrate the different ways in which the issues discussed manifest themselves in Francophone African film, and explore individual works in the light of these representation and identity questions.

This book will also position the region's filmmaking in relation to the Western imagery that its filmmakers have reacted against. However, the commonalties and shared preoccupations in the work of these filmmakers who come from highly divergent backgrounds and cultural spheres, can never be placed above their pronounced diversities and individual creative agendas.

The films selected for analysis reflect a degree of personal preference, but have above all been chosen for their representativeness, filmic qualities, and pertinence to the issues discussed. This selection was determined after having viewed at least 80% of the entire corpus of Francophone African films at the time of writing, and thus provides a balanced sample of the range and diversity of the films being produced in the region. The intrinsically related context, content and form of the films in question are analysed: context is shown to influence directorial intent, and thus form and content. Whilst the methodology is primarily empirical, analysis is set within the context of a range of theories of a multi-disciplinary scope. These theories include contemporary film criticism, African cultural studies, feminist theory, and especially the representation and postcolonial theories developed by numerous critics and scholars, including Stuart Hall, bell hooks, Ella Shohat, Teshome Gabriel, Kobena Mercer, Clyde Taylor, and Kwame Appiah. Although not always specifically related to the African and/or film contexts, these theories provide relevant insights into the questions explored in Francophone African film. Prime importance is also accorded to the filmmakers' own discourses, which help to illuminate their understanding of film and its role in Africa.

The book is divided into six chapters, the first of which places Francophone African filmmaking in its wider international context and considers whether or not the existing, predominantly Western, critical models can be usefully applied to African film. By examining the origins of contemporary critical theory, the chapter argues that certain critical

8 Public meeting with Gaston Kaboré, op. cit.

legacies are indeed problematic when applied to this field. It also demonstrates how the universal application of Western paradigms can produce misguided or reductive readings of culturally divergent works by failing to recognise their own specific influences and models. At the same time, the chapter situates Francophone African cinema in its own postcolonial context, thereby helping to ascertain why the questions of representation, identity, voice and alterity have become so predominant, even if they are not necessarily exclusive to it. In the light of these findings, the chapter concludes by proposing more appropriate critical paradigms.

With this more appropriate critical framework, Chapter 2 explores the central questions of representation, identity and voice. By examining the political climate in which Francophone African film was born and by considering how the cultural debates of the independence era have informed filmmaking agendas and conceptions of the role of filmmaker, this chapter considers exactly why the representation and identity issues have taken on such importance in Francophone African film. In order to help ascertain how Francophone African directors have used film to express their own cultural identities, the chapter proceeds to discuss the ways in which the African continent and its people have, and continue to be, portrayed in Western imagery, thereby again highlighting the particular urgency of representational questions. Like other hitherto marginalized or silenced groups, Francophone African filmmakers have used the film medium to redefine and reaffirm their identities and cultures, thereby restoring a polyvocal African voice and perspective that challenges the hegemony of the West. Bearing in mind that identities themselves are multiple and evolving, the chapter looks at how these representations have diversified to reflect Francophone Africa's own changing contexts.

Chapter 3 examines the cultural context in which Francophone African filmmaking has evolved. This helps to provide the necessary cultural framework for evaluating the ways in which filmmakers have integrated their own cultural codes – and particularly the oral traditions – into the universal film medium as they have appropriated and articulated their identities and realities on the screen. By defining both these determining cultural forms, the characteristics of the artistic environment and role of the artist in Francophone Africa, this chapter also explores the crucial question of how its filmmakers view their own role, demonstrating how this conception in turn reflects their specific cultural environment.

The remaining chapters focus on three recurrent thematic concerns that clearly illustrate representation and identity questions. Chapter 4 looks at the frequently articulated notions of memory and history, establishing the ways in which they are central to the quest to redefine cultural identity, as directors challenge the West's former erasure and denial of African history and African interpretations of that history. After briefly examining Western attitudes to Africa's past, the chapter examines a range of films that explore memory or history from a specifically African point of view, narrating episodes and providing filmic perspectives absent from Western historiographies. The chapter also considers how several of these films introduce a highly personal voice and deliberately transgress generic boundaries as directors find ways of recovering local memory. These 'counter-memory' films, which clearly play an important role in the reappropriation of representation, also perpetuate one of the key functions of many Francophone African oral cultures, namely interrogating the past to inform the present and future.

Chapter 5 examines the numerous Francophone African films set in Europe, that evoke the immigrant experience. Although shot outside the continent, these films deal with the same kinds of representational and identity questions found in locally based films, and thus reflect similar filmmaking styles and concerns. Given European stereotypes and/or the complete absence of African immigrant characters in European films, this chapter particularly considers how Francophone African directors working in Europe have used their images to foreground the concerns and conditions of immigrant communities, again revealing an alternative African perspective in their films. The chapter also considers how these images have evolved over the years as socio-cultural conditions have changed. Finally, it discusses where these films stand in the French cinematic landscape and considers what this says about the situation of African immigrants in France, and attitudes towards them.

Finally, Chapter 6 looks at both female and male directors' frequent focus on women's issues in their films. Such films again challenge the absence, silence, or misrepresentation of female African characters in Western films. Drawing on the work of non-Western and black feminist writers, whose insights provide pertinent theoretical and critical frameworks for the discussion of representations of women from a different cultural zone, the chapter highlights the striking ways in which many Francophone African filmmakers have formulated empowering representations of African women. The films in question are shown to foreground African women's frequently overlooked pivotal role in daily and political struggles, and/or to provide critiques of traditions that continue to oppress African women. The work of three prominent Francophone African women filmmakers is highlighted, illustrating how they foreground women's perspectives and voices, creating images and styles that challenge both Western and patriarchal authority and preconceptions about African women.

All of the films discussed in Chapters 4, 5, and 6 thus provide examples of what is referred to in the title as the Francophone African directors' alternative perspectives. These are shown to challenge existing images and establish African viewpoints and representations firmly in the crucial process of reappropriating and articulating individual identity, thereby reclaiming a proud and independent voice. But first, it is important to outline the development and evolution of Francophone African film to provide a general background to these issues.

Development and evolutions: a brief history of sub-Saharan Francophone African film

Filmmaking did not develop in sub-Saharan Francophone Africa until after independence. The colonial regime was guided by the logic of what the French authorities referred to as their *mission civilisatrice*, which aimed to 'civilise' Africans by imposing French cultural modes and norms. Naturally, it preferred to import French films that reinforced perceptions of French moral and technological 'superiority' than to teach or encourage Africans to make their own films. As early as 1900, the Lumière brother's *L'Arroseur arrosé* was thus first publicly screened in Dakar and a network of cinemas showing imported films was set up in the French African colonies after the First World War.

Not content simply to promote its own films, the colonial authorities soon actively sought to discourage the development of any African filmmaking activity, apparently recognising the potentially subversive nature of film (discussed more fully in Chapter 2). The 1934 Laval Decree, for example, which stipulated that all film projects set in the French African colonies be submitted for prior approval, allowed the colonial authorities to contain or eliminate any films likely to counter or challenge official colonial discourse. Senegalese filmmaker Paulin Soumarou Vieyra was thus refused permission to shoot in Senegal in the Fifties and the authorities used the decree to censor the rare anti-colonial French films of the time, including Réné Vautier's *Afrique 50* (1950) and Alain Resnais and Chris Marker's *Les statues meurent aussi* (1953). Despite the authorities' manifest reluctance, a few individual French filmmakers, including René Vautier and the ethnographic filmmaker Jean Rouch, did take the personal initiative of familiarising Africans with the medium by employing them as technicians and actors on their films set in West Africa.[9] Furthermore, a handful of French West Africans, including Vieyra, managed to attend film school in Paris.

It was only when the colonies finally gained independence, and Franco-African cultural, political and economic ties were sealed through cooperation agreements, that the French authorities significantly changed their attitude. Manthia Diawara suggests that this change was prompted by the combined pressure of the African film students in France, individual French filmmakers, and by the film historian Georges Sadoul who, in the Fifties, repeatedly attacked France's lack of development of filmmaking in the colonies.[10] More cynically, it also undoubtedly reflected the realisation that the French film industry would also directly benefit from backing Francophone African film. Under the auspices of the new Ministry of Cooperation and its Bureau du Cinéma set up in 1963 and run by Jean-René Débrix, France thus began to play an instrumental and often controversial role, providing technical and financial assistance to Francophone African filmmakers, part of which was obligatorily spent in paying French technicians and French post-production services.

9 Directors Oumarou Ganda (Niger) and Safi Faye (Senegal), for example, both started filmmaking after acting in Rouch's films *Moi, un noir* (France, 1957) and *Petit à Petit* (1968) respectively.

10 See Manthia Diawara, *African Cinema: politics and culture* (Bloomington & Indianapolis: Indiana University Press, 1992).

7

Introduction

11 Burkina Faso is a notable exception. Successive Burkinabè governments have quite exceptionally chosen to back their national cinema. In 1970, for example, the government nationalised the Burkinabè cinemas. The two French distribution companies, SECMA (Société d'Exploitation Cinématographique Africaine) and COMACICO (Compagnie Africaine Cinématographique Industrielle), who jointly controlled 80% of the film distribution market in Francophone West Africa, flooding its cinemas with cheap, trashy films and refusing to screen the emerging African productions for fear that audiences demand different types of film, retaliated by shutting down their Burkinabè distribution circuits. This starved the country of films and forced the government to negotiate a compromise that allowed them to continue to operate in the country. The Burkinabè government also set up its own state distribution company in 1970, now known as the SONACIB (la Société Nationale du Cinéma Burkinabè). The SONACIB continues to support Burkinabè filmmakers by buying their films and by levying a tax on foreign films shown in the country which is then used to help finance local films. The SONACIB also finances the DIPROCI (Direction de la production cinématographique) whose film equipment and technicians are employed on shoots throughout West Africa. Private initiatives have unfortunately proven to be short-lived due to insufficient demand. Burkina Faso's state structures have nonetheless provided the country with the most efficient film structures and facilities in West Africa.

12 Cited in Oliver Barlet, *African Cinemas: Decolonizing the gaze*, translated by Chris Turner (London: Zed Books, 2000), p 263.

13 Whilst *Borom Sarret* was the first film shot by an African filmmaker in sub-Saharan Africa, directors had sporadically been making films in North Africa since the Twenties, and Egyptian

Whilst the modalities of the diverse subsidies available to Francophone African filmmakers have continually evolved over the years, the basic funding structures still exist today and France remains one of the main financiers of African film. Although this undeniably helps filmmakers work in countries where local state and private backing remains virtually non-existent, such technical and financial aid has nonetheless frequently been attacked for perpetuating neo-colonial dependence on France and promoting films that conform to French expectations of what should constitute an African film.[11] Olivier Barlet highlights this tendency, citing Frédéric Bontems, director of the Ministry of Cooperation's Bureau des Médias: 'It's not for us to dictate their subjects to [African] filmmakers ... but to emphasize the risk of marginalization they run in terms of funding if they don't meet the expectations of their audiences more fully' – audiences clearly being defined here first and foremost as Western.[12] Similarly, the inter-ministerial 'Fonds Sud' subsidy to Francophone African filmmakers was, until very recently, only awarded to films located principally in Africa, a condition which effectively determined where African filmmakers were allowed to direct their cinematic gaze.

On the eve of Independence, a handful of Francophone Africans mostly attracted to filmmaking by their own film-going experiences, and who had received film training in European film schools in some cases, finally began making films in the spirit of the liberation movement. Senegalese directors Paulin Soumarou Vieyra, Mamadou Sarr, and the Groupe africain du cinéma made the first Francophone African film, *Afrique sur Seine*, in Paris in 1955. In 1963, Senegalese filmmaker Ousmane Sembene, the doyen of black African cinema, made *Borom Sarret*, the first film actually shot in Francophone West Africa. Its thematic activism and social realist style immediately set a trend that would remain predominant in Francophone African film circles for many years to come.[13]

In the Sixties and Seventies, several key tendencies marked emergent Francophone African film. Many films showed deep political commitment in reflection of the committed socio-political climate of the time. As shall be discussed in Chapter 2, the decolonisation era was indeed a time of widespread theorising on the identities and future of the newly independent African nations which stimulated a general questioning of values and mores. As the films discussed in this book indicate, such debates clearly informed a range of art forms, including film. Influenced by the liberation theories developed in Africa and elsewhere, Africa's first generation of filmmakers thus formulated their own responses to the new nations' pressing questions of identity, representation, and liberation. Adopting the traditional community-based role of the artist (discussed further in Chapter 3), sub-Saharan Francophone Africa's filmmakers tended to situate their work in the socio-educational vein, using their films to reflect upon the key issues of the time, thereby fully assuming their political responsibility as artists. At the same time, directors sought to foreground a sense of African dignity that widely disrupted existing Western literary and filmic representations. Right from its formative years, Francophone African filmmaking was characterised by its frequently overt desire to educate and to contribute to socio-political debate.[14]

This committed stance and the categorical embracing of a sense of responsibility as artists – both of which are clearly stipulated in the filmmakers' joint Algiers and Niamey Charters of 1975 and 1982 – can, of course, be found in other film movements around the world, some of which have undoubtedly influenced certain African filmmakers. Several filmmakers claim, for example, to have taken inspiration from the Italian neo-realism of the Forties and Fifties and the way its directors addressed socio-political questions in their films, focused on the lives and realities of 'ordinary' people, and used lightweight film equipment, natural settings, and non-professional actors. Other directors have also cited the politically committed style and concerns of Brazil's Cinema Nuovo or early social realism in the USSR as sources of inspiration that provided alternatives to mainstream Euro-American models. It must also be pointed out that certain European and American independent filmmakers became similarly politicised in the Sixties and Seventies when leftist, anti-capitalist politics, the rise of the women's movements, and the anti-war sentiment fuelled by the colonial wars in Vietnam and Algeria radicalised the Euro-American socio-political climates.

Many Francophone African films in the Sixties and Seventies consequently focused on the social issues facing the new nations. They provided critiques of archaic and oppressive traditions, or attacked the rapacious and corrupt new ruling elites and their neo-colonial behaviour. Films by Ousmane Sembene (*Mandabi*, 1968; *Xala*, 1974), or the Malian filmmakers Souleymane Cissé (*Baara*, 1977; *Finyé*, 1982), Cheick Oumar Sissoko (*Nyamanton*, 1986; *Finzan*, 1989), and Adama Drabo (*Ta Dona*, 1991), for example, all address issues of social injustice, corruption, and oppression in a predominantly realist vein that prioritises their politically strident content. This overt political vein has not necessarily excluded stylistic innovation nor the adopting and adapting of oral narrative codes, however, as shall be discussed in Chapter 3. This social realist style, which is sometimes referred to as the 'Sembenian' school after its earliest practitioner, can still also be identified in a number of contemporary films. Recent examples include Clarence Delgado's *Niiwam* (Senegal, 1991), which is in fact adapted from a short story by Sembene, or short films such as Issa Serge Coelo's *Un taxi pour Aouzou* (Chad, 1994) *Daresalam* (2000), and Mahamat Saleh Haroun's *Maral Tanié* (Chad, 1994).

In the late Sixties and Seventies, several other major filmmaking trends and styles began to emerge. In his first film *Soleil O* (1969), the French-based, Mauritanian filmmaker Med Hondo adopted a radically politicised and experimental style. This blending of genres and registers is clearly marked by both the non-linear, fragmentary constructions found the West African oral traditions, and by the deconstructionism of Brechtian theatre. Hondo's generic blending and politically strident voice still find an echo in the later works of other politically vociferous

13 (cont.) film production really took off in the inter-war years. See Roy Armes & Lizbeth Malkmus, *Arab & African Film Making* (London & New Jersey: Zed Books, 1991), pp 28– 32.

14 Teshome Gabriel rightly points out that the distinctions between 'educational' and 'entertainment' film are subtle. Hollywood productions, which are usually considered the epitome of commercial entertainment film, for example, most definitely impart clear ideological messages, just as more the educational and sometimes didactic African films also entertain. See *Third Cinema in Third World: The Dynamics of Style and Ideology* (Ann Arbor, Michigan: U.M.I Dissertation Services, 1979), p 205.

filmmakers, such as the Cameroonian Jean-Marie Teno, who also combines formal experimentation and overt political reflection.

In the same period, the late Senegalese filmmaker Djibril Diop Mambety introduced a new and original style of filmmaking that was formally experimental, highly symbolic and at times surreal. Although not as politically strident as much of the filmmaking of the time, Diop Mambety's films remain socially conscious, containing their own form of reflection and critique. The 'popular' urban influences of cartoons, music and the B movies and Westerns commonly screened in African towns blend with more 'traditional' Senegalese influences in an up-beat and hybrid intertextual collage. This has clearly influenced the work of a number of later filmmakers, who have adopted Diop Mambety's playful, resolutely urban, and often-symbolic style. Some such films include Amet Diallo's *Boxulmaleen!!* (Senegal, 1991), José (Zeka) Laplaine's *Le Clandestin* (Democratic Republic of the Congo, 1996), which contains clear references to Diop Mambety's *Badou Boy* (1970), and Jean-Pierre Bekolo's *Quartier Mozart* (Cameroon, 1992).

Finally, the Seventies also saw the development of a more humorous, light-hearted vein of filmmaking that has frequently been attacked by other filmmakers for being too commercial and vacuous. The Cameroonian filmmaker Daniel Kamwa's *Pousse Pousse* (1975) was one such pioneering film, combining light-hearted comedy and social critique in a way that made it a West African box office hit at the time. Ivoirian director Henri Duparc has continued to develop this commercial, humorous film style in his films *Bal Poussière*, 1988; *Rue Princesse*, 1993; and *Une Couleur Café*, 1997, all of which similarly deal with 'serious' social issues, such as polygamy, prostitution, AIDS, and immigration, through caricature and comedy, which has also been popular with audiences throughout West Africa. Duparc defends the 'seriousness' of this form, arguing that 'l'humour est une arme puissante pour faire passer des idées ... on rit, mais après on réfléchit ... Si je caricature, c'est pour avoir le courage de nous regarder tels que nous sommes pour nous corriger' ['humour is a powerful means of getting ideas over ... people laugh, but think later ... If I use caricature, it is to give us the courage to look at ourselves as we really are so that we can mend our ways'].[15] Other filmmakers have similarly integrated humour and satire into their works without necessarily adopting a more commercial style, notably Ousmane Sembene in *Xala* (1974), Cheick Oumar Sissoko in *Guimba* (1995), Adama Drabo in *Taafe Fanga* (1997), Jean-Pierre Bekolo in *Quartier Mozart* (1992) and *Le Complot d'Aristotle* (1997), José (Zeka) Laplaine in *Le Clandestin* (1996), and Burkinabè director Fanta Regina Nacro in *Un Certain Matin* (1991), *Puk Nini* (1995), and *Le Truc de Konaté* (1997).

Since the late Seventies, Francophone African film has continued to diversify, giving rise to numerous forms that defy simplistic categorisation. A notable evolution is the way in which film is increasingly used to interrogate Africa's past to inform and reflect upon the present and the future (as will be shown more fully in Chapter 4). Similarly, there is an

15 Oliver Barlet, 'Entretien avec Henri Duparc', *Africultures*, 12, novembre 1998, pp 16 & 17.

increasing tendency to blend Africa's diverse cultural traditions and film, both in stylistic and thematic terms. Ousmane Sembene was again one of the first directors to use his films to reflect upon historical subjects and periods in his films *Emitaï* (1971), *Ceddo* (1976), and *Camp de Thiaroye* (1988), before returning to contemporary issues again in *Guelwaar* (1992) and *Faat Kine* (2001). This tendency to focus on the past became increasingly diversified and developed in the Eighties as filmmakers consciously embraced and re-evaluated African cultural forms in an effort to develop their own culturally specific film styles. Oumarou Ganda's *L'Exilé* (Niger, 1980), for example, is not only set in the past, foregrounding both West African traditional oral cultures and the place of the spoken word, but is also actually structured like a West African tale. Other filmmakers have similarly juxtaposed oral narrative and other local cultural forms in their works, exploring the predominantly rural environments of the past. Many such works are strikingly infused with African mythology and supernatural beliefs. The filmmakers tend to re-evaluate and reclaim such beliefs rather than systematically condemning them in the name of modernity, as was often the case in earlier Franco-phone African film. Frequently dubbed 'return to the source' films, such works by filmmakers as diverse as Idrissa Ouedraogo, Gaston Kaboré, Souleymane Cissé and Cheick Oumar Sissoko, have tended to abandon the didacticism of the earlier social realist films whilst nonetheless continuing to address politically committed issues. This more coded, often allegorical approach confounds the criticisms of certain critics and other African filmmakers that the 'return to the source' films have lost their political edge, or that directors have become more concerned with satisfying Western desires for exoticism than with addressing African agendas. (This view is discussed in more detail in Chapters 2 and 3.) Whilst it is true that certain Western spectators have failed to understand the political nature of such films, the messages are still there. These films have apparently not sacrificed the interests of audiences in Africa, where they have often been huge popular successes.[16] The 'return to the source' films' move away from political didacticism can be better understood as reflecting Africa's changing socio-political climates. As many of the new African leaders have often proved themselves to be ineffective, dictatorial and corrupt, earlier liberation euphoria has given way to increasing disillusionment. This has stimulated a more complex analysis of Africa's situation, an interrogation of earlier ideals, and more acceptance of Africa's own share of responsibility in this situation; such changes are echoed in Francophone African filmic discourses. In cultural terms, these changing styles are also symptomatic of individual filmmakers' desire to experiment further. They seek to develop the narrative and aesthetic pleasure of film as they explore traditional narrative forms and focus more on the quality of the images themselves. The 'return to the source' films' emphasis on orature and its stylistic influences also remains strong today, as can be seen in recent films such as Dani Kouyaté's *Keïta! L'Héritage du Griot* (Burkina Faso, 1995) and *Sia, le rêve du python* (Burkina Faso, 2001), Cheick Oumar Sissoko's *Guimba* (Mali, 1995), and

16 Reliable box office figures are only available in Burkina Faso where the SONACIB closely monitors ticket sales. SONACIB figures compiled in March 1997 confirmed that the so-called 'return to the source' films, such as Gaston Kaboré's *Wend Kuuni* and *Buud Yam*, Idrissa Ouedraogo's *Yaaba*, *Tilaï*, and *Samba Traoré*, Souleymane Cissé's *Yeelen*, Dani Kouyaté's *Keïta!*, and Cheick Oumar Sissoko's *Guimba*, were all hugely popular in Burkina Faso. Similarly, Adama Drabo's *Taafe Fanga* and Sissoko's *Guimba*, whose entrance figures were compiled by the directors themselves as there is no compre-hensive monitoring system in Mali, also reveal that both films, and particularly *Taafe Fanga*, were huge popular successes in Mali. Neither film found a distributor in France, which confounds the argument that such films cater more to Western audiences.

Introduction

Adama Drabo's *Taafe Fanga* (Mali, 1997), which will be explored more fully in Chapter 3.

The Nineties have confirmed this diversification and what Ella Shohat has aptly referred to as the continuing emergence of 'collisionary tendencies', or the mixing of different styles and generic forms in Francophone African film.[17] Many filmmakers have increasingly experimented with styles and forms, making it impossible to class their work in a single category. Earlier genres, such as social realism, have also continued to be explored and developed, as can be seen in a range of contemporary films including Clarence Delgado's *Niiwam* (Senegal, 1991), or Pierre Yameogo's *Laafi* (Burkina Faso, 1990) and *Silmandé* (1998).

Directors have also moved beyond the filmic and even geographic and linguistic boundaries of predominantly West African film production. Some have challenged the definitions of documentary and fiction, for example, as shall be seen in a number of films discussed in Chapter 4. Others, including Jean-Pierre Bekolo and Idrissa Ouedraogo, have moved outside the habitual West African or European spaces to shoot their recent films: *Le Complot d'Aristotle* (1997) and *Kini and Adams* (1997) were made in Zimbabwe with English-speaking South African and Zimbabwean actors. Joseph N Kumbela similarly shot his latest short film *Feizhou Laona*i (DRC-China, 1998) in China, exploring the issues in Europe-based immigration films that will be referred to in Chapter 5.

Films by a number of younger directors particularly reflect the cultural synthesis that characterises both the contemporary African urban centres, where African and international cultural values coexist, and the rural areas which are increasingly susceptible to urban influences. The Nineties have thus seen a spate of fast, hybrid, urban films that freely juxtapose popular cultural forms of all origins with more specifically African cultural references. Jean-Pierre Bekolo's *Quartier Mozart* is one such example. Snappy, urban youth culture cohabits with traditional supernatural beliefs in a fast, quirky style reminiscent of the early Spike Lee whom many younger filmmakers, including Bekolo and Kumbela, cite as an influence. In Bouna Medoune Seye's *Bandit Cinéma* (Senegal, 1993), Bekolo's *Le Complot d'Aristotle*, and Gahité Fofana's *Immatriculation Temporaire* (France-Guinea, 2000) the directors focus on petty criminality in the urban environment, often drawing freely on the cinematic references of the second-rate action and karate films shown in Africa's urban cinemas. Fofana's short film *Temèdy* (Guinea, 1994), his feature *Immatriculation Temporaire*, and Bouna Medoune Seye's *Saï Saï By* (Senegal, 1995) develop experimental styles that strikingly capture the twilight ambiance and moods of the bars and clubs frequented by an urban youth facing the problems of AIDS, drugs, poverty, and unemployment. José (Zeka) Laplaine's *Macadam Tribu* (DRC-Mali, 1996) focuses on the lives and concerns of a group of young city-dwellers, integrating popular sports, such as boxing, into the heart of the narrative. These and other recent urban films, such as Drissa Touré's *Haramuya* (Burkina Faso, 1995), all tend to develop their different characters' multiple stories in a fragmented style that reflects the chaotic

17 Speaking at the British Film Institute's *Screen Griots Conference*, London, 9-10 September, 1995.

pace of life in African urban centres. Such works also feature contemporary music forms, abandoning the kinds of reservations towards foreign cultural influences shown in earlier Francophone African works. They uninhibitedly embrace the reality that contemporary African culture is hybrid, international, and continually evolving. This younger generation of filmmakers no longer seems to be interested in pitting the 'modern' against the 'traditional' within the African space, accepting that the two coexist. This shift in attitudes no doubt mirrors the directors' changing preoccupations and frequently international life-styles. As many directors become more culturally internationalised, often travelling and/or living between Europe and Africa, some have also tended to move away from the earlier, typically African conception of the filmmaker's socially responsible role. Several of these younger Europe-based Francophone African directors have even begun to make films in Europe which might be better classed as 'European', although this movement remains embryonic. Examples include Isabelle Boni-Claverie's first short film *Le Génie d'Abou* (France, 1997); Mama Keita's still unreleased *Le 11e commandement* (France, 1997); Jean Odoutan's *Djib* (France-Benin, 2000); *Mama Aloko* (France-Benin, 2002), and Zeka Laplaine's *(Paris : xy)* (France-DRC, 2001).

This survey would not be complete without a brief mention of the production and distribution of Francophone African film.[18] Mention has already been made of the financial and technical backing France has traditionally granted to Francophone African filmmakers through a range of subsidies allocated by the Agence de la Francophonie and the Ministry of Cooperation, which became part of the Ministry of Foreign Affairs in 1999.[19] Added to these is a system of bilateral co-production agreements that allow filmmakers from certain countries to apply for France's Centre National de la Cinématographie (CNC) grants. Although France's pre- and post-production aids undoubtedly inject vital finances into film in the Francophone countries, it is important to emphasise that the French film industry also benefits from these agreements. Funding is frequently granted on the condition that post-production work is carried out in France, that a French co-producer work on the film, and/or that a specified number of French technicians be employed on the shoot. This funding also raises the problematic question of whether Francophone African directors are forced to adapt their work to suit the tastes of their Western financiers. Other non-African funding sources include the European Union, and an increasingly rare handful of television channels such as France's Canal +, Britain's Channel 4, and Germany's ZDF.

Alternative funding sources on the continent are limited, and very few states are willing to subsidise their own filmmakers. Burkina Faso is the notable exception. Filmmakers have little other choice than to seek funding elsewhere. The relative paucity of alternative funding sources means that filmmakers often spend many years and much energy trying to get their projects financed. Once they have managed to scrape together enough resources to shoot, directors are often forced to double up as producer and/or distributor due to the lack of willing and reliable

18 Other studies give more detailed descriptions of the conditions of production and distribution, for example part 3 of Oliver Barlet, *African Cinemas: Decolonizing the gaze*; and Manthia Diawara, *African Cinema: politics and culture*.

19 The 1999 merger signalled the end of the Ministry of Cooperation's system of direct aids to feature and short films made by directors from the Ministry's predominantly French-speaking African partner countries. Indirect ADCSud (Appui au développement des cinemas du Sud) subsidies are now available to feature films only, made by directors from the entire 'zone de solidarité prioritaire' ['priority solidarity zone'], which has considerably intensified competition.

13

collaborators. The absence of national, or global West/Francophone African film industries and infrastructures does not make production any easier. Directors are forced to work with European laboratories whose high costs may represent up to a third of a total film budget. In recent years, however, there have been increasing moves to use Zimbabwean and South African film facilities. More and more directors have started setting up their own production companies and have collaborated on each other's projects in order to become less dependent on European producers. Idrissa Ouedraogo produced Cheick Oumar Sissoko's *Guimba*, for example, and Pierre Yameogo produced Dani Kouyaté's *Keïta!*

Distribution also remains a fundamental problem for African filmmakers. Whilst they are not alone in this respect, as all independent directors worldwide face similar difficulties in a market totally dominated by mainstream American productions, the problems are often more acute in Africa. Very few African cinemas are actually in working order. Those that are generally belong to foreign distributors who prefer to block-book cheap foreign films that have already recouped their production costs on international circuits. This explains the predominance of second- and third-rate action films, karate films, and 'Bollywood' productions in Africa. As a result, directors who succeed in finishing their films can rarely get them screened in their own countries. As cinema owners and distributors seem reluctant to change the standard film fare made available to African audiences, directors are frequently forced to tour their films themselves if they want them to be seen. The frequent claims that local audiences are not interested in African films are confounded by the rare distribution figures available, which reveal that African films tend to do well at the box office when they actually get shown.

Given the limited number of cinemas throughout Africa, directors obviously have to target other markets in order to recover their costs. The only real market in Africa is South Africa where television stations have shown a new interest in Francophone African productions since the end of apartheid. Outside Africa, African cinema is often confined to the international festival circuit. It occasionally finds limited release in art-house cinemas, but rarely receives adequate promotion and media coverage. Like other non-mainstream productions, African films appear to be at the mercy of fashions and fads, although this is difficult to quantify with precision. It can be noted, however, that whilst directors like Idrissa Ouedraogo and Souleymane Cissé generated much interest and adulation in Europe in the Eighties, winning prizes at Cannes and other major festivals and registering substantial box-office figures in France, the same festivals have tended to 'snub' equally strong Franco-phone African films in recent years. Selections indicate that there is now a marked preference for Asian cinema. High-quality films such as Cheick Oumar Sissoko's *Guimba*, which won the main 'Etalon de Yennenga' award at the Ouagadougou Pan-African Film and Television Festival (FESPACO) in 1995, and Adama Drabo's *Taafe Fanga* (winner of the FESPACO Special Jury Prize in 1997, and selected at Cannes and other prestigious international festivals) have not managed to find commercial distributors in France despite France's policies to encourage the (albeit limited) distribution of independent, non-Western films. Filmmakers are battling on, devoting energy to promoting their work, as can be seen from initiatives taken by individual filmmakers and collectives such as the FEPACI, or the Guilde africaine des réalisateurs et producteurs (The African Guild of Directors and Producers). Set up in 1999 by a group of African filmmakers living in France, notably Jean-Marie Teno, Fanta Régina Nacro, and Balufu Bakupa-Kanyinda; the Guild tries to make filmmakers collectively more visible and to share their experience and skills. In recent years some directors have also started using digitial video to cut productions costs. Zeka Laplaine's *(Paris : xy)*, for example, was shot on digital video before being transferred onto film. In spite of such efforts, production and distribution remain urgent problems for Francophone African film.

1 Critical Paradigms

Outsiders only see what they know.
African proverb.

*'If you wish to know who I am,
If you wish me to teach you what I
know,
Cease for the while to be what you are
And forget what you know.'*
Tierno Bokar, sage of Bandiagara.[1]

1 Cited in Amadou Hampaté Bâ , 'The
Living Tradition', in Joseph Ki-Zerbo
(ed.), *General History of Africa vol. I*
(Paris: UNESCO, 1981), p 203.

2 Such contrasts echo the racist essen-
tialism predominant in much Western
thought since the Enlightenment that
was later echoed by the Senegalese
writer-president Léopold Sédar Senghor's
much criticised assertion that 'l'emotion
est nègre, comme la raison hellène'
['emotion is black, just as reason is
Hellenic']. Léopold Sédar Senghor, 'Ce
que l'homme noir apporte' in *Liberté I*
(Paris: Editions du Seuil, 1964), p 24.

3 Chinua Achebe, *Arrow of God*, in *The
African Trilogy* (London: Picador, 1988),
p 365. (*Arrow of God* first published in
1964).

Before examining the questions of representation and identity, it is
important to acknowledge the exteriority of my own critical gaze. It is
also necessary to consider whether the dominant modes of film theory
and criticism developed and based on the filmmaking traditions and
practices of the West can usefully be applied to Francophone African film.

Whilst Francophone African film has developed in a specific geograph-
ical and socio-cultural zone, and reflects this, its filmmaking practices
have naturally not developed in a cultural vacuum cut off from all other
exogenous artistic and critical traditions. Francophone African filmmakers, many of whom have studied film and/or lived in various European countries, are familiar with Euro-American film, its images of
Africa, and its critical debates in a way that is rarely reciprocated in the
West. It could be argued that it is almost impossible to separate Francophone African filmmaking traditions from the questions and concerns of
dominant film theory and criticism. The kind of essentialist dualism that
seeks to contrast so-called 'First World theory' and 'Third World practice'
serves Francophone African filmmakers badly by ghettoising their work.[2]
Until recently, Western hegemony and imperialism left little space for
alternative viewpoints and articulations. However unsavoury this
historical reality might be, the centrality of Western critical theory makes
it difficult to ignore. The increasingly prolific non-Western critical voices
that have emerged since the Sixties' and Seventies' liberation
movements started to emancipate a range of populations; such groups
continue to challenge and deconstruct the hegemonic position of these
Western critical paradigms. Whilst this has provoked a diversification of
artistic critical practices and forced scholars to recognise that Western
modes of thought cannot always be satisfactorily applied to non-
Western art forms, the legacy of Eurocentrism remains prevalent. It is
therefore still important to examine Western critical tools closely and to
acknowledge both their partialities and limitations. This will particularly
help to avoid the kinds of misinterpretations and shortsighted readings
of culturally unfamiliar film texts that have often transpired when
Western scholars unquestioningly project their own critical paradigms
onto non-Western art forms. Rather than simply assuming that existing
Western critical paradigms can adequately highlight the specificities and
unfamiliar sensibilities of Francophone African film, this chapter will
attempt to establish a more appropriate critical framework, bearing in

mind the words of the Nigerian writer Chinua Achebe, 'The world is like a Mask dancing. If you want to see it well, you do not stand in one place'.[3]

The problematic legacy of Eurocentrism

Whilst it would be reductive to dismiss all Western critical theory as irrelevant to African film, it is important to recognise that certain attitudes and assumptions have at times been carried over from other, more problematic periods of critical thought and thus risk obfuscating our readings. This is certainly the case with what can be described as the lingering tendency to Eurocentrism in much critical work.

Critics such as Sylvia Wynter or Clyde Taylor have already highlighted this Eurocentric tendency in Western critical theory, tracing it back to Europe's eighteenth-century Enlightenment period, when beliefs in the universal validity of Europe's civilisations and critical modes were established.[4] Whilst it is common for groups to take their own culture as a reference when evaluating what is unfamiliar to them, the Eurocentrism that became established in nineteenth-century thought is particularly problematic for the study of African film given, as is now widely acknowledged, that this attitude was originally couched in notions of racial superiority. European cultural norms such as Universalism, Reason and Humanism were not simply taken as normative and therefore exportable, but were later used to justify the belief that European civilisations could and should be universally imposed through empire-building projects. These functioned by excluding, silencing, or explicitly reviling all that deviated from these established 'norms'. Any group not conforming to and/or having alternative thought systems or modes of reasoning was thus negatively marked as 'other', as representing all that Europeans were not.[5]

The Enlightenment era also saw the emergence of the 'scientific' investigation and classification of racial difference. This laid the foundations of the nineteenth-century 'scientific' racialist doctrines that castigate non-European peoples. Whilst it is not within the scope of this book to discuss the beliefs in the physical and intellectual superiority of white people expounded at the time by thinkers such as Hume, Kant, Hegel, Frobenius, Voltaire, Montesquieu, Diderot, and Gobineau, these beliefs in a racial hierarchy that situated black people at the bottom of the human ladder in both aesthetic and intellectual terms have had long-lasting repercussions for the African continent and its people and the way in which they have been perceived in Western thought.[6] The firm belief in scientific reason and the subsequent assumption that the written word was the only measure of humanity and authority has, for example, often encouraged Western scholars to see black Africans, whose culture was predominantly (but not exclusively) oral, as intellectually inferior and thus incapable of contributing to learning and the arts, blinding Westerners to the richness and diversities of Africa's multiple civilisations.[7]

4 See, for example, Sylvia Wynter, 'Africa, the West and the Analogy of Culture: the Cinematic Text After Man' (paper given at BFI *Screen Griots Conference*, London 9-10 September 1995), Clyde Taylor, 'Black Cinema in the Post-aesthetic Era', in Jim Pines & Paul Willemen (eds.), *Questions of Third Cinema* (London: BFI, 1989), pp 90-110, and 'We Don't Need Another Hero: Anti-Theses on Aesthetics', in Mbye B. Cham & Claire Andrade-Watkins (eds.), *Blackframes: Critical Perspectives on Black Independent Cinema* (Cambridge, Massachusetts: The MIT Press, 1988), pp 80-85.

5 V.Y. Mudimbe has commented on the way in which positioning the 'other' has helped define the 'self', pointing out that, since the slave trade, Africans have been classified 'according to the grid of Western thought and imagination, in which alterity is a negative category of the Same ... The African has become not only the Other who is everyone else except me, but rather the key which, in its abnormal differences, specifies the identity of the Same'. See *The Invention of Africa: Gnosis, Philosophy and the Order of Knowledge* (Bloomington & Indianapolis: Indiana University Press, 1988), p 12.

6 It is important to remember that these theories continue to resurface in the American and European extreme right-wing today whenever national identities and boundaries are perceived to be in flux and certain groups feel the need to denigrate and distance themselves from others in order to reaffirm their own supposedly 'threatened' identities.

7 The Malian sage Tierno Bokar has identified and attacked this confusion between writing and knowledge, pointing out that, 'Writing is the photograph of knowledge but it is not knowledge itself. Knowledge is the light that is in man'. (Cited by Amadou Hampaté Bâ, in 'The Living Tradition', p 166).

Critical Paradigms

Numerous examples testify to the ways in which the negative marking of and disregard for African culture in the nineteenth century continues to manifest itself today. For example, John D. H. Downing has rightly pointed to the lack of interest prominent critical journals such as the *Cahiers du Cinéma* show for African film compared with other non-European cinemas. Olivier Barlet has referred to the way in which many Western film critics reproach African films for being too slow, while accepting this same internally justified rhythm in Asian films.[8] As the apparent lack of interest and respect for African film shared by Western critics and distributors alike usually bears no correlation to the actual quality of the films themselves, one must assume that it reflects traditional Western prejudices concerning African art and culture. This view is confirmed elsewhere in the arts. It was not until revered modernist artists such as Picasso and the Surrealists acknowledged the influence of African statuary and masks on their own work, for example, that Western art critics first accepted the notion that African art could have an aesthetic, rather than simply ethnographic value, even if the modernists' appraisal was of course formulated very much in Western terms. By suddenly elevating African masks and statutory to the realm of 'high art' – a concept which, as shall be seen later, has no place in traditional African understandings of art – the modernists failed to recognise the equally important ritual functions of these objects, just as earlier ethnographers had failed to appreciate their aesthetic worth. This once again reflects the type of oversight which can arise when non-Western cultural forms are evaluated purely in Western terms.

This tendency continues today, as certain critics persist in taking Western forms as a normative model rather than seeking to understand the non-Western influences at play in culturally unfamiliar texts. Teshome Gabriel has highlighted the way in which many Western film critics are still tempted to position all film movements in relation either to the dominant (Hollywood) model, or to counter-dominant models, such as the European avant-garde.[9] This inevitably posits a reductive binary model whose fixed boundaries automatically situate 'counter-cinemas', such as Francophone African film, in a simply oppositional, reactive role. This encourages critics to overlook the specific identities and other merging influences in these works, thereby foreclosing the possibility of diversity. The way in which some critics have disparagingly read certain popular Francophone African films, such as Henri Duparc's comedy *Bal Poussière* (Côte d'Ivoire, 1988), as simple imitations of mainstream Western cinema, completely fails to consider the various other non-mainstream influences at play in the film. For all its light-heartedness and its overtly commercial nature, *Bal Poussière*'s thematic and satirical registers are far closer to other West African films and narrative traditions than they are to Western cinema. This is immediately apparent if the film is situated in its own cultural context.

Kobena Mercer has similarly pointed to what he identifies as the Eurocentric desire to refer all filmic experimentation to the Euro-American cinematic avant-garde. While affirming that this in itself is not

8 John D.H. Downing, 'Post-Tricolour African Cinema', in Dina Sherzer (ed.), *Cinema, Colonialism, Postcolonialism: Perspectives from the French and Francophone Worlds* (Austin: University of Texas Press, 1996), footnote 3, p 223; Olivier Barlet, 'La critique occidentale des images d'Afrique', *Africultures*, 1, octobre 1997, pp 5–11.

9 Teshome Gabriel, 'Thoughts on Nomadic Aesthetics and the Black Independent Cinema: Traces of a Journey', in Mbye B. Cham & Claire Andrade-Watkins (eds.), *Blackframes: Critical Perspectives on Black Independent Cinema* (Cambridge, Massachusetts: The MIT Press, 1988), pp 62–79.

necessarily problematic, Mercer rightly claims that it does nonetheless testify to 'an underlying anxiety to pin down and categorise a practice that upsets and disrupts fixed expectations and normative assumptions about what "black" films should look like'.[10] This indeed denies the existence of experimentation in non-Western cinemas and again overlooks alternative influences. The common tendency to describe the fragmented and deconstructed narrative of Med Hondo's first film, *Soleil O* (Mauritania, 1969), as 'Godardian', for example, despite the fact that the film was actually shot (but not released) prior to Godard's own late Sixties/Seventies experimentations with Brechtian deconstructionism, clearly illustrates the assumptions Mercer describes. Whilst Hondo was certainly not impervious to contemporary French cinematic influences and had encountered Brecht's ideas when acting in his plays, critics who foreground this aspect of his film language completely ignore the director's own explanation that the fragmented nature of the film's narrative structure is first and foremost characteristic of the West African oral traditions in which digression and multiple, layered narrative threads are common.

Other critics with equally Eurocentric perspectives continue to reductively categorise all non-Western cultural forms as essentially 'other' to Western models. This once again creates an oppositional paradigm that, by confining African culture to this otherness, pre-determines – and thereby limits – expectations of what these forms 'should' or 'should not' be like. Such conceptions of alterity have their foundations in the Humanist philosophies discussed above. Whilst few people in the West would now categorise non-Western populations as 'other' (read: inferior) to the so-called 'civilised' (hu)man, however, Africa is still nonetheless frequently positioned as 'other' to the 'politically sophisticated and economically developed' West.[11]

Perceptions of alterity are, however, always relative. As already seen above, Western ideas about Africa are inevitably more a reflection of our own self-image and perceptions than of African understandings. This makes it all the more important to avoid projecting preconceived, Eurocentric perceptions if we are to remain receptive to African expressions of identity. The failure to do so has led to a range of critical aberrations. Some contemporary Western critics have gone so far as to reject work that does not correspond with their own notions of alterity. Others, whilst embracing the 'other' voices that Western scholarship once suppressed or ignored, assume that these voices must be different, that they must necessarily represent the notions of alterity that the West itself has created. This key issue has been addressed in the writings of the critics and writers bell hooks and Trihn T. Minh-ha. Objecting to the way in which she has often been expected systematically to affirm her ethnic and/or gender identities in her work, Trihn T. Minh-ha has written:

> Now, i am not only given the permission to open up and talk, i am also encouraged to express my difference. My audience expects and demands it; otherwise people would feel as if they have been cheated: We did not come to hear a Third World member speak about the First (?) World, We came to listen

10 Kobena Mercer, 'Diasporic Culture and The Dialogic Imagination: The Aesthetics of Black Independent Film in Britain', in Mbye B. Cham & Claire Andrade-Watkins (eds.), *Blackframes: Critical Perspectives on Black Independent Cinema*, p 51.

11 Worrying stereotypes of 'primitive' African tribes nevertheless still find their way into contemporary Hollywood films, for example in the 1995 film *Ace Ventura: When Nature Calls*.

Idrissa Ouedraogo, Tilaï, 1990. Popular for what Western audiences took to be its 'exotic' images of distant, rural Africa.

(Courtesy of Idrissa Ouedraogo)

to that voice of difference likely to bring us *what we can't have* and to divert us from the monotony of sameness. They ... are in a position to decide what/who is 'authentic' and what/who is not.[12]

This demonstrates the way in which the West still often positions itself as the normative centre. In filmmaking terms, the Francophone African films that have received the most critical acclaim in the West and have registered the highest box-office figures – Souleymane Cissé's *Yeelen* (Mali, 1987), or Idrissa Ouedraogo's *Yaaba* (Burkina Faso, 1987) and *Tilaï* (1990), for example – are those which, often inadvertently, conform to and confirm Western notions of an exotic, fundamentally 'other', pre-colonial Africa. This preoccupation with exotic alterity fails to recognise the vital political messages behind the beautiful images, however, and thus deflects many Western viewers' readings away from the key allegorical issues explored in such films.

Francophone African film directors have also frequently complained that Western producers and distributors reject or criticise their scripts and films for not being African enough, which means that they do not conform to Western conceptions of what is 'African'. Western critics and festivals' unjust disenchantment with African cinema in recent years no doubt reflects the fact, as Olivier Barlet rightly points out, that many films no longer coincide with what Western critics now seem to want from

12 T. Minh-ha Trinh, *Women, Native, Other: Writing Postcoloniality and Feminism* (Bloomington & Indianapolis: Indiana University Press, 1989), p 88.

Africa's filmmakers, namely contemporary, urban productions that chronicle Africa's current geo-political crises. When Francophone African cinema persists, as Barlet puts it, in not conforming to what Westerners want it to be, critics tend simply to write it off *per se*, rather than seeking to understand what those films are trying to portray.[13] At the same time, Francophone African filmmakers, like all independent directors in the world, are also faced with contradictory pressures to conform to the increasingly globally imposed Hollywood cinematic model, which naturally reflects a very narrow creative viewpoint.

The pressure placed on African artists to foreground their 'otherness' in their work risks masking the multiplicity of their identities. Ali Mazrui describes these identities as being marked by at least a triple heritage of 'traditional' African influences, Islamic influences (introduced when the religion started to spread in West Africa in the seventh century), and Western influences (encountered during the slave trade, Christian evangelisation, and colonisation).[14] This plurality needs to be given the chance to express itself unhindered by Western expectations. Similarly, frequent references to a 'timeless' Africa, which can be seen as part of a more general 'heritage mentality' in the West that embraces 'safe' and unchallenging visions of history, are also a Western myth. This denies the rich hybridity of contemporary African cultures in which the hi-tech coexists with calabashes and ritual masks. It is important to recognise cultural difference, therefore, to avoid essentialist notions of 'other'. Michel Foucault makes this clear when he argues that, 'The freeing of difference requires thought ... without dialectics, without negation; thought that accepts divergence ... thought of the multiple – of the nomadic and dispersed multiplicity that is not limited or confined by the constraints of similarity'.[15]

It is thus clear that Western critics need to approach Francophone African cinema with an open-mind, accepting the filmmakers' diversity and recognising that African films will not always fit comfortably into their own critical paradigms. Whilst this has become something of a commonplace in the contemporary 'postmodern' era, the following discussion of the modernism/postmodernism debate serves to reveal that certain Eurocentric tendencies, and not least the continuing habit of unquestioningly – and often misleadingly – projecting Western local cultural concepts onto the non-Western world, continue to prevail.

Postmodernism or postcoloniality?

Western critics' frequent use of the term 'postmodern' to describe more recent Francophone African films, such as Jean-Pierre Bekolo's *Quartier Mozart* (Cameroon, 1992) and *Le Complot d'Aristotle* (1997), Djibril Diop Mambety's *Hyènes* (Senegal, 1991), or Souleymane Cissé's *Yeelen* (Mali, 1987), offers an interesting illustration of continuing Eurocentrism in contemporary critical thought. This tendency is all the more marked given that the postmodern era has heralded a new interest in non-Western texts and influences in the West, causing formerly marginalized

13 Olivier Barlet, 'La critique occidentale des images d'Afrique', p 7.

14 See Ali A. Mazrui, *The African Condition: A Political Diagnosis* (Heinemann: London, 1980). References to a 'traditional' Africa are, of course, problematic, as the term has often been used to connote lack of change in Africa, as shall be seen in more detail in Chapter 3. Here, the term 'traditional' is used simply to refer to cultural customs that existed in Africa prior to contact with Europe, and which were in no way static.

15 Michel Foucault, *Language, Counter-Memory, Practice: Selected Essays and Interviews*, translated by D. F. Bouchard & S. Simon (New York: Ithaca, Cornell University Press, 1977), p 185.

voices to become more centred on the Western cultural stage. If we look closely at the actual characteristics of postmodernism, it soon becomes apparent that the very facets of the African works seen as corresponding with the postmodern traits of the West often have very different significations and implications. These risk being overlooked if they are simply described as 'postmodern'.

The term 'postmodernism' has been so liberally applied to such a wide range of artistic practices in the West since the Seventies that it has become notoriously hard to define. Jean-François Lyotard aptly describes the shift in sensibilities and practices that constitute the 'postmodern condition' as a result of the collapse of the modern era's founding 'grand narratives', including Humanism and Patriarchy.[16] It is clear from its name that postmodernism is intrinsically related to 'modernism', even if only in oppositional terms. It is therefore important to define what we mean by modernism, and to consider whether or not one can talk of modernism in African art before going on to talk about postmodernism.

As the cultural manifestation of the West's modern era, which began in and reflected the rationalisation of the Enlightenment and later saw the advent of democracy and the development of industrialisation in the nineteenth century, modernism reflects a specific period of European socio-cultural history. It is thus clearly a unique, logocentric phenomenon. In spite of its developments and diversifications in the nineteenth and twentieth centuries, Andreas Huyssen has rightly identified a constant and defining trait in modernism and modernist practices that is relevant to this discussion, namely modernism's volatile relationship between 'high art' and the 'mass culture' born out of the industrial era. According to Huyssen, 'Modernism constituted itself through a conscious strategy of exclusion, an anxiety of contamination by its other: an increasingly consuming and engulfing mass culture', thereby causing most modernist artists – with the exception of certain avant-garde artists – to separate art from everyday life, elevating it above the 'mundane' of social and political concerns, and giving rise to such concepts as 'art for art's sake'.[17] In the same vein, modernist artists tended to reject realism and verisimilitude, to favour formalistic concerns over content, and to seek to create a self-referential art that reflected the sensibilities of its individual creator. Whilst this is not the place to explore or comment on the diverse reasons behind the modernists' attitude to art, it is clear that these defining characteristics immediately and fundamentally distinguish modernist artistic precepts from attitudes to the arts in Africa. As shall be seen in more detail in Chapter 3, art in the sub-Saharan Francophone continues to be intrinsically linked to and part of everyday life in a range of societies that rarely distinguish the aesthetic from the functional, content from form, or one genre or artistic medium from another. Similarly, art continues to be closely related to the social and the political, which, in this context, means that the notions of 'high' and 'low' art, or 'art for art's sake', have little or no relevance.

Despite this fundamental difference between European modernist and African art, it is tempting to talk about 'modernist' African art when

16 See Jean-François Lyotard, *La Condition postmoderne: rapport sur le savoir* (Paris: Les Editions de Minuit, 1979).

17 Andreas Huyssen, *After the Great Divide: Modernism, Mass Culture, Postmodernism* (Bloomington & Indianapolis: Indiana University Press, 1986), p vii.

describing works related to Africa's own 'modern' colonial and post-colonial periods. This is all the more so when discussing film, which only emerged in Africa after the colonial encounter with the West. However, it has to be acknowledged that modernity has been experienced under entirely different terms and conditions in Africa, and has thus generated quite different 'modernist' aesthetics. If we are to use the term 'modernism', therefore, it needs to be 'decolonised', as Ali Mazrui would argue, so that modernism is no longer simply equated with 'Euro-modernism'.[18] The fundamental societal changes that took place in the European modern period are usually understood to have been liberating, freeing Europe from its autocratic feudal and theocratic systems and inspiring profound confidence in Western civilisation. However, Clyde Taylor rightly points out that this very same modern period saw the introduction of Western slavery, colonialism, and an exploitative system of industrialisation in the non-Western world, making the need to redefine 'modernism' all the more urgent.[19]

Africa's 'modern' period is indeed equated with the European colonial powers' introduction of repressive systems and was thus the time when Africa's anti-colonial, liberation movements were born. Referring to the emergence of liberation theorists such as Franz Fanon, Amilcar Cabral, or Kwame Nkrumah, Taylor thus argues that, 'If there is an African modernity ... then it is a counter-modernity, a movement in opposition to the debilitating effects of Euro-modernism'.[20] African modernism thus tends to revolve around the overtly political questions of liberation and decolonisation, rather than the kinds of generally apolitical agendas articulated by modernists in Europe. The radically different, committed nature of art in Africa is particularly clear in its filmmaking which has been singularly marked by its inception in the liberation era. The liberation theorists' call for culture to be used to reclaim the popular cultures and histories undermined by years of colonial domination thus both echoed and reinforced traditional African conceptions of the artist's communal role. It encouraged the new generation of filmmakers to use their work to reappraise and reconstruct local identities and values and to challenge continuing neo-colonialism or the corruption of the new African ruling elites. In addition to this fundamentally different approach to political commitment, Francophone African modernist films, such as the works of the Senegalese director Ousmane Sembene, further differ from their European counterparts in that they both recognise and embrace Africa's sociological and artistic traditions, even if this recognition has often involved a critical revaluation and selective appropriation of traditional beliefs.

Another fundamental point of divergence has been the tendency amongst Francophone Africa's modernist directors to embrace cinematic realism as they prioritise the political urgency of their works over formal experimentation. In this sense, modernist Francophone African filmmaking is closer to the overtly socio-political Italian neo-realist filmmaking agendas of the Forties and Fifties, cited by a number of Francophone African filmmakers as a point of reference. Like the early generation of

18 See Ali Mazrui, *World Culture and the Black Experience* (Seattle & London: University of Washington Press, 1974).

19 Clyde Taylor, 'Searching for the Post-Modern in African Cinema' (paper given at BFI *Screen Griots Conference*, London 9–10 September 1995).

20 Clyde Taylor, ibid.

Critical Paradigms

Francophone African directors, the Italian neo-realists tended to be more concerned with the politics of Italy's liberation and post-war reconstruction than with the kind of formal experimentation and rupture with classical filmic traditions (such as verisimilitude) that characterised the French New Wave movement in the Sixties. Many of the radical thematic projects of the Francophone African filmmakers are often overlooked by Western critics, however, who are still influenced by the modernist highlighting of formal concerns. This characteristic Western critical practice fails to recognise that African cultures rarely privilege aesthetic concerns over content and the functional and/or spiritual nature of a work. This point has been stressed by Olivier Barlet who further notes that, 'Critiquer [un] film pour ce qu'il est plutôt que ce qu'il dit, c'est voir l'Autre comme un objet et non comme un sujet ... C'est s'intéresser à lui sans s'intéresser à ce qu'il produit, à son texte, à son oeuvre, à sa parole' ['Criticising a film for what it is rather than what it says amounts to seeing the Other as an object, rather than a subject ... It amounts to taking an interest in him or her without taking interest in what he/she produces, his/her text, work, or word']. This suggests that this 'oversight' perpetuates the dominator-dominated paradigms that have long characterised Euro-African relations.[21] Concepts of modernism can thus clearly be seen to diverge in Africa and the West. It will therefore necessarily follow that experiences of postmodernism diverge too. It is essential to bear this in mind in any critical discourse, and especially in work that deals with a non-Western context.

As the emancipatory decolonisation and feminist movements began to challenge white, patriarchal hegemony in the Sixties and Seventies, and deconstructed binaries such as 'civilised vs. primitive' and 'progress vs. backwardness', belief in modernism's position of authority and confidence in its projects was shaken, heralding what has become known as the postmodern era. Postmodernist sensibilities in the arts, which Huyssen succinctly defines as being characterised by the blurring of the rigid boundaries that distinguished 'high modernist art' from 'mass culture'; the blending of the new and the past traditions formerly rejected by modernists in the name of modernity and an eclectic mixing of the Western and the non-Western, clearly reflect this loss of faith and questioning of modernist precepts.[22] Critics remain dubious about whether this has led to the creation of genuinely new aesthetic forms, arguing that postmodernism has simply used parody and pastiche to recycle modernist forms.

Whilst the collapse of modernist authority has unsettled some Western quarters, it is important to acknowledge that it has been empowering for the groups formerly suppressed and silenced by the now de-centred (white, male) authoritative voice. The demise of notions of Western authority has heralded a multiplication and/or centring of alternative voices in the postmodern age. This in turn has destabilised the very notions of 'margin' and 'centre' and raised issues of subjectivity, of *who* is speaking. It is precisely postmodernism's polyvocality that has led a number of Western artists and critics to assume that these newly

21 Olivier Barlet, 'La critique occidentale des images d'Afrique', p 10.

22 See 'Mapping the Postmodern' in Andreas Huyssen, pp 178-221.

embraced voices are themselves 'postmodern' – a reaction that immediately questions whether or not those voices are really being heard, however, or whether they are only accepted when they appear to correspond to Western postmodernist expectations.

Although there is more interest in non-Western and other 'alternative' voices in the West, James Snead has attacked what he qualifies as the paradoxical racism by exclusion of postmodern theory (as opposed to practice) informed by the post-structuralist writings of Barthes, Derrida, Kristeva, Eco, Foucault, and others, declaring that 'the black is the signifying absence, the signifying other in the text of post-modernism'.[23] Despite the influences that women and non-Westerners' changing roles have had on Western thought, issues of gender and ethnicity have indeed been largely absent from the modernism/postmodernism debate. One explanation is that post-structuralist deconstructionist theory has tended to separate the text from authorial intent, thereby distancing the very notions of subjectivity and agency that have allowed the formerly marginalized groups to express their own perspectives.[24] Even the names of non-Western artists are often strikingly absent from postmodern theoretical works. This has caused Michele Wallace to comment that, 'Euro-American Postmodernism emerges as the lily white pure blooded offspring of an inbred and dishonest (in the sense of not acknowledging its mixed blood) Modernism and Poststructuralism'.[25]

Such evaluations inevitably raise questions about exactly how 'post-', or different, postmodernism really is. One may wonder whether the postmodern crisis of authority has really gone as far in deconstructing Western cultural theory's inherent Eurocentrism as it would at first seem and whether the new focus on the work of non-Western artists has really fragmented notions such as 'centre' and 'margin', 'self' and 'other'. Has this embracing of 'difference' really deconstructed oppositional and over-simplistic binary paradigms? Is there a risk of conflating all non-Western, non-male voices under the apparently homogeneous banner of difference? Whilst 'post', as Kwame Appiah comments, has traditionally been understood to mean 'after' and 'beyond' since the European Enlightenment period, and that, 'to step forward (in time) has been ipso facto to *pro*gress', one indeed begins to wonder how many presuppositions of the modern era have been recycled into postmodern theory in the same way that postmodern practices have recycled modernist forms.[26]

Ella Shohat defines the prefix 'post-' in her article 'Notes on the "Post-Colonial"', in which she writes, 'its emphasis is on the new modes and form of the old colonialist practices, not on a "beyond"'.[27] This may also be applied to postmodernism which appears to have inherited the Euro-centric tendency of taking its paradigms to be universally relevant. The temptation to seek postmodern signs in African film has no doubt been all the greater given that many Francophone African films do address a number of the concerns brought to the fore by postmodernism – notably representation, cultural identity, voice – and do at times use hybrid forms that mix different artistic registers. A more detailed consideration of the Francophone African cultural context soon reveals, however, that such

23 James Snead, 'Racist Traces in Postmodern Theory and Literature', *Critical Quarterly*, vol. 33, 1, cited by Clyde Taylor in 'Searching for the Post-Modern in African Cinema'.

24 Concepts of ethnicity are not only absent from postmodernist debate. Black lesbians, homosexuals, and feminists have similarly all drawn attention to the ways in which the Eurocentrism of 'official' (white) feminist and gay discourse has excluded their concerns. (See, for example, the writings of bell hooks, Angela Davis, Audre Lorde, Kobena Mercer & Isaac Julien.)

25 Michele Wallace, 'Modernism, Postmodernism and the Problem of the Visual in Afro-American Culture', in Russell Ferguson *et al* (eds.), *Out There: Marginalization and Contemporary Cultures* (New York & Massachusetts: The New Museum of Contemporary Art & The MIT Press, 1990), p 46.

26 Kwame A. Appiah, *In My Father's House: Africa in the Philosophy of Culture* (New York & Oxford: Oxford University Press, 1992), p 141.

27 Ella Shohat, 'Notes on the 'Post-Colonial', *Social Text*, 31/31, 1992, p 106.

concepts and styles are more typical of certain African cultural traditions and preoccupations, rather than being typically 'postmodern'.

The tendency to read African history in the light of Western history risks overlooking the two regions' different experiences of modernisation, as was discussed earlier, and assumes that Africa is destined to follow the same modern-postmodern paradigm as the West. Moreover, if we accept that postmodern art has emerged from, and thus reflects, a specific period in Western history that has seen the decline of its empires and their founding narratives, it is also important to recognise that in Africa, 'the source of dis-integration came from European invaders centuries ago, when nobody would have named it postmodern. Fragmentation (and other features of post-modernism) operates in the African context as a reflection of incomplete recovery from a regime of oppression – an incomplete modernity, not a 'post' one'.[28] This analysis again indicates that Africa and the West's experiences are fundamentally different, and must be clearly acknowledged as such if we are to understand and appreciate the specificities of Francophone Africa's cultural manifestations.

For all the above reasons, Francophone Africa's contemporary cultural condition is thus better described as 'postcolonial', rather than 'postmodern'. Postcolonial theory has itself at times been attacked for continuing to take Europe's imperial history as its defining reference despite its purported efforts to dismantle Eurocentrism, and for conflating the different European and African countries' experiences of colonisation and decolonisation. Postcolonialism remains a valid term, however, if, like postmodernism, it is understood in terms of continuity and discontinuity, rather than as an actual rupture with colonialism. It is clear that *neo*-colonial influences are still prevalent in Africa today. Furthermore, one cannot escape the fact that contemporary African cultures have, 'been influenced, often powerfully, by the transition of African societies *through* colonialism', giving rise to a cultural syncretism that is marked by colonial interaction in many domains.[29] Much contemporary African art thus emerges as a refreshingly positive amalgamation of African and other international forms, as is certainly the case with filmmaking in Francophone Africa. Being open to other cultural references is a traditional feature of Francophone African art, as indeed is the refusal to accept rigid generic and stylistic categorisations. Francophone Africa's art practices are open and fluid by tradition and inclination, which again undermines references to the 'new' or 'postmodern'.

Further divergences emerge when one considers other features found in both the African and Western postmodern contexts. The tendency to blend the old and the new in Francophone African film has little in common with the way in which postmodern works in the West refer to the past. Whilst Kobena Mercer characterises the latter as being, 'implicated in a logic that problematizes the recent past by creating ironic distance between "then" and "now"', and as featuring 'the pervasive mode retro, nostalgia and recycling aesthetic, or the prevalence of pastiche and parody', in the Francophone African context, references to

28 Clyde Taylor, 'Searching for the Post-Modern in African Cinema'.

29 Kwame A. Appiah, *In My Father's House: Africa in the Philosophy of Culture*, p 149.

the past and past traditions fulfill an entirely different function.[30] Informed by both the works of liberation theorists and the kinds of belief that characterise many Francophone African cultures' attitudes to the past and the ancestors (discussed further in Chapter 3), Francophone African film works posit the past as a site to be revisited in the vital reconstructing of postcolonial identities and memory. They thus use the past to reflect on both the present and the future. Such attitudes clearly distinguish these postcolonial works from the 'ironic distancing' of their postmodern counterparts.

With the exception of the film *Afrique sur Seine*, which was shot in Paris by the Senegalese filmmakers Paulin S. Vieyra and Mamadou Sarr in 1955, Francophone African cinema belongs to the postcolonial era. As discussed earlier, many of the films, particularly those shot in the early years, are profoundly marked by the intellectual climate of the independence era and by Africa's postcolonial concerns. This justifies once more references to a postcolonial rather than a postmodern context. It is precisely this postcolonial legacy discussed in Chapter 2 that has brought questions of both cultural identity and representation to the fore in Francophone African film. This point is particularly clear in the Pan-African Federation of Filmmakers' (FEPACI) 1975 Algiers Charter and 1982 Niamey Manifesto's call for film to be used as an educational, political tool that challenges existing stereotypes of the continent. African directors have been prompt to respond to such liberationist visions of culture as a way to reconstruct the formerly colonised nations' identities.

Even though this overtly political conception of film has evolved as Africa's own socio-political climates have changed, and the focus of much film work adapted and diversified, many directors' profound commitment to the advancement of Africa has, on the whole, remained unshaken. The politicisation of filmmaking reflects a profound commitment to humankind that is again specific to the African context, and is clearly illustrated by filmmaker Ousmane Sembene's call for the emergence of a new African culture that places respect for man at its centre, because 'Man is Culture'.[31] In addition to Africa's own existing conceptions of art and the role of the artist, the unique nature of sub-Saharan Francophone Africa's colonial experience and its ensuing postcolonial concerns have thus profoundly marked its contemporary cultural forms. It is in this context that the questions of identity, representation, and memory have to be situated. They cannot simply be conflated with similar issues that have emerged in the West's very different postmodern climate if we are to help break with the long tradition of analysing African concerns through a Eurocentric prism.

Towards new critical paradigms

Whilst it is clear that existing Western critical paradigms can be limited and ill-adapted if rigidly applied to artistic practices from different cultural locations, it is nonetheless essential to recognise areas and instances in which they are relevant. Contemporary critical discourse aims not only

30 Kobena Mercer, 'Welcome to the Jungle: Identity and Diversity in Postmodern Politics', in Kobena Mercer, *Welcome to the Jungle: New Positions in Black Cultural Studies* (New York & London: Routledge, 1994), p 267.

31 See Ousmane Sembene, *Man is Culture*. The Sixth Annual Hans Wolff Memorial Lecture. (Bloomington: African Studies Program, Indiana University, 1979).

to deconstruct the myths of a universally applicable paradigm, but also to construct new approaches to critical assessment. The tendency to identify postmodernism everywhere must be avoided, but we can recognise that the postmodern climate has introduced a progressive receptivity to a diverse range of critical voices in the West, challenging former notions of authority and objectivity. This is particularly clear in the work of both feminist and non-Western writers who have sought to interject a personal, voluntarily subjective voice into their critical works. The move away from the notion of an authoritative voice and a definitive critical work is paramount. It is particularly relevant in relation to my own position as a European critic of African film whose critical gaze, however well-informed, will necessarily always remain an external one.

Given the long-standing tendency in the West to speak about and for non-Western peoples and to define their realities and identities, thus effectively silencing their voices, it is important to stay receptive to the critical voices and alternative perspectives of Africa's scholars and avoid the habitual oppressive subject-object dichotomies.[32] Without belittling the insights and observations Westerners might make about African films – for it naturally goes without saying that African cinema merits the attention of a multiplicity of critical viewpoints – it is thus worth accepting that our own readings of these films will be more complete if informed by the interpretations of local critics working within the cultural sphere in which these films are set. Furthermore, Western readings of African film will ultimately be more useful if taken to be part of an on-going critical dialogue, rather than a definitive statement, which thus requires that we accept that our critical paradigms be constantly challenged. This requires a move away from notions of closure in criticism, a point which is all the more important in a cultural sphere where artistic forms and thought-systems are opposed to this very notion.[33]

As Western critics, we need to be ready to accept the diversity of Francophone African film and to evaluate it on its own terms rather than continuing to project preconceived ideas about what constitutes an African film. The Burkinabè director Idrissa Ouedraogo has stressed the importance of recognising this diversity by insisting, 'We don't all share the same vision of the world just because we're all African filmmakers ... It's the diversity of ideas, of opinions that will lead to the creation ... of thriving African cinemas.'[34]

Contextualisation can also help develop more appropriate critical tools. Recent critical thought has re-established the importance of text-milieu, which was hitherto undermined by modernist structuralists' and semioticians' tendency to discount data external to the text itself. Placing culturally unfamiliar works in their own context helps to understand their various stylistic and thematic influences, their directors' creative agendas, and the role film plays in a given context. For these reasons I have taken a predominantly contextualising approach in the following chapters, which is particularly important considering that creativity is expressed, evaluated and appreciated in a variety of ways according to its

32 See bell hooks' essay 'feminist scholarship: ethical issues' (in bell hooks, *Talking Back: thinking feminist, thinking black* (Boston, MA: South End Press, 1989), pp 42-48.), which provides some pertinent reflections on the question of evaluating the work of artists of other genders/ethnic groups.

33 It is quite common for Francophone African films to avoid narrative closure, as shall be seen in more detail in Chapter 3. This traditional narrative device encourages audiences to participate in the conclusion or moral of the narrative. Many African peoples also have a cyclical, rather than linear conception of life that similarly defies closure, as is apparent from traditional beliefs in the deceased's presence amongst the living and, in some areas, beliefs in reincarnation.

34 Interview with the author. Ouagadougou, February 1995.

original context. Acknowledging the importance of this socio-cultural setting also helps to break away from the Eurocentric practice of taking Western paradigms and generic boundaries, such as 'mainstream' and 'experimental', or 'documentary' and 'fiction', as the normative points of reference, and of the insistence 'on a correspondence within African culture to the institutionalised discourses of the West'.[35]

In a similar effort to avoid postulating rigid practices and/or definitive critical criteria, Mbye Cham has called for critical practices that are, 'conceptualized as dialogic, nomadic and transient', and thus capable of responding to the different and ever-changing syncretic postcolonial cultural environments in which Francophone African films are made.[36] This approach has the added advantage of facilitating the necessary move away from the restrictive preconceptions already referred to in this chapter, remembering, in the words of Amadou Hampaté Bâ, that, 'Pour se comprendre mutuellement, il est bon d'oublier un moment qui l'on est et ce qu'on sait' ['it is good to forget who you are and what you know for a moment in order to understand one another'].[37] After all, as one African proverb puts it, 'a full calabash holds no new water', an attitude that I propose to bear in mind in my analysis of Francophone African film.

35 Kwame A. Appiah, *In My Father's House: Africa in the Philosophy of Culture*, p 68.

36 Mbye Cham, 'Introduction', in Mbye B. Cham & Claire Andrade-Watkins (eds.), *Blackframes: Critical Perspectives on Black Independent Cinema*, p 11.

37 Amadou Hampaté Bâ, *Aspects de la civilisation africaine* (Paris & Dakar: Présence Africaine, 1972), p 82.

2 Cultural Identity, Representation & Voice

The highly charged Sixties' decolonisation period in which Francophone African filmmaking was born has been extremely important in shaping its present aspect. Further clarification of this context is needed in order to appreciate Francophone African cinema's diverse agendas and to identify some of the ways in which the questions of cultural identity, representation, and voice have become so central in Francophone African film.

If we accept that all art forms reflect their socio-historic context to some degree, it is not surprising that Francophone Africa's new generation of filmmakers was profoundly affected by the important political debates that marked Africa's anti-colonial, liberation era. Most influential of all was liberation theory's focus on culture as a means of affirming local identities and memories after years of colonial domination.[1] Filmmakers working in this context could hardly ignore the representational questions inherent to the visual medium, questions which were all the more pressing for populations traditionally so widely misrepresented in Western film. As they embraced this new medium, Francophone African film directors were inevitably conscious of the cinema's ability to affirm and create identities by influencing the images people have of themselves and they seized the opportunity to address the question of African self-representation in their work. The very medium used to propagate profoundly damaging and demeaning images of Africa in both the colonial era and today has thus become the means for challenging the visual hegemony of the West.[2] However, before discussing the questions of cultural identity and representation and the ways in which Francophone African directors have used cinema to disrupt Western imagery, it is first of all important to establish exactly how Western discourse and film have positioned the African continent and its inhabitants.

1 The question of memory is so central to Francophone African film that it will be discussed in a separate chapter (see Chapter 4).

2 Jackie Buet identifies the same process amongst women filmmakers who appropriated the film medium in the Sixties to explore and to testify to their own emancipation, thereby challenging the mainstream representations that confined women to subjugated roles. (cf. Jackie Buet, 'Les femmes et l'image', CinémAction, 67, 1993, p 11).

Representing Africa: the Western imagination

The traditionally negative representations of Africa in Western discourse and film can be seen as part of an overall hegemonic strategy born out of the European nations' desire to expand their economic and imperial influence in Africa. Historian Basil Davidson has made this point particularly clearly, arguing that it was the advent of the slave trade in approximately 1560 that first brought about a radical change in Western attitudes to Africa. Before that, accounts written by the European sea traders who first made contact with West African coastal populations in the early sixteenth century were predominantly respectful, even flattering.[3] It was not until the slave trade escalated and became institutionalised and the European nations later began to explore, covet and evangelise inland Africa in the nineteenth century, that the so-called 'scientific' racialist discourses referred to in Chapter 1 began to emerge, castigating the Africans and extolling the virtues of Western 'civilisation'. Such imperialistic attitudes are reflected in the words of the French Minister for the Colonies, Albert Sarraut, who wrote in 1923: 'Nous avons tout de même sur [les races indigènes] ... des siècles d'avance, de longs siècles au cours desquels ... s'est constitué le patrimoine magnifique de science, d'expérience, de supériorité morale qui nous confère le titre éminent à la protection et à la direction des races en retard sur nous' ['We are centuries ahead (of the indigenous races) ... long centuries during which a magnificent patrimony of science, experience and moral superiority has been established, giving us the eminent duty to protect and lead the races who have fallen behind us'].[4]

It was in this context that the colonial authorities rapidly took advantage of the new film medium, which emerged at the same time that the European colonial nations quartered the African continent, a process settled at the 1894 Congress of Berlin. The authorities recognised that film's ability to recreate impressions of reality made it a potentially powerful propaganda tool.[5] This is reaffirmed in the words of the French explorer and empire-builder Colonel Marchand: 'Au-delà de l'avantage de désarmer l'homme primitif et de le faire rire, le cinématographe comique est, de toute évidence, l'arme de conquête de l'Afrique' ['In addition to the advantage of disarming the primitive man and making him laugh, comic cinema is quite clearly the perfect weapon for conquering Africa'].[6] Cinema had the double advantage of demonstrating the colonial rulers' technological superiority and reproducing and sanctifying the kind of images of Africa already propagated in the West's 'scientific' and racialist discourses. Films produced in the colonial era thus reinforced Western perceptions of both colonial ruler and subject. They helped to determine not only how Western audiences, who had little or no real contact with Africans, imagined Africa and its people, but also, more damagingly, how African audiences exposed to these films saw themselves.

When the colonising nations first began to produce documentary films and newsreels in Africa, they continued to justify the imperial project by lauding the actions of the coloniser and establishing Western lifestyles as the norm. At the same time, they portrayed African beliefs and customs as 'primitive' or 'backward'. Completely partial documentary newsreels focused on the colonial authorities' efforts to bring 'progress' and 'modernity' to 'deepest, darkest' Africa. They filmed the new colonial railways, roads, schools, and medical centres, and the smiling faces of the 'contented' African subjects whilst paternalistic, triumphant voice-overs

3 See Basil Davidson, *The Story of Africa* (London: Mitchell Beazley/ Channel 4 Books, 1984).

4 Albert Sarraut, 'La Mise en valeur des colonies françaises', 1923, cited in Nicolas Bancel & Pascal Blanchard, 'De l'indigène à l'immigré, messages et réalités', *H&M*, 1207, pp 16-17.

5 Bertholt Brecht was amongst the earliest theoreticians to insist that the cinematic image was not an innocent photographic reproduction of reality, but an ideological tool. The influence of Brechtian theory and later semiotics and structuralism on film triggered a widespread understanding of the subjective and constructed nature of the film image.

6 Cited by François Vokouma, 'Produire Nos Propres Images ... Malgré l'Etat de l'Afrique', in FEPACI (ed.), *L'Afrique et le Centenaire du Cinéma* (Paris & Dakar: Présence Africaine, 1995), p 270.

Cultural Identity, Representation & Voice

7 An excerpt from the French Centre National de la Cinématographie's newsreel archives shown at the 1995 FESPACO film festival in Burkina Faso.

8 Interestingly, colonial authorities were equally sensitive to the kinds of images of white people African audiences were allowed to see. Charlie Chaplin films were censored in the British colonies, for example, because of their disrespect for Western symbols of authority such as the police and the clergy, just as they were later censored in France for being subversive under the Vichy regime. Such attitudes are clearly confirmed in Sir Robert Horne's speech before the British Parliament, in which he claimed, 'I do not suppose that there is anything which has done so much harm to the prestige and position of Western people and the white race as the exhibition of films which have tended to degrade us in the eyes of peoples who have been accustomed to look upon us with admiration and respect'. Cited in Lizbeth Malkmus & Roy Armes, Arab & African Film Making (London & New Jersey: Zed Books, 1991), pp 18–19.

9 Youssef El Ftouh denounces the hypocrisy of the French authorities who, since 1987, have promoted Afrique 50 in their overseas embassies to prove that anti-colonial discourse was tolerated in France at the time. (cf. Olivier Barlet, 'Ce que filmer veut dire: entretien avec Youssef El Ftouh', Africultures, 3, décembre 1997, p 14).

enumerated colonial achievements and assured viewers of the Africans' gratitude and devotion to the colonial 'motherland'. One French newsreel commentary from the period typically informs viewers, for example, 'Ces gens primitives ... honorent leurs chefs, mais ils aiment la France. Ils la clament du Sénégal à la Mauritanie, du Cameroun au Togo ... "La France est notre Mère"' ['These primitive folk ... honour their chiefs, but they love France. They proclaim from Senegal to Mauritania, from Cameroon to Togo ... "France is our Motherland"'].[7] This reinforced the belief that Africans were contented, passive and essentially childlike or immature colonial subjects, and reassured the French of their innate superiority, their fixed position in the universe, and of the superiority and wisdom of their own nation.[8]

What is particularly striking, however, is the Africans' total silence in these films. There is naturally no suggestion of an African point of view or discourse, nor are there any references to the often brutal realities of colonial domination and economic exploitation. Any suggestions of African animosity or discontent are completely absent. One striking example of this is the way in which footage showing French colonial forces being enlisted always ignores the reality of the African revolts against forced conscription. At the same time, any Western film that challenged the dominant imagery or questioned the colonial project in any way was quite simply censored. The French authorities tried to prevent René Vauthier from completing Afrique 50 (France, 1950), already referred to in Chapter 1, because the film focused on the colonial forces' brutal suppression of political uprisings in the French colonies of Côte d'Ivoire and Upper Volta (now Burkina Faso), and virulently criticised the colonial administration. When Vauthier managed to complete the film illegally, it was banned in Africa and France until 1987, and Vauthier was condemned for shooting it without authorisation.[9] Chris Marker and Alain Resnais's 1953 film Les statues meurent aussi, which criticises the West's habit of pillaging and storing traditional African artefacts in Western museums, was also perceived as an outright challenge to colonial authority and banned for ten years, before a cut version was released. It was not until 1995 that the full version of the film was finally shown on the Franco-German cultural television channel ARTE.

Colonial documentaries and newsreels were soon complemented by Hollywood and European fiction films, which began to feature the African continent at the beginning of the twentieth century. After an initial spate of exotic 'explorer' films, the African adventure genre soon emerged. Both revealed the same kind of attitudes to Africa and its people as the colonial newsreel productions. Standard African adventure films, such as the Tarzan features, MGM's Trader Horn (1930), King Solomon's Mines (the 1950 remake of an earlier British version), or the Hollywood classic The African Queen (1951), are striking for the way in which they positioned African characters as background 'props', who are little more than geographic markers to remind the spectator that the film is set in Africa. This is most revealing of Western attitudes to Africans at the time and their perception of Africans' (lack of) importance and place in their own land. The only other more detailed images of African characters generally serve to contrast or highlight the importance of the films' central, intrepid white explorers and adventurers. Whilst white characters are given individual filmic treatment as they bravely wrestle with wild animals (*Tarzan*), save white women from treacherous African populations in hostile landscapes (*Trader Horn, Tarzan*), battle through the jungle in search of unspeakable treasures (*King Solomon's Mines*), or protect 'good' (loyal), childlike Africans from other 'bad' (disloyal) Africans (*Sanders of the River*, 1935), African characters only come in anonymous groups that epitomise danger and savagery, or serve as 'domesticated' houseboys or soldiers, thereby accentuating the inherent superiority of the white heroes, their values and lifestyles. The concerns, viewpoints and realities of the African characters do not feature in these films, nor are they considered important.

These films' 'African' settings, dreamed up by people who more often than not had never set foot on the continent, said more about the West's exotic fantasies than they did about Africa. Like those of its people, representations of Africa itself bore no correlation to the geographic or sociological realities and complexities of the continent. Africa was thus systematically represented as an ethnically and geographically homogeneous zone, covered in hostile jungle. All culturally specific details, such as language or dress, were erased and/or apparently considered to be totally spurious or without interest. Hence as late as 1940, the voice-over in Paul Heofler's American (pseudo-) documentary *Leopard Men of Africa* could still boom, 'Afr-r-r-ica!', the 'land of sorcery, witchcraft, and mumbo-jumbo! Shrouded in the dark jungle – Africa! Crowded – primitive – lusty – still ruled by fang and claw!', in a typical display of ignorant partiality.[10]

Whilst such representations seem ludicrously exaggerated today, at the time they were as close to discovering 'Africa' as the majority of Western spectators would get. Their veracity would not have been doubted, for film was marketed at the time as being a 'realistic' window on the world. Kenneth Cameron has rightly pointed out in his study of the representation of Africa in Western film that the danger of these films was that they tended to reinforce not only Western audiences' inaccurate and grossly exaggerated image of Africa, but also that of other filmmakers. When directors went on location to shoot in Africa, they set out to find and to record the images that had already been shown, rather than to discover what the continent actually had to offer. When the local realities failed to live up to expectations, filmmakers would get local inhabitants to enact what they wanted to see, replacing reality with fiction and thus perpetuating and enhancing myths about the continent.

Certain archetypal African characters began to emerge as an increasing number of mainstream fiction films were set in Africa.[11] Cameron identifies several of these archetypes, notably the frequently represented 'Good African' who, like his American 'Uncle Tom' counterpart, is usually the white hero's childlike, faithful and obedient

10 Cited in Kenneth M Cameron, *Africa on Film: Beyond Black and White* (New York: Continuum, 1994), p 54.

11 As the title of Donald Bogle's book *Toms, Coons, Mulattoes, Mamies and Bucks: An Interpretive History of Blacks in American Films* indicates, similar essentialist stereotypes of African-Americans also emerged in Hollywood's silent films. Whilst such stereotypes have evolved with their times and/or new stereotypes have emerged, their underlying characteristics have remained remarkably persistent.

companion/servant whose life is regularly sacrificed to save the white master/mistress. The predominance of 'Good African' servants and other anonymous houseboys reinforced white beliefs that Africans were naturally destined to serve the 'superior' European. Such attitudes are further confirmed by the ways in which such African characters are usually filmed in such works. Faces are often poorly lit, for example, thus accentuating the impression of anonymity and deliberately failing to highlight those individual, 'humane' characteristics that define the white characters, reinforcing notions of white superiority.[12]

In belated recognition of the fact that Africans had been attending European universities for some years and that, in France, Blaise Diange, the first African deputy, had even been a Member of Parliament since 1914, the new 'Educated African' archetype began to appear in European films after World War Two. 'Educated African' characters are invariably portrayed to be uppity trouble-makers, who, unlike 'Good Africans', can rarely be trusted, thus mirroring representations of Europe's rigid class systems which similarly indicted characters who tried to rise above their station.

African women characters are most noticeable for their complete absence from the screen. On the rare occasions that they are actually singled out from the anonymous crowds in films from the colonial period, African women (often played by white women in blackface in the early years) are usually portrayed as sexually rampant creatures who ensnare unwitting white men, accelerating their downfall. Many films function as cautionary tales about young men who 'go native', stop shaving, take to the bottle, and finally succumb to the forbidden charms of what Cameron describes as 'Black Eve' characters. The implication here is that it is just as sinful to stray outside one's race as it is to escape one's class.

What is most striking about these representations, however, is not so much the fact that films from the colonial era misrepresented Africa through their reductive stereotypes, but rather that elements of these early stereotypes continue to emerge in film today, albeit in updated forms. These constantly renewed stereotypes reflect developments in attitudes and imaginations concerning the colonial subject. It is precisely this adaptability that enables such stereotypes to withstand both the passage of time and socio-historical change. As Françoise Lorcerie argues, it is the fact of re-producing stereotypes and their fundamental motivations that remain unchanged, rather than the stereotypes themselves.[13] Homi K. Bhabha develops this analysis further, suggesting that the need to rearticulate and reiterate the stereotype actually stems from its fundamentally ambivalent nature. On the one hand an extreme, arrested marker of alterity with a fixed and limiting set of characteristics that define the racial, cultural and historical difference of the other, the stereotype is at the same time a means of transforming that unknown other into the familiar and thus safe, into something that can be controlled. This explains the need to repeat the stereotype, which, although *a priori* an arrested form of representation, thereby becomes a contradictory, polymorphous construct.[14] Recognition of this character-

12 In the French film *Le Crime de Monsieur Stil* (Claire Devers, 1995), discussed in more detail later, Stil's houseboy is almost exclusively shot in the shadowy corners of the rooms, his face never lit, thereby confirming the impression that, in the eyes of his employers at least, he does not exist beyond his role as a servant.

13 Françoise Lorcerie, 'La catégorisation sociale de l'immigration est-elle coloniale?', in *H&M*, 1207, p 82. For further, highly informative reading on the nature of colonial stereotypes see also: Homi K. Bhabha, 'The Other Question... Homi K. Bhabha Reconsiders The Stereotype and Colonial Discourse', *Screen*, vol. 24, 6, 1983, pp 18–36; and Nicolas Bancel & Pascal Blanchard, 'De l'indigène à l'immigré, messages et réalités', pp 6–29.

14 See Homi K. Bhabha, 'The Other Question...', p 18.

istic helps to explain why so many contemporary Euro-American films set in Africa continue, often unconsciously, to present the same sorts of construction as in the colonial films.

Two recent French films amongst many others – *Le Crime de Monsieur Stil* (Claire Devers, 1995), which is set just before Africa's independence, and *L'Etat Sauvage* (Francis Girod, 1978), which takes place immediately after decolonisation – provide good examples of this process of reiteration, showing how traditional archetypes can be rearticulated to suit contemporary contexts. Both films are set in unspecified countries in Africa, reinforcing traditional representations of the continent as a homogeneous entity. Both films also feature trouble-making 'Educated Africans'. In *Le Crime de Monsieur Stil*, Diallo poses as a government official in order to take revenge on the expatriate community. Whilst we can guess at his motivations, Diallo is never actually allowed to explain and/or justify his actions himself, thereby reinforcing the impression that he is little more than an impostor. In *L'Etat Sauvage*, Dumbe is a somewhat aloof character who makes waves by trying to fight corruption in his country's newly independent government. In so doing, he inevitably upsets both his fellow cabinet members and the neo-colonial powers that continue to govern behind-the-scenes. The expatriate communities and, in Dumbe's case, the other African deputies from whom he alienates himself, view these two characters with intense hostility. Significantly, both have also unpardonably transgressed what is clearly represented as the ultimate taboo: being sexually involved with white women. Diallo and Dumbe are murdered before the end of each film, apparently punished for challenging the colonial and/or neo-colonial order and for flouting the rigid sexual barriers. The elimination, and thus ultimate subordination of the 'Educated African' is retold.

In both films 'Good African' characters serve as assistants to the (white) police commissioners. Both have learnt their masters' lessons well, remaining passive when the 'Educated Africans' are eliminated. These modern-day 'Good Africans' continue to preserve the status quo, to know their 'place', and to be loyal.[15] Female African characters are notably absent in both films, only allowed into the narratives as the 'local girls' who are purely the objects of the white men's exotic sexual fantasies. Similarly, these updated 'Black Eve' characters are quite literally discarded as soon as the men's ('superior') white wives or girl-friends enter the picture (literally).

Whilst *Le Crime de Monsieur Stil* and *L'Etat Sauvage* paint harsh critical portraits of the expatriate communities in Africa, neither film really breaks away from traditional representations of Africans. In other words, both illustrate the ways in which a whole range of contemporary films in the West continue to deny African characters any real cinematographic respect, treating them as little more than visual, scenic details, or portraying them as servants whose status continues, perhaps unconsciously, to reaffirm notions of white supremacy.

Other filmic examples demonstrate how elements of various stereotypes have been blended and rearticulated to form new archetypes as

15 It is interesting to note that an updated version of the Good African/ Uncle Tom character emerged in the Hollywood 'buddy' movies of the Eighties in which a kind-hearted black partner (often a police partner) always gets murdered, giving the 'sensitive' white hero the opportunity to avenge his death and save the day.

socio-historic contexts have changed. Cameron notes the emergence in the Fifties of a new archetype – the 'Dangerous African' – rightly suggesting that this is an update of the obsolete 'Savage African' archetype, similar to the Hollywood 'Black Buck' stereotype, first incarnated in D.W. Griffiths' *Birth of A Nation* (USA, 1915). Both convey the threat to the virtue of the white woman in reflection of the Westerner's simultaneous fear of and fascination with black sexuality. As anti-colonial agitation intensified in Africa, the 'Savage African' character thus evolved into the new 'Dangerous African' killer/freedom fighter archetype who habitually commits violence against white people in the quest for power and freedom. Interestingly, the 'Dangerous' and 'Educated African' archetypes also merge on several counts, no doubt reflecting the actual threat many colonialists felt when faced with the emergence of a Western-educated African elite. Both also share qualities that hitherto defined the earlier 'Savage' stereotype (threat to the white man, sexual threat to the white woman, etc.).

Other contemporary examples also indicate how the same kinds of essentialist construct are used to define the African continent in both past and contemporary discourse, even when the stereotypes themselves have changed. The recent images of an eternally unchanging continent inhabited by natives in war paint and leopard skins in the Hollywood Ace Ventura comedy *When Nature Calls* (USA, 1995), or the 1996 remake of the *Tarzan* series, suggest, for example, that old clichés concerning the 'Dark Continent' as the site of savagery, degeneracy, primitiveness, and superstition, continue to defy the passage of time. Similarly, the resurgence of a series of backward-looking 'empire nostalgia' films in the Eighties, which use colonial Africa as a backdrop for otherwise routine adventures and/or romances – for example *Out of Africa, White Mischief, Mister Johnson, White Hunter, Black Heart* – continue to deploy the same, tired stereotypes and to reinforce the invisibility of African characters. The highly selective reading of history articulated in such films is, of course, symptomatic of a yearning for Europe's 'good old' colonial past at a time when Europe's own identity and position are perceived by some to be in a threatening state of flux.[16]

More common still, however, are today's representations of Africa as the site of famine, poverty, disease and war, or, in other words, as 'Other' to the 'economically developed', safe West. Despite claiming to challenge the Western media's reductive and pessimistic representations of the continent, Raymond Depardon's apocalyptic documentary *Afriques, comment ça va avec la douleur?* (France, 1996) focuses solely on moments of pain, death, illness and suffering as the director journeys across the continent. The film thus reinforces this habitual image of Africa, one that the passers-by randomly questioned in the Zimbabwean director Moise Matura's German documentary *News Blues* confirm. None of the people Matura questioned had been to Africa, and all say that their source of information is the media, thereby confirming the powerfully influential role visual representation can play in forming people's perceptions.

16 In his essay 'Recoding Narratives of Race and Nation', Kobena Mercer suggests that these African empire films, and the series of British television films about the Raj constitute 'a remythification of the colonial past', which is symptomatic of the desire to revive the master narrative of Empire in an attempt to 'stabilize the "imagined community" of the nation'. See Kobena Mercer (ed.), *Black Film British Cinema* (London: ICA Documents 7, 1988), pp 12–13.

Alternative perspectives, or reassessing identity through film

This overview of past and present Western representations of Africa demonstrates quite to what extent the African filmmakers coming to voice in the independence era were not – and to a large degree are still not – negotiating an innocent terrain. The existence of this kind of dominant Western imagery and discourse has confronted African film-makers with the urgent task of displacing its authority and challenging its negative stereotypes. Faced with what Kobena Mercer aptly describes as this 'specific, if not unique, set of representational problems that constitute a particularly difficult "burden of representation"', filmmakers have not been free simply to make images 'innocently', nor have they been able to ignore the issue of representation.[17] What clearly emerges in Francophone African film is a specific understanding of filmic representation that Stuart Hall rightly defines as playing 'a *constitutive*, and not merely a reflexive, after-the-event role'.[18] Filmic representation is thus understood not as a 'neutral' reproduction of reality, but as an active means of defining identities and interrogating reality. Similar reflections on representation are also manifest in other, earlier African art forms, such as literature and theatre. This confirms that the colonial authorities' systematic castigation of the fundamental markers of identity – indigenous culture and history – has inevitably brought these issues to the fore.[19] It is clearly important to situate Francophone African cinema, and in particular its early films, in this unique context if we are fully to understand the issues that inform many of these works.

Liberation theorists' writings on culture provide a vital analysis of the colonial cultural policies that marked the colonial era and influenced the work and concerns of Africa's artists seeking to challenge imperial hegemony. By identifying the colonial authorities' attempts to undermine African culture, language, religion, and history as part of a policy to guarantee political stability and colonial economic domination, Frantz Fanon and Amilcar Cabral reveal how colonial film propaganda or the mass destruction and/or banning of cultural and religious objects and forms specifically aimed to reinforce the colonial subject's own sense of inferiority. Both authors also provide insight into the concerted effort to eliminate anti-colonial protest. African school children were encouraged to identify with French culture and history, thereby reinforcing their loyalty to the colonial power and again undermining potential challenges to its authority. Children were frequently punished for speaking their own languages, as is clearly illustrated in Ahmadou Diallo's short film *Le Symbole* (Senegal, 1994), in which a child incurs his mother's wrath when he addresses her in French as instructed by his teacher, and is then punished at school for having tried to explain the situation to her in Fulani. Local history was erased as school children were taught to recite phrases such as 'France is our Motherland' and 'Our ancestors, the Gauls', legitimating Fanon's argument that, 'Colonialism is not satisfied

17 Kobena Mercer, 'Recoding Narratives of Race and Nation', p 9.

18 Stuart Hall, 'New Ethnicities', in Kobena Mercer (ed.), *Black Film British Cinema*, p 27.

19 Questions of identity tend to take on importance when that identity is perceived to be threatened. If similar issues have become significant in the postmodern West, it is precisely because postmodernism heralded the collapse of the modernist narratives that previously defined Western identity. It is significant that extreme right-wing parties, like the French National Front, have gained support by promising to defend an imaginary 'homogeneous' nation at a time when definitions of 'Frenchness' or 'Britishness' are shifting in our increasingly cosmopolitan world.

Cultural Identity, Representation & Voice

merely with holding a people in its grip and emptying the native's brain of all form and content. By a kind of perverted logic, it turns to the past of the oppressed people, and distorts, disfigures and destroys it'.[20]

Considering the efforts made to annihilate the colonial subject's sense of cultural identity, it is easy to understand the desire and need of artists and intellectuals – many of whom had suffered the greatest degree of acculturation as a result of their passage through the colonial school system – to prove the value of their own culture.[21] The Negritude literary movement of the Thirties is indeed symptomatic of that desire. Founded by the Paris-based African and Antillean students Léopold Sédar Senghor (Senegal), Aimé Césaire (Martinique), and Léon G. Damas (French Guyana) at a time when black people all over the world were oppressed by white imperialist regimes, the Negritude writers used their poems and essays to celebrate and affirm their blackness. By evoking the position of black people, refusing oppression, and revaluating what they personally defined as their positive African values and heritage, the Negritudinists aimed to define a new black collective identity to counter the negative attributes of racist discourse. In so doing, they also sought to restore and prove to the Western world what had hitherto been denied to them – their dignity. It is interesting to note that the recurrent theme of dignity in literature is equally central in Francophone African film, which confirms the influence that the colonial period had on a range of contemporary art forms in the region. From *Borom Sarret* (Senegal, 1962) to his most recent film *Guelwaar* (1992), filmmaker Ousmane Sembene has, for instance, focused on the dignity of the oppressed, who, despite their poverty and hardship, refuse to compromise their ideals and pride.

Whilst the reactions of the Negritudinists were the logical antithesis of white supremacy, and no doubt played a vital part in restoring the pride of a despised people, the movement itself has been criticised by subsequent generations of African writers and intellectuals, including the Nigerian writer Wole Soyinka, for articulating its celebration of blackness in the same rigid and essentialist terms that the earlier racist scholars used to construct the image of a backward and eternal Africa. The Negritudinists have also been widely criticised for their excessively romantic treatment of Africanity and for their uncritical celebration of even the most oppressive aspects of African tradition.

However, the Negritude movement was certainly not the only one to have replaced a negative, essentialist construct with an equally essentialist, positive one. Whilst this has ultimately failed to offer a truly radical redefinition of identity, it has constituted a necessary *first step* in a long process of revaluation. Movements such as Negritude must be seen in their original cultural and historical contexts, recognising that their concerns naturally evolved over time. The Nigerian writer Chinua Achebe confirms this analysis when he writes, 'owing to the peculiar nature of our situation, it would be futile to try and take off before we have repaired our foundations ... This, I think, is what Aimé Césaire meant when he said that the short cut to the future is via the past'.[22] It

20 Frantz Fanon, *The Damned*, translated by Constance Farrington (Paris: Présence Africaine, 1963), p 170.

21 It is important to qualify the notion of acculturation in the colonies. Whilst some members of the educated elite and other groups in close contact with the colonial structures may have been problematically 'torn between two worlds' and led to reject their heritage, one must not forget the far greater majority who lived in relative isolation from the centralised colonial influences and who were thus far less likely to question their indigenous customs and culture in the same way.

22 Chinua Achebe, 'The Role of the Writer in a New Nation', in G.D. Killam, (ed.), *African Writers on African Writing* (London: Heinemann, 1973), p 10.

is precisely this kind of 'repairing of foundations' that emerges in a number of Francophone African films and is crucial to our understanding of how many 'first generation' Francophone African directors see their work. According to Malian filmmaker Souleymane Cissé, 'La première tâche des cinéastes africains est d'affirmer que les gens d'ici sont des êtres humains, et de faire connaître celles de nos valeurs qui pourraient servir aux autres. La génération qui nous suivra s'ouvrira sur d'autres aspects du cinéma. Notre devoir à nous est de faire comprendre que les blancs ont menti par leurs images' ['African filmmakers' first task is to show that people here are human beings and to help people discover the African values that can be of service to others. The following generation will branch out into other aspects of film. Our duty is to make people understand that white people have lied through their images'].[23] Or, in the words of the Burkinabè director Idrissa Ouedraogo, 'Nous tournons par urgence ... Peu importe le style du film, nous partageons tous le même désir de donner une certaine fierté au public et au peuple africain' ['We shoot as a matter of urgency ... Whatever the style of the film, we all share the same desire to give the African audiences and people back their pride'].[24] This confirms that the desire to challenge and/or to rectify the existing (mis)representations of African people and to restore their sense of pride remains very present in many filmmakers' minds, even if this general consensus has naturally not excluded a diversity of approaches and directing styles. Francophone African film has certainly evolved and diversified since its inception, but it remains crucial to understand what is still perceived as the urgency of this question of representation, which continues to inform the work of many directors.

Sub-Saharan Francophone Africa's first wave of post-independence filmmaking similarly needs to be situated in the wider contexts of decolonisation and the Sixties 'Third World' liberation euphoria if we are to understand its cultural agendas. The publication of Teshome Gabriel's book *Third Cinema: The Aesthetics of Liberation* in the Eighties confirmed the tendency to see the most overtly political or socially committed African films as part of a wider, global movement or trend referred to as 'Third Cinema'. This concept, which evolved in Latin America in the Sixties, is generally understood to refer to all progressive, socially and politically motivated film from the Third World.[25]

Whilst as a general concept, the term 'Third Cinema' tends to mask the diversity of the agendas and influences of filmmakers who come from very different regions of the globe, it points to a real sense of solidarity and a shared conception of cinema as a form of opposition to all kinds of colonial, neo-colonial, cultural or political imperialism and oppression. This aspect has led Teshome Gabriel to define it as 'an alternative cinema, a cinema of decolonisation and for liberation'.[26] Third Cinema also refers to the formerly subjugated peoples' shared desire to use film to reappraise their history, restore popular memory, and denounce social ills as they counter existing misrepresentations and affirm a new sense of identity. The Pan-African Federation of Filmmakers' (FEPACI) call in

23 Speaking in Rithy Panh's documentary *Souleymane Cissé* (Cambodia-France, 1991).

24 Speaking at the British Film Institute's *Screen Griots Conference*, London, 9-10 September, 1995.

25 The concept of Third Cinema evolved in Latin America in the Sixties, inspired by the 1959 Cuban revolution, Brazil's Cinema Nuovo and Italy's Neo-Realist movement. It reflected the desire to use film as a tool for liberation from all forms of oppression. Two manifestos defined its goals, namely Octavio Getino & Fernando Solanas' 'Towards a Third Cinema' (1969), and Julio Garcia Espinosa's 'For an Imperfect Cinema' (1970). Third Cinema was defined as rejecting both dominant mainstream 'First Cinema' and apolitical *auteur* 'Second Cinema'.

26 Teshome Gabriel, *Third Cinema in Third World: The Dynamics of Style and Ideology* (Ann Arbor, Michigan: U.M.I Dissertation Services, 1979), p 3.

Cultural Identity, Representation & Voice

27 Frantz Fanon, *The Damned*, translated by Constance Farrington, pp 187–188.

28 Cheick Hamidou Kane, 'The African Writer and His Public', in G.D. Killam, (ed.), *African Writers on African Writing*, p 69.

29 The radical US-based Ethiopian filmmaker Haile Gerima has criticised such African films for becoming 'respondent to European needs. If Europe needed exotic cinema, we supplied it to the brim. ... in the 1980s innovativeness was abandoned for imitativeness' (Onyekachi Wamby, 'Decolonizing Film: Interview with Haile Gerima', *Black Film Bulletin*, vol 3, 2/3, Summer/Autumn 1995, p 14). Critic Clyde Taylor also describes 'return to the source' films as muting political discourse to facilitate reception by non-African audiences. ('Searching for the Post-Modern in African Cinema', paper given at BFI *Screen Griots Conference*, London 9–10 September 1995). Tunisian filmmaker and critic Férid Boughedir has similarly described Cissé's *Yeelen* as 'escapist Africa offering a journey for the European spectator, with no contemporary political reference'. ('African Cinema and Ideology: Tendencies and Evolutions', paper given at BFI *Screen Griots Conference*). All of the 'return to the source' directors cited here have also made overtly politically and morally committed social realist films, for example Kaboré's *Zan Boko* (1988), Cissé's *Baara* (1977) and *Finye* (1982), Ganda's *Saitane* (1972), and Sissoko's *Nyamanton* (1986) and *Finzan* (1989). Explaining this change in style, Cissé explains in an interview with Manthia Diawara, 'there was also tension building around me because of my previous films, and it was clear that if I wanted to stay in my country and enjoy a degree of freedom of expression, I had to lighten things a bit, or to make a different type of cinema'. ('Souleymane Cissé's Light on Africa', *Black Film Review*, vol 4, 4, 1988, p 13).

their Algiers and Niamey manifestos of 1975 and 1982 for cinema to be used as a means of questioning, consciousness-raising, and redefining identities and dignity is informed by the kinds of responses to questions of liberation prevalent throughout the oppressed regions of the world at the time. This politically committed approach to filmmaking also reflects the understanding of culture as a means of liberation articulated in the work of theorists such as Fanon and Cabral. Indeed, as Fanon argues in *The Damned*:

> To fight for national culture means in the first place to fight for the liberation of the nation ... A national culture is the whole body of efforts made by a people in the sphere of thought to describe, justify and praise the action through which that people has created itself and keeps itself in existence. A national culture in under-developed countries should therefore take its place at the very heart of the struggle for freedom which these countries are carrying on.[27]

Fanon suggests that the need to affirm one's culture is much stronger and even vital when that culture has recently been denied. In this context, culture is clearly situated at the heart of the quest to reclaim identities and freedom. Furthermore, the vision of culture's role in the decolonisation struggle articulated by both Fanon and Cabral is particularly pertinent in the Francophone African context where the functional and educational aspects of culture have traditionally been as important as their aesthetic, or entertaining roles. As the writer Cheick Hamidou Kane affirms, African art is 'functional, not because it rejects aesthetic intentions, but because it does not separate aesthetic pleasure from the rest'.[28]

It is hardly surprising in this context that certain Francophone African filmmakers working in the Sixties and Seventies – notably Ousmane Sembene, Med Hondo, or Souleymane Cissé – responded by making politically committed social realist films that reflected the liberation agendas and attitudes to culture and addressed urgent contemporary socio-political issues. More recent film genres and styles, which have at times been criticised for allegedly abandoning this political engagement to pander to Western desires for exoticism, maintain a politically committed attitude to filmmaking that remains informed by the intellectual concerns of the liberation era, even if the political analyses of these films adopt a different, more covert, allegorical style.[29] Notable among these are the Eighties and Nineties films situated in pre-colonial Africa that have often, somewhat disparagingly, been referred to as the 'return to the source' films (including Oumarou Ganda's *l'Exilé* (Niger, 1980), Gaston Kaboré's *Wend Kuuni* (Burkina Faso, 1982), Souleymane Cissé's *Yeelen* (Mali, 1987), or Cheick Oumar Sissoko's *Guimba* (Mali, 1995). Cheick Oumar Sissoko insists upon the continuingly political nature of such works, arguing that 'We insisted on the style of the film because audiences are often uncomfortable when a film tries to be very political in the banner-waving sense of the term. I think that the message can be got over better when a work is made artistically', and 'we address the past by referring to what is happening today. That is what you could call a "political" use of this past', demonstrating filmmakers' diverging conceptions of their filmmaking agendas.[30] Sissoko's attitude, which is echoed in the works of the other filmmakers cited above, reflects both the liberation theorists' conception of the past as source of inspiration for the future, and echoes attitudes that are fundamental to Francophone Africa's oral traditions, which we shall consider in the following chapter.

It is important to stress that decolonising images of the continent has not simply involved countering the negative stereotypes perpetrated by the West. Defining, or rather confining Francophone African film to a purely oppositional role would be reductive. There is not necessarily unanimity amongst African directors about the kinds of films they should be making, as the aforementioned debates about the 'return to the source' films demonstrate. As Francophone African film has developed, its approaches and concerns have naturally diversified. However, the challenging of such stereotypes has certainly been *a part* of the effort to reconstruct images of Africans from African points of view, or to make films which, to cite the Burkinabè filmmaker Gaston Kaboré, function as 'une passerelle vers une autre observation de l'Afrique' ['a gateway to another view of Africa'].[31] This remains a pertinent, even urgent process in the light of the reductive representations of Africa that continue to be produced in the West. The deconstruction of stereotypical representations is not simply limited to reversing existing stereotypes and binary paradigms, even if some directors have produced some equally simplistic and reductive images that position all that is African as good and all that is Western as bad. More typically, the process of deconstruction has been about formulating *alternative* representations, and about reclaiming the right to represent one's self rather than simply being represented.

The need and desire to identify with representations of the self is an issue that has faced all groups silenced or marginalized by the hegemony of a dominant discourse. In the introductory chapter of *European Identity in Cinema*, Wendy Everett refers to similar kinds of representational issues facing filmmakers from marginalized countries such as Scotland, Ireland and Wales, whose populations have also been limited by the stereotypical representations of the British media for a long time.[32] Without wanting to conflate the diverse experiences of all marginalized groups, parallels can also be drawn between the issues facing other categories and groups. Teresa de Laurentis's pertinent argument that it is vital that women 'who have never before represented ourselves as subjects, and whose images and subjectivities – until very recently, if at all – have not been ours to shape, to portray, or to create', gain access to image-making mechanisms so that they too can make, and thus identify with, their own images, can similarly be applied to the African context.[33] Kwame Appiah makes the same point: 'For those of us raised largely with texts that barely acknowledged the specificity of our existence, each work that simply places before us the world we already know – and this is a point that has been made eloquently by feminism – can provide a moment of self-validation'.[34]

30 Interview with the author. Ouagadougou, February 1995.

31 Speaking at the British Film Institute's *Screen Griots Conference*, London, 9–10 September, 1995.

32 Wendy Everett (ed.), *European Identity in Cinema* (London: Intellect, 1996).

33 Teresa de Laurentis, 'Aesthetic and Feminist Theory: Rethinking Women's Cinema', in Arlene Raven, Cassandra Langer & Joanna Frueh (eds.), *Feminist Art Criticism: An Anthology* (New York: First Icon, 1991), p 135.

34 Kwame A. Appiah, *In My Father's House: Africa in the Philosophy of Culture* (New York & Oxford: Oxford University Press, 1992), p 67.

Cultural Identity, Representation & Voice

Like those from other marginalized groups, many Francophone African filmmakers have sought to remedy the fact that, whilst there are myriad images of Africans as the *object* of representation, there are far fewer which position Africans as *subjects*. Filmmakers highlight the dangers of this lack of representation. The Tunisian Nouri Bouzid claims that 'Sans l'image, nous deviendrons des voyeurs incapables de voir nos propres corps' ['Without images, we will become voyeurs, incapable of seeing our own bodies'], thereby leading to a situation in which external influences and realities become the only point of reference and aspiration, accentuating the loss of identity.[35] Gaston Kaboré also warns of this risk of acculturation, arguing that, 'Une société quotidiennement et quasi exclusivement submergée par des images absolument étrangères à sa mémoire collective, à son imaginaire, à ses références et à sa valeurs sociales et culturelles perd peu à peu ses repères spécifiques et son identité' ['A society that, every day and quasi-exclusively, is swamped by images that are completely alien to its collective memory, its imagination, its references, and its social and cultural values gradually loses its own specific markers and identity'].[36]

In this charged context of always having been represented and spoken for, the struggle to 'come to voice' itself constitutes an act of resistance. Given the increasingly US-dominated world cultural stage, it is obviously important for Francophone African directors that their voices be heard. The Mauritanian filmmaker Med Hondo makes this point clearly: 'Je ne vois pas pourquoi les Africains seraient condamnés à occuper des strapontins sur la scène culturelle mondiale. Nous devons occuper toute la place qui nous revient, continuer à témoigner' ['I don't see why Africans should be condemned to the backseat of the world cultural stage. We have to occupy the entire place that is due to us and continue to testify'].[37] Africans are not the only people concerned, of course. Europe's (and particularly France's) insistence on writing a 'cultural exception' clause into the 1994–1995 GATT world trade agreements to protect Europe's cultural industries from US domination, shows the importance certain European nations attach to safeguarding their culturally-specific voice.

bell hooks has described this 'act of speech', of 'talking back', as an act of liberation that allows formerly oppressed groups to become subjects rather than remaining the voiceless objects of dominant discourse whose realities and identities are perpetually defined by others. Speaking back, appropriating the camera thus becomes a way of defining oneself. The introduction of new voices and narratives disrupts and challenges the fixed and limiting constructs formulated by the colonial West. By 'identifying themselves as subjects, by defining their reality, shaping new identities, naming their history, telling their story', the oppressed are thus able to counter the dominating forces.[38]

Hostile reactions in France to Med Hondo's *Sarraounia* (Mauritania, 1986), or Ousmane Sembene's *Camp de Thiaroye* (Senegal, 1988), which 'tell their story' as they depict French colonial involvement in Africa from an African point of view, indicate how powerful, or threatening this voice

35 Speaking at the British Film Institute's *Screen Griots Conference*, London, 9–10 September, 1995.

36 Gaston Kaboré, 'L'image de Soi, Un Besoin Vital', in FEPACI (ed), *L'Afrique et le Centenaire du Cinéma* (Paris & Dakar: Présence Africaine, 1995), p 21.

37 Cited in Ibrahima Signaté, *Med Hondo: Un Cinéaste Rebelle* (Paris & Dakar: Présence Africaine, 1994), p28.

38 bell hooks, 'feminist scholarship: ethical issues', in bell hooks, *Talking Back: thinking feminist, thinking black*, p 43.

can be perceived to be. *Sarraounia* was given an extremely limited distribution in France, where the critics attacked it for being overly polemical, and *Camp de Thiaroye* was only released when Med Hondo distributed it himself in 1998, despite the fact that it won the Special Jury Award at the 1988 Venice Film Festival. The fact that both films offer alternative African readings of history that specifically reclaim and reinterpret collective memory must be recognised, as the liberation theorists frequently claimed, as a fundamental stage in the quest for self-definition. Reminding us that Michel Foucault posits memory as a site of resistance, which, in this context, can be understood to mean that the expression and/or reinstatement of African memory is a defiant act that challenges the interpretations and/or erasures of dominant discourse, bell hooks thus rightly argues that revised readings of history, such as those articulated in Hondo and Sembene's films, produce a vital counter-memory that contributes to the necessary process of 'speaking back', as discussed above.[39]

A certain understanding of cultural identity seen to emerge in the above discussions needs to be qualified to consider the ways in which Francophone African filmmakers have used the cinema to construct and express their cultural identities. Given the filmmakers' apparent desire to use cinema to challenge existing representations of Africa and to constitute African identities as filmmakers reconstruct their 'disfigured selves' in film, to cite the Ethiopian filmmaker Haile Gerima, identities are conceived not as a stable and fixed constructs, but as something that is in the making *within* representation.[40] South African filmmaker Mickey Madoda Dube confirms this: 'For too long now we have been defined by the images created about us ... That is why it is crucial for us to create images that we know, that we experience, *so that we actually become the images themselves*'.[41] Rather than simply being a mirror that reflects identity, film is a kind of screen onto which emergent identities can be projected. Stuart Hall clearly shares this understanding of identity when he writes,

> Cultural identity ... is a matter of 'becoming' as well as of 'being'. It belongs to the future as much as to the past. It is not something which already exists, transcending place, time, history and culture. Cultural identities come from somewhere, have histories. But like everything which is historical, they undergo constant transformation.[42]

Hall's point also highlights the ever-changing nature of identities, and the importance of exploring identity in film. Such attitudes to identity are significant, given that in the past people have tended to define identity in terms of the culture shared by people with a common history and ancestry. Identity was often considered a stable point of reference and self-definition, irrespective of the changing or disruptive nature of actual historical experience. This traditional view of identity is increasingly challenged by the realities of the contemporary world, particularly of the erosion of homogeneous communities. Moreover, as Kwame Appiah argues with regard to African identities, such earlier definitions tended to

39 bell hooks, 'The Oppositional Gaze', in bell hooks, *Black Looks : Race and Representation*, p 131.

40 Speaking at the British Film Institute's *Screen Griots Conference*, London, 9–10 September, 1995.

41 Interview with the author. Ouagadougou, February 1995. (My emphasis).

42 Stuart Hall, 'Cultural Identity and Cinematic Representation', *Framework*, 36, 1989, p 70.

Cultural Identity, Representation & Voice

reaffirm the constructs originally imposed by Europe with its reductive perceptions of the continent and the African 'race', rather than reflecting the genuine cultural or metaphysical commonalties and the shared experience of colonialism that exist in Africa.[43] Negritude or Pan-Africanism's espousal of the belief in a single and fixed African identity unwittingly continued to promote what the philosopher Paulin Houn-tondji has dubbed 'unanimism', or the belief that there is a central body of ideas shared by all Africans. Both Appiah and Hountondji argue that this 'unanimism' has done Africa a disservice, as it has effectively continued to do exactly what the Western world has done for too long – namely silence Africa's diversity. Colonial and postcolonial experiences in Africa have, however, forced us to see cultural identities in a new light. Francophone African film work, and in particular its articulations of identity, has contributed to this reappraisal by highlighting both points of difference and similarity. Above all, it has illustrated that identities are not monolithic and homogeneous constructs beyond the influences of culture and time.

Francophone Africa's increasingly diverse film styles are both characteristic of the region's multiple identities and contribute to the ongoing process of evaluation and assessment of those identities. As such, this diversification can be seen as a sign of Francophone African cinema's maturity and increasing richness, rather than a 'loss of authenticity' as is sometimes claimed. As we have seen, numerous directors have moved away from the overtly political styles of the early years as they develop more reflexive works that seek to interrogate local cultures and history. Other filmmakers, such as Djibril Diop Mambety, have opted for more experimental, intertextual forms whose fragmented narrative structures and fast rhythms reflect the vibrant hybridity of contemporary African urban environments, addressing issues specific to the cities, such as petty crime, prostitution, and drugs. Numerous other works evoke the mutual influence and inter-penetration of the urban milieu and rural zones, and thus clearly illustrate that the boundaries between the two are shifting and fluid.

It is precisely this move away from monolithic definitions of African identity that has permitted an uninhibited embrace of indigenous and non-indigenous, 'traditional' and 'contemporary', rural and urban elements, as Appiah confirms when he writes, 'we are all already con-taminated by each other ... there is no longer a fully autochthonous echt-African culture awaiting salvage by our artists'.[44] The works of many of today's younger Francophone African filmmakers, including Jean-Pierre Bekolo (Cameroon), Issa Serge Coelo (Chad), Joseph Kumbela (DRC), Zeka Laplaine (DRC), Gahité Fofana (Guinea), or Bouna Medoune Seye (Senegal), amongst many others, fully acknowledge the syncretic cosmopolitanism that characterises contemporary African cultures and identities. Their blend of generic styles and mediums in a dance of continuities and discontinuities goes well beyond the simplistic binary oppositions of 'tradition' and 'modernity'. Jean-Pierre Bekolo's *Quartier Mozart* (Cameroon, 1992) and *Le Complot d'Aristotle* (1997), for example,

43 See Kwame A. Appiah, *In My Father's House: Africa in the Philosophy of Culture.*

44 Ibid, p 155.

44

foreground contemporary urban youth culture, fashion, music, and the 'creolised' forms of African French and English. Both films juxtapose African and non-African references and filmic influences in an upbeat and bitingly ironic style. They weave extraneous genres, such as the *photo-roman* into the filmic text and use sharp, bright colours, fast music, freeze frames, rapid montage, acutely high and low-angles and tight close-ups to give the films a resolutely urban, youthful feel that sharply contrasts with the more static long shots and slow rhythm often associated with Francophone African films set in the rural milieu.

In *Le Complot d'Aristotle*, Bekolo takes references to imported culture to extremes. By adopting and parodying the styles of the Western B movies, karate and action films avidly consumed by young cinema-going audiences in Africa today, he develops a humorous reflection on the tensions and contrasts between this kind of cinema and African film. When African filmmaker Essomba Tourneur – whose initials, E.T., or 'extra-terrestrial', make a clearly ironic reference to Spielberg's blockbuster film and to the filmmaker's own 'alien' position as the sole defender of an African cinema – tries to impose African films on local film fans nicknamed Nikita, Bruce Lee, Saddam, Van Damme and Scharzenegger, the youngsters revolt. The fiction of the films they like rapidly takes over reality as the opposing clans battle it out in a brilliant parody of a Hollywood action film. Ultimately, despite the film's warning against cultural mimetism, Bekolo advocates a cultural synthesis capable of embracing all influences, as one of the characters exclaims, 'We're building the new thing. New Africa. We take what we can get. If it's old and it's good, fine. If it's new and it fits, excellent.'

The multiplicity of Francophone African identities is also manifest in the linguistic choices made in its films. Given the tight correlation between identity and language, the latter being one way in which people define their identity, Francophone African filmmakers soon recognised that they could represent their own cultures and identities by using local languages in their works, so reaffirming both. Since the early Sixties, therefore, the majority of Francophone African films reflect the region's true polyvocal linguistic make-up. Filmmakers generally prefer to opt for languages that faithfully represent that multiplicity, rather than choosing a *lingua franca* such as French which, whilst it may well be more easily understood by a greater number of people throughout the region, would continue to erase a vital facet of that local identity rather than enhance it. After initially using French in *Borom Sarret* (Senegal, 1962), *Niaye* (1964), and *La Noire de...* (1966), Ousmane Sembene was one of the first directors to insist on using Wolof in his subsequent film *Mandabi* (1968) in an effort to reach his home audiences better. Sembene's later work *Emitaï* (1971), which is a Jola-language film, also reflects the linguistic diversity in Senegal. Cheick Oumar Sissoko's *Guimba* and Souleymane Cissé's *Yeelen* and *Waati* (Mali, 1995) feature a whole range of different West African languages, accentuating Africa's linguistic diversity and rejecting the imposed language of the foreigner. Such films acknowledge that there is no single, 'authentic' African voice or style, but rather a multitude of vital and distinctive expressions.

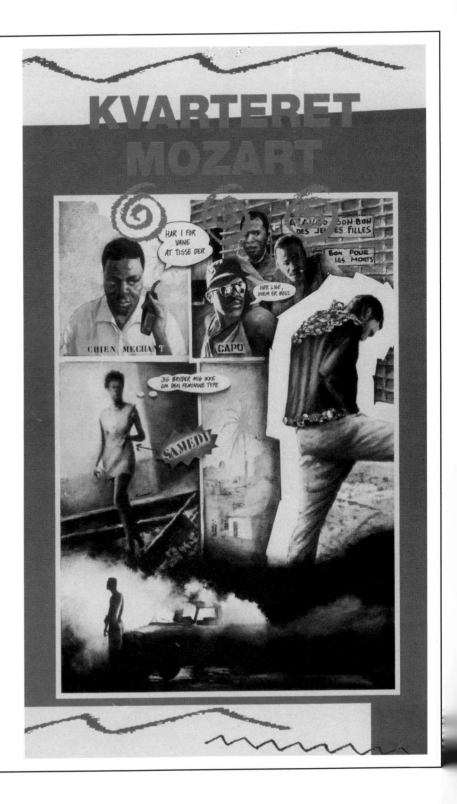

*(Opposite and top) Jean-Pierre
Bekolo,* Quartier Mozart, *1992.
Foregrounding contemporary urban
youth culture in a parody of the
photo roman.*
(Courtesy of Jean-Pierre Bekolo)

(Middle) Jean-Pierre Bekolo, Le
Complot d'Aristotle, *1997. Acute
low angles give the parodic film a
resolutely urban, up-beat feel.*
(Courtesy of Jean-Pierre Bekolo)

(Bottom) Jean-Pierre Bekolo, Le
Complot d'Aristotle, *1997. The
local 'gangsters', Nikita, Bruce Lee,
Saddam, Van Damme and
Schwarzenegger live out their
favourite action films.*
(Courtesy of Jean-Pierre Bekolo)

**Cultural Identity,
Representation & Voice**

This examination of Western representations of Africa and of the unique decolonisation climate in which Francophone Africa's directors first began making films helps to evaluate the importance of representation and identity, which the directors themselves often describe as fundamental.[45] In this respect, their attitude to film is summarised in the words of Dr Tafataona Mahoso:

> Like the cook who asks the child to hold the light so she can cook, African films should hold the light out to Africans so they can see how to live. The light that is the film should enable people to open up to explore their own consciousness, their own memory, their own space ... People should see their own lives, their own dignity, their own shame ... These films should help people in exploring African consciousness and spirituality and epistemology, rescuing them from the European exoticism which is standing in the way of our understanding of the importance of our own consciousness.[46]

Filmmaking can play a valuable guiding role in the revaluation and reassessing of postcolonial identities in the Francophone African context, as it has in the past. The majority of filmmakers adhere to the vision of their works as a means of expressing an African voice, rather than simply being a form of entertainment: the predominance of the questions of representation and identity and their influence on filmmaking agendas can clearly be recognised in the specific ways in which filmmakers articulate their cultural identities: they adapt local cultural forms to film, address questions of memory and history, and challenge the misrepresentation and visual absence of specific African groups, such as women and African immigrants in Europe. These responses are explored in further chapters. The predominance of such expressions of identity and voice provides every reason to look at Francophone African cinema in the light of these questions in order to understand some of the essential characteristics and agendas of Francophone African film more thoroughly.

45 See the author's interviews with various filmmakers in the appendices.

46 Tafataona Mahoso, 'Unwinding the African Dream on African Grounds: Audiences and the Critical Appreciation of Cinema in Africa' (paper given at BFI *Screen Griots Conference*, London 9–10 September 1995).

3 Screen Griots
Orature & film

When cinema was first invented at the end of the last century, Western filmmakers naturally integrated elements of their own cultures into the new art form, thereby developing the new cinematic codes and narrative conventions that have continued to evolve and diversify. By the time Francophone African filmmakers started experimenting with film in the early Sixties, therefore, cinema was by no means a neutral technological tool. African filmmakers adopting the medium appropriated Western filmic traditions, with which they were familiar, at least as spectators. But whilst film was an imported art form, it did not develop in a cultural void. When local directors started making films, they too integrated their own cultural forms, and notably their story-telling codes, adapting the new medium to suit and express their own realities and agendas.[2] In the same way that the previous chapter examined the socio-historic context of Francophone African film, Francophone African filmmaking also needs to be situated in its specific cultural context to highlight the ways in which local cultural and oral storytelling traditions have been adapted to the film medium. Without wanting to be too essentialist, this analysis will show that this has conferred a certain cultural identity on Francophone African film. But first it is important to clarify some of the general characteristics of the cultural environment of Francophone African filmmaking.

Living traditions: the cultural context

Given that the term 'traditional' African culture has often connoted 'rigidity' or 'fixedness' in much Western scholarship, it must first of all be made clear that the use of the term here in no way suggests that homogeneous, static cultures existed in Africa before contact with the West. James Clifford has rightly pointed out that Western anthropologists have often tended arbitrarily to focus on the elements of African culture that confirm their conception of tradition. As a result, all that is 'hybrid or "historical" in an emergent sense has been less commonly collected and presented as a system of authenticity'.[3] Whilst certain cultural continuities can be identified in both pre- and postcolonial Africa, it is important to remember that African cultures – just like any other culture in the world – have evolved as lifestyles or ruling dynasties have changed, new religions been introduced, and populations migrated and

'Un conte est un miroir où chacun peut découvrir sa propre image' ['A tale is a mirror in which everyone can discover his or her own reflection'] Amadou Hampaté Bâ[1]

1 Amadou Hampaté Bâ, *Contes initiatiques peuls* (Paris: Editions Stock, 1994), p 17.

2 As Susan Hayward writes, citing Graeme Turner, whilst 'narrative form probably serves the same function in all cultures, ... the specificity of its articulation is determined by the particular culture'. (Susan Hayward, *French National Cinema* (London & New York: Routledge, 1993), p 9).

3 James Clifford, *The Predicament of Culture: Twentieth-Century Ethnography, Literature, and Art* (Cambridge, Massachusetts & London: Harvard University Press, 1988), p. 231.

travelled. What has commonly been referred to as 'traditional' African culture in the past has generally been understood in opposition to 'modern' culture. As discussed in Chapter 1, 'modern' culture is understood to be the 'Euro-modern' culture imposed by the European colonial powers. This implies that the two are fundamentally opposed when there is more often a syncretism and/or harmonious coexistence of several cultures (explored in the previous chapter). In the same way that many formerly polytheistic Africans integrated the Christian or Muslim Gods into their 'traditional' belief systems, most contemporary African cultures have blended pre- and postcolonial elements. Elements of so-called 'traditional' culture are also still very much alive today, whether in their 'original' or updated forms and are not simply relics of an unchanging past. It is more useful to think in terms of Amadou Hampaté Bâ's 'living traditions'. It is also important to avoid the assumption that past cultural forms are more 'authentic' than those of the present. Just as contemporary African statues often represent figures in colonial pith helmets or on bicycles, Francophone African filmmakers have also blended 'traditional' cultural forms into the 'new' cinematographic medium, and have sometimes even thematically addressed the question of cultural synthesis and the relations between the 'traditional' and the 'new' in their work.

In order to appreciate how filmmaking has been integrated into this cultural sphere and, by extension, to understand the position filmmakers occupy in their respective African societies, some of the principal characteristics of the cultural environment and the role of the artist must be explored. Although we need to remember that the Francophone African countries form a vast and heterogeneous geographic space, inhabited by a multitude of different ethnic groups who all have their own cultural traditions, there are points of convergence that are particularly enlightening here. For all their diversities, certain West African ethnic groups do, for example, share cultural references that stem from their common historical legacies. Many ethnic groups belonged to the same empires in the past, were related through extensive ethnic alliances and trade links, and/or were subjected to the same system of French colonial rule. This has conferred a degree of cultural convergence without excluding significant diversities. The well-known Burkinabè actor and griot Sotigui Kouyaté remarks: 'When you look at ... western Africa and the Sahel in particular, you realise that the cultural bases ... [and] the points of view concerning the philosophy linked to existence and the human being are the same'.[4] The same is true of certain regions of West Africa. The Mande region, incorporating most of modern-day Mali, parts of Senegal, Mauritania, Niger, Burkina Faso, Guinea and Côte d'Ivoire, which constituted Sunjata's Mali Empire from the thirteenth to fifteenth centuries, still maintains its cultural and linguistic unity today.

Whilst pointing to the general, however, it is salutary to bear in mind Michel Leiris's observation that Western critics of African art often overlook its diversity because 'we are less able to appreciate the respects in which cultures or things unfamiliar to us differ from one another than the respects in which they differ from those to which we are used',

4 Jadot Sezirahiga, 'Every man has something of the divine in him. Speaking to Kouyaté', *Ecrans d'Afrique/ African Screen*, 13–14, 3rd–4th quarter, 1995, p 10.

causing us 'to see a certain resemblance between them, which lies, in point of fact, merely in their common differentness'.[5] So, whilst we can at times usefully highlight certain cultural continuities in a region as vast and heterogeneous as Francophone West Africa, such similarities should not cause us to lose sight of what are often the greater degrees of diversity. We must avoid falling into the trap of reductively treating African cultures as homogeneous entities, as has so often been the case in the past. If we acknowledge that there are similarities and differences between individual African cultures, we also need to recognise that there are also both differences *and similarities* with more distant cultural spheres.

As dominant beliefs concerning people's place in the universe are fundamental to any understanding of the cultural context and the role of the arts in Francophone Africa, it is useful to begin by considering the region's creation myths, which convey a profoundly holistic understanding of people, the community, and their environment, and which in turn points to the traditionally communal nature of many societies, their art forms and the role of the arts. These beliefs' emphasis on community is particularly relevant to this analysis of Francophone African film as they have profoundly influenced conceptions of filmmaking and creative choices.

Unlike contemporary Western cultures, which tend to privilege the individual and to value personal initiative and achievement, most Francophone African cultures consider people to be part of a community whose harmony and equilibrium takes precedent over notions of individual fulfilment. This does not necessarily mean that individuality is actually excluded, rather that people are expected to abide by community values, even in countries where massive urbanisation has weakened (but not necessarily eradicated) this village-based organisation. Many Francophone African filmmakers reflect the importance that their cultures confer on the group when they define their artistic role as being at the service of their people, as shall be discussed later.

Given that individuals are first and foremost considered to be part of the community, it follows that the human community is also taken to be an inseparable part of immediate surrounding environment. Whilst most creation myths situate humans at the centre of the universe, they are not deemed to master it. They are expected to respect the environment and the natural balance thought to exist between all beings and things. Interesting manifestations of this symbiosis can be identified in the spatial organisation of a number of Francophone African films, which accord as much importance to the surrounding landscape as to individuals in their shots. Directors will often hold shots of the skies, trees, water, or landscape once the characters have left the scene. Slow sweeping pans that give a sense of the unity and vastness of the landscape and reinforce identification with those surroundings are often included. Contrary to the style of many mainstream Western films, spatial considerations can take precedent over temporal concerns, explaining why many Francophone African directors film entire journeys, emphasising the spatial dimension rather than replacing the journey with an ellipse. These episodes are

5 Michel Leiris, 'The African Negroes and the Arts of Carving and Sculpture', in *Interrelations of Cultures* (Westport, Conn.: UNESCO, 1953), p 351.

Screen Griots:
Orature & Film

6 See André Gardies' fascinating book *Cinéma d'Afrique Noire Francophone: L'Espace Miroir* (Paris: L'Harmattan, 1989) for a more detailed discussion of this symbolic use of space in Francophone African film.

7 John S. Mbiti comments that, religion 'is integrated so much into different areas of life that in fact most of the African languages do not have a word for religion as such'. (*Introduction to African Religion* (London: Heinemann, 1975), p 12).

8 See Ousmane Sembene, *Man is Culture* (Bloomington: African Studies Program, Indiana University, 1979).

9 Gérard Meyer comments on these participatory practices in the introduction to his anthology of Mande tales: 'Beaucoup de contes, en effet, sont entrecoupés de chants, qui font partie intégrante du récit ... Ces chants sont repris par l'auditoire qui participe de manière très vivante. D'ailleurs, avec le conteur il y a toujours quelqu'un qui intervient après chacun de ses énoncés, qui ponctue en quelque sorte son récit en disant *naamu* (qu'on pourrait traduire par oui, certes, j'écoute!) Le conte est ainsi un véritable dialogue'. ['Many tales are indeed dotted with songs which form an integral part of the narrative ... The actively participating audience joins in with these songs. Moreover, there is always someone with the storyteller who intervenes after each of his statements, who effectively punctuates the narrative, saying *naamu* (which could be translated as yes, that's right, I hear you!) The tale is thus a real dialogue'.] (in *Contes du pays mandingue* (Paris: CILF & EDICEF, 1988), pp 3–4).

rarely gratuitous in the narrative, but take on a symbolic signification, notably in the numerous films that contrast the town and village, Africa and Europe (A theme developed in Chapter 5).[6]

Relations between the individual and the environment are also reflected in the way many filmmakers also favour long or medium shots that frontally frame characters in groups in relation to their surroundings, rather than isolating them. Idrissa Ouedraogo's two-shots in *Tilaï* (Burkina Faso, 1990) are a good example. The characters are systematically positioned together looking out at the fixed camera, rather than being singled out in the kind of separate shot-counter-shots that would generally be considered 'more natural' in mainstream Western film. *Tilaï* breaks the 'rules' of classic Western film narrative and may seem theatrical and stylised to viewers more used to film traditions that have striven to distinguish themselves from theatre. The film's shot composition openly embraces and recreates the kind of 'performance space' characteristic of West African traditional outdoor communal theatre performances. Once again, the aim is to reinforce this community-based spatial organisation.

To return to the Francophone African cultural environment, the same kinds of holistic understanding of the relation between humans and the forces of the universe, whether living or dead, sacred or profane, similarly apply to the relation between people and the arts.[7] Music, song, dance, and orature are totally integrated into and related to people's daily existence. The Senegalese writer and filmmaker Ousmane Sembene insists that art is not just ornamental in West Africa, pointing out that the word 'art' does not actually exist in the region's languages, Man himself being the symbol of art.[8] In most Francophone African cultures, art forms are traditionally destined for the whole community, irrespective of status or lifestyle, and frequently play a functional role. In both rural and urban environments, song and dance continue to play an integral role in various farming and domestic activities and social occasions.

Audiences also play a central role in all artistic performances. Although specific members of the community traditionally play music or sculpt by birthright, all members of the community actively participate in such events. When oral tales are narrated, for example, audiences regularly join in to sing the codified 'call-and-response' refrains or clap accompanying rhythms.[9] It is interesting to note that at popular films, audiences in Africa often transfer such participatory practices to the non-live imported medium. Western spectators in an African cinema are often struck by the way in which audiences participate in the film, interjecting remarks, clapping along to songs, and sometimes even providing running plot commentaries, especially in the rarely subtitled Indian or Kung-Fu films.

This holistic approach to the relations and interaction of people, their environment, and the arts influences the way in which different art forms are interrelated and/or juxtaposed in many Francophone African societies. Music rarely goes unaccompanied by song or dance, which are woven into the narrative structures of both contemporary theatre and film, providing the same kinds of structuring mechanisms as in the oral tales. Song and dance are not simply illustrative or decorative but play an integral role in either the narrative development or the overall meaning of an event. The lack of division between different art forms or their aesthetic/functional character also gives rise to the mixing of film genres. For this reason Teshome Gabriel calls African film a 'nomadic cinema', unconstrained by traditional filmic boundaries.[10] Like the tales, numerous Francophone African fiction films include 'documentary' moments, especially when directors film customary rituals and festivities in real time. This is also particularly common when the narrative touches on, and becomes a vehicle for educational or sociological issues, highlighting film's functional role. Examples include Cheick Oumar Sissoko's *Nyamanton* (Mali, 1986) and *Finzan* (1989), Adama Drabo's *Ta Dona* (Mali, 1997), Safi Faye's *Kaddu Beykat* (Senegal, 1975), *Fad'jal* (1979), and *Mossane* (1996), Jean-Marie Teno's *Clando* (Cameroon, 1996), Jean-Pierre Dikongue Pipa's *Muna Moto* (Cameroon, 1975), and Desiré Ecaré's *Visage des Femmes* (Côte d'Ivoire, 1985).

This emphasis on the functional does not mean that aesthetic qualities are neglected, however. Francophone African art rarely separates the two, reflecting the holistic understanding of the relation between the different elements in the universe. When a narrator tells a tale, which is often a vector for transmitting social codes, he or she will always seek to entertain and to engage the audience by bringing the tale to life 'like a film that unreels from beginning to end, ... restoring it *in the present*'.[11] The successful reception of the narrative will depend on the narrator's performance skills, particularly as audiences in Africa will often be familiar with the narrative or its stock characters and situations. Tales are judged for their perspicacity and delivery, rather than for their originality, a concept that rarely evokes the same deference as in Western artistic circles where individual, original artistic creation is more valued.

The actual message of a tale will usually be conveyed through a rich metaphorical language interpreted on different levels by different members of the audience, whether children, adults, initiates, or non-initiates. Gérard Meyer confirms the importance of the power of suggestion in this system of values, conveyed through images and a metaphoric language that rarely contains an explicit moral.[12] This complex layering of meaning hidden behind a beguilingly simple facade is explained in the introductory text to *Kaïdara*, one of the principal Fulani initiation tales, which traditionally begins:

> Pour les bambins qui s'ébattent au clair de lune, mon conte est une histoire fantastique. Pour les fileuses de coton pendant les longues nuits de la saison froide, mon récit est un passe-temps délectable.
> Pour les mentons velus et les talons rugueux, c'est une véritable révélation.
> Je suis à la fois futile, utile et instructeur.
> [For the children playing in the moonlight, my tale is an imaginary story.
> For the women spinning cotton through the long, dry season nights, my tale is a delectable pastime.
> For the bearded chins and rugged feet, it is a veritable revelation.
> I am at once futile, useful and instructive][13]

10 See Teshome Gabriel, 'Thoughts on Nomadic Aesthetics and the Black Independent Cinema: Traces of a journey', in Mbye B. Cham & Claire Andrade-Watkins (eds.), *Blackframes: Critical Perspectives on Black Independent Cinema* (Cambridge, Massachusetts: The MIT Press, 1988).

11 Amadou Hampaté Bâ, 'The Living Tradition', in Joseph Ki-Zerbo (ed.), *General History of Africa vol. 1* (Paris: UNESCO, 1981), p 199.

12 Gérard Meyer, *Contes du pays mandingue*, pp 4–5.

13 Amadou Hampaté Bâ, *Contes initiatiques peuls*, p 251.

**Screen Griots:
Orature & Film**

A number of Francophone African filmmakers have adopted a similar metaphorical approach to avoid being overtly didactic, as shall be seen in more detail later. Their films reflect the same kind of close relation between the functional and the aesthetic, content and form found in other art forms in the region.

The central position that the oral traditions and other art forms occupy in Francophone African societies reflects their significant societal role. Amadou Hampaté Bâ describes the tales, myths and legends as, 'the great school of life ... [which are] at once religion, knowledge, natural science, apprenticeship in a craft, history, entertainment, recreation ... Based on initiation and experience, oral tradition engages man in his total being'.[14] Through tales and myths, children learn the organisational structures and moral codes regulating their society and encounter their ancestral history and the belief systems of their community. Epic tales of past heroes, which the narrator often directly relates to present-day events, help to convey a sense of pride and belonging to a given community, setting accepted behavioural patterns and reinforcing social cohesion. Other tales serve as a vehicle for addressing all kinds of potentially problematic issues, ranging from family relationships to generational conflicts, or relationships with the surrounding animal and spirit environments. Such tales generally reinforce the moral order, with villains being punished and conflicts resolved. Given these key societal functions, it is hardly surprising that other new art forms, such as film, have adopted them.

It is important to note that storytellers frequently adapt the narrative details of a tale to suit the mood and tastes of their different audiences. This is particularly clear from the way tales are constantly modernised so that they continue to reflect changing socio-cultural realities. So-called traditional tales frequently contain anachronistic references to towns, colonialism, modern communications, or divorce, and the same tales may have different conclusions at different times. Christopher Miller describes this renewal of the oral traditions: 'the lessons of the past are ... constantly translated into the terms of the present'.[15] This suggests that it is the evolutive, rather than the static or obsolete aspects of these traditions that continue to be perpetuated. It also explains how orature, which is such a prominent part of Francophone Africa's cultural heritage, has managed to remain so very much alive today.

In addition to playing an educational role, oral tales and other live performances, such as song and theatre, have always provided a forum for protest and criticism. The focus is often the abuse of power, and is usually articulated through satire. The traditional outdoor theatrical performances of the Koteba in Mali continue to serve as a vehicle for social commentary as the younger generations satirise and mock the behaviour of their elders. Likewise, many contemporary musicians use their songs to comment on current issues and politics.

In this traditionally committed context, it is not surprising that many Francophone African filmmakers have conserved the political, societal aspect of the oral traditions. Such conceptions are clear from both

14 Amadou Hampaté Bâ, 'The Living Tradition', p 168.

15 Christopher Miller, *Theories of Africans: Francophone Literature and Anthropology in Africa* (Chicago: University of Chicago Press, 1990), p 98.

filmmakers' individual declarations and from the joint positions expressed in their diverse manifestos. The Pan-African Federation of Filmmakers' 1975 Algiers Charter declares, for example, that:

> ... the cinema has a vital part to play because it is a means of education, information and conscious raising, as well as a stimulus to creativity. The accomplishing of these goals implies a questioning by African film-makers of the image they have of themselves, of the nature of their function ... The stereotyped image of the solitary and marginal creator which is widespread in Western capitalist society must be rejected by African film-makers, who must, on the contrary, see themselves as creative artisans at the service of their people.

This again highlights how filmmaking has been integrated into Africa's existing artistic structures and practices. This politically committed view continues to prevail today, as the Malian filmmaker Adama Drabo makes clear:

> I don't want to make films just for their beauty, just for the aesthetics. I am accountable to a people who expect a lot of me because you're incredibly lucky to find yourself behind a camera in our countries and you have to make the most of it every time you can to encourage people to think, to encourage people to ask themselves questions, to surpass themselves, and thus to participate in the effort to reconstruct our countries.[16]

Numerous filmmakers thus use their work to address a whole range of social and political issues. One could say that filmmaking itself is a political act in Africa, where filmmakers are inevitably forced to confront the hegemony of Western representations and paradigms (as already discussed in Chapter 2).

Various African art forms remain profoundly marked by the predominantly (but by no means exclusively) oral nature of culture in sub-Saharan Africa.[17] The transmission of learning via a system of codified tales, myths, legends, riddles and proverbs helps to account for the predominant role orature continues to play in Francophone Africa's still widely non-literate societies and also explains the extensive influence it has on more recent cultural forms, such as literature, theatre, and cinema.

The centrality of the oral traditions reflects the profound reverence that traditionally surrounds the spoken word in many Francophone African societies. This deference is best understood in terms of what many of the African creation myths referred to earlier describe as the sacred origin of the word. According to Bambara cosmogony, for example, the diverse forces constituting the human only became activated and thus complete when Maa Ngala, the Supreme Being, breathed the god-given and unique force *Kuma*, or Word, into human beings. Both the Bambara and Dogon peoples of Mali, amongst many others, also traditionally believe that this 'divine' spoken word can activate the life forces not only in, but also around, people. In so doing, word is thought to instigate a process that can either harmonise or upset the natural balance between all things. As words are considered capable

16 Interview with the author. Ouaga-dougou, February 1997.

17 Arabic script was widely used in the Islamised regions of sub-Saharan Africa long before the arrival of the first European missionaries and traders, and certain groups, such as the Bamoun in modern-day Cameroon, or the Bambara in Mali, had developed ideograms and written forms of their languages.

of influencing this equilibrium, their ritualised forms play a key role in all ceremonies that seek to modify the balance of forces. Speech thus frequently fulfils a highly symbolic and complex function, and controlled speech is highly valued and cultivated in such societies where, as Sory Camara points out, elders and dignitaries prefer to express themselves in riddles to conserve the mysterious dimension of things and to conserve the purity of the word.[18]

The preference for restrained, 'coded' speech also explains Africans' predilection for proverbs, or 'the palm-oil with which words are eaten', to cite the Nigerian writer Chinua Achebe.[19] According to Isidore Okpewho, proverbs are 'the storehouse of the wisdom of the society'. He adds that, 'Most proverbs have a philosophical depth which is the result of a careful and sensitive observation of human conduct and experience of the surrounding nature ... Proverbs ... are treated with authority and respect because they are regarded as truth tested by time.'[20] Proverbs, like tales, are part of the codified system through which learning and experience are transmitted and thus play a central regulatory role.

Francophone African film unsurprisingly reflects these local speech codes and perpetuates reverence for the spoken word. Characters' words are often peppered with proverbs as they seek to clarify a point, conclude a discussion, or diffuse overt tension. Ritualised moments of speech are also accorded an importance in the narrative that reflects the place speech traditionally occupies in most Francophone African societies. This can clearly be seen from the diegesis' frequent inclusion of the traditional decision-making sessions known as the *palabre* [palaver] in Francophone Africa, in which villagers gather to resolve communal questions.[21] This perhaps also reflects a conscious or unconscious desire to reappropriate the word, and thus an African voice, after years of being silenced by Western colonisers.

Whatever the motivations, the importance accorded to speech often disconcerts Western audiences who are used to logical, linear narrative development and clear dialogues that advance the narrative. Rather than being superfluous or tedious appendices, these long discussions, greetings and palavers are very much part of the overall internal rhythm and logic of the films and the cultures they portray. André Gardies recognises this point, remarking that in many African films, 'La parole ne sert pas à écourter, pas plus qu'elle ne saurait être écourtée. Au contraire, elle demande à être écoutée'. ['Speech is not a short-cut, nor can it be cut short ... On the contrary, it is there to be listened to'].[22]

Such ritual moments of speech are often distinguished from moments of simple conversation by their poised delivery and ritualised settings. Whether in the urban or rural environment, discussions usually take place in the shade of the 'palaver tree', on an elevated platform, or under some kind of canopy. The camera is often static and unobtrusive. By not drawing attention to itself or directing/controlling the viewer's gaze, this allows the spectator to concentrate on what is being said. The whole group is often filmed from the front at the beginning and end of the sequence before the camera focuses on individual speakers, emphasising

18 See Sory Camara, *Gens de la Parole: Essai sur la condition et le rôle des griots dans la société malinké* (Paris/Conakry: ACCT, Karthala, SAEC, 1992).

19 Chinua Achebe, *Things Fall Apart*, in *The African Trilogy* (London: Picador, 1988), p 20.

20 Isidore Okpewho, *African Oral Literature: Backgrounds, Character, and Continuity* (Bloomington & Indianapolis: Indiana University Press, 1992), p 235.

21 It is interesting to note what the generally negative connotations of this word in Europe says about the Europeans' view of traditional decision-making institutions in Africa.

22 André Gardies, *Cinéma d'Afrique Noire Francophone: L'Espace Miroir* (Paris: L'Harmattan, 1989), p 137.

the unity of the group rather than any individual. The speaker is also usually positioned in the centre of the shot, highlighting the centrality of the spoken word.

Cheick Oumar Sissoko's film *Finzan* contains several good examples of this process. Sissoko gives the lengthy exchanges between the village chief and his intermediaries their own filmic space, focusing primarily on the gestures and stances of the characters, rather than on the 'action'. He avoids close-ups and tight focus which might single out the individual. Sissoko's directorial choices reflect the community-based conception of the individual already described, for, as Sissoko himself insists, 'It's not one person but the group effort that influences events'.[23]

Given the importance of orature, it comes as little surprise that specific members of diverse Francophone African communities are often considered to be specialists of the spoken word. Although such individuals are commonly referred to by the non-indigenous generic term 'griot', which is thought to be a corruption of the Portuguese word 'criado', it is widely accepted that the name in fact masks a multitude of different statuses and roles.[24] Amadou Hampaté Bâ distinguishes between what he refers to as the 'traditionalists', or Master Initiates – known as *domas* or *donikebas* in Bambara, the highly-respected scholars who often travel far to expand their own knowledge and to teach, and who are characterised by their measured speech – and the endogamous hereditary griot caste known throughout the Mande region as *djeli*.[25] The hereditary griot traditionally play a range of roles such as highly-respected mediators, advisors, and spokesmen-cum-ambassadors to individual rulers or ruling noble families, providing a counter-balance in power relationships; learned genealogists, historians, poets, singers, musicians and storytellers responsible for safeguarding and transmitting popular memory; and 'henchmen', or salacious scandalmongers with infamously sharp, gossiping tongues. Griots enjoy different degrees of respect according to their diverse roles. In general they are always both feared and revered for their mastery in manipulating the dual creative and destructive forces of the spoken word.

Whatever their exact status or name, hereditary griot have always played an essential role in West African societies and their arts. This has influenced contemporary filmmakers, becoming a point of reference. In particular, the hereditary griot – like the royal jester or fool in Medieval Europe – traditionally enjoy a far greater degree of freedom of speech than other individuals, allowing them to broach all subject matters and, if necessary, to openly criticise abuses of power and authority. Nowadays, griots often continue to perform as storytellers and musicians, perpetuating the oral traditions. Some have adapted to postcolonial social structures by offering their services to the new rulers or by continuing to exercise their prerogative to criticise abuses of power. Sory Camara comments: 'Certaines chansons de griots relèvent incontestablement de ce que l'on appelle l'art engagé. L'art des griots a toujours été engagé politiquement, du fait même des rapports étroits qu'ils ont avec le pouvoir et les réalités politiques de leurs pays.' ['Certain griot songs can

23 Pat Aufderheide, 'Interview with Cheick Oumar Sissoko', *Black Film Review*, vol 6, 2, 1990, p 6.

24 Given that each language in the region has a range of terms describing the different kinds of 'griot', the admittedly nebulous generic term will nonetheless be used here.

25 Referred to as *mabow* and *tyapurtaw* by the Fulani, *gaulow* by the Wolof, and *funew* by the Soninke. (cf. S-M Eno Belinga, *La littérature orale africaine* (Issy les Moulineaux: Les classiques africains, 1985). Many ethnic groups throughout West Africa are traditionally organised into castes. The Bambara, for example, are divided into the *horon*, or 'noble' caste that includes rulers, warriors and farmers; the endogamous *nyamakala*, or artisan caste comprising smiths, potters, weavers, wood and leather workers, and the *djeli*; and the *jon* who were captives originally taken in battle. According to Hampaté Bâ, the concept of higher and lower castes, or classes, did not originally exist, but seems to have become more prevalent in some regions later on.

incontestably be defined as *engagé*. The griots' art has always been politically committed due to their close relationships with their countries' authorities and political realities'].[26]

Despite the profound changes that have taken place in contemporary Africa, especially in urban areas, griots continue to play a fundamental societal role, widely reflected in contemporary art forms including film. As Francophone African filmmakers have appropriated their medium to express their own cultural specificities and forms, they have been influenced not only by the thematic and stylistic characteristics of the oral tales, but also by the role of the griot itself. Strikingly, many Francophone African filmmakers have described their own role as that of the 'modern griot', thereby confirming the parallels between filmmaking and orature. Ousmane Sembene was one of the first to embrace a socially and politically committed vein of filmmaking, arguing that, 'the artist must in many ways be the mouth and ears of his people. In the modern sense, this corresponds to the role of the griot in traditional African culture'.[27] He has also regularly called for African films to be night-schools to replace traditional storytelling sessions.[28] Senegalese director Djibril Diop Mambety echoes Sembene's words, declaring: 'the word griot ... is the word for what I do and the role that the filmmaker has in society ... the griot is a messenger of one's time, a visionary and the creator of the future'.[29] The Malian filmmaker Adama Drabo adds, 'I at times identify with the griot's way of telling stories. As the griot says at the start of [*Taafe Fange*], it's my duty to capture the past to prepare the present and the future. African filmmakers work in the same spirit, in the same direction.'[30] These views highlight the way in which both Francophone African film and orature strive to interrogate the past in order to reflect upon and to forge the present and the future. This process is particularly clear in the 'return to the source' films mentioned in Chapter 2 and in the series of historical films discussed in Chapter 4 which, since the Seventies, refute 'official', predominantly Western readings of history, redefining the past.

Whilst not all filmmakers describe themselves as modern griots, the oral tales remain the predominant narrative articulation in the region, continuing to be a common point of reference for contemporary writers and filmmakers alike. Although efforts to determine whether or not there is a specifically Francophone African film language risk falling into the same kind of reductive and essentialist categorisation that has characterised Western discourse on Africa in the past, African societies clearly have their own culturally-specific narrative forms which influence their filmmakers consciously and unconsciously. Cameroonian filmmaker Jean-Marie Teno has claimed, for example, that, 'tales ... are a part of my childhood and thus are amongst the things that are totally unconscious in my work ... [They] belong to the dramatic art in a given space that I know, in which I grew up'.[31] The Burkinabè filmmaker Dani Kouyaté, himself a member of the well-known Kouyaté griot family, also claims to take direct inspiration from the oral traditions and the performance of the griots, stating, 'Griots ... tell stories all night long ... They have techniques

26 Sory Camara, *Gens de la Parole*, p 347.

27 Ousmane Sembene, 'Filmmakers and African Culture', *Africa*, 71, 1977, p 80.

28 See Ousmane Sembene, *Man is Culture*.

29 June Givanni, 'African Conversations: Interview with Djibril Diop Mambety', *African Conversations*, published in conjunction with the *Screen Griots Conference* (London: BFI, 1995).

30 Interview with the author. Ouagadougou, 1997.

31 Interview with the author. Paris, August 1997.

to stop the audience from getting bored ... We ought to try to understand the griot's techniques and adapt them to the new media'.[32]

Given the hybrid nature of contemporary cultural forms in Africa, it is important to recognise that other local and/or imported forms also complement these traditional oral influences. Keyan Tomaselli and Maureen Eke thus aptly refer to such new, orature-influenced forms as 'secondary orality', reminding us that whilst filmmaking may be an articulation of traditional orature, it cannot be confused with orality itself.[33]

The stylistic and structural influences of orature on film

A multitude of stylistic and structural oral influences can be identified in Francophone African film. This is particularly clear in a series of films directly inspired by traditional narrative styles and techniques that confirm the importance of these narrative traditions by adapting tale formats and their narrative codes to the screen and using griot characters to introduce and/or to narrate the main filmic diegesis in the form of a tale. Examples include Oumarou Ganda's *L'Exilé* (Niger, 1980), Ababacar Samb Makharam's *Jom* (Senegal, 1981), Dani Kouyaté's *Keïta! L'Héritage du griot* (Burkina Faso, 1995) and *Sia, le rêve du python* (2001), *Guimba* by Cheick Oumar Sissoko (Mali, 1995), and Adama Drabo's *Taafe Fanga* (Mali, 1997). Many other films weave narrated tales into the main diegesis, for example Jean-Marie Teno's *Afrique, je te plumerai* (Cameroon, 1991) and *Clando* (1996), Souleymane Cissé's *Waati* (Mali, 1995), *Fad'jal* by Safi Faye (Senegal, 1979), and *Djeli* by Fadika Kramo Lancine (Côte d'Ivoire, 1980). Several other filmmakers, including Mustapha Dao (Burkina Faso), Kadiatou Konaté (Mali), Cilia Sawadogo (Burkina Faso), Mansour Sora Wade (Senegal), and the pioneer of the filmed tale format, Mustapha Alassane (Niger), have adapted actual tales to the cinema, often using puppets, animal masks, and animation.

Tale structures

Oumarou Ganda's *L'Exilé*, one of the first films to overtly adapt a tale structure, opens with the politician-in-exile, Ousseini, telling an African tale at a drinks party in Europe. As the story unfolds, developing the theme of keeping one's word, it becomes obvious that Ousseini has chosen it to explain his own reasons for resigning from his country's government. His allegorical use of the tale immediately echoes the metaphorical function of many oral tales. Ousseini's central position in the circle of guests recalls the centrality of the narrator in traditional storytelling sessions. As the frontal shot of Ousseini fades into an African village landscape whilst Ousseini is heard narrating the beginning of his tale in voice-over, the traditional accompaniment of the *ngoni*, a small three-stringed elongated guitar, reinforces the traditional storytelling context.

The tale's opening words – 'A long, long time ago in virgin Africa ... word was sacred'[34] – immediately mirror the central theme of the whole

32 Interview with the author. Ouagadougou, February 1995.

33 Keyan Tomaselli & Maureen Eke, 'Secondary Orality in South African Film', *iris*, 18, Spring 1995, pp 61–71.

34 All quotes from the films discussed throughout this book are translated from the original French subtitles.

film, the theme of the tale, and the theme of the second tale told within the former. As the events of the embedded narrative begin to unfold, Ousseini's explanatory voice-over fades, and the tale becomes the central narrative of the film. However, periodic shots of Ousseini narrating to the listening guests and Ousseini's intermittent voice-overs constantly remind the spectator of his presence.

In the first tale, a king, who is described as deeply respecting his word, decides to put two brothers to the test when he overhears them swearing to give their heads in return for a night with the king's daughters. One year after the two couples are married, the king summons the brothers, Marafa and Sadou, to remind them of their words. Here, and each time the king holds an audience in the film, he is always filmed in a central position elevated on a kind of platform, flanked by a *ngoni* player and encircled by his courtiers. They in turn are encircled by the low court wall, which creates a ritual circle that visually accentuates the sacred nature of the word. The film's pace is particularly measured as Ganda allows the spoken word to unfold. Camera movements are limited so as not to deflect the viewer's attention away from what is being said. Reminding Marafa that 'one's word is a thing that must be treasured like a fortune', the king proceeds to tell his own story to clarify the way in which he expects his son-in-law to act. In this second tale within Ousseini's tale, a king decrees that he will behead the first person to announce the death of his favourite horse, but is tricked into saying it himself by the clever griot who comes to announce the news. Having sworn to honour his word, this king thus orders his own execution. Marafa, who knows 'the value of one's word', immediately understands the king's allusion and agrees to die to honour his word. Sadou agrees too, but is ultimately persuaded to flee by his wife.

In exile, Sadou's word and that of his wife Miriama are put to the test three times. When Sadou is bewitched by a spirit outside the first village they come to, Mariama accepts the help of Sougorez Zima, 'the greatest diviner of all times', on condition that Sadou marries his daughter Hadio. When Sadou, Mariama and Hadio settle in a second village, Sadou agrees to marry the king's daughter in return for her help in answering the king's trick questions which, if answered wrongly, are punishable by death. When Sadou is summoned, the king is again seated in the centre of the frame, flanked by his courtiers and *ngoni* players in a composition that recalls the first court and thus reinforces the embedded narrative. When Sadou answers the questions correctly, the king accepts his own fate and is beheaded, Sadou thus succeeding to the throne.[35]

At this point in the tale, Ousseini is seen narrating to the listening guests once more. This time, the sounds of the village can be heard, suggesting that the tale setting has become so tangible in the telling that it permeates the European sitting room. As we return to the African space one final time, Ousseini's off-screen voice remains present as he narrates the end of the tale. Sadou, who is now king and father of several children, agrees to sacrifice himself to the village's divinity to save his people from famine. The film ends with shots of the guests, a frontal

35 *L'Exilé* is clearly based on a common Senegalese/Guinean tale in which a man is saved three times by each of his three wives. At the end of this tale, the man arrives in a village where newcomers have to correctly answer an 'impossible' question and is saved when the chief's daughter intervenes to help him. This 'impossible task' theme is also very common throughout West Africa, as shall be seen in more detail later.

close-up of Ousseini, and a shot of the first king speaking to Sadou, thereby voluntarily confusing our understanding of who is telling which tale to whom and thus confirming that the different tales' messages can be related to each time-period in the film. Not only does Ganda successfully adapt the tale structure and theme to his film, using the embedded narrative structures common in the oral tales to build up successive layers of meaning, but also structurally and thematically he accords a key place to the spoken word, thereby intrinsically linking the form and content of the film.

Ababacar Samb Makharam's *Jom* similarly comprises three disparate parts related to a common theme. At the start of the film, set in the present, Khaly the griot, who serves as the link between the conflated past and present 'tenses' of the film, narrates an episode of recent Senegalese history to a group of friends and neighbours who are on strike. Once again, the audience is gathered in a circle in a hut, their unity emphasised by the circular panning movements of the camera. As Khaly starts to tell his tale, both the film characters and the spectator are party to his role and his storytelling techniques.

The theme of Khaly's tale, 'jom', or 'dignity' in Wolof, is clearly choosen to galvanise the strikers' resolve, for he begins his tale by saying, 'He who listens to me will not lose his way.' To illustrate exactly what he means by 'jom', Khaly takes inspiration from a photo of a colonial officer parading a Senegalese man's head on top of a spear (shown in close-up on the wall of the hut), declaring, 'Let's examine the past to answer this question'. This highlights the way in which griots habitually refer to the past to inform the present, the shot fading into a sequence set sometime at the beginning of the century. Khaly's narrative voice continues off-screen to the sound of the *kora*, a twenty-one stringed harp-lute that is often used to accompany the oral tales. As in *L'Exilé*, West African audiences familiar with the instrument and its role in oral performance will immediately recognise the association between the film and traditional storytelling sessions.

Over images of Westernised Africans at a colonial officer's garden party, Khaly introduces what will later be understood to be a common leitmotif in the film's different stories: 'When we lost our freedom, people had two choices – to collaborate ... or live in refusal and preserve their *Jom*. That meant hunger, destitution, and death, but it also meant preserving one's dignity too.' As he strides into the shot himself, dressed in exactly the same way as in the present tense of the film, Khaly becomes physically present in each of the tales he narrates. This helps to link the film's disparate elements and quite literally illustrates the idea that the griot is always a witness to collective memory and perpetuates past events. Spatio-temporal continuity is disrupted, therefore, as is common in the oral tales. Khaly evokes this discontinuity himself as the film returns to its present tense, the panning camera shot emphasising the episode's circular structure: 'Time has no hold over me. I pass through and outlive the different periods ... I am the passing of time. I am the memory of the people and history ... I am continuity.'

In this past episode, Khaly both narrates and participates in the story of Dieri, the Senegalese prince seen earlier in the photo, who resisted the colonial regime before finally being killed by his collaborating cousin. Each of the film's episodes is characterised by this 'mirror' structure, commonly found in the oral tales, in which two protagonists react in opposite ways to the same situation. These two different characters, the 'positive' and 'negative' heroes, will be understood to represent man's dual nature, offering examples of how or how not to behave. The tale of Dieri's resistance is clearly related to the strike sequences set in the present tense of the film. Madjembe, one of the characters present when Khaly tells the story of Dieri, refuses his boss's bribes aimed at breaking the strike, unlike one of his other colleagues. Whilst the community celebrates Madjembe's action, with Khaly calling him 'Dieri's spiritual son', the collaborator's wives leave him, declaring, 'We entered this marriage with our dignity intact and we refuse to relinquish this virtue.' Encouraging the other strikers to maintain their resolve, Madjembe frequently refers to the importance of their 'jom', suggesting that he at least has heeded Khaly's lesson.

Towards the end of the film, Khaly's own 'jom' is tested when he is summoned to the house of a wealthy Senegalese family who ask him to perform at a party. Noticing how badly they treat their maid, Khaly narrates another story to explain his refusal. As he announces, 'I sing all that is beautiful and majestic', the second story unfolds. Again in the presence of Khaly, the famous dancer Koura Thiaw publicly defends badly treated maids, singing, 'Being an employee does not make you a slave. There are no stupid professions, only stupid people.' The 'mirror' structure is present again in this episode as Koura's kindness is contrasted with her hostesses' cruelty. As Khaly finishes his narrative, the scene returns to the sitting room of the rich man's house. Despite the obvious implication of the tale, the rich man insists on trying to pay Khaly who simply answers, 'Do I have to repeat myself ... I was born a griot. I live on what people give me. My tools are my memory and my word and I only sing what is beautiful.' His words are an explicit resumé of the process already seen at work throughout the film and reaffirm the way in which orature uses the past to contemplate the present.

Based on the famous legend of Sunjata Keita, the thirteenth-century founder of the Mande Empire, Dani Kouyaté's *Keïta! l'Héritage du Griot* is another particularly interesting example. Not only does the film use an embedded narrative structure to bring part of the Sunjata legend directly to the screen, but also questions the role of orature today and its relation to Africa's contemporary, Western-style education. Here, the griot Djeliba Kouyaté comes to Ouagadougou on a mission to teach the young Mabo Keita the story of his ancestors, Maghan Kon Fatta Konate and Sunjata Keita.[36] Every time Djeliba narrates an episode of the legend to Mabo (the two filmed increasingly close together in the same frame as their complicity grows), the episode unfolds in flashback, initially accompanied by the *ngoni*. However, Djeliba's narrative voice or Mabo's off-screen questions constantly recall the storyteller's presence. As the film

36 Throughout the Mande region, the Kouyaté are the Keita family's hereditary griot. The director's father, Sotigui Kouyaté, who plays the role of Djeliba, is a well-known actor and griot.

(Top and middle) Dani Kouyaté,
Keïta! L'Héritage du Griot, *1995.
Djeliba and Mabo's increasing
proximity in the frame reflects their
growing complicity.*
(Courtesy of Dani Kouyaté &
Jean-Christophe Dupuy)

(Bottom) Dani Kouyaté, Keïta!
L'Héritage du Griot, *1995. Mabo,
narrates the Sunjata legend to his
friends up in the branches of the
tree, a common symbol of
transmission.*
(Courtesy of Dani Kouyaté &
Jean-Christophe Dupuy)

progresses, Mabo himself becomes the narrator as he tells the tale to his school friends, again showing the process of oral transmission at work. In these scenes, the three boys are always seated around a huge tree, or up in its branches – the tree commonly being associated with transmission in many West African traditions – and Mabo is always centre frame, accentuating both his position as narrator and his words.

Djeliba's storytelling sessions alternate with scenes set in the present. This present-day intrigue ultimately interrupts the legend to question the role of orature in contemporary society. As Mabo becomes increasingly absorbed in the tale, his schoolwork begins to suffer, much to his teacher's and his mother's consternation. When Mabo's father refuses to intervene, insisting that Djeliba's teachings are part of the tradition, his mother retorts, 'Times have changed. Tell your griot that there is school now.' Things go from bad to worse at school, making Mabo's mother increasingly irate, so she confronts Mabo with the impossible choice of the tale or his education. These two approaches are best summed up when Djeliba confronts Mabo's teacher, reproaching him for teaching Mabo that his ancestors descended from the apes whilst he himself tries to teach Mabo that his ancestors were great rulers. Recognising the tension his story is creating, Djeliba finally decides to leave, disappearing as suddenly as he arrived. The rest of the story is left untold, implying that it is up to Mabo himself (and the spectator) to go on searching. In the final shots of the film, Mabo significantly looks up into the sky at the circling vulture, Djeliba's totem, which, as Hampaté Bâ explains, 'est un animal hautement significatif. Son symbolisme est multiple. Parce qu'il niche souvent sur des sommets inaccessibles ... il est le symbole même de l'initiation, c'est-à-dire la connaissance difficile à atteindre' ['(the vulture) is a highly significant animal. Its symbolism is multiple. As it often nests up on inaccessible summits, ... it is the very symbol of initiation or, in other words, knowledge that is difficult to attain'].[37] In the same way that Khaly is physically present and thus links the disparate elements of the film *Jom*, the 'magical' Do hunter who mysteriously appears at key moments of the film's past and present tenses, appears in the street to comfort Mabo. This second apparition in the present tense of the film thus echoes its opening sequence, when the Do hunter first sends Djeliba on his mission, thereby completing the filmic cycle that is characteristic of oral tales.

Cheick Oumar Sissoko's *Guimba, un tyran, une époque* not only adopts the tale structure, but emphasises the oratory skills of the main griot character. The film opens with a lateral tracking shot of the griot-narrator walking along the banks of a river playing the *sokou*, a small two-stringed fiddle that commonly accompanies tales, as his opening narrative sets the scene to come. A flashback shows Guimba's son being betrothed at birth to Kani, the daughter of a Sitakili family, before the camera returns to the griot. As the camera pans down onto the griot's reflection in the water, the image dissolves directly into the main diegesis and the film leaps forward in time to Kani as an adult and Guimba a much-feared tyrant. Spatio-temporal continuity is distorted, as in oral tales.

37 Amadou Hampaté Bâ, *Contes initiatiques peuls*, note 61 of *Njeddo Dewal*, pp 368–369.

Cheick Oumar Sissoko, Guimba, un tyran, une époque, *1995.
Guimba's intimidating aura is accentuated by his central, raised position and the fact that his face is always hidden.*
(Courtesy of Cheick Oumar Sissoko)

Guimba is generally accompanied by his faithful griot (far right).
(Courtesy of Cheick Oumar Sissoko)

Guimba's personal griot plays a key role in the film as an ambassador and advisor. He nearly always accompanies him, highlighting the relation between the griot and his 'master'. Guimba is always positioned in the centre of the shot, on a raised platform in his court, or on horseback in the streets, symbolising his power. His intimidating and mysterious aura is accentuated by the use of low-angle shots and the way that long fringes of his hat hide his face from his subjects. As Guimba's regime is authoritarian and corrupt, the griot is by extension corrupt, in contrast to the more noble types of griot seen in all the films mentioned so far.[38] His incredibly quick tongue and masterfully applied

38 Ousmane Sembene's short film *Borom Sarret* (Senegal, 1962) also features a parasitical, 'corrupted' griot who unscrupulously feeds off people poorer than himself.

proverbs are an art in themselves, even if they are spent singing the praises of 'the generous and selfless noble' Guimba, in flattery clearly at odds with Guimba's tyrannical behaviour. Every time the griot goes to visit Kani's family, whom he knows to be hostile to Guimba and his son, he tries to flatter them, citing their noble lineage, with a verbose stream of calming proverbs. Kani's parents, Mambi and Meya, are not deceived, however, and treat the griot with all the contempt that his allegiance to Guimba merits.

As the film closes, the original griot-narrator is seen walking by the river playing the *sokou*, thanking the audience for its attention, reminding them that the central narrative is only a tale. The camera pans down onto his reflection in the water, accentuating the kind of circular structure common in the oral traditions, before returning to the final shots of Sirriman the hunter as he leaves Sitakili. As this griot's voice-over gives the final details of the story, his restrained style and integrity again contrasts with the compromised flamboyance of Guimba's griot.

The opening sequence of Adama Drabo's *Taafe Fanga* is particularly explicit in its affirmation of orature's contemporary role. The griot Sidiki Diabaté enters a crowded urban compound where the children are gathered watching a black and white Hollywood musical on TV, nonchalantly flicking off the television before sitting to play his *kora* and opening the night's story-telling session. As the camera zooms in on the griot and pans round the compound to show the gathered audience clicking their fingers to the music, the griot asks, 'which past shall we visit tonight?' This stresses the fact that the story-telling sessions are a collective occasion, the circular panning shots again accentuating the harmony of the group. When a mysterious woman enters the compound, provoking a scuffle by going to sit with the men who loudly protest, 'Don't upset the order! Trouser-wearers here. Skirt-wearers over there', she floors her male adversary, much to everyone's astonishment. The griot takes inspiration from this exceptional incident, just as Khaly in *Jom* takes inspiration from the photo in the hut, highlighting the way in which griots draw lessons from the events around them. Declaring, 'Beautiful stranger, spirit or human, I sing your amazing feat. It takes me far back in time to the Dogon women's revolt on the Bandiagara Escarpment in our fine Mali. Honourable audience, let's borrow the legend to visit this people reputed for its conception of the universe', the griot relates the lessons of the past to the present.

Sidiki Diabaté's *kora* is heard over the first establishing shots of the Dogon village, linking the film's contemporary present tense to the main body of the film, set in the past. Throughout the rest of the film, the griot's presence is recalled every time the *kora* punctuates the narrative and whenever the *kora* serves as a musical interlude between scenes, linking time and place. As the tale in the Dogon village of Yanda begins and Timbé learns that her elderly husband Ambara is about to take a young second wife, Timbé is seen walking dejectedly through the labyrinthine streets. The words of a song are used in the background to comment, 'O World, made by and for men. Your children's lot is lack of sympathy and suffering'. This use of song recalls the way in which the old tales incorporate songs to comment on narrative action.

When Yayèmé steals the sacred Albarga mask from the magical Andoumboulou, using it to scare the men into accepting a reversal of male-female roles in a 'take-over' scene that marks the culmination of the first 'act' of the film, the *kora* is heard off-screen, before the camera slowly zooms in on Sidiki Diabaté playing in the compound.[39] This device reminds viewers of the griot's (omni)presence, that they are watching a tale within a tale, and encourages spectators to find the links between the past and present. After creating a reflective pause in the dramatic narrative, the griot briefly comments on the events seen so far as the film returns to the scenes of the women celebrating their victory over the men. The Yanda narrative thus becomes the main diegesis of the film again. In the following scene, song plays a predominant narrative role, with the griotte (female griot) celebrating:

Who ever saw a goat bite a dog? O night of power. The extraordinary has happened. Being a woman isn't a weakness; it's believing so that is. The women have been given power. They will keep it. If you attack the Mande women, they will sell your hide for a cola nut. Take a look over here! The skirt has floored the trousers.

As the women circle round the griotte dancing and clapping, the song's final words echo those of the man who defied the stranger at the beginning of the film, linking the film's structure.

The tale of the Yanda revolt also includes its own story-telling sequence when Yandju, the Andoumboulou, is caught looking for her stolen mask on the night Kouni's friends come to her compound to hear one of her father's tales. As in the Bamako compound at the beginning of the film, the camera focuses on the whole group, highlighting its unity, while Yandju tells the children her story from centre frame. The children respond in unison to the opening storytelling formulae, revealing the collective participatory nature of the tales, while the images of the tale itself take over. Meanwhile, Yandju's narrative voice is occasionally heard off-screen. The same actress plays Yandju and the stranger from the beginning of the film, suggesting that both the fight incident and the actual characters inspire Sidiki Diabaté, which further blurs the boundaries between the film's 'reality' and its 'fiction'. It also highlights the 'magical' quality of the film and, through the Yandju/stranger character, the link between the past and present tenses of the film. The vivid red clothes worn by both Yandju and the stranger visually accentuate this 'confusion'. The stranger's red *boubou* is decorated with Dogon crosses in a reference to the Yanda part of the film.

As the story set in Yanda draws to an end, the *kora* is heard and the griot's voice intervenes off-screen to conclude that even though the women finally lose control of the mask, 'from North to South, East to West, they are winning their rights and establishing an equality that respects difference'. This statement brings us back to the present and yet

39 *Taafe Fanga*'s theatrical structure, character and camera movements, and acting styles are characteristic of Mali's popular theatre traditions which several Malian directors, including Adama Drabo and Cheick Oumar Sissoko, cite as a source of inspiration. Adama Drabo was also a playwright before he become a director, and *Taafe Fanga* is an adaptation of one of his own plays, which also helps to explain the theatrical style of Drabo's work.

echoes Kouni's final words in the tale. It is the Yanda griotte who has the final word, singing over the film's last images, 'we have tasted freedom and we won't ever forget it. So beware!' Her song clearly has resonance in both the Yanda tale and the whole film, explicitly linking its two tenses and reminding us how the lessons of the past inform the present.

Several other films include tale sequences, such as the opening of Souleymane Cissé's *Waati*, where an aerial camera scans the abstract forms of the ridges and shadows of the desert below. As the camera gradually descends and the landforms become clearer, the minimalist soundtrack gives way to the ethereal voice of an old woman who tells how the earth was created out of wind, water and fire. The voice slowly loses its ethereal, distant quality and becomes anchored in the present as the landscape is replaced by the image of a South African family seated round a fire at night. The camera slowly pans full circle around the listening audience and back to the grandmother, establishing the ritualised storytelling circle, the sense of communion in the group, and the grandmother-narrator's centrality. This centrality develops as the camera zooms in on her, literally drawing the spectator and her absorbed audience into the animal creation tale she narrates.

The power and land struggles she describes allude to the anti-apartheid power struggle to be portrayed. The grandmother's concluding words, 'It was necessary to go to the school of life to grow strong', also 'prophetically' announce the transcontinental initiatory journey that her granddaughter Nandi (one of the small children listening to the tale), will make later in the film. The old woman's mystical voice continues to play a guiding role throughout the rest of the film, encouraging Nandi on her quest for knowledge and freedom, in the same way that the griot's voice seeks to guide and advise the community.

One last example is Jean-Marie Teno's *Clando*, in which an inter-mittently narrated hunter tale allegorises the Cameroonian expatriate Rigobert Chamba's difficulties in Germany. The working out of this tale helps Chamba find a solution to his problems. The first part is heard in voice-over when the main protagonist, Sobgui, is still in Cameroon, and the second part is told much later when Sobgui is in Germany. The relationship between this 'old' tale and Chamba's present experience only becomes apparent when the third and final episode is narrated as Rigobert Chamba is 'reunited' with his estranged father on the telephone, thus retrospectively illuminating the meaning of the first two parts of the tale. The fragmented delivery of the tale and the intentional ambiguity about who is actually narrating forces the film's characters – and the spectator – to work at unravelling the different layers of meaning. This freedom of interpretation ultimately augments the tale's dramatic impact and echoes the metaphorical function of the traditional genre.

Allegory and satire
The allegorical nature of the hunter tale in *Clando* is characteristic of the way allegory functions in oral tales. Numerous other directors have adopted these structures and leave their conclusions open-ended,

Cheick Oumar Sissoko, Guimba, un
tyran, une époque, *1995.*
*Guimba's tyrannical reign: a clear
allegory for contemporary
dictatorships in Africa.*
(Courtesy of Cheick Oumar Sissoko)

encouraging audiences to interpret the symbolism of the story in the
same way that static or minimal camera movements leave spectators free
to direct their own gaze. As Dany Kouyaté explains, 'Griots ... address
everyone. They take fateful, fundamental stories and turn them into
amusing legends. All those with experience, who are perspicacious, who
read between the lines, will understand their meaning.'[40]

A number of directors exploit the satire in allegory traditionally used
to mock symbols of authority. Kenyan writer wa Thiong'o Ngugi claims
that 'Satire is certainly one of the most effective weapons in oral
traditions'.[41] Griots frequently resort to satire when exercising their

40 Interview with the author. Ouagadougou, February 1995.

41 wa Thiong'o Ngugi, *Decolonising
the Mind: The Politics of Language in African Literature* (London/Nairobi: James
Currey/Heinemann, 1986), p 81.

Screen Griots:
Orature & Film

42 Cited by Françoise Pffaf, *The Cinema of Ousmane Sembene, A Pioneer of African Film* (Westport, Connecticut: Greenwood Press, 1984), p 74. In, 'Cinema and Development in Africa', the Burkinabè historian Joseph Ki-Zerbo comments, 'one of the film-maker's arms is the African laugh. Africans laugh a great deal, perhaps to mask centuries of oppression and depression, but also because laughter is an essential part of the celebration of fraternity which is so striking in oral cultures based on personal dialogue. These smiles and laughter are ... varied and meaningful ... Yet many foreigners have reduced the African laugh to what could be adapted to their system of oppression, characterised by the dialectic of master and slave: the infantile or servile laugh, the irresponsible, gaping, blissful laugh, the 'Banania' laugh'. See Imruh Bakari & Mbye Cham (eds.), *African Experiences of Cinema* (London: BFI Publishing, 1996), p 74.

43 Citing Zahan and Dieterlen's *Textes sacrés d'Afrique Noire*, S-M Eno Belinga informs us that Bambara men may become initiates of secret societies which form the basis of Bambara cultural, philosophical and spiritual organisation. According to Belinga, there are six secret societies (some other sources mention seven) – the *n'domo*, the *komo*, the *nama*, the *kono*, the *tywara*, and the *kore* – each of which represents one of the different stages of initiation. The *kore* represents the supreme degree of knowledge and mystical life. (See also S.-M. Eno Belinga, *La littérature orale africaine* (Issy les Moulineaux: Les classiques africains, 1985). As the opening titles of the film also explain, the Komo is 'l'incarnation du savoir divin. Son enseignement est basé sur la connaissance des "signes" des temps et des mondes. Il embrasse tous les domaines de la vie et du savoir' ['the (Komo) is the incarnation of divine knowledge. Its teaching is based on the understanding of time and the world's "signs". It incorporates all domains of life and knowledge'].

traditional right to criticise, in order to protect themselves from the potential wrath of the objects of attack and to encourage reflection through laughter. Ousmane Sembene stresses the serious potential of satire: '[it] makes people laugh, but it also makes them think. For us laughter is a social phenomenon'.[42] Humour, therefore, does not diminish the seriousness of a film's message.

Some filmmakers working under dictatorships or other repressive governments in Africa have chosen allegorical forms to avoid the political repercussions of their often bitingly satirical portrayals of authority. Some of the best examples include Ousmane Sembene's *Xala* (Senegal, 1974), Souleymane Cissé's *Yeelen* (Mali, 1987), Djibril Diop Mambety's *Hyènes* (Senegal, 1991), Gnoan M'bala's *Au Nom du Christ* (Côte d'Ivoire, 1992), Cheick Oumar Sissoko's *Guimba* (Mali, 1995), Adama Drabo's *Taafe Fanga* (Mali, 1997), and Balufu Bakupa-Kanyinda's short film, *Le Damier* (DRC, 1996). All of these deal more or less overtly with the abuse of power and related conflicts, which are common themes in oral tales where the weak often battle against the strong, the good versus evil. It is vital to recognise the place of allegory and satire in many African narrative forms, in order to appreciate the multi-layered and often highly political implications of such works.

Souleymane Cissé's *Yeelen*, which recounts the bitter confrontation between Nianankoro and his father Soma, an initiate of the Bambara's sacred Komo secret society, can be read as an allegory for both generational conflicts and as a challenge to a stagnating and oppressive order.[43] This has profound political implications given that the film was made in the final years of Moussa Traoré's brutal dictatorship in Mali. Unable to bear the idea of his son outdoing him in his quest for knowledge, Soma ruthlessly sets out to destroy Nianankoro, ignoring all pleas for clemency and abusing his sacred powers. *Yeelen* thus also offers a key reflection on the nature of the transmission of knowledge in traditional African societies.

Soma's refusal to be equalled by a member of the younger generation is clearly expressed during the Komo ceremony when he says, 'If Nianankoro is the blade of the knife, I, Soma, am the haft. Even the most pointed blade cannot cut its haft'. Nianankoro refutes this, 'The snake's slough is not the snake. The python's son can grow up to rival its father', alluding to the Malian youth's real struggle against Traoré's autocratic regime. Father and son meet in a final confrontation that is prefigured by both the film's parallel montage, which charts Soma's relentless approach, and by its imagery of conflict. When the mother performs a ceremony to implore the Goddess of water to protect her son, two bowls are seen, for example, to float and knock as if drawn together by some implacable force. Although both men are ultimately destroyed, out of the final confrontation comes light, for, as Soma's twin brother, Djigui, tells Nianankoro, 'All upheavals bear hope' – a hope which Nianankoro's young son clearly embodies at the end of the film.[44]

In the press book of the film, Souleymane Cissé confirms the allegorical nature of his work, 'La rencontre entre le père et le fils, leur lutte,

symbolise la guerre, la grande tuerie, la folie de l'homme' ['The father
and son's encounter, their fight, symbolise war, widespread slaughter,
and human madness']. Djigui's prediction that the land of the Bambara
will undergo profound changes as its people are reduced to slavery and
the country itself become subject to conflicts can be read as referring to
the colonial era and to the disorder of Moussa Traoré's twenty-three-year
regime. Set some ten centuries ago, *Yeelen* is thus an allegory for
contemporary abuses of political power and the quest for knowledge. The
way in which filmmakers such as Souleymane Cissé embrace traditional
allegorical forms to evoke politically contentious contemporary issues
confounds the criticism discussed in Chapter 2 that their works are
apolitical and primarily cater to Western desires for a bygone, exotic
Africa.

Loosely adapted from Friedrich Dürrenmatt's parodic play *The Visit*,
Djibril Diop Mambety's film *Hyènes* is a scathing allegorical 'assault on
ongoing economic imperialism ... and a mournful commentary on the
current state of African communalism'.[45] When Linguère Ramatou –
'Linguère' meaning the 'sole queen', and 'Ramatou' a bird incarnating
the souls of the dead[46] – returns to her impoverished sleepy village of
Colobane 'richer than the World Bank', she makes the village an offer it
cannot refuse. Her promise of 'one hundred billion' in return for the life of
her former lover, Draman Drameh, initially shocks the inhabitants of
Colobane, who insist, 'we may well be in Africa, but drought hasn't
turned us into savages yet'. However, they are soon driven by their own
wretchedness and cupidity to abandon Draman, who finds himself
condemned for having brought disgrace on Ramatou. Thirty years earlier
he refused to recognise the paternity of their child, forcing her to leave
the village and driving her into prostitution. The theme of prostitution is
in itself a powerful metaphor in a film that questions the relationships
between those who hold financial power (the West and Western financial
institutions such as the IMF and the World Bank) and those who do not
(the African states).

Whilst Ramatou's unwavering determination to see justice done seems
ruthlessly cruel, Diop Mambety refuses to portray her simplistically as an
'evil' character. Not only does he evoke the motivations for her actions,
but also reveals the inhabitants' and Draman's own share of
responsibility in his ultimate fate. For all its mercilessness, Ramatou's
offer unmasks the villagers' own equally ruthless latent materialism,
suggesting that even the most morally upright are open to corruption. As
Ramatou showers gifts on the impoverished villagers, shipping in all
kinds of increasingly extravagant commodities, the villagers quickly
forget their initial indignant moral stance. Their change of heart is
observed by Ramatou's all-seeing, watchful valet, Gaana, the former
judge of Colobane, played by Diop Mambety himself (in another layer of
symbolism), who peers down on the villagers like a bird of prey from the
balcony of his hotel. Even Ramatou is surprised at the speed with which
the villagers abandon Draman. Her exclamation, 'Already! The reign of
the hyenas has begun', becomes a leitmotif that raises the question of

44 Twin characters are also commonly
found in 'mirror' oral tales, each twin's
behaviour representing opposing poles
of behaviour, as shall be seen in more
detail later on.

45 Richard Porton, 'Mambety's Hyenas:
Between Anti-Colonialism and the Critique of Modernity', *iris*, 18. Spring,
1995, p 96.

46 Angelo Fiombo, 'Africa up for auc-
tion', *Ecrans d'Afrique/African Screen*, 2,
1992, p 25.

Djibril Diop Mambety, Hyènes,
*1991. The popular and respected
Draman leads the welcome
committee that fêtes Linguère
Ramatou's return home.*

*Now isolated and abandoned,
Draman is sacrificed for
material gain.*
(Courtesy of Pierre Alain Meier,
Thelma Films)

Djibril Diop Mambety, Hyènes,
*1991. Linguère Ramatou: 'The
world made a whore of me. I want to
turn the world into a whorehouse.'*

Djibril Diop Mambety, Hyènes,
*1991. Ramatou and Draman
reminisce about their youth.*
(Courtesy of Pierre Alain Meier,
Thelma Films)

corruption and corruptibility in the film.[47] The hyena leitmotif is echoed by Diop Mambety's periodic inclusion of shots of circling hyenas, suggesting that it is only a matter of time before the village acquiesces and moves in for the kill. At the end of the film, a series of signs that have presaged Draman's death in every scene come to mind, beginning with the teacher's early recollection that, as a child, Ramatou 'never forgot a thing'.

Like all tragic heroes, Draman reaches a state of inner calm and self-knowledge before his death, and willingly accepts his fate. He is completely free of rancour in the final Ramatou-Draman scene. As the couple sit overlooking an expanse of sea that evokes the vastness of eternity, their mood echoes the other tender moment of intimacy earlier in the film when they sat reminiscing about their youth. Ramatou has remained resolutely emotionless until this final moment, when she tells Draman, 'You will be by my side for eternity. Go, die and join with me again', suggesting that her relentless desire to see Draman dead is not simply motivated by revenge, but ultimately by a need to be united with him. His death makes possible what his life denied her.

As the council of initiates gather to condemn Draman, their judgement being a foregone conclusion, they encircle Draman under the watchful eye of Gaana. Draman disappears beneath their feet, in the tradition of the legendary West African warriors, such as al-Hajj Umar or Soumangourou, who 'evaporated' in a veil of mystery rather than be defeated by their enemies. Ultimately, if Draman is found guilty of his original betrayal, he maintains his dignity. The villagers, on the other hand, are condemned for abandoning their principals. In the final shots of the film, bulldozers close in on sleepy Colobane, the cityscapes on the horizon indicating that speculators are about to raze the village. This is the price the villagers have to pay for selling their souls for material wealth. This pessimistic conclusion is summed up in Diop Mambety's own words, 'We are done for ... I'm not just referring to Africans but to the entire human race. We sold our soul too cheaply'.[48] His harsh judgement is quite unusual in Francophone African film. Although the film provides a critique of human behaviour, it is not so much the protagonists that Diop Mambety ultimately condemns, but rather the dehumanising conditions in which they live. Once again the allegorical implications of the film are far-reaching and universal, as are all the messages of the oral tales.

Like *Hyènes*, Balufu Bakupa-Kanyinda's uncompromisingly satirical black-and-white short film *Le Damier* also refuses to provide an optimistic closure. The central President character clearly resembles Zaire's former dictator Mobutu Sese Seko, with his leopard skin hat and thick-rimmed glasses, overtly satirising the former regime and providing a more general reflection on the nature and abuse of power. Tired of beating his own Mobutu-style, brutal Presidential Guard at draughts, the insomniac 'President for Life' has the best draughts-player in town brought to the palace. His decision is set against the almost surreally remote backdrop of a government reshuffle and the President's staunch refusal to accept

47 Symbolic of 'trickery and social marginality' and 'notoriously known for its greed and mischievousness', the hyena is a recurrent animal character in West African oral tales. (Nwachukwu Frank Ukadike, *Black African Cinema* (Berkeley/Los Angeles: University of California Press, 1994), p 176).

48 Jean Servais Bakyono, Baba Diop & Clement Tapsoba, 'I went to compare, not to compete. Speaking to Mambety', *Ecrans d'Afrique/African Screen*, 2, 1992, p 12.

multiparty politics, hints of which only penetrate the calm of the luxurious presidential palace via a series of TV and radio news flashes. As the essence of the game lies in the elaborate insults the opponents launch at one another – examples of which are heard as two soldiers play – the intimidated, downtown draughts champion cannot play properly. The inequality of the two men's positions is highlighted throughout the film by the fact that the President's face is only seen on television or in official photos. The camera instead focuses on his impatiently tapping foot, the back of his head, his body, and so forth, as if the lens, like the draughts champion, could never 'dare' look the President in the eye. In contrast, the camera bears down on the champion draughts player in high-angle shots, starting with a crushingly vertical high-angle when he first arrives in the palace hall that makes him look rather like a disposable piece on a chessboard himself.

Fed up with winning so easily, the President threatens to have his 'opponent' punished. The player pleads for food and marijuana to recreate more 'natural' playing conditions. Losing all his inhibitions, he really begins to play well – much to the indignation of the Presidential Guard, listening over the walkie-talkie system, and to the angry surprise of the President. As the player's insults increasingly demystify the Presidential aura, the camera finally focuses on the President's face for the first time. They player's lack of respect cannot be tolerated, however. The President requests that the player remain silent the next time he comes to play and the thuggish Presidential Guard interpret this as the go-ahead to give the player 'a hiding he'll never forget'. A radio flash announcement ends the film as it started (adopting the circularity common in orature), laconically reporting that the player 'was the victim of a nasty fall'. The allegory is unequivocal, the film's satirical form allowing Bakupa-Kanyinda to treat a highly serious subject with a large dose of disrespectful humour.

Finally, in *Taafe Fanga*, Adama Drabo satirises power relations between men and women by bringing a traditional Dogon myth to the screen in the form of a tale. Although the main body of the film is set in a Dogon village in the past, its message is unambiguously linked to the present as the griot who narrates the myth himself states when he begins to perform before the contemporary Bamako audience. The drama shows how the formerly subjugated women use the power of the sacred Albarga mask to force the men to accept a role reversal. In a series of hilarious sequences, the men, now dressed in women's wrapper skirts, learn to cook, winnow, carry pots on their heads and babies on their backs, whilst the women strut about in men's clothes, ordering their husbands around and spending their time drinking together in the shade of the palaver spot just as the men did before. Only Timbé, an older aunt, recognises that the women's power lacks the necessary stabilising economic base, in an analogy to the African continent and the continuing neo-colonial economic imperialism there today.

Lacking these strong foundations, the women's power is ultimately overthrown, leaving the final message of the film that it is better to

Balufu Bakupa-Kanyinda, Le
Damier, *1996. The high-angles and
shot composition accentuate the
division between the all-powerful
President and the lowly downtown
draughts player.*
(Courtesy of Balufu Bakupa-Kanyinda)

Balufu Bakupa-Kanyinda, Le
Damier, *1996. The draughts player
loses his inhibitions and the
President his all-powerful aura.*
(Courtesy of Balufu Bakupa-Kanyinda)

recognise each other's differences and to work together as equals rather than for one group to try to dominate the other. (As Yayèmé, one of the principal female characters remarks, 'If you return the donkey's kick, you are no better than the donkey'). This representation of male–female power relations can again be seen as an allegory for a range of relations, just as the past serves as an allegory for the present. All of these films clearly show how numerous Francophone African filmmakers have adapted allegorical and satirical structures commonly found in Francophone Africa's oral narrative traditions. This technique enables filmmakers to address serious, and often complex social issues in an entertaining and thoughtful way, thereby perpetuating the critical role of the griot to which many filmmakers aspire.

Common tale structures

A number of filmmakers have adopted some of the structural characteristics of the oral tales without necessarily opting for an overt tale format or style. In *La mère dévorante*, Denise Paulme identifies a range of recurrent structures found in the oral tales, which can also be seen in a number of Francophone African films.[49] These include the 'ascendant tale', which moves from an initial lack, or problematic situation, to the resolution of the lack/problem; the 'descendant tale', in which the status quo is upset or a stable situation deteriorates due to the arrival of a new disruptive influence in the community or the protagonist's ill-judgement or greed. (In the later case, the character responsible for upsetting the original order will be integrated, distanced or punished.) A third type is the 'cyclical tale', in which the status quo is upset, leading to the same consequences for the guilty party and the restoration of order, before the situation is upset again for different reasons, and the events repeated, or, lastly, the 'mirror tale', already mentioned earlier, in which two protagonists react in opposite manners to the same challenges (one good, the other bad).

Whilst not exhaustive, Paulme's classifications provide a useful introduction to some of the different schema at work in many Francophone African films. Identifying these structures' oral origin thus confirms the close ties between orature and film. Filmic examples of these classifications are multifarious. Djeliba the griot's sudden disruptive eruption in the Ouagadougou family household in Dani Kouyaté's *Keïta!*, or Ramatou Linguere's cataclysmic return to Colobane in Djibril Diop Mambety's *Hyènes*, are both characteristic of the 'descendant tale' structure in which an outsider's arrival upsets the status quo. In other films, the outsider's arrival represents a timely and necessary challenge to the existing order, as when Sirriman the hunter comes to confront the tyrannical ruler in Cheick Oumar Sissoko's *Guimba*, or when the Albarga mask erupts amidst the Dogon villagers in Adama Drabo's *Taafe Fanga*. Idrissa Ouedraogo's *Tilaï* offers an example of the 'cyclical tale' structure in which the status quo is upset and restored twice by both of Saga's homecomings.

'Mirror tale' structures are also frequent in film, as has already been demonstrated. In both Moussa Touré's *Toubabi* (Senegal, 1991), or Jean-

49 Denise Paulme, *La mère dévorante: Essai sur la morphologie des contes africains.* (Paris: Editions Gallimard, 1976).

Marie Teno's *Clando*, for example, one character's successful experience of Europe is contrasted with another's disastrous one. In Drissa Touré's *Laada* (Burkina Faso, 1990), Do and Demba's decision to leave the village for the town where they become involved in crime contrasts with Sina's decision to stay in the village where he is initiated into the village's traditional teachings. At the end of the film, Demba's renouncing of criminality and his reintegration into village life is also contrasted with Do's lack of repentance and his subsequent exclusion from the community.

Narrative layering

Other stylistic features influence Francophone African film structures and narrative codes. Non-linear forms have already been shown to arise when griots digress to develop a point or a lesson before coming back to the original tale. Not only have an increasing number of directors opted for the tale within a tale format discussed earlier, but many films are also marked by this characteristic layering of narrative threads. These are often related to a common theme, as in *L'Exilé* or *Jom*, or linked by a single character. In Adama Drabo's *Ta Dona* (Mali, 1991), for example, Sidy's job as a government agricultural advisor enables Drabo to address both questions concerning the rural environment and corruption in the civil service/political sphere. At the same time, Sidy's personal quest for the 'seventh clay pot' also allows Drabo to introduce elements of traditional esoteric Bambara learning. Drabo explicitly relates this narrative layering to the oral traditions, acknowledging the influence of oral narrative techniques when he remarks that:

> griots ... start telling stories that they can decide to break off at any moment to address the listeners directly, to ask them questions, before taking off in another direction, controlling the digression before bringing it back to the original story. I tried to follow the same procedure in *Ta Dona*. You start the story off, head in one direction, you appear to stray, circle round, come back and take up the original story again.[50]

Western spectators accustomed to narrative causality may find the fragmentary layering, parallel developments, and shifts of point of view in time and space disconcerting. Many Western critics, who often fail to recognise the specificity of these narrative codes, frequently complain that such African film narratives are 'poorly constructed'. African audiences are familiar with such narrative structures, as filmmaker Jean-Marie Teno confirms: 'there are so many tales in which someone tells a story, and in that story there is another character who tells another story. You can end up with two or three superimposed layers ... Africans follow [this kind of narrative construction] easily'.[51] Other films, such as Med Hondo's *Soleil O* (France-Mauritania, 1969) and *Watani, un monde sans mal* (1998); Abderrahmane Sissako's *Octobre* (Mauritania, 1992); Djibril Diop Mambety's *Touki-Bouki* (Senegal, 1973) and *Le Franc* (1994), similarly have sophisticated and challenging non-linear structure's inspired by such narrative techniques, but which are frequently associated in the West with the self-conscious, Euro-American cinematic avant-garde.

50 Interview with the author. Ouaga-dougou, February 1997.

51 Interview with the author. Paris, August 1997.

In more recent years, directors whose films are often situated in Africa's fast-moving, syncretic urban environments, have pushed this non-linear fragmentation to the extreme in their efforts to capture the chaotic city ambience. In Drissa Touré's *Haramuya* (Burkina Faso, 1995), the narrative constantly shifts from one story or group of characters to another as Touré gives fragmented glimpses of a wide range of characters' lives – students, employees, prostitutes, con artists, rich Lebanese traders, and a bigoted religious head of a polygamous family – rather than building the intrigue up to an overall climax. Several of the pivotal characters serve as 'bridges' between the disparate groups who meet and diverge again throughout the film. The upbeat, contemporary feel of such films still has its roots in the narrative layering traditionally found in the oral tales.

Circularity

The circular structures commonly found in the oral tales have also been adopted in film, as already mentioned. Numerous films open and close on the same shot, whose symbolic meaning only becomes apparent when it is seen again the second time. Near the beginning of Sissako's *Octobre*, for example, shots of Idriss phoning at the airport are punctuated by the camera panning over a vast desolate wasteland. It is not until the film comes full circle and the shots of him buying his plane ticket home are followed by the same wasteland images that we understand that what appeared to be the film's direct events were in fact situated in the past. Temporal continuity and our perception of the film's narrative tense are disrupted. In Souleymane Cissé's *Finyé* (Mali, 1982), the mysterious opening shots of the small boy superimposed over a stretch of water only take on their symbolic meaning when the same child is later seen in Bâ's symbolic hallucinatory dream sequence.

Protagonists in what will later be seen to be orature-inspired 'quest' films tend to find themselves back at their initial point of departure, but they are changed by the events narrated in the film. Jean-Marie Teno's *Clando* ends as it starts, with shots of Douala filmed from inside a moving car. However, Sogbui's final voice-over conversation with Irène indicates that their meeting in Germany has helped him find the resolve to act. Similarly, as Nandi tells the daughter of the oppressive farmer Baas Hendricks when she returns to South Africa in Souleymane Cissé's *Waati*, 'the experiences of my life have changed me', now giving her the strength to assert her own identity and will.

Interestingly, the very concept of the circle is integral to the structure of *Waati*. In a number of scenes, the camera movements actually trace a circular pattern. When Nandi confronts the white mounted policeman on the beach, Cissé alternates dizzily circling low-angle shots from Nandi's family's point-of-view, with menacing high-angle shots from the police-man's perspective, using their constantly spiralling movement to accentuate the spiralling tension in the scene. Cissé explains, 'je voulais que [la scène] s'articule à partir de mouvements circulaires. Pas seulement pour mettre en place une chorégraphie dramatique, mais aussi pour reprendre la figure du cercle cosmique qui apparaît juste après le générique' ['I wanted (the scene) to adopt a circular movement, not just to develop a dramatic choreography, but to echo the figure of the cosmic circle that appears just after the credits too']. This cosmic circle symbolises 'toute la cosmogonie de l'univers, de l'existence du monde et de l'au-delà. C'est un cercle parfait, on est dedans et on ne peut plus sortir' ['the entire cosmogony of the universe, of the existence of the world and the beyond. It's a perfect circle. We are inside it and can no longer get out'].[52] Cissé's inclusion of the circular motif in the film's very structure sets up a thematic and metaphysical echo and logic. The circle, representing both Nandi's circular initiatory journey and symbolising the culturally-specific understanding of life that gives meaning to Nandi's voyage, confers a powerful internal coherence on a film that spans very different geographic settings and periods.

Repetition

The repetition of musical and/or visual leitmotifs, narrative incidents, and standardised call-and-response formulae that enable the audience to answer the griot's periodic interjections with set replies are all common structuring devices found in oral tales. In Francophone African cultures, this repetition, which can also be seen in the circular repetition of musical rhythms, the cyclical nature of regenerative religious festivals, or the cyclical view of human existence, does not bear the same negative connotations (duplication, lack of originality, and so forth) associated with repetition. (Most Western cultures have long privileged linear progression.)

This is most apparent in films' common 'quest' motifs, which borrow both structural and thematic forms from the oral tales, as shall be seen in more detail later. Characters are repeatedly faced with a set of tasks or challenges. When a poor and illiterate man, Ibrahim Dieng unexpectedly receives a money order from his nephew in Paris, in Ousmane Sembene's *Mandabi* (Senegal, 1968), he tries to complete an impossible task: to cash the money order whilst fending off his neighbours, all of whom hope to share his good fortune. Dieng is seen heading into the hostile town centre over and over again, where unhelpful officials send him from one administrative office to another. Along his way, he meets a series of unscrupulous characters who take advantage of his naïveté by robbing him.

Repetition also acts as a structuring device in Idrissa Ouedraogo's *Tilaï* as Saga, then Nogma, go to and fro between their home village and their village of exile. Saga returns to his home village twice in the film. On both occasions, his presence triggers a confrontation. The montage and shot compositions of both return sequences are strikingly similar. Blowing his horn to announce his arrival, Saga is first of all seen up on the escarpment overlooking the village and the huddle of inhabitants below on the distant plain. On both occasions, Saga's brother Kougri is singled out from the crowd as he advances alone on the plain, a physical isolation that later echoes his psychological distancing from the other villagers when he refuses to comply with harsh traditional law. Each of

52 Jean-Marc Lalanne and Frédéric Strauss, 'Entretien avec Souleymane Cissé', *Les Cahiers du Cinéma*, 492, juin 1995, p 58.

the brothers' two meetings is preceded by a frontal shot of Kuilga warning her mother that there is going to be trouble, followed by a fixed mid-shot of the brothers, face to face. After each confrontation, one of the brothers is seen having to leave the village, the whole of the second sequence giving the spectator a sense of déjà-vu that builds the suspense at the end of the film. The spectator's knowledge of the outcome of the first meeting accentuates the dramatic irony, creating a sense of foreboding. This film thus expresses the notion of fatality incorporated in many culture's belief systems.

Musical leitmotifs

One final structural parallel is the way in which a number of Francophone African filmmakers have adopted orature's practice of rhythmically punctuating narrative with musical leitmotifs, song, and dances. In oral performance, different narrative themes are often accompanied by a musical leitmotif that audiences will quickly recognise. Music and song may serve as a transition between different episodes of a tale, particularly when the tale comprises a number of digressions. The song or music facilitate narrative development and lend an overall structural coherence and rhythm to the tale. Moreover, the lyrics of songs frequently provide a commentary on elements of the film's plot, or narrate some episodes, adding another voice to the diegesis, and recalling the interjections and commentaries habitually provided by the griot.

Desiré Ecaré was one of the first directors to develop this structure in *Visage des Femmes* (Côte d'Ivoire, 1985). The importance of the music is immediately apparent when the film opens with a long, *cinéma-vérité* style documentary sequence of a village dance that sets the scene and introduces one of the film's two narrative threads. This sequence is repeated as the film closes, providing a fresh commentary on the film's overall meaning and highlighting the circular structure common in oral narrative.

When the young dandy, Kouassi, returns to the village from the town and slowly seduces his sister-in-law, N'guessan, the film cuts back periodically to documentary-style shots of a group of village women dancing and beating a rhythm as they sing in the traditional call-and-response style. The words of their song comment on the events in the main narrative, or narrate events that are about to happen. When N'guessan's husband accuses her of having an affair before she actually has, the women sing, 'Men never trust us ... They see evil everywhere ... What does a jealous man deserve? Just one thing ... to be cheated on.' They continue to mock their menfolk's jealous behaviour and introduce the ensuing events singing, 'I'm going to tell you what I do to my man ... who is always spying on and suspecting me. Follow me and you'll see the life I make him lead.' Images of N'guessan and Kouassi meeting by the river replace the shots of the women, the song fading as the couple start to make love. The song links the different episodes, allowing greater temporal flexibility without losing narrative coherence. The director thus layers all readings by introducing the village women's exterior point of view and opening up the dialogic possibilities of the film.

In three more recent Senegalese films, songs also complement the main narrative. In Mansour Sora Wade's moving short film *Picc Mi* (Senegal, 1992), Modou, a fatherless child entrusted by his mother to an unscrupulous imam, makes his way through the streets of Dakar begging, doing odd jobs and playing with another street child. A song-tale is intermittently heard off-screen, parts of which are repeated, adding another narrative dimension to the film. The song/tale about the caiman and the abandoned little bird on whom the caiman preys is clearly related to Modou's own story. This is made clear when Modou returns to the Koranic school alone in the dark, handing his earnings over to the greedy imam, seated under the tree, as the song continues off, 'The bird was tired and hungry. He knew that the caiman was even hungrier than him ... The caiman said: Bird, your mother is my friend. I'm here at the foot of the tree watching over you for your own good.' But as Modou huddles up with the other sleeping children, he dreams that he flies away like a bird, accentuating the parallel between the tale-song and the film narrative. The singing voices repeat over and over, 'Mother, come and save me!', whilst an adult voice sings in increasingly slow motion, 'What have you done with what you earned begging today?', the child's reality thus filtering into his dream.

Safi Faye's striking film *Mossane* (Senegal, 1996) is also punctuated by the haunting voice of the famous Serer griotte Yandé Codou Sène. As the film opens on the waterfront at sunset, alternating long silhouette shots of the tragically beautiful young protagonist, Mossane, and mid-shots of three strange Pangool water 'spirits', a voice-over sings – 'when Mossane bathes ... the Pangools, who disappeared at the height of their youth, come to contemplate their chosen one.' Both the imagery and the film's storyline are thus given a tragic cast. Throughout the rest of the film, Yandé Codou Sène's song is associated with each apparition or evocation of the Pangool, the words of the song always stressing Mossane's beauty and the solitude and unhappiness it causes, as is witnessed in the main plot of the film. As the film closes, Mossane's dead body is found by the waterside. The Pangool huddle together in the foreground echoing the film's opening, the voice-over song praising Mossane's beauty and bringing the narrative to a close as the villagers slowly file into the distance and out of the fixed long shot.

In all of these films, music and song play the same integral, functional role as in the oral traditions. They serve as a structuring narrative device, rather than simply being an 'exotic' or aesthetic embellishment. The oral tales' structural and stylistic influences are thus clearly as deeply rooted as they are multiple, as is also the case with the thematic influences discussed below.

Thematic influences

Thematic studies of Francophone African film frequently point to the parallels between the themes and archetypal characters found in both the oral tales and films. The well-known traditional narratives of Francophone African orature often consciously or unconsciously inspire filmmakers who adapt its standard themes and characters to the film medium. Even when the thematic content of a film has been updated to reflect the contemporary realities and context of the film, it is possible to identify the same characters or situations habitually found in the tales.

African audiences familiar with such tales since childhood will immediately recognise and interpret both the traits associated with these characters, and the symbolism of given situations and themes. Amadou Hampaté Bâ explains how the characters in tales represent us all. Good and evil characters 'sont en nous comme deux pôles extrêmes ... Notre être est le lieu de leur combat ... C'est en nous-même, et non dans des catégories sociales extérieures, qu'il faut chercher les correspondances, les qualités et les défauts des personnages' [(Good and evil characters) 'are like two opposite poles within us ... Our being is the site of their combat ... It is within us, and not in external social categories, that one needs to look for the character's similarities, qualities and faults'].[53] Some Western viewers more used to film characters being given an individual psychological development may mistakenly interpret this tradition as poor or incomplete characterisation. African audiences, however, will immediately recognise the cinema's frequently portrayed corrupt politicians or rapacious traders to be representations of what Emmanuel Obiechina identifies as the 'trickster archetype', who is often positively incarnated as the cunning hare and negatively incarnated as the deceitful hyena in oral animal tales.[54]

In the same way that the heroes of the tales are often exceptional and/or magical child characters (described by Denise Paulme as the 'precociously clever child' archetype) who defy or outwit the representatives of authority, many filmic characters also defy the symbols of power.[55] In Cheick Oumar Sissoko's *Finzan*, the villagers successfully defy the government officials who come to levy unfair taxes. Sidy, in Adama Drabo's *Ta Dona*, risks his own position as a civil servant by refusing to compromise, and confronts the film's corrupt government officials. Nianankoro stands up to his ruthless father in Cissé's *Yeelen*, and the inhabitants of Sitakili ultimately overthrow their tyrannical ruler in Sissoko's *Guimba*. Other films feature predestined or precociously clever children: Kouni, the exceptionally quick-witted, high-spirited child protagonist in Drabo's *Taafe Fanga*, plays a pivotal role in the film's action. She represents a bastion of stability and reason when the world 'turns upside down', acting as a link between the 'warring' men and women. As the film reaches its climax, it is Kouni who has the final word of reconciliation and hope, telling her mother, 'thanks to you, an eternal flame has been lit. We will win not power, but an equality that respects our differences.' Audiences familiar with the popular clever child archetype will positively identify with its contemporary filmic variants, reinforcing the progressive behaviour of such characters and/or their message in these films.

53 Amadou Hampaté Bâ, *Contes initiatiques peuls*, p 16.

54 Emmanuel N. Obiechina, *Language and Theme: Essays on African Literature* (Washington DC: Howard University Press, 1990). Many West African tales are situated in the animal world, but the animals' traits and characteristics are clearly related to those of humans.

55 In oral tales, the 'clever child' archetype represents abnormally precocious, pre-destined children who immediately distinguish themselves from 'common mortals' by speaking from their mothers' wombs, birthing and naming themselves. (cf. Denise Paulme, *La mère dévorante: Essai sur la morphologie des contes africains*).

**Screen Griots:
Orature & Film**

In the same way that oral tales evoke a wide range of social issues, set precedents for behaviour, and regulate inter-community relations, the vast majority of Francophone African films do the same, whether the films are realist, symbolic, experimental, surreal, or comic. Certain themes are recurrent in both tales and films. These include family relations (generational conflicts, polygamy, forced marriage, patriarchal domination, impossible love, etc.), greed and corruption, the abuse of power, the battle between good and evil, health and the environment (AIDS, the fight against desertification, etc.), education and the quest for knowledge, the contrasts between the rural environment and the towns, and the lot of the poor and social outcasts. The treatment of such issues in films by directors such as Ousmane Sembene, Med Hondo, Souleymane Cissé, Cheick Oumar Sissoko, or Adama Drabo, has given rise to a number of highly committed and at times overtly political films, although individual styles vary enormously.

The 'quest', or journey theme

A significant number of films have adapted orature's common 'quest' or journey structure, where the protagonist faces a series of challenges before accomplishing a specific task. In many such films and tales, the quest or journey itself is as much a theme as a structuring device. Journeys often provide the central motor to events in the narrative and symbolise some form of initiatory quest for knowledge and wisdom, or battle between good and evil. Referring specifically to the Fulani initiation tale *Njeddo Dewal*, Amadou Hampaté Bâ describes such journeys as an unending abundance of wild events, fantastical combats, perilous journeys, successes and failures that follow a non-linear path to their final happy conclusion.[56]

The quest for (self) knowledge is present in a number of films, notably in Souleymane Cissé's most recent films, *Yeelen* and *Waati*. In *Yeelen*, Nianankoro is pursued by his father, who is jealous of his son's acquisition of the secrets of the Komo initiatory society. At the beginning of the film, Nianankoro claims to be ready to confront his father, but accepts his mother's advice that he should continue on his journey to find his uncle Djigui and give him an object whose value is unclear. On his way, Nianankoro is faced with a series of challenges. Captured in the Fulani kingdom, he escapes death by using his supernatural powers firstly to overcome the Fulani warriors, then to help the Fulani king combat his enemies and to cure Attou, the king's wife, of infertility. Betrayed by his own sexual urge during the ceremony, however, he sleeps with Attou. When Nianankoro admits what has happened, the king repudiates Attou and gives her to Nianankoro.

Unwittingly, Nianankoro fulfils his mother's prayer that 'grass not cover the house of the Diarra'; Attou is pregnant with his child. When Nianankoro finally reaches the Dogon country, he and Attou symbolically purify themselves in the sacred spring, echoing the images of Nianankoro's mother pouring the milk over herself as she prays to the water goddess. Djigui's sermon, which also symbolically lasts throughout

56 Amadou Hampaté Bâ, *Contes initiatiques peuls*, p 10.

the night, heralds a new dawn, and helps Nianankoro to understand his relationship with his father, the meaning of their confrontation, and the mystery of the transmission of knowledge. When Nianankoro gives Djigui what turns out to be the 'eye' of the magic Koré wing, the wing is at last complete. As the new day dawns, Nianankoro is at last fully spiritually armed to confront his father. Although he is consumed in the confrontation, evil is eradicated and new hope is born in the film's final images of Nianankoro's young son, to whom Attou entrusts Nianan-koro's *boubou* and the sacred Koré wing, so that his learning will be perpetuated. Like all quest tales, Nianankoro's fulfilment of his challenges brings him the necessary understanding and knowledge to challenge the corrupt and stagnating order that his father represents.

In *Waati*, Nandi grows up on an Afrikaner farm where her parents work, the farm itself being both typical and a microcosm of South Africa's oppressive apartheid regime. Later, Nandi flees to West Africa where, guided by the voice of her grandmother, she learns the lessons of 'the school of life' in a personal quest for self-knowledge that ultimately enables her to affirm her own identity and to 'reclaim' South Africa. Those who have historically negated black South Africans are overcome in her story. Nandi's return to South Africa signals that the film has come full circle, that her initiation is complete. All this is prefigured by the circular Bambara ideogram that appears just after the credits.

The different sections of the film represent stages of Nandi's long initiation journey. In South Africa, she leaves her home to go to school, where she acquires the learning that reinforces her spirit of revolt. On her first day at school, she draws a doorway, symbolising how education is her doorway to freedom. When she returns home to the farm several years later, the actual journey representing her maturity, she has gained the assurance to confront Baas Hendricks and the policeman on the beach. Forced into exile, she flies to Côte d'Ivoire. Here, in a totally different, free West African environment, she continues her studies at university, where she discovers some of the key foundations of African culture denied her under the apartheid system and thus begins to discover her own identity. When she first arrives in Côte d'Ivoire, she repeats as she learns French, 'I look up at the sky', evoking the new horizons that are now open to her, far from the restrictive climate of apartheid South Africa. Shortly afterwards, she has her hair braided and dons West African style clothing, these external accoutrements mirroring her psychological embrace of an African identity.

In Nandi's doctoral exposé on ritual African masks, during which her own face is lit against a dark backdrop so that it too resembles a mask, Nandi affirms the value of Africa's cultural systems and reflects on her own and her people's journey of discovery. The choice of the mask is not innocent, as director Cissé confirms, explaining that the mask connotes knowledge and understanding.[57] As Nandi's exposé demonstrates, she has reached a state of self-knowledge and, as the words of the wise old man in the party sequence make clear, the understanding that her education needs to be put at the service of her people. Having discovered

57 Gaillac-Morgue, 'Entretien avec Souleymane Cissé', *Le Film Africain*, 20, mai 1995, p 2.

herself, Nandi is ready to go to the desert to help the Tuareg people. This decision represents the final stage of her initiation, after which she is psychologically able to return to the recently liberated South Africa despite the suffering it still represents to her. Nandi tells Baas Hendricks' daughter at the airport: 'I'm different. The experiences of my life have taught me a lot.' Nandi's spiritual journey is thus complete, and she is able to re-embrace the land that once rejected her, and her people. The film's circularity is evident in its final images and sound effects, echoing those at the beginning of the film.

In his first film, *Ta Dona*, Adama Drabo weaves his hero Sidy's quest to discover the secret of the 'seventh clay pot', one of the 'profundities of the Bambara world', into the film's other main narrative threads. As the different initiated elders guide Sidy from village to village in a series of scenes that are always set inside darkened huts, far from prying eyes and ears, the audience gradually gathers information about the healing powers of the 'seventh clay pot'. But the knowledge Sidy seeks requires that he prove his worth along the different stages of his search. As Balbé, one of the elders tells him, 'Son. Bambara society only gives true knowledge to those who are worthy of it.' Sidy, who claims to want the 'seventh clay pot' for the good of mankind, is distinguished by his exemplary behaviour throughout the film. He strives to help the villagers combat deforestation and defends them before contemptuous government officials whose corruption is vividly denounced. Once he has successfully been put to the test by a mysterious elder who makes him accomplish a number of tasks, he acquires the two halves of a symbolic bracelet. Sidy finally arrives in Dogon country, where he meets an old woman who, in an eerie, magical sequence, finally initiates him before dying.

Elderly characters often appear at critical moments of the quest tales to help protagonists who have proven their worth by helping the elder first. Gaston Kaboré's *Buud Yam* (Burkina Faso, 1997) relates its protagonist's quest to find the only healer capable of saving his sick adoptive sister, thus reconciling him with his own difficult past. When the hero, Wend Kuuni, makes a typical elderly woman character a fire near the start of the film, she gives him the first clues to help him find what he is seeking. She also gives him a bobbin of spun wool that will later help save his life. In both films, Sidy and Wend Kuuni's quests are central to the narrative, and both films include archetypal characters associated with the quest theme in the oral tales.

Symbolic and real voyages are often central in Djibril Diop Mambety's films, notably in *Touki-Bouki* (whose title means 'the voyage of the hyena'), and, more recently, in *Le Franc*. The surreal and highly symbolic film *Touki-Bouki* follows the efforts of a 'marginal' young couple, Mory and Anta, as they try to scrape enough money together to go to Paris, the city of their dreams. They journey around Dakar on Mory's motorbike, the cow horns on its handlebars recalling the opening and closing shots of the film which depict a child riding a cow. The direct transition from the shots of the child to a shot over the motorbike's cow horns clearly suggests that the small boy is Mory himself. When Mory and Anta are

Djibril Diop Mambety, Le Franc,
*1994. Marigot's 'pilgrimage' to
cash his winning lottery ticket.*
(Courtesy of Silvia Voser, Waka Flms)

finally about to embark on the ship for France, the ship horn's cow-like
bellowing makes Mory change his mind. He is torn by his African 'roots'
symbolised by the shots of his childhood with the cattle and the horns on
his bike. As Mory runs off, leaving Anta alone on the ship, he finds his
bike smashed up by a surreal 'spirit' character (who had appeared earlier
in the film). Whilst Mory 'nurses' the broken cow horns, which symbolise
his broken dream, the ship pulls away, The film ends on the same
opening shots of the child on the cow. The repetition of the images of
Mory's childhood seem to suggest that, ultimately, Mory chooses his
attachment to his African roots rather than the mythical lure of Europe.
It is only once he fulfils his symbolic journey through Dakar, however,
that he can come to this realisation.

In *Le Franc*, Marigot journeys backwards and forwards into the centre
of Dakar via a desolate urban rubbish dump in a desperate effort to earn
back his *congoma*, confiscated by his 'devilish' landlady in lieu of unpaid
rent.[58] His fragile, on-the-edge existence is visually accentuated by
alarming camera angles and by his own disarticulated movements.
When he finally wins the lottery, Marigot heads off on what turns out to
be a veritable pilgrimage to cash the ticket, which he had stuck to the
door of his room for safety. He carries the door on his shoulder, looking
like some kind of Biblical martyr, the door and its promise of fortune
symbolising the terrible burden of poverty. Marigot's final journey takes
him not to his death, however, but to an 'illumination' or 'redemption'.

In a number of other films, such as Ousmane Sembene's *Borom Sarret*
(Senegal, 1962), Clarence Delgado's *Niiwam* (Senegal, 1991), Moussa
Sene Absa's *Yalla Yaana* (Senegal, 1994), Amet Diallo's *Boxulmaleen*
(Senegal, 1991), Issa Serge Coelo's *Un taxi pour Aouzou* (Chad, 1994),

58 All of the main protagonists in
Diop Mambety's *Badou Boy, Touki-
Bouki,* and *Le Franc* are 'persecuted' by
a 'devilish' female character to whom
they owe money, and who is always
played by the same actress, Aminata
Fall. The same distorting close-up shots
of the woman scolding them occur
from film to film as a leitmotif.

Ousmane Sembene's Borom Sarret,
*1962. The cart-driver's journey and
thoughts offer a panoramic view of
Dakar society.*
(Courtesy of Férid Boughedir)

and José (Zeka) Laplaine's *Le Clandestin* (DRC, 1996), the protagonists
also make protracted journeys through various towns, which serve as
'windows' on several characters and situations. The journeys themselves
are very often filmed in their entirety, rather than being approximated in
ellipses, even when the film is not overtly a quest/initiation film, giving
them a symbolic dimension. As Teshome Gabriel notes, 'Viewed as a
whole, a pattern seems to emerge around the journey theme: wandering,
exile, migration and homeland. Journeys acknowledge encounters with
others, with known and unknown forces, happy and horrendous.'[59] The
journey becomes an integral site for meetings and transformations that
are both real and symbolic.

Ousmane Sembene's *Borom Sarret*, which follows a cart driver through
Dakar as he scrapes together a living, was the first film to adopt this
'panoramic' approach. The driver's voice-over reflections and the different people he meets en route – an unemployed youth, a trader, a crippled
beggar, a pregnant woman, an unscrupulous griot, a man carrying the
body of his dead child, and a young member of the new African elite –
offer insights into the difficulties and injustices facing the destitute in the
newly independent capital.

Based on a short story by Ousmane Sembene, Clarence Delgado's
Niiwam bears a number of resemblances to Sembene's much earlier
Borom Sarret. When the main protagonists' young child dies in Dakar,
the fisherman has to take a bus across Dakar to the cemetery, which
clearly echoes the cemetery incident in *Borom Sarret*. A whole range of
characters get on and off the bus along the way, provoking a number of
diverse incidents, all of which are commented by the fisherman who sees
the city folk through his mistrusting village eyes.

Similarly, Moussa Sene Absa's *Yalla Yaana* takes place in a public
minibus that also crosses Dakar, focusing on the interaction between the

59 Teshome Gabriel, 'Thoughts on
Nomadic Aesthetics and the Black
Independent Cinema: Traces of a jour-
ney', p 72.

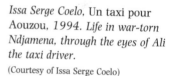

Issa Serge Coelo, Un taxi pour
Aouzou, *1994. Life in war-torn
Ndjamena, through the eyes of Ali
the taxi driver.*
(Courtesy of Issa Serge Coelo)

different passengers. Issa Serge Coelo's *Un taxi pour Aouzou* follows Ali, an endearing young taxi driver at work in Ndjamena, the capital of Chad, on the day that his wife gives birth to their first child. Again, the incidents with each of Ali's different passengers, his voice-over reflections, and the interactions with his taxi driver colleagues, allow Coelo to paint a realist portrait of a cross-section of the city's inhabitants and to raise questions about social conditions in Chad after years of civil war. *Boxulmaleen*, a colourfully surreal and satirical film in the vein of Diop Mambety's work, portrays a range of bizarre characters in a poor suburban neighbourhood. A group of street children weave their way through the streets, stealing and playing tricks as they try to rustle up enough money to buy their sick crook/hero's prescription. In all of these films, the journey itself is an integral part of the narrative. It links the disparate characters and situations portrayed, and becomes the central thematic focus of the film.

Adaptations of traditional themes

Other examples of the thematic influences of oral traditions show that filmmakers do not only borrow, but also adapt oral themes. Manthia Diawara's thorough analysis of Gaston Kaboré's *Wend Kuuni* (Burkina Faso, 1982) illustrates how Kaboré alters familiar themes to suit the film's more contemporary message.[60] As Diawara indicates, the film combines elements of three different oral themes. These include the 'missing husband' (a husband's absence triggers a search process that leads to the reunion of the husband and wife), the 'wanted son' (the lack of child is established, the quest to get a son narrated, and the son is found), and a more contemporary addition found in both literature and film, the 'emancipated daughter/female'. This last theme not only stresses the important role women play in the liberation of Africa, but also involves the denunciation of patriarchal domination.

60 Manthia Diawara, 'Oral Literature and African Film: Narratology in Wend Kuuni', in Jim Pines & Paul Willemen (eds.), *Questions of Third Cinema* (London: BFI, 1989), pp 199–211.

Adapted forms of the first two 'traditional' themes can be identified in *Wend Kuuni*, but familiar stages of their development are eliminated or inverted so that a new story and a new message emerge. Although we know, for example, that the husband/father is missing, we do not learn of his mother's search for him until the child narrates it in flashback at the end of the film. By this time, however, we already know that the mother has died, eliminating any possibility of reunion. It is therefore more important that Wend Kuuni has found his voice, and himself, at the end of the film, than his father. The child found is named Wend Kuuni, or 'Gift of God', and is adopted by a family that has no son. He is seen in numerous scenes working with his adoptive father, all of which point to the 'wanted son' myth, yet the film only shows the stage in which the son is found. The 'wanted son' and the 'emancipated daughter' themes (the latter being centred on Pongneré, who defies parental authority to follow Wend Kuuni, and through whose eyes many of the events are seen) are intertwined rather than being developed separately. Kaboré thus modernises the film's impact, adapting the traditional themes to suit contemporary circumstances.

Many other directors have also adopted this approach. Traditional themes are often updated to convey more progressive messages and to denounce oppressive or obsolete social codes. Numerous filmmakers have up-dated oral tales' 'difficult girl' theme, in which daughters refuse their parents choice in marriage. In orature, this defiance usually has disastrous consequences. Jacques Chevrier demonstrates the way in which such desires for independence are generally harshly dealt with in traditional tales.[61] Directors rarely criticise the 'difficult girl' in their films; preferring instead to attack the institution of arranged marriage itself, even if the outcome of such films is also often tragic due to the pressures of the community or family. In Safi Faye's film *Mossane*, for example, the central character repeatedly refuses to marry the wealthy emigrant chosen by her parents. When her parents go ahead with the wedding plans, blinded by the promise of the fortune the marriage will bring – as Mossane's mother says to her griot confidante, 'If you own a cow, you have to milk it' – Mossane boldly addresses the guests at the wedding ceremony, publicly voicing her refusal. Her unprecedented *cri de coeur* goes unheard, however, and she drowns when trying to escape in the night. Throughout the film, members of the family who sympathise with Mossane repeatedly criticise the girl's parents, reinforcing the condemnation of this type of marriage.

Idrissa Ouedraogo's *Tilaï* also implicitly condemns traditional marital customs. When Saga returns to his village after a long absence, he discovers that his own father has married his fiancée, against her will. The young couple defy all the social codes and continue to see each other in secret, ultimately destroying their own families and leading to Saga's death. The film's construction, and in particular the sympathetic point of view of Kuilga, Nogma's endearing little sister, encourage the spectator to empathise with the star-crossed lovers.

In Jean-Pierre Dikongue Pipa's *Muna Moto*, N'dome and Ngando's

61 Jacques Chevrier, *L'Arbre à Palabres: essai sur les contes et récits traditionnels d'Afrique noire* (Paris: Hatier, 1986), p 92.

marriage is prevented when Ngando's childless, polygamous uncle Mbongo refuses to help Ngando pay the high bride price that N'dome's parents demand. He decides to marry N'dome himself, in a desperate bid to have his own child. As Ngando, a poor young fisherman, cannot financially rival his uncle, N'dome's father, who is again driven by the prospect of financial gain, decides to force his daughter to marry Mbongo. Hoping to thwart her parents' plans, the desperate N'dome insists that she and Ngando make love hoping that Mbongo will no longer want to marry her if she is not a virgin, and forcing her parents to lower her bride price. When the marriage goes ahead anyway, despite the fact that N'dome is already pregnant, Ngando simply has to accept that it is his uncle who officially fathers his child. When Ngando and N'dome later try to flee together, their friend's words express the general spirit of the film: 'We young people have always obeyed. People have to start listening to us now too.' The director alters the traditional message of the tales to attack unjust and obsolete, seeking to promote social changes that reflect the younger generation's values.

Magic realism

Numerous directors' use of the supernatural elements omnipresent in both oral tales and the contemporary and traditional societies they portray offers one final example of the thematic parallels between the two artforms in Francophone Africa. Filmmaker Adama Drabo has commented, 'We are steeped in this atmosphere all our lives, so it seems completely normal to me that my films, which ... come from my whole culture, inevitably be tinged with this knowledge that people call magic.'[62] Characters therefore often use the magical, supernatural powers that play an integral role in many African societies where initiated individuals are considered to have the power to manipulate natural forces and to communicate with the spirits.

As the Tunisian filmmaker and critic Férid Boughedir has pointed out, the negative portrayals of such beliefs and practices found in earlier films such as Oumarou Ganda's *Saitaine* (Niger, 1972), which showed diviners to be charlatans who manipulate people's credulity, have gradually given way to less judgmental and less inhibited evocations, since the mid-Eighties.[63] These clearly differ radically from the 'hocus-pocus, mumbo-jumbo' mystification of traditional African beliefs found in many Western films even today. They are now generally shown, as Drabo states above, to be a logical part of the socio-cultural environment in which the films are set. In works such as Cissé's *Finyé*, *Yeelen*, and *Waati*, Drabo's *Ta Dona* and *Taafe Fanga*, Touré's *Laada*, or Sissoko's *Guimba*, characters frequently use their supernatural powers to both good and evil ends, as the directors film real rituals and use special effects to create a magical dimension in their works. In the same way that in many traditional African thought systems, 'il n'y a pas de séparation réelle entre la vie et la mort. Cela s'imbrique comme des écailles' ['there is no real division between life and death. They interlock like fish scales'], these directors shift between 'natural' and 'supernatural' registers with no great to-do.[64]

62 Interview with the author. Ouaga-dougou, February 1997.

63 See Férid Boughedir, 'African Cinema and Ideology: Tendencies and Evolutions' (paper given at BFI *Screen Griots Conference*, London 9-10 September 1995).

64 Souleymane Cissé speaking in the documentary *Souleymane Cissé*, by Rithy Panh (Cambodia-France, 1991).

Screen Griots: Orature & Film

Cissé's *Yeelen*, which is infused with traditional Bambara mysticism, brings a hitherto secret Komo ritual to the screen in its entirety, emphasising its rich complexity and symbolism. As Cissé himself explains:

> For the first time, a film decodes the secret ritual described by the song [Malians are used to hearing] on the radio. The film interprets this ritualistic song ... [thus inviting] the spectator to go deeper in imagining the significance of the Komo beyond the literal meaning of the song, beyond the film ... The codic meanings of the song ... contain the secrets of the universe. My film positions the spectator in the midst of these secrets and keeps him/her busy looking, interpreting, discovering.[65]

This 'initiation' reflects that of the main protagonist, Nianankoro. In Adama Drabo's *Taafe Fanga*, the sacred sanctuary sequence enables Drabo to transmit elements of the Dogon creation myth and its rich conception of the spiral of order and disorder in a magical *mise en scène*. Drabo places what have often been criticised as 'primitive' African beliefs in a new light. This uninhibited representation of the supernatural and mystical practices situates Francophone African cinema at the heart of traditional cultural forms and beliefs, its filmmaking practices reflecting elements characteristic of that cultural sphere.

The aim of this appraisal has been to offer an understanding of the multiple ways in which local African cultural forms and artistic codes have been blended into the universal cinematographic medium as filmmaking has broadened and been adapted to reflect African sensibilities. This has unquestionably helped 'construct different meanings out of the same system of signs', thereby conferring a certain specificity on Francophone African film without limiting its expressive possibilities.[66]

This analysis of the characteristics of Francophone African orature and the ways in which its techniques, themes and styles have been adapted, updated and integrated into film to create new syncretic forms, also demonstrates that orature, which is itself a marker of cultural identity, plays a central role in the construction of identities in a wide range of Francophone African films. Understanding the nature of orality helps to show how the hybridity and/or transgression of genre boundaries found in the work of certain younger filmmakers in particular is typical of so-called 'traditional' orature. That tradition has always freely incorporated new, outside elements and blended genres and forms. Even the most experimental and contemporary works can thus be analysed in terms of orality's influences. This fundamental influence on such a wide range of Francophone African films justifies the importance accorded to orature here and confirms Hampaté Bâ's view of orality as a 'living tradition'.

Being aware of the specific cultural context in which Francophone African cinema has developed helps unfamiliar audiences understand the complexities of its filmmaking practices, particularly when these diverge from Western cinematic codes. This contextualising approach demonstrates that Francophone African film is very much part of its cultural environment, incorporating values and customs that have a long tradition in the region.

65 Manthia Diawara, 'Souleymane Cissé's Light on Africa', *Black Film Review*, vol 4, 4. Fall 1988, p 15.

66 Kobena Mercer, 'Black Art and the Burden of Representation', in Kobena Mercer (ed.), *Welcome to the Jungle: New Positions in Black Cultural Studies* (New York & London: Routledge, 1994), p 257.

4 Memory, History
Other stories

It is impossible to ignore the prominent place accorded to memory and history in Francophone African film. Identifying memory as one of the constants of African film, the Tunisian filmmaker Nouri Bouzid explains, 'the word "memory" recurs very often in our cinema since the Eighties ... We are in the presence of men and women at the crossroads of lost paths, but with a knowledge of their past. They know nothing of the future; they only have a past. They are very often searching for an identity.'[3] This characteristic recurrence needs to be situated within the overall quest to redefine cultural identity described in Chapter 2. Filmmakers working in the postcolonial context have found themselves confronted with a legacy of distorted, demeaning images created by the European colonisers. Both the liberation discourses and works of contemporary filmmakers frequently accord history and memory a major role in reworking this imagery. Reassessing and interrogating the past are posited as a means of recreating and redefining the present and the future. Telling one's own story, recounting history from one's own point of view to reappropriate collective memory and to challenge the erasures of Eurocentric readings of history have become a vital part of the postcolonial process of self-definition.[4] Such explorations of the past rarely involve the nostalgic overtones associated with certain mainstream European productions.[5]

This effort to uncover, revalue, and restore memory and history is all the more significant given the traditional Western attitudes to Africa and its history. As the nineteenth-century Enlightenment scholars became obsessed with tracing European origins back to a 'noble' Ancient Greek ancestry, it logically followed for them that Africans could not possibly share this, or for that matter any other, legitimating history. Hegel's famous introduction to *The Philosophy of History*, published in 1837, characteristically articulated the widespread belief that Africa was a continent without history that showed no signs of historical development.[6]

Scientific rationalism's classing of history as a 'scientific' discipline in the same period also played a determining role in Western perceptions of African history. Assuming that 'history' was impartial, other interpretative modes of historic study were gradually effaced by the notion of a 'single', linear narrative truth – i.e. that of the West. As the European countries colonised Africa, their education and propaganda machines

'You say "History" but that means nothing. So many lives, so many destinies, so many tracks go into the making of our unique path. You dare say History, but I say histories, stories. The one you take for the master stem of our manioc is but one stem among many others...'
Patrick Chamoiseau[1]

'History is a legend, an invention of the present. It is both a memory and a reflection of our present'.
V.Y. Mudimbe[2]

1 Patrick Chamoiseau, *Texaco*, translated by Rose-Myriam Réjouis and Val Vinokurov (London: Granta, 1997), p 88.

2 V.Y. Mudimbe, *The Invention of Africa: Gnosis, Philosophy and the Order of Knowledge* (Bloomington & Indianapolis: Indiana University Press, 1988), p 195.

3 Nouri Bouzid, 'On Inspiration', in Imruh Bakari & Mbye Cham (eds.), *African Experiences of Cinema* (London: BFI Publishing, 1996), pp 52-53.

4 This process can unsurprisingly be identified in the films of all marginalized or subjugated peoples, whether in Africa or elsewhere. Various studies, such as Wendy Everett's (ed.), *European Identity in Cinema* (London: Intellect: 1996) have shown that the concepts of history and memory also play a key role in films by Europe's traditionally marginalized minorities and/or nations.

Memory, History:
Other Stories

5 Salman Rushdie deplores the way in which 'Raj nostalgia' films made in Britain in the Eighties, including David Lean's *A Passage to India* (1987) or the television series *A Jewel in the Crown*, yearn for the 'glorious' colonial past. Wendy Everett points to the comforting, escapist nostalgia of British 'heritage' films, such as Merchant Ivory's *Howards End* (1991), or *The Remains of the Day* (1993). France's former colony Indochina has also become the focus of comparable nostalgic revisitations in French films, such as Régis Wargnier's *Indochine* (1992) and Jean-Jacques Annaud's adaptation of Duras's *L'Amant* (1984). (cf. Salman Rushdie, 'The Raj Revival', *The Observer*, April 1984; Wendy Everett, 'Framing the fingerprints: a brief survey of European film', in Wendy Everett (ed.), *European Identity in Cinema*, p 19; and Panivong Norindr, 'Filmic Memorial and Colonial Blues', in Dina Sherzer (ed.), *Cinema, Colonialism, Postcolonialism: Perspectives from the French and Francophone Worlds* (Austin: University of Texas Press, 1960, pp 120-146).

6 In this book Hegel writes, 'Africa proper, as far as History goes back, has remained ... shut up ... it is no historical part of the world; it has no movement of development to exhibit. Historical movement in it – that is in its northern part – belongs to the Asiatic or European World ... What we properly understand as Africa, is the Unhistorical, Undeveloped Spirit, still involved in the conditions of mere nature and which had to be presented here only as on the threshold of the World's history'. Cited by George Lamming, 'The Occasion for Speaking', in Bill Ashcroft, Gareth Griffiths & Helen Tiffin (eds.), *The Post-Colonial Studies Reader* (London & New York: Routledge, 1995), p 15.

7 Bill Ashcroft, Gareth Griffiths & Helen Tiffin (eds.), 'Introduction to Part XI', *The Post-Colonial Studies Reader*, p 355.

began to impose this historical interpretation. In this context, 'the myth of a value-free, "scientific" view of the past ... as a single representation of the continuity of events, authorized nothing less than the construction of world reality. This was a time in which the European nations ... "absorbed into themselves the whole of world history".'[7]

Even though Western attitudes to Africa and its past evolved in the twentieth century, remnants of these nineteenth-century attitudes still formed the philosophical foundations of colonial discourse. Education programmes in Africa particularly reflected such attitudes. In the French colonies, children were thus taught to identify with the French 'Mother country' and its history, to the extent that they had to recite, 'Our ancestors, the Gauls'. At the same time, their collective memories and histories were devalued, especially as these were generally, but not exclusively, orally transmitted. Such oral data was perceived as unreliable, inaccurate, partial, and thus unhistorical in rationalist terms.[8] As a result, Africans today now find themselves confronted with 'written histories that erase and deny' their points of view and experiences.[9]

It is easy to understand the urgency of telling one's own history/ies and experiences in Africa's vital process of rediscovery and self-definition. History and memory are thus positioned here as a form of resistance, giving African scholars, artists and filmmakers the 'liberté de dire tout haut ce que quatre-vingt-dix ans d'oppression ne nous permettaient pas de dire' ['the freedom to say out loud what ninety years of oppression forbade us from saying'].[10]

The 'colonial confrontation' genre

Representations of history and memory in Francophone African film fall into two broad categories. Rather than being mutually exclusive, these two categories tend to reflect a shift in sensibilities, priorities and understandings of history. In chronological terms, this shift is more or less concomitant with recent re-evaluation of personal readings of history that has caused the boundaries between memory and history to become blurred. Whilst this process is not specific to Africa alone – Wendy Everett has, for example, pointed to the emergence of personal and subjective forms of historical film in Europe[11] – it is certainly a main tendency in Francophone African film, mirroring the way that the reappropriation of African history as a counter-memory has evolved. Both categories' reworking of history/memory from an African point of view illustrates the issues of representation discussed throughout this book. The second category's introduction of a personal voice makes these films particularly interesting, creating a distinctive Francophone African film genre. Whilst taking both categories into consideration, this chapter will focus on several of these more recent 'memory' films.

The first 'wave' of history films to emerge in Francophone Africa, which Manthia Diawara aptly describes as the 'colonial confrontation genre', echo the liberation theorists' calls for the reinterpretation of history.[12] Set in the past, these films articulate alternative, African readings of episodes of colonial history that have either been overlooked or excluded from Western historical sources. They bring to the screen rarely-mentioned examples of African resistance to colonial penetration in a clear challenge to Western readings of the period. Veteran Senegalese filmmaker Ousmane Sembene was one of the first filmmakers to offer a re-reading of colonial history. His 1971 film *Emitaï* narrates the events that took place in Effok, a rice-growing village in the southern Senegalese region of Casamance, in 1942. The opening shots of young village men being conscripted by force into the French colonial forces immediately challenges the absence of this reality in French colonial films and histories. The rest of the film chronicles the French forces' massacre of the Effok villagers when they refuse to hand over their requisitioned rice harvests, an episode which is again either glossed over, or absent from most French sources.

The soldiers' arrival prompts the village women to quick action, hiding the rice at night. In the absence of the enlisted younger male villagers, the village elders ineffectively implore the gods for guidance. The women's resolve remains unshaken, however, even when the soldiers take them hostage. Although forced to sit in the blazing sun without food or water, the women's singing and silence actively challenges the soldiers. When the elders finally capitulate and take the rice to the soldiers, the women once again symbolically resist, defying the French commander's order not to bury the only elder to have challenged the soldiers. Hearing the women sing the men's traditional funeral song in the distance, the menfolk regain their courage and refuse to hand over the rice, but are mown down by the French forces. The film thus sheds light on the French colonial authorities' under-reported brutality, the local population's resistance, and, in particular, the decisive resistance of the women.[13]

Med Hondo's *Sarraounia* (Mauritania, 1986) similarly highlights women's key role in the fight against colonial domination whilst also shedding light on a particularly bloody episode of French colonial conquest in West Africa. The film narrates a series of historically documented events in the late nineteenth century by focusing on the warrior queen Sarraounia's efforts to resist both the Sokoto Fulani's attempts to Islamise the region and the murderous onslaught of the columns led by Captains Chanoine and Voulet.[14]

Hondo's *mise en scène* deconstructs the myth of France's peaceful *mission civilisatrice* – that habitual justification for French colonial engagement in Africa. In the film's early animation sequence, the map of Africa burns, rips and bleeds as the Europeans penetrate the continent, contrasting starkly with the map sequences typical of colonial films that show the 'dark' continent turning progressively white as the European colonisers bring it 'light'. The series of scenes with Chanoine, Voulet and their African *tirailleur* infantrymen murdering, raping, pillaging, and burning the villages in their path, reveals the colonial forces' increasingly deranged sadistic brutality. Certain local chiefs' complicity with the

8 Amadou Hampaté Bâ refutes such accusations, insisting that when he collected the oral material necessary to write his *History of the Fulani Empire of Macina in the Eighteenth century* that, 'on the whole my thousand informants had respected the truth of events. The thread of the story was everywhere the same. The differences, which affected only minor details, were due to the quality of the reciter's memory, or his particular spirit ... [but] did not change the basic data.' In 'The Living Tradition', in Joseph Ki-Zerbo (ed.), *General History of Africa, Vol. I* (Paris: Unesco, 1981), p 198.

9 bell hooks, 'Representations of Whiteness', in bell hooks, *Black Looks: Race and Representation* (Boston, MA: South End Press, 1992), p. 172.

10 Jean-Marie Teno, 'Liberté, le pouvoir de dire non', in FEPACI (ed), *L'Afrique et le Centenaire du Cinéma* (Paris & Dakar: Présence Africaine, 1995), p 375.

11 Wendy Everett, 'Framing the fingerprints: a brief survey of European film', p 20.

12 Manthia Diawara, 'African Cinema Today', in *Framework*, 37, 1989, pp 110–128.

13 Several other African films from outside the French-speaking zone also focus on the role women have played in various African resistance struggles. Sarah Maldoror's *Sambizanga* (Angola, 1972), Flora Gomez's *Mortu Nega* (Guinea Bissau, 1988), and Ingrid Sinclair's *Flame* (Zimbabwe, 1997), dramatise the African wars of independence fought in Angola, Guinea Bissau, and Rhodesia (Zimbabwe) respectively. Each film focuses on one or several female protagonists' part in the struggle against the brutal, torturing colonial powers.

14 Referring to this episode of colonial conquest, Webster and Boahen's *The Growth of African Civilisation: West*

French is not overlooked in the film, avoiding both reductive binary paradigms that pit 'good Africans' against 'evil Europeans' and the mythification of a pre-colonial Africa free of rivalry and strife. French critics of the film who accused *Sarraounia* of being too polemical have overlooked this point. Unlike the other local chiefs in the film, Sarraounia chooses to resist the French with her army of men and women soldiers, defeating Voulet and Chanoine at the battle of Luga. Shaken by a defeat that undermines the European officers' invinciblity, their infantrymen revolt, shooting the two power-crazed captains in an act of resistance that has also rarely been reported in French historical sources.

Ousmane Sembene's *Camp de Thiaroye* revisited the 'colonial confrontation' genre in 1988. Dramatising another largely overlooked episode of colonial brutality, the film narrates the fate of a regiment of *tirailleurs* in 1944, recently returned from fighting in Europe in World War Two. Waiting for demobilisation in the Thiaroye camp outside Dakar they stage a revolt against their inferior status and poor conditions, and are massacred. Comparing Thiaroye to a German prisoner of war camp and, by extension, comparing colonial France to Nazi Germany, Sembene focuses on the African soldiers' poor conditions and the majority of French officers' racist contempt for them, tracing the *tirailleurs'* political awakening. The film's detailed portraits of the individual infantrymen, of the initially 'assimilated' Sergeant Diatta, and of the soldiers' increasing engagement offers an unusual image of the *tirailleur*, a far cry from the obedient, silent masses that they are usually portrayed to be. The emphasis is placed on resistance, with the French colonial authorities' contempt and brutality clearly portrayed.

Finally, Bassek Ba Kobhio's *Le Grand Blanc de Lambaréné* (Cameroon, 1994) offers an African perspective on the life of one of France's renowned colonial figures, the Nobel Prize-winning Dr Albert Schweitzer. Famous for founding a hospital in Lambaréné, Gabon, where he treated and evangelised the local inhabitants in the colonial era, Schweitzer is generally seen in France as a benevolent and altruistic hero, a kind of precursor of the modern-day aid worker. However, Ba Kobhio demystifies this image in his film. Set in the period from 1944 to Schweitzer's death in 1965, shortly after Gabonese independence, Ba Kobhio's film shows him to be a far more ambiguous figure whose medical practices were often sub-standard and whose condescension towards 'his natives' reeked of colonial paternalism.

At the beginning of the film, Schweitzer is portrayed as both a benevolent patriarch and an irascible old man. Initially, he is shot from imposing low-angles that echo the representations of white 'heroes' in Western colonial films, as he quite literally lords it over the locals. Despite the huge energy he invests in the local population, he is shown to be incapable of treating Africans as his equals and never deigns to understand or participate in their customs. As the film progresses, Schweitzer's practices and attitudes are increasingly challenged as a number of 'outsiders' begin to penetrate his domain and as national political changes begin to reverberate in the local community. This is

14 (cont.) *Africa Since 1800* notes: 'Another [column] under Voulet and Chanoine left a trail of fire and blood behind them as they burnt villages and executed friends and foes alike ... Their advance was slowed by water shortage, the vast quantity of booty they carried, and slaves. The French government sent a political officer to report on them and they so resented this action that they killed the political officer and declared their independence from France. However, their soldiers mutinied and killed both officers. It now appears that Voulet and Chanoine had gone mad with blood lust.' (London: Longman, 1967), p 29.

particularly the clear when the young African soldiers return home from the Second World War with stories of the French army's treachery. These fuel the growing antagonism towards the country's colonial authorities. The character Koumba personifies the challenge to Schweitzer and the colonial order he represents. Although shown to revere the doctor as a child, Koumba studies medicine and begins to challenge the doctor, repeatedly confronting him about his methods. When his authority is challenged, Schweitzer withdraws into himself, unable to comprehend the aspirations of the people amongst whom he lives and unable to adapt to the changing times. He tells another European doctor, 'Don't upset our natives' habits', and is bitter when the country gains independence. His European staff become increasingly hostile to the local inhabitants once their order collapses. Schweitzer dies an isolated and lonely old man who, despite his good intentions, is shown never to have adapted to, nor understood, the people he came to 'save'.

Each of the above films gives an alternative African perspective on episodes of colonial history. They highlight the dehumanising effects of colonisation, while foregrounding the African populations' efforts to preserve their own freedom and integrity. All of these films can also be seen either as allegories or lessons for the present in the same way that history is often referenced in the oral tales (discussed in Chapter 3). Their challenge to Western historiographies and continuing relevance today explains the hostile reception they have often received in France. *Emitaï*, was not distributed for six years and, due to pressure from France, was banned in a number of Francophone countries. *Camp de Thiaroye* was only distributed after Med Hondo screened the film in Paris in 1998, and *Sarraounia* was given a very limited screening after being harshly attacked by French critics for being exaggeratedly anti-French. One can only assume, therefore, that their alternative readings of history touch a raw nerve, confirming how powerful this alternative African voice can be.

Memory-history films: *Afrique, je te plumerai*; *Asientos*; *Allah Tantou*; and *Fad'jal*

In more recent years, a second category of memory-history films has emerged, four examples of which shall be discussed here: Jean Marie Teno's *Afrique, je te plumerai* (Cameroon, 1991), François Woukoache's *Asientos* (Cameroon, 1995), David Achkar's *Allah Tantou* (Guinea, 1990), and Safi Faye's *Fad'jal* (Senegal, 1979). These films, which tend to reflect the more personal, at times autobiographical, approach to history discussed above, differ significantly from the 'colonial confrontation' films. Their interrogation or re-creation of the past is conducted from a point of view situated clearly in the present. In this highlighting of the relation between the past and the present, these four films offer innovative approaches to film structure, generic boundaries, and thematic considerations, while developing highly personal filmic voices.

Memory, History: Other Stories

As shown in Chapter 3, such characteristics are commonly found in Francophone Africa's traditional narrative forms, which suggests that all four films explore relations between cultural identity, memory-history and voice.

Before looking at how Jean-Marie Teno, François Woukoache, David Achkar, and Safi Faye address these issues, it is useful to consider their form and common stylistic characteristics. Each film is technically classed as a documentary, yet their recourse to fiction positions them beyond the 'traditional' boundaries of that genre. Each film 'transgresses' what André Gardies describes as one of the principal credos, namely that documentaries directly film 'real' life, which means that all reconstitutions are viewed as suspect and that authenticity is considered the ultimate value.[15] According to these criteria, the four films cannot be described as documentaries, but neither are they fictions. Traditional classifications are thus too rigid to be adequately applied to these films.

The generic blending referred to here finds an artistic and expressive justification in each individual's film. Jean-Marie Teno comments, 'What matters most is ... to let oneself be transported by an emotion, a line of thought [rather] than trying to work out whether a scene is enacted or not.'[16] This blending characterises the oral traditions in which storytellers often change registers as they digress from the original narrative to related tales and/or real life incidents. The parallels with orature are further accentuated by these films' non-linear constructions which owe more to the narrative discontinuity of the tales than to the chronological linearity of Western historiographic traditions. This relation is also highlighted by the way these histories are fragmented and interspersed with other related elements. In *Afrique, je te plumerai*, Teno's personal memories and his filmed investigation into the Cameroonian publishing sector are woven into disparate episodes of Cameroonian colonial history. In *Asientos*, real footage of refugees at the time of the Rwandan genocide and various fictional scenes punctuate the description of the African slave trade, while scenes of village life intersperse *Fad'jal*'s chronicle of how a Serer village was founded. These films' generic blending can be seen to be consciously or unconsciously influenced by the traditional narrative schema found in the region's storytelling and historical narrative. In filmic terms, it has contributed to creating a new and dynamic hybrid genre.

Other features of *Fad'jal*, *Allah Tantou*, *Asientos*, and *Afrique, je te plumerai* diverge from established documentary criteria. Shifting freely through a wide variety of styles and modes of address from the most unobtrusive, *cinéma-vérité* type filmmaking to the most self-conscious subjective camera work and styles, these four films mix film formats, archive footage, newsreels, photos, newspaper articles, and drawings that build up layers of images, meanings and texts. This formal experimentation is a far cry from what Gardies describes as documentary filmmaking's zero degree of writing.[17]

Finally, one of the most interesting and original features of these films

15 A. Gardies & P. Haffner, *Regards sur le Cinéma Négro-Africain* (Bruxelles: Editions OCIC, 1987), p 177. A number of Francophone African fiction films, and particularly social realist films, inversely contain documentary moments. Jean-Marie Teno and Safi Faye's only fiction films to date – *Clando* (Cameroon 1996) and *Mossane* (Senegal, 1995) – are, for example, strongly marked by the documentary vein.

16 Interview with the author. Paris, August 1997.

17 A. Gardies & P. Haffner, *Regards sur le Cinéma Négro-Africain*, p 178.

is the filmmaker's personal presence and/or voice-over intervention. This personal, subjective voice disrupts the claims to objectivity associated with Western historic and documentary discourse. The filmmakers embrace a more personal, autobiographical stance, so that they are never above or separate from the subjects explored. This does not stop them from weaving other voices and discourses into the films. Referring to *Allah Tantou* and *Afrique, je te plumerai*, N. Frank Ukadike, remarks that, 'On the level of delineation ... we find a constant shift in the voice of authority, as the form of narration turns to what we might term a filmed essay in documentary dialect. The many kinds of presentation within the films ... diversify the authoritative voice.'[18] Unlike certain Western historic texts, these personalised expressions of memory and history do not exclude alternative points of view. They allow the filmmakers, just like the griot in orature, to explore the dialogic and interpretative possibilities offered by film.

Direct authorial intervention is particularly marked in *Afrique, je te plumerai* and *Allah Tantou*. In *Afrique, je te plumerai*, Jean-Marie Teno's voice is ever-present as the director comments, analyses, and narrates in a series of incisive, subjective, first-person voice-overs that convey his highly committed point of view. The voice-over texts provide an ironic counterpoint to the images themselves, distancing, deconstructing, and contradicting what the images show. Teno comments, 'things can always be read on several levels ... There is always a distance between what people say and what they really are ... The sounds and images should [thus] enrich and complete one another, clash.'[19] Interestingly, Teno is also physically present in the film, the camera at times assuming his subjective point of view as if to reinforce his own commitment. Teno's centrality is complemented or at times countered by his layering of other voices and material that reinforce the dialogic nature of the film.

David Achkar's *Allah Tantou* is notable for the filmmaker's deeply personal direct involvement. Achkar tells the story of his father, a key political figure and UN representative in the early days of Guinean independence. He was later imprisoned on trumped-up charges of conspiracy, tortured, and murdered by Guinea's increasingly paranoid and autocratic leader, Sekou Touré. Perhaps more important, is the way in which Achkar also creates a space to articulate his father's voice. Via readings of the diaries Marof Achkar wrote in prison, this device permeates the whole film. Achkar only intervenes in direct voice-over to introduce the film, or occasionally to provide complementary information on his father's life and key events in Guinean history. His tone is understandably partial; he addresses his father directly as if he were talking to him, explaining details his father could not have known (for example, 'July 1971, we are deported. Mother does everything she can to find out where you are ... 26 March 1984, Sekou Touré dies of a heart attack in Cleveland. On 3 April there is a military coup, the jam-packed camps are opened, but no sign of you'). This conversational form of address heightens the highly personal, autobiographical register of the film.

18 N. Frank Ukadike, 'The Other Voices of Documentary: *Allah Tantou* and *Afrique, je te plumerai*', iris, 18, Spring 1995, p 91.

19 Interview with the author. Paris, August 1997.

François Woukoache is less obviously present in *Asientos*, which is nonetheless a highly personal and lyrical film. It is introduced by the voice of a woman who is never identified. Speaking in the first person, she articulates the preoccupations and reflections of an unspecified 'he', who could be the fictional male character in the film, and/or its director. Woukoache maintains this ambiguity between himself and the character, ultimately creating the impression that it is his own voice that is expressed through his fictional character.

Finally, it is not so much the direct intervention of the Safi Faye's voice that is striking in *Fad'jal*, even though Faye does very occasionally interject to illuminate certain episodes in the village sequences, but rather the space she gives the villagers to express their voice. Faye has stressed the importance of this element in her work: 'I give people a voice, they are able to speak about their own problems, to show their reality, and I take a position within that. I situate myself on one side or another, my voice criticises what is open to criticism or I provide some small explanation.'[20] Here the onus is on the collective voice. In the traditional village environment in which the film is set, this voice is as personal as the individual voice. In each of these four films, the directors' decision to adopt a direct and personal tone effectively restores their own memories and voice, as each one strives to reclaim their histories and narrative modes.

Afrique, je te plumerai: recovering historical interpretation

Jean-Marie Teno's *Afrique, je te plumerai* is one of Francophone African film's most memorable examples of an attempt to offer what the director describes in voice-over at the beginning of the film as his own 'indigenous reading of Cameroonian history'. He aims to end 'the torment of a history with which we have not yet come to terms'. Identifying writers as the witnesses of their epoch – a role traditionally played by the griot – the film sets out to survey writing and the written text in contemporary Cameroon. In the process, Teno analyses Cameroonian history from the colonial era to the present to explore both how Cameroonians have either collaborated with the coloniser or resisted colonisation through history, and to show what remains of Cameroonian culture today. Reappraising Cameroonian history is also an attempt to understand the repressive, neo-colonial political climate of a country ruled by the same leader since 1982, whose reluctant conversion to multi-party politics in 1992 convinced neither opposition politicians nor international observers.

The film's non-linear sequences fall into three main groups interspersed throughout the film. Firstly, there are the sequences that illustrate Cameroon's situation at the time the film was made. These comprise both live footage of the early Nineties' pro-democracy demonstrations, and both a 'documentary' and 'fictional' filmed investigation into the situation of publishing and broadcasting in Cameroon. This raises questions about European cultural neo-colonialism, State repression, and censorship. Secondly, there are sequences that provide a

20 Cited in Angela Martin, 'Four West African film-makers', *Framework*, 11, Autumn 1979, p 18.

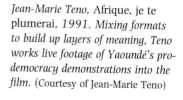

Jean-Marie Teno, Afrique, je te
plumerai, *1991. Mixing formats
to build up layers of meaning, Teno
works live footage of Yaoundé's pro-
democracy demonstrations into the
film.* (Courtesy of Jean-Marie Teno)

non-chronological overview of modern Cameroonian history. The
montage of colonial film footage and interviews constitutes a body of
material that counters the authority of the Western historic voice and
documents episodes absent from the history books. These include the
questions of forced labour in the colonies; the suppression of indigenous
cultures; abusive land exploitation; the repression of the nascent trade
union movement that founded a 'tradition' of political repression later
perpetuated by the Cameroonian Presidents Ahidjo and Biya; and the
existence of the written Sho-mon alphabet developed by the Sultan
Ngoya in 1895. Finally, the film includes a series of fictionalised black
and white autobiographical childhood memory sequences narrated in
voice-over by the director that are both related to the issues dealt with in
the rest of the film and intended to off-set the 'official' history in the film
with personal memory. The film's oscillation from past to present
reinforces the notion that historical analysis can be used to reassess the
present and future, as Teno later makes explicit in the film, with a
Chinese proverb, 'A people with no past has no present and no future'.

Afrique, je te plumerai opens with a pre-credits sequence that
establishes the turbulent political climate of the early Nineties when the
Cameroonians' demands for multi-party politics were violently repressed
by Paul Biya's regime, one of the themes explored and analysed
throughout the film, while announcing the tone and intent of the work.
As the camera pans slowly past a contemporary Yaoundé townscape, the
apparent 'normality' of the shot is disrupted by the director's uncompromising voice-over: 'Yaoundé. Cruel town. You have stuffed our heads

full of your official lies. You have trampled our distress into your arrogant filth. You answer your children's cries for freedom with the rattle of machine-gun fire ... Yaoundé, cruel town, you have sown the seeds of shame.' A montage of live footage showing contemporary pro-democracy demonstrations, the military police, and an assassinated demonstrator lying on the ground immediately corroborates this abrupt and vehement voice-over. The brutality of the shots is accentuated by their juxtaposition with a joyful sequence of black and white archive footage of Cameroon's Independence celebrations, ironically accompanied by the famously optimistic 'Independence Cha Cha' song. As elsewhere in the film, the montage plays a key dramatic role. The irony of the independence scenes is further undermined by Teno's voice-over, which relentlessly interprets the 'official' historic facts of the independence period, and contextualises the contemporary political situation:

> After three centuries of slavery and colonisation, a light appeared at the end of the tunnel. All over Africa, Africans were taking charge of their countries' affairs. At last, we thought, things were about to change. On 1 September 1966, Mr Ahidjo, 'Father of the Nation', united all Cameroonians under the banner of the single part, granting himself full power. Cameroon was about to experience its darkest hour.

Over Sixties' archive footage of army vans, riot police firing at fleeing demonstrators – images which clearly resonate with the contemporary footage just seen – the voice-over continues to trace Cameroon's recent political history, describing how the equally repressive Paul Biya became president in 1982. After a short extract of Biya's official address to the nation, in which he confirms his rejection of democracy, and contemporary documentary shots of young men grouped around the dead body of a demonstrator (partially covered with a poster of President Biya), three titles read:

> To all those
> Who have given their lives
> In the name of freedom

followed by the film credits.[21] By juxtaposing the black and white archive footage and details of Cameroonian history with contemporary, hand-held camera documentary material, this violent and unequivocally critical pre-credits sequence establishes the country's climate of repression. Teno thus makes clear that he intends to examine how the colonial past has contributed to the country's present situation, and to unravel the 'mystery' of why, 'a country made up of such well-structured traditional societies has failed to organise itself into a state'.

Afrique, je te plumerai is a complex collage of sequences which, for the sake of analysis, can be divided into two broad, interrelated strands revolving around the quest to reclaim the past and reinterpret the present. The film explains contemporary repression and censorship by tracing the country's history of repression. Secondly, it reveals a tradition of cultural domination that has created a class of rulers willing to perpetrate the same kind of oppression that already existed in the colonial

21 David Achkar's *Allah Tantou* also begins with the inscription, 'This film is dedicated to my father and all the prisoners in CAMP BOIRO and else-where', both films thus addressing the hitherto silenced theme of political repression in Africa.

era and to allow neo-colonial influence to continue. It also focuses on pockets of resistance to this pattern, allowing an alternative African voice to permeate the film.

Teno raises the question of cultural domination from the start, demonstrating the extent to which the colonial authorities used schools to impose their own cultural norms. Teno reminds us that this legacy continues today, notably amongst Cameroon's decision-makers, particularly in a fictionalised re-enactment of an interview with the Chief Executive of the national television station. As Teno makes his way through corridors to the office, the hand-held camera gives a subjective point of view, and his voice-over informs the viewer that he intends to discuss the possibility of broadcasting the film he is in the process of making on Cameroonian television. As the director/camera enters the office, the Chief Executive can be seen behind his desk playing a computer game, with a portrait of the omnipresent President Biya behind him on the wall. The ensuing 'live interview' sequence encapsulates the impossibility of broadcasting local productions given the continuing foreign domination of the market:

Chief Executive: How much?
Off, Teno: What do you mean, how much?
Chief Executive: How much will you pay for us to show your stories on the national television? We get films like *Dallas*, *Dynasty*, *Châteauvallon*, *Derrick*, *Mademoiselle* for free. And the people are happy.

In a later sequence, Teno's reporter friend, Marie interviews librarians at the French, British, and German cultural centres in Yaoundé to find out how many African books they have in their collections. The interviews confirm that these centres' vocation is to promote European culture, or as Teno comments, 'Wherever you look, it's Europe again.' In a series of interviews with two Cameroonian publishers, we learn that local publishing is still unprofitable, even though the film shows that they have the technical resources to print books, because French publishers continue to dominate the most lucrative school textbook market. Teno concludes:

Our universities are full of graduates who regularly write on a whole range of subjects. We have the necessary infrastructures to produce books in the country. What's more, we are in charge of our own school syllabuses. So, how can we explain this dependency on France? Literature will die in our country if only foreign publishers profit from the book market. By killing literature, thought and collective memory are being killed.

Having denounced the state of the Cameroonian book market, Teno revisits his own childhood memories of learning through a series of fictionalised black and white sequences narrated in voice-over, introducing personal memory alongside 'official' history. They reveal the kind of imported culture to which his post-independence generation was exposed, repeating the neo-colonial domination which the preceding sequences have already shown still exist. As the camera zooms in on the pages of a book in Yaoundé's present-day second-hand book market, a new sequence begins with the filmed pages of a Tarzan comic book, complete with jungle sound effects off-screen. As the camera zooms back out to show a child reading the book in a playground, the switch to black and white indicates that we are now in the realm of Teno's memory. Teno's voice-over describes, 'This was how we learnt to read, between the interminable football matches. An unforgettable moment that we shared with the neighbourhood cinema.' Despite the somewhat nostalgic mood of the rest of the sequence – a nostalgia that his voice-over later self-mockingly acknowledges[22] – the subsequent close-up shots of comic book cowboy scenes, fairy-tale white princes and princesses, white adventurers speaking roughly to a caricatured African (set to the sounds of the jungle), and long extracts of a Bollywood Indian film at the local cinema, are interspersed with close-up shots of the children's transfixed faces, all emphasise that these children's early visual/literary education is made up of primarily imported matter.

Two further sequences complete the picture of cultural imperialism. Firstly, Teno edits together extracts of French colonial film footage, boasting about the creation of colonial schools in which (the original voice-over commentary informs us), 'the young blacks receive a sound education that directs expectations towards a normal life. The schools train them to be shop assistants, craftsmen and, above all, well-informed farmers.' By positioning this colonial voice in the context of the rest of the film, however, Teno reveals the prejudice of this approach, highlighting the fact that the colonial powers considered African children incapable of receiving the same level of education as children in the West. In reality, they had no desire to educate them any more than their own needs required. The myth of France's supposedly altruistic desire to 'educate the natives' is further deconstructed by the preceding sequence on the written script developed by the Sultan Ngoya and taught in indigenous Cameroonian schools as of 1895. These schools were shut down when the French took control of what was originally a German colony after World War I, as they were considered 'an obstacle to colonial action'.

Secondly, Teno sets up a thematic circularity around his initial premise that colonial rule established the lasting notion that Western-style education was the only way to become 'like a white man' and thus to succeed in life. He traces the emergence of an educated Cameroonian elite who, despite reaching the top of the social ladder, were still treated as sub-humans in their own country. Quoting the poetry written by this educated elite, who are seen in a montage of photos from the colonial era wearing Western suits, top hats and wedding dresses ('Blinded by love, I have lost my mind. I am black, and you a beautiful blonde', or, 'Oh France, our only hope. No, you will not die. You will always be the guardian angel of the black man'), Teno reveals the extent of their conditioning. If he adds that, 'their desire to please the white man is disturbing', it is clearly because he identifies them as the predecessors of today's ruling elite, by extension denouncing what he sees as the latter's continuing state of submission.

22 As the sequence draws to an end, Teno mockingly sighs, 'Ah childhood, independence', immediately disrupting any wistfulness by recalling the repressive violence of the period. His words are reinforced by an extremely jarring silent sequence of black and white archive footage of policemen beating a man, accompanied only by the dull thuds of their blows.

Elsewhere in the film, Teno addresses another closely related question. In a montage of colonial footage, with interviews and voice-overs that trace key moments of twentieth-century Cameroonian history, Teno illustrates how today's 'tradition' of political repression has its antecedents in the colonial period. It will be recalled that *Afrique, je te plumerai* opens with shots of the Nineties' pro-democracy demonstrations being violently repressed. In a long following sequence, Teno explains how, when he started shooting the film in 1991, history unexpectedly accelerated. The Cameroonian newspaper, *Le Messager*, published journalist Célestin Monga's virulently critical letter to President Paul Biya, denouncing the President's arrogant style of rule, Cameroon's lack of democracy, human rights abuses, and widespread poverty and corruption. After reading extracts of the letter in voice-over, the film traces the subsequent arrest and trial of Monga and the newspaper editor, and the banning of *Le Messager* and other newspapers which triggered demonstrations for freedom of speech and democracy. Teno's montage of newspaper headlines, extracts of an interview with the newspaper editor, and documentary footage already hint at the complicity between autocratic African leaders like Biya and certain Western powers. He ironically juxtaposes an extract of the interview with the *Messager* editor (who explains that the Monga trail exacerbated the newspaper's already extremely fraught relationships with the regime, and led to the sudden suspension of the paper), with a shot of a French newspaper headline stating 'Cameroonian censorship is more symbolic than real'. The question of censorship also relates this part of the film to the sequences examining the state of the Cameroonian book market, which conclude that the dearth of local publications is part of an overall strategy to stifle free expression. These contemporary examples of the lack of freedom of speech echo the repressive measures of the colonisers, characterised in the film by the closing of the Sultan Ngoya's schools.

This comparison is euphemistically alluded to in the ominous words of one extract of colonial film footage which refers to how Cameroon became a French territory in 1916, and states: 'the country then had to be pacified to give the blacks an understanding of a necessary discipline'. Examples of this 'pacification' and 'discipline' include sequences of black and white footage of police beatings and the revelation of how the colonial authorities violently repressed the nascent Cameroonian trade union movement. Mixing footage from the time with voice-overs and interviews with a former trade unionist, the historian Jean-Pierre Essomba, and the father of one of the UPC party leaders, Teno documents how the colonial authorities violently repressed the Douala general strike in September 1945.[23] Ten years later, the same authorities launched an attack to eradicate the UPC, killing thousands, banning the party, and arresting its leaders. Archive footage from the time, which is not dissimilar to that of the Nineties' demonstrations, shows French soldiers in armoured vehicles patrolling deserted streets littered with dead bodies, firing, beating, and smiling. The similarity between the actions of the new African leaders and the colonial

23 Founded in 1948, the 'Union des Populations du Cameroun' (UPC) was the country's first political party and was closely affiliated with the French Communist Party.

authorities is accentuated by giving the dates of the deaths of the three assassinated UPC leaders, one of whom was killed in 1971, well after independence. Inclusion of the famous footage of the Congolese leader Patrice Lumumba's arrest in 1961 also links Cameroonian repression to the general climate of repression that characterised the early independence era, when certain Western powers did not hesitate to help eliminate the African politicians who appeared to threaten their neo-colonial and/or Cold War interests.

The question of the unions, the neutralisation of certain political leaders, and the contemporary struggles of the journalists and young people in the fight for democracy and freedom bring us back to the notion of resistance established at the beginning of the film. This introduces the second focus of *Afrique, je te plumerai*, which documents this resistance, giving it a voice. The film thus offers alternative readings of the period and sheds light on a struggle which, for obvious reasons, has rarely been acknowledged by the authorities. Elsewhere in the film, Teno creates a space in which other alternative voices challenge the falsifications of Western colonial history and formulate new, specifically African perspectives on Cameroonian history. At the same time, the achronological, non-linear structure of the film disrupts and challenges the 'rules' of Western historiographic presentation.

One of the first examples of this alternative reading comes in the black and white childhood memory sequence in which Teno recalls the metaphoric tale his grandfather used to tell him to explain the advent of independence. Set in the prosperous land of skylarks, the story tells of the arrival of foreign hunters who settle the land, exploit the hospitality of the skylarks, and install a new chief when they leave:

> The chief was exactly the kind of chief the hunters wanted. Some even said that he was a very old hunter-sorcerer who, realising he was about to die, found the strength to leave his terrestrial envelope. He rushed into the first hut and entered the body of a newborn skylark. Ever since that time, a very strange race of skylarks had lived in that village who showed their brothers absolutely no respect.[24]

The tale clearly illustrates the way in which oral traditions use allegory to interpret contemporary realities. At the same time, it provides an entirely different perspective and interpretative mode than that likely to be taught in Africa's Western-style education system. In this same childhood memory sequence, Teno debunks two Western myths about Africa, namely that the continent was without writing (an interviewee describes the development of the Sultan Ngoya's Sho-mon alphabet), and without history (we are shown the original book of the Bamoun people's history, written in the Sultan's script in 1911).

Later in the film, Teno goes even further in his explicit deconstruction of colonial narratives. As already seen in Chapter 2, colonial 'documentary' films are striking for their lack of an African viewpoint. By editing together extracts of these same films and juxtaposing them with his own alternative voice-over commentaries or the words of Cameroonian

24 The reference to skylarks ('alouettes'), retrospectively explains the significance of the musical leitmotif created by the repetition of the well-known French song, 'Alouette, je te plumerai' ['Skylark, I will pluck you clean']. The film title is, of course, a play on the words of the song, which allegorise the violation/exploitation of the African continent.

Jean-Marie Teno, Afrique je te
plumerai, *1991. Colonial film
extracts showing men and women
hard at work is deconstructed by
Teno's voice-overs, which highlight
the exploitative nature of the
colonial regime.*
(Courtesy of Jean-Marie Teno)

historians and individuals who had lived through that time, Teno
challenges the authority of these films. He begins with a montage of
colonial film extracts showing men and women labouring, steam trains
laden with produce, shots of goods being loaded onto docked ships
accompanied by triumphant voice-over commentaries describing the
construction of modern ports, the use of modern equipment and the
production of raw materials destined for Europe. Then Teno's voice-overs
cut in to explain that many Cameroonians died during the construction

Memory, History: Other Stories

of these 'modern' roads and railways due to the lack of safety measures, medication and food. The filmed interviews with the historian Jean-Pierre Essomba, the elder Nji Fifen, and ex-trade unionist Leopold Moume-Etia re-write the absences of the colonial films as they also describe forced labour practices in the colonies, how chiefs were paid for each man they managed to send to work, and the brutal working conditions where beatings, insults, and docked wages were common fare.[25] This information makes it impossible to take the following extract of colonial footage at face value, with its characteristic images of colonial officials distributing pay and rewards and claims that, 'France has always prided itself on peacefully conquering overseas' hearts.'

In a second sequence of colonial films, Teno's own voice-over replaces the original commentary, again subverting the original message of the film. Over shots of men carrying the colonial masters through the jungle, felling huge trees as the disproportionately amplified thudding sound of their chopping recalls that of the man being beaten by the police earlier, women harvesting cotton, depositing loads of palm nuts, Teno scathingly comments,

> Our lands were labelled 'colonies'. People don't behave like they do at home in a colony. They take all there is, pillage, garner, and destroy ... Europe has taken everything, leaving us its toxic waste and hunger in return ... When I hear people talking about Third World debt, I realise that some people's cynicism knows no bounds.

The distorted nature of the colonial narrative is again driven home by Teno's montage, which juxtaposes his incisive critique and more jubilant colonial footage celebrating how France's 'children' willingly contributed raw materials and men to help save France in the Second World War.

25 Nji Fifen's description of this system throws light on an earlier, un-explained sequence in which a group of men led by a chief (designated by his colonial-style pith helmet) are seen going to arrest a young man who is hidden under his bed. In retrospect, we understand that this was in fact a dramatisation of how labourers were force-fully recruited. Once again, therefore, the film moves away from traditions of chronological narration.

As the film draws to an end, Teno moves back into the 'present tense' to show two final examples of resistance that complement the film's rejection of oppression. Commenting that, 'Throughout this century, we have drowned our bitterness in beer. The alternative to death is silence or exile. Humour is the only form of speech tolerated', Teno films a sketch by comedian Essini Mindja, who parodies a dictator's press conference and the journalists' embarrassing questions about human rights abuses, the single party state, and the President's Swiss bank accounts. Afterwards, Teno films a father that he has seen, teaching his young son and daughter to read and write by the roadside because he cannot afford to send them to school. As Teno comments in voice-over, 'For me, this man was a resistance fighter, because an educated man can speak out and be free'. The director's critical analysis of the past thus brings us full circle back to the present. The film constitutes a journey whose alternative, challenging perspectives offer the viewer a far greater, new understanding of both history and the present.

Asientos: archaeology of memory

François Woukoache's *Asientos* is a rich and powerful film that deals explicitly with the question of representation and memory – or, to be more precise, lack of memory, as is clear from the quotation on the first page of the film's press book: 'L'Histoire avance en se bouchant la mémoire comme on se bouche les oreilles' ['History advances, blocking memory like we block our ears'].[26] The film sets out to document what the director considers to be an under-represented, and thus not yet fully assimilated period of history: the slave trade. Woukoache describes his project as an attempt to 'Filmer pour la Mémoire, contre l'oubli. Filmer pour lutter contre l'amnésie sélective ... faire le deuil de ce "moment historique"' ['To film for the sake of memory, against oblivion. To film to combat selective amnesia ... to grieve for this "historic moment"'].[27] For Woukoache, there needs to be a process of mourning if this painful chapter of history is to be rightfully acknowledged, but first, there needs to be a process of remembering.

The film's quest to reconstruct this memory, to recover a 'lost' period that has left little visual documentation and even fewer testimonies from enslaved Africans, and whose sites are gradually being eroded, forces the director to deal with the difficulty of expressing 'une souffrance qui a eu lieu il y a plus d'un siècle alors qu'on a déjà tant de mal à faire accepter celles d'il y a 50 ans, et que celles d'aujourd'hui semblent laisser indifférent ... Comment dire cette mémoire sans témoins et dont les lieux subissent les assauts terribles du temps?' ['a suffering that took place over a century ago when we already find it so hard to accept those that took place fifty years ago, and when today' sufferings seem to leave us indifferent ... How to speak this memory that has no witnesses and whose sites are subjected to the terrible assault of time?'].[28] *Asientos* brings to mind the words of bell hooks: 'To bear the burden of memory one must willingly journey to places long uninhabited, searching the debris of history for traces of the unforgettable, all knowledge of which has been

26 From Chris Marker's film *Sans Soleil*. (France, 1982).

27 François Woukoache. Introduction to the *Asientos* press book.

28 François Woukoache. ibid.

François Woukoache, Asientos,
1995. The young man and the
elusive woman staring out to sea,
the rolling waves creating a visual
and aural leitmotif that represents
both the passing of time and the
passageway to the Americas.
(Courtesy of PBC Pictures SPRL.
All rights reserved)

François Woukoache, Asientos,
1995. The woman character finally
glancing at the main protagonist
(and spectator).
(Courtesy of PBC Pictures SPRL.
All rights reserved)

suppressed ... Travelling, moving into the past ... [one] pieces together fragments ... For black folks, reconstructing an archaeology of memory makes return possible.'[29]

The film is a tapestry of non-linear sequences that fall into three main interwoven groups. The first explores the factual, 'official' historical data on the slave trade period through shots of display cases at the Nantes slave museum in France; shots of the Gorée Island slave house in Senegal; photos; and factual voice-over texts. This precise 'official' version of history is interspersed with beautifully filmed fictional scenes. Featuring a mysterious old man, who appears to represent the voice of the dead, an elusive woman, and Super-8 images of a child, these are accompanied by pensive voice-over texts that take us into the realm of a young man's imagination. He struggles to come to terms with a past that eludes him, thereby raising the question of the difficulty of reconstructing a memory one has not experienced. In a third strand, Woukoache includes contemporary images of the 1994 Rwandan genocide. These draw a parallel between the past horrors of slavery and the modern day, introducing a reflection on the repetitions of history and the significance of memory if we are to learn from past errors. The raw horror of these images becomes the object of a reflection on the question of representation in general and of the African continent in particular.

The film opens with a written text that explains the meaning of 'asiento' (a licence to deliver slaves to the King of Spain, first granted in 1528), thereby immediately establishing the factual, historical setting of the period in question. Fragments of historical data are interspersed throughout the rest of the film, gradually building up an inventory of the slave trade. Woukoache films the remaining tangible evidence of the slave trade period, including exhibits from the Nantes museum and the Gorée Island slave house where slaves were sorted and held before being shipped to the Americas, while voice-over texts provide information on when and why the slave trade started, how long it lasted, how the trading was organised, who benefited, the conditions in which the slaves were held, the criteria of choice of slaves, and so forth. Although this accumulation of data provides a historical outline of the period, Woukoache emphasises the lack of personal testimony and lack of an African point of view. Throughout the film, he reminds us of those 'lost forever in the cracks of history'. It is precisely because, in the words of the old man, 'My brothers, your ancestors ... have disappeared in history', that the film sets out to acknowledge this absence and to restore memory.

The second sequence immediately introduces the film's two other key preoccupations. Over images of the young man looking out to sea – the sea becoming a visual and aural leitmotif in the film, its rolling waves marking the passage of time that erases memory and symbolising the passageway to the Americas – an unidentified female voice-over (fictitious or real), describes, 'The first time we met ... I listened to him speak. Too many images here in Europe, he said. Too many helpless images. Too few images over there. The difficulty of filling his memory's empty spaces'.[30] On the one hand 'he' (the director? the fictionalised

29 bell hooks, 'Representations of Whiteness', pp 172–3.

30 The 'empty space' motif is visually reiterated throughout the film, Woukoache insistently filming the empty cells of the Gorée slave house and the empty huts of the fictionalised sequences.

Memory, History:
Other Stories

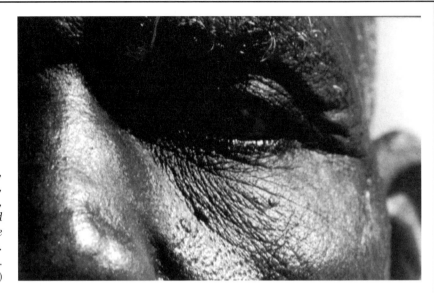

François Woukoache, Asientos, 1995. Close-up shots of textures, such as the old man's wrinkled skin, give form to the absences highlighted in the film, as if to arrest the ineluctable erasure of time.
(Courtesy of PBC Pictures SPRL.

young man?) is confronted by the predominance of European representations of Africa and, on the other, by 'official' history's lack of African voice, which makes it all the more difficult to reconstitute memory.

An old man and the woman appear in the fictionalised sequences, representing in the young man's imagination the 'spirits of the dead', and embodying this distant and intangible past.[31] Throughout the film, they are separated from the young man by an insurmountable gulf. The old man never acknowledges the young man's presence as he sits staring out to sea even though he addresses him in voice-over. The woman, who is always filmed walking out of the frame or disappearing from the shots, leaving a resonant emptiness behind her, remains completely inaccessible. Her final glance towards the young man literally blinds him as the image of her burns out, giving way to the unbearable images of the Rwandan genocide. The old man's words squarely confront the young man/director with the dilemma of the film. He demands to be remembered: 'I have come here every day. I have waited for you every day. I wanted to talk to you. Where were you?' or 'My body was lost in a shipwreck. I rejoined my brothers piled with no names in the cracks of history. I don't exist anymore. Do something for me. Remember.' Paradoxically, he affirms that the memory is irrevocably lost: 'What do you want? Leave me alone. You'll get nothing from me. I am dead. You can't enter death', and 'You can't unbury the dead, nor their cries, their revolts, their wounds. I died and you weren't even born. I died without leaving you a thing, orphan of those who left, who never came back, your ancestors, my brothers.' These words echo the director's own dilemma as he tries to depict a past that both haunts and eludes him. The woman's voice-over confirms, 'There where I suffer, he said, there is nothing to suffer or to bear this suffering. How to reach the site of this suffering? How to know what happened? There is nothing to show. Nothing.'

31 The term is borrowed from the opening voice-over of Haile Gerima's feature film *Sankofa* (Ethiopia-USA, 1993): 'Spirit of the dead rise up. Those stolen Africans, step out of the ocean, from the wounds of the ships and claim your story. Lingering spirit of the dead rise up and possess your bird of passage'.

François Woukoache, Asientos, 1995. The video footage played on the television stacked in an attic shows Western journalists intrusively photographing Rwandan refugees, with no regard for their suffering. This obtrusive saturation of images contrasts with the lack of representation of the slave trade highlighted in the film, both silencing an African voice.
(Courtesy of PBC Pictures SPRL. All rights reserved)

The director seeks to give form to this absence, turning his camera to film and re-film slow, close-up tracking shots of the flaking walls of the empty Gorée slave house, its cells and passage ways, interspersed with shots of the ebbing and flowing waves, of cloth blowing in the wind, and the wrinkled skin of the old man's ageing body, as if to arrest the ineluctable erasure of time. Given the silence surrounding this past – as the woman's voice-over says, 'Over there, he said, you don't speak about the difficult things you experience. The serious things remain silent' – the director strives to capture the silences of these empty memory-ridden places, the silences of the old man. The closing words of the film evoke his desire 'to listen to the silence, to learn to look again to see the unspeakable'. Long moments of the film, such as the slow tracking shots, or the long fixed takes of the three characters as they stare out to sea are purposefully wordless. The silence of the shots creates a space for the viewer to listen and reflect too, as the beautifully composed images focusing on textures, forms, and colours complement the absences evoked in the film.

Asientos's inclusion of video footage of the terrible Rwanda genocide opens up a wider, related reflection on both questions of memory and representation. Projected on a television stacked in an attic, which is in itself symbolic of memory, images of dead bodies being unceremoniously dumped with other debris, and emaciated refugees surrounded by masked Western journalists intrusively taking photos in complete disrespect for their suffering and dignity, immediately bring to mind the opening words of the film, 'Too many images here in Europe ... Too many helpless images.' Woukoache raises the question of how the Western media continues to represent the African continent through only its tragedies, completely disarming and silencing the people concerned, as is clear from the silence of the refugees as they stare fixedly into the video camera. Woukoache expresses his concern that this intense media coverage ultimately engenders a dangerous widespread indifference that fosters the 'selective amnesia' already referred to in the film, thereby bringing us back to the central question of memory.

The Rwanda images also serve to represent how history is likely to repeat itself if we fail to come to terms with the past. As the woman's voice-over at the beginning of the film describes, 'He is scared, scared that it might happen again elsewhere. Here, now, it's beginning to happen again. Why carry on trying to flee the past?' The suffering of contemporary Rwanda mirrors the suffering of the slave trade. The saturation of (the wrong kind of?) contemporary images is contrasted with the lack of representation of the slave trade, but we are still no closer to hearing an African voice. History is repeated. The parallel between the past and present is accentuated as shots of the slave ship model and shackles in the Nantes slave museum adjoin the woman's voice-over reflection on the Rwanda images. Her reference to a 'commerce' of images also echoes the commerce of people, suggesting that such images deprive the continent and its people of a certain freedom.

The repetitions of particular shots and sequences in the film formally echo the message that history is being repeated. A black and white Super-8 sequence of the child running on the beach accompanied by an extract of Aimé Césaire's *Journal of a Return to the Native Land* is constantly repeated, with this choice of author and text further evoking the question of slavery and the African diaspora. Certain shot compositions are also repeated, such as the camera's revolving movement around the heads of the young man and woman as he repeatedly tries to approach her, or the way in which the young man repeats the old man's ritual libation gestures to honour the ancestors, symbolic of the past. The repetition of motifs confers a cyclical structure on the film, which brings Woukoache's (re)presentation of history closer to African historiographic traditions and to the cyclical conception of time in orature. Memory is restored in the process, giving this historical reconstruction a highly personal and moving tone.

Allah Tantou: personal memory, public testimony

Achkar's *Allah Tantou* is an emotive and powerful testimony that highlights relations between the spheres of personal memory and politics/history by piecing together fragments of the filmmaker's father's private and public experiences. It seeks to restore the memory of Marof Achkar, the Guinean ambassador to the United Nations in the early Sixties, who was imprisoned on charges of conspiracy and executed without trial by the increasingly paranoid Sekou Touré, the independence hero turned autocratic leader. The film gives form to a less well-known and sometimes deliberately erased facet of a historical period and a regime, and addresses the wider issue of political oppression, as is indicated in the film's opening title: 'This film is dedicated to my father and all the prisoners in CAMP BOIRO and elsewhere.' By literally giving his father a voice and piecing together his hitherto suppressed memory,

Allah Tantou constitutes a counter-memory, or a means of 'speaking back' on behalf of both Marof Achkar and all other victims of political repression.

Right from the start, director David Achkar clearly positions himself in relation to his subject matter. Over extracts of family Super-8 footage in which he is seen with his father as a young child, he comments, 'Many sons admire their fathers. I barely knew mine. All I know about him is what my mother or his friends told me, and what he wrote to us in prison.' By acknowledging his relationship and, in a sense, acknowledging that the film is partly a quest to 'discover' his own little-known father, Achkar recognises his own obvious partiality and places the film outside the Western tradition of historic 'objectivity'. Whilst the film addresses history, therefore, it tells first and foremost the filmmaker's and his father's personal stories.

As in *Asientos*, *Allah Tantou* seeks to give form to an absence – that of the little-known father – and to create a space in which the father's silenced voice can at last be heard. Through a montage of diverse elements including Marof Achkar's prison writings, other personal documents (photos, family Super-8 film), 'official' archive material (newsreel footage, newspaper headlines, photos, footage of UN meetings), 'fictional' re-enactments, and the filmmaker's own voice-over commentaries, Achkar pieces together a multi-faceted portrait of his father and a certain period of Guinean history. The film recovers two lives, the public and the private, portraying the man whose status and importance become clear through the extracts of archive film footage of Marof Achkar speaking before the United Nations, visiting a plethora of countries with international delegations, or appearing before acclaiming crowds in Guinea. This public image is developed through filmed extracts of international newspaper headlines reporting Achkar's struggle against the South African apartheid regime, official photos, and occasional voice-over details. All of this 'official' material retraces Marof Achkar's rise from musician in the Guinean national dance troupe to Guinean ambassador to the United Nations when the country gained independence in 1958. Later, he became Chairman of the UN Special Committee on Apartheid, an aspect of his career that also situates the question of repression on a continental level – the irony being that this spokesman for African freedom should end up a political prisoner in his own country. The reconstructed scenes where Marof Achkar, tied and suspended in a dark cell, is tortured, are all the more poignant when juxtaposed with footage of the same man at the height of his career.

The film simultaneously portrays a far more private Marof Achkar, showing him as a family man in the home movie footage, and giving voice to his thoughts and reflections in prison. Information from the prison diaries also enables Achkar to highlight Sekou Touré's increasingly dictatorial stance and the waves of political assassinations perpetrated by his regime. This material and the film's personalised re-interpretation both challenge the official government version of Achkar's father's arrest and the generally accepted, positive image of

Sekou Touré as the 'first president of Guinea and undaunted pan-Africanist'.[32]

Marof Achkar's prison writings cover many subjects: the circumstances of his arrest and the squalid and humiliating conditions in which he is held, the tortures to make him sign a forced confession; his own realisations about the nature of the regime; his reflections on Africa's plight; his ideas on freedom and religion; his evolving states of frustration, anger and finally of joy as he finds inner harmony or release through his ordeal. David Achkar, the director, thus allows his father's own voice to permeate the very texture of the film, conferring a far greater resonance on the rest of the factual documentary material.

The 'fictionalised' recreation of the prison and torture episodes, which are played by an actor with Marof Achkar's writings as voice-over narrative and direct speech, encourage the viewer to identify emotionally with his ordeal. By including shots of the actual texts themselves, however, Achkar reminds the viewer that this is reality, not fiction, a knowledge which makes the emotional weight of the film harder to bear. This 'play' on fiction/reality is used most poignantly at the end of the film when (over shots of a bush track filmed from a moving vehicle) we hear the actor/father's voice saying, 'It was on a morning like this, on a road like this, that I was shot in January 1971' – words which Marof Achkar obviously did not write. This is followed by a fixed shot of the bottom of a written page that jars us back to reality. On it we can read, 'your triumph is INEVITABLE. Signed Marof David Achkar. DEDICATED to my son F.M. DAVID ACHKAR on his 10th birthday. Dated 26 Jan 70'. By closing on Marof Achkar's dedication to his son, the film also sets up a mirroring effect: Marof Achkar dedicates his writings to his son, who centres the writings in a film whose very content is dedicated to his father. David Achkar thus chooses to conclude on a highly personal note that emphasises the personal dimension behind 'official' history as it interweaves and juxtaposes the two.

Fad'jal: oral transmission and memory

Our last analysis focuses on Safi Faye's Fad'jal, a chronicle of day-to-day life in a Serer village in southern Senegal, which combines both the 'ordinary' (harvesting, gathering salt, cooking) and the 'exceptional' (a birth, a death, a traditional wrestling ceremony). As the French subtitle of the film, 'Grandfather recounts', indicates, the film is concerned with the living memory of the village and how this memory is orally transmitted, contrasting this continuity of rural traditions with the incursion of contemporary Senegalese life. The film provides a space in which the village elders narrate and perpetuate village history. In so doing, they affirm this history and their perennial community values and also reveal how such memory is an integral part of their way of life.

Fad'jal opens with a pre-credits sequence that explicitly contrasts the nature and mode of transmission of the village's collective memory with the Western-style models imposed since the colonial era. In a classroom next to the church – the physical presence of which, and the off-screen

32 N. Frank Ukadike, 'The Other Voices of Documentary: *Allah Tantou* and *Afrique, je te plumerai*', p 88.

116

religious music immediately associating the school with the European missionaries and colonial authorities – children are seen reciting their history lesson in unison: 'Louis XIV was the greatest French monarch. He was called the Sun King.' This sequence is literally divided from the rest of the film by the credits, indicating that, unlike local oral history, the history of a bygone French king is in no way integrated, nor indeed relevant, to daily village life. The fact that neither church nor school reappear in the course of the film confirms the point. One cannot escape the irony of these children still being taught 'official' French history, even after the advent of political independence. By filming the elders as they transmit their own communal memory, however, Safi Faye chooses to pay tribute to a form of history long denigrated and ignored by what she clearly shows to be an ill-adapted education system imposed by colonial authorities. Amadou Hampaté Bâ's famous quotation, 'En Afrique, un vieillard qui meurt est une bibliothèque qui brûle' ['In Africa, when an elder dies, a library goes up in flames'] is superimposed over the following long shot of a cart cutting across an open landscape that contrasts strikingly with the preceding closed space of the classroom. Throughout the film, Faye pays tribute to the elders and griots who, as *Fad'jal* clearly demonstrates, play a vital role in transmitting collective memory and history.

Amongst the sequences that build up a detailed portrait of village life, Faye includes a series of sequences in which an elder narrates the village history and explains its communal values to a group of boys. This fragmentary, non-linear presentation is in itself typical of the digressive narrative style of the oral traditions discussed earlier. The elder narrates some of the scenes in real time, whilst others are enacted in fictionalised sequences, the narration actually 'coming to life'.

At the start of the film, a group of young boys walk into the shot to join the elder seated on a mat in the shade of a large tree. The boys each greet the elder and sit in a circle round him, creating a ritualised space in which the narration can begin. Each time the elder addresses the youngsters throughout the film, the circle is formed, usually in the shade of a tree, that in itself symbolises the circular process, the link between the living and the dead, and cultural transmission in many West African traditions.[33] Once the children have settled, they ask the elder to tell them about their history. In the following narrative sequences, the boys (and the audience) learn how the village was founded and how it thrived, so that it became common knowledge that, 'Fadial means work. He who works will be happy. He who does not will become the laughing stock'. One of the village's communal values is thus established. The boys also learn about the origins of the matriarchal system, how land was traditionally distributed – a system which is threatened by a new law that will make the State the sole owner of the land. The film also teaches how the village was destroyed by King Latsouk Fagname of Sine, before being founded again on its present site. During both the storytelling sessions and, later, celebrations held to honour the newborn child and deceased elder, the village griot, Latyr, often intervenes to recite the

33 In the film we also learn that a tree is planted every time a child is born. When the children ask the elder how old he is, he tells them to compare the size of their trees to find out. The tree thus also appears to symbolise the continuity of life.

genealogy of the ancestors, always starting with the formula, 'I have something to add. Let's list our ancestors.' These events highlight the importance of genealogy in Serer (and indeed other African) traditions and history, and show its oral mode of transmission. At the end of the film, the children in turn recite snippets of the elder and the griot's teachings as they sit perched in the branches of the tree. As André Gardies points out, the understanding is that the youngsters will in turn pass on the lessons of the past, the tree itself symbolising such transmission.[34]

The presentation of several narrative incidents in *Fad'jal* is revealing. Whilst most of the story is narrated directly as the children are seen gathered round the elder, episodes concerning the downfall and re-founding of the village are narrated in voice-over in a series of fictionalised scenes that mix both dramatised re-enactment and contemporary documentary footage of village life. This technique brings history to life and places it at the heart of the village's contemporary existence. The downfall episode begins with a long, lateral tracking shot of King Latsouk Fagname riding across the screen in the distance, flanked by his courtiers. It is not until the voice-over intervenes to narrate the story a moment later, that we realise that this is an enactment. As the voice-over continues to describe the prosperity of the village at the time, we see contemporary 'documentary' shots of the villagers tying bundles of millet, women pounding corn or cattle drinking. Although the images situate us in the 'present tense' of the film, there is a direct link to the past setting of the tale. Over a fixed frontal shot of the king and his entourage, the elder's voice-over tells how the king was jealous, 'and so he said...'. The king character takes over, addressing the camera directly, 'I will destroy Fadial without a single shot.' The narrated sequence thus becomes a direct re-enactment. The deliberate ambiguity between the two modes continues as 'real' shots of the contemporary villagers preparing a feast are juxtaposed with images/sound of the king laughing, while the elder narrates in voice-over how the king abused the villagers' hospitality, exhausting its stores and forcing the people to leave. The 'confusion' is maintained as we see a contemporary family preparing to leave the village in what initially seems to be a 'real' scene. They come across Latyr, the real village griot, who explains that he is also leaving because he refuses to become the king's griot, once more taking us back to the narrated story. The sequence ends with a shot of the elder telling the story to the children, concluding, 'At that time, everybody emigrated to survive', in a clear reference to the contemporary rural exodus. This conflating of the past and present stresses the lack of Western-style linear chronology in the oral transmission of history. Moreover, it demonstrates how the past and the present are intrinsically related in orature, the past serving to inform the future and the present.

The different approaches to history and memory explored in all of these films restore a specifically African perspective as they strive to give space and voice to episodes hitherto neglected by 'official' history. Each

34 A. Gardies & P. Haffner, *Regards sur le Cinéma Négro-Africain*, p 190. It is also interesting to note that when the child Mabo in turn starts telling his friends the Sunjata story told to him by the griot in Dani Kouyaté's *Keïta!*, the storytelling sessions also take place at the foot of a huge tree, or up in its branches.

film provides a historical re-reading of history that challenges the received, often Western points of view. The alternative cinematic approaches to the past confirm the development of a less conventional vein of politically committed and personalised historical filmmaking that frequently incorporates an overtly subjective and/or autobiographical voice. These films tend to draw freely on a range of film styles and formats, blending them with traditional African narrative techniques to create an alternative space in which other formerly suppressed viewpoints and histories can be developed. Such approaches, adopted by numerous Francophone African filmmakers, reveal the importance of such questions in the wider quest to redefine identities.

5 Filming the Immigrant Experience
Francophone African cinema in Europe

'La doctrine de l'intégration impose de nouveaux repères. Comme lors de la période coloniale, l'Autre ne doit pas être ce qu'il est, mais doit correspondre à ce que le pays d'accueil souhaite qu'il soit.'
['The integration doctrine imposes new markers. Just as in the colonial period, the Other must correspond to what the host country wants him to be, rather than what he really is.']
P. Blanchard & N. Bancel[1]

1 P. Blanchard & N. Bancel, 'De l'indigène à l'immigré, le retour du colonial', H&M, 1207, mai-juin 1997, p 107.

2 France's continuing economic and cultural ties with its former colonies have often been accused of being neo-colonial. De Gaulle certainly never disguised the real motivations behind France's 'cooperation' (technical assistance) policies set up in the Sixties, affirming that France would get back three francs for every franc it invested in Africa. As already mentioned in the introduction, French subsidies available to African filmmakers follow this logic. Production deals stipulate that sums equivalent to those given have to be spent in French film laboratories and studios, or on the salaries of a certain number of obligatory French technicians. Most contentious of all, however, were the clauses in certain subsidies, such as the Fonds Sud, which, until very recently, was only awarded to films set mainly in Africa. Such clauses were attacked for curtailing freedom of expression and creative choice. Whilst European funding has undoubtedly allowed many African films to exist, there are legitimate

Given the continuing, often contentious cultural and economic ties between Africa and its former colonial powers and the lack of technical and financial aid available to filmmakers in Africa, Europe has traditionally attracted African filmmakers who have little other choice but to go there for training and funding.[2] Ever since Francophone African filmmaking began, a significant number of directors have chosen to set their works in Europe in a reflection of these migratory trends. These European-based films can be seen as constituting a genre in their own right, and are significant both for the ways in which they portray immigrant realities, especially the conditions and concerns of Europe's African communities, and for their fidelity to the thematic and stylistic agendas highlighted throughout this book. Even set outside Africa, such films continue to reflect the kinds of preoccupations that characterise works from the African continent. Their exploration of the relations between the former colonising and colonised nations places them firmly within the overall framework of Francophone African film. By bringing characters to the screen who reflect Europe's cosmopolitan make-up, they also reflect a resolutely African point of view that challenges the absences, stereotypes and misrepresentations of immigrant characters in the vast majority of European films.[3] By exploring the very nature of identity, the values and place of the immigrant communities in Europe, these films affirm the multiple identities and cultural forms re-evaluated in other Francophone African films. Finally, directors' efforts to inscribe an African voice in a country such as France, where, as Olivier Barlet rightly points out, the official policy of integration by definition refuses to acknowledge the existence of immigrant 'communities', can once again be seen as an act of resistance, of 'speaking back'.[4]

This chapter examines the European films made by a number of Francophone African directors who are permanently or temporarily resident in France and other European countries. It will consider the kinds of images and concerns they have chosen to portray as they represent the experiences of Africa's immigrant communities. This analysis will help to illustrate how such representations are similar to those found in other Francophone African works. It will also consider the ways in which such representations have evolved.

Setting a precedent: *Afrique sur Seine*

Afrique sur Seine, the very first film made by the group of black African directors, Paulin Soumarou Vieyra, Mamadou Sarr, and the Groupe africain du cinéma, was shot in Paris in 1955. It set a precedent that offers an interesting example of Francophone African filmmaking in Europe and continues to be influential today.[5] The film is both typical and atypical of the two waves of European-based, Francophone African films that have followed – the first of which spanned the ten or so years between Ousmane Sembene's *La Noire de...* (1966) and the mid-Seventies; the second emerging in the Nineties after an almost complete absence of European productions in the late-Seventies and Eighties. *Afrique sur Seine* introduces a number of archetypes, themes and concerns that have been explored in later works. Whilst a number of these themes have remained consistent over the years, their treatment has radically diversified in keeping with socio-cultural changes and evolutions in filmmaking preoccupations and styles.

One of the defining characteristics common to all these European-based films is the way in which they centre the black experience. As Mauritanian filmmaker Med Hondo puts it, '[they bring] some Black faces to the lily-white French screens which have been ignoring us for years'.[6] Made at a time when African characters were either entirely absent or visually marginalized in French film productions, *Afrique sur Seine* was the first work to provide a panoramic overview of the African community in France. The film also focuses on Paris and its monuments to such an extent that they too become a subject rather than just a setting, avoiding simply reversing the ethnographic gaze that characterised so many Western representations of Africa at the time. This allusion to 'an ethnographic gaze' is not fortuitous, for the film, whose opening credits present 'under the patronage of the Museum of Mankind's ethnographic film committee', widely adopts the contemporary ethnographic film-making style.[7] This is conveyed through the characteristic exteriority of the filmic gaze, the physical distance from the characters (most of the film is shot in long and mid-shot), and the silence of the characters whose voices are replaced by the film's omniscient voice-over commentary and music.

Like *Afrique sur Seine*, all the films discussed in this chapter centre their African characters and/or communities. Many of them include 'random' street scenes that highlight the presence of black individuals as if simply to testify to their otherwise ignored presence in Europe. The majority of these films consciously highlight their respective protagonists' immigrant status, positioning it as a prominent if not defining feature of their identity. This immigrant status effectively situates the characters both in relation to the host country – providing a portrait of Europe and its inhabitants through the eyes of the immigrant character – and in relation to the character's country of origin. In the same way that the spectre of Europe is often present in films set in Africa, the African space is equally represented in these European-based films. This clearly evokes

2 (cont.) fears that it puts pressure on directors to produce works that conform to the European public's expectations of what an African film should be like.

3 Such European films include Thomas Gillou's comedy *Black micmac* (France, 1985), which, despite its efforts 'to engage positively with cultural differences', offers a grossly caricatured and stereotypical portrayal of life in an African hostel. See Carrie Tarr, 'French Cinema and Post-Colonial Minorities', in Alec Hargreaves & Mark McKinney (eds.), *Post-Colonial Cultures in France* (London & New York: Routledge, 1997), p 67. Similarly, despite its critical portrait of the day-to-day workings of the drugs squad, Bertrand Tavernier's very different film *L.627* (France, 1991) also reductively depicts all its black characters as drug dealers and addicts.

4 See Oliver Barlet, *African Cinemas: Decolonizing the gaze*, translated by Chris Turner (London: Zed Books, 2000), pp 117–118.

5 Ironically, Vieyra and Sarr shot the film in Paris when the colonial authorities refused them permission to shoot in Senegal. This refusal confirms quite how tendentious the issue of African cinematic self-representation was in the colonial era.

6 Cited by Françoise Pfaff, *Twenty-five Black African Filmmakers* (Westport, Connecticut: Greenwood Press, 1988), p 161.

7 French ethnographic filmmaking boomed in the Forties, largely inspired by the work of Marcel Griaule, who called for the then new lightweight 16 mm cameras and sound recording equipment to be used to document ethnographic field work in Africa. Jean Rouch was one of the main ethnographers to turn to filmmaking, gradually applying his (allegedly objective) ethnographic film techniques to improvised fictional stories. This in

Filming the Immigrant Experience

the real fluidity of borders brought about by European colonisation and subsequent African emigration to Europe.

Before focusing on the African community in France, *Afrique sur Seine* opens with a short sequence set in Africa that introduces a 'contextualising' African space. Over images of a group of playing children, the narrative voice-over describes an idyllic and carefree childhood before the images cut to pan across the Paris skyline, where tall buildings and bustling, busy streets offer a stark contrast to the adobe huts, the banks of the Niger, and the bush path. The African song and *balafon* music heard in the opening sequence continue in transition over the two visual spaces. This symbolic use of music is repeated throughout the film: African music, jazz, and salsa evoke an African and/or cosmopolitan presence in the Parisian landscape. African music is commonly used in the French space, therefore, in the same way that films such as Ousmane Sembene's *Borom Sarret* (Senegal, 1962) use Western classical music to evoke expatriate presence in the up-market Plateau neighbourhood of Dakar, or that Djibril Diop Mambety's *Touki Bouki* (Senegal, 1973) recurrently uses the 'Paris, Paris, Paris' song to evoke Anta and Mory's dream city.

In Ousmane Sembene's *La Noire de...*, Moussa Touré's *Toubabi* (Senegal, 1991), and Jacques Trabi's short film *Bouzié* (Côte d'Ivoire, 1996), this African space contrasts with the films' French environments.[8] In *La Noire de...*, which traces the unhappy existence of a young Senegalese woman who comes to France to work for the expatriate family that employed her in Dakar, flashbacks to the relatively carefree period before Diouana's departure emphasise the misery of her present condition. In these sequences, the white expatriates' world itself represents an extension of the French space in the African setting, where large houses and luxuriant gardens hidden behind tall walls and guarded by barking dogs contrast starkly with the sprawling labyrinth of houses and yards in the Medina district where Diouana's family lives. At this point in the narrative, Diouana clearly aspires to this French expatriate world, her admiration conveyed by the low-angle vertical panning shots that accentuate the imposing nature of the modern apartment blocks.

Toubabi and *Bouzié* also begin by situating the characters in their respective African spaces so that their close-knit communities and/or family environments later contrast with the lifestyles they encounter in France. In both films, France is also already a major presence in the African space. In *Toubabi*, the bundles of second-hand clothes from Europe seen in the opening shots represent a European presence in Africa. Later shots of the main protagonist, Soriba, in France, wearing the same overcoat he managed to grab in the Dakar market reinforce the inter-penetration of the two spaces. In *Bouzié*, a child comes to announce that Zébia has sent his mother a letter with a plane ticket for France. As in a number of films, the letter establishes a physical link between the two continents. Both protagonists, who are so clearly positioned in their respective African spaces at the outset of each film, are unusually characterised by a predominantly exterior gaze when in France, maintaining their African, rather than immigrant, identities.

7 (cont.) turn gave rise to the French *cinéma-vérité* tradition. Rouch continued to shoot many of his fiction films in West Africa, where he initiated several African directors to the medium. These ethnographic/*cinéma-vérité* films have been the object of much debate, however. Ousmane Sembene, for one, famously remarked that Rouch's films scrutinised Africans as if they were insects.

8 The transition from the Ivoirian village to Paris in *Bouzié* is very similar to the transition in *Afrique sur Seine*. The final shot of the village women walking along together is followed by a pan across the Paris skyline, the women's song similarly linking the two spaces.

Afrique sur Seine's opening sequence ends with a shot of two children heading off into the distance as if setting out on a journey. The voice-over intones, 'We would of course grow up and leave the country for Paris, capital of the world, capital of black Africa.' This notion of ineluctability and the glowing terms in which Paris is described introduce the recurrent 'myth', or 'lure' of Europe, a theme revisited in many other works. Faraway Europe indeed represents an eldorado for many of the films' characters, thanks to the lingering legacies of colonial propaganda and the comparative luxury of both the expatriates' lifestyles in Africa and the relative wealth of Africa's emigrant communities. In *Afrique sur Seine*, the voice-over refers twice to the gold-lined streets of Paris described in the 'tales for black children'. Mory is obsessed with going to Paris in *Touki Bouki*, thinking that, 'When I come back, people will call me SIR!', and in Jean-Marie Teno's film *Clando* (Cameroon, 1996), Sobgui's interior monologue describes the image many Africans hold about emigration: 'To leave is to succeed. Even when you wore a nice suit as a tiny child, your friends would look at you enviously and say "he's gone".' This gives an ironic twist to the saying, 'Partir, c'est mourir un peu' ['To leave is to die a little'], suggesting that many such dreams are dashed by the harsh realities of immigration. Numerous films, notably those of the first wave, also depict this process of disillusionment.

Afrique sur Seine differs most from later works in this respect. Its uncharacteristic optimism – 'We bow to the genius of the men of liberty and equality. We bow to all the Paris monuments, the testimony of grandeurs past and present', or 'The people of the Latin Quarter gather, assimilate, melting the ancient barriers of prejudice and the monuments to hatred in the sun of love, growing closer, understanding one another' – no doubt reflect the relatively convivial climate of the student milieu in the Fifties. Judging by the films of the Sixties and Seventies, however, this convivial optimism did not last.

After the establishing shots of Paris, *Afrique sur Seine* focuses on a range of (literally) passing individual African characters who, although never actually given a direct voice, provide glimpses of African life in the student district. The film establishes a gallery of 'archetypes' that frequently reappear in later films. The African student seen jumping on and off the bus at the beginning of the film, provides a visual narrative thread when he pops up in later scenes, and becomes the 'student archetype' found in a number of other works. The young, cosmopolitan student milieu offers fleeting portraits of mixed-race couples, who become both an archetype and a more extensively developed theme in later films.

Afrique sur Seine introduces other recurrent themes and images, suggesting a harsher immigrant reality. As the camera weaves its way through the streets of Paris, one African character is seen asking other Africans for money, and two students cross paths with a down-and-out African drinking in the street. The film also offers a brief shot of an African prostitute who spins away from the camera and a lonely old African who asks an African street sweeper for a cigarette as the voice-over comments, 'The Paris of days without bread. The Paris of days without hope.

The Paris of loneliness, compensated by eternal fraternity.' This reference to a certain inter-community solidarity is developed in later works to such a degree that it actually emerges as one of the immigrant community's defining characteristics. The street sweeper figure also becomes a constant, epitomising the exploitation of African immigrant workers, who are repeatedly shown to do the most unrewarding and despised jobs.

The myth of Europe: illusions and delusions; integration or return?

Over the years, Francophone African directors have continued to develop the thematic concerns explored in *Afrique sur Seine*. Many of the first wave films focus on the sense of disillusionment experienced when immigrant characters find themselves confronted with the realities of life in Europe and notably its hostile, discriminatory climate. Based on a true story published in *Nice-Matin* in 1958, Ousmane Sembene's *La Noire de...*, follows Diouana, the Senegalese nanny-cum-maid, in her downward spiral from her initial state of excitement about going to France to her final, defiant suicide, which she sees as the only escape from exploitative and unsympathetic employers. In addition to charting the destruction of Diouana's illusions, the film raises the question of the exploitative nature of relations between French employers and their African employees. This clearly symbolises the relationship of domination and subordination that persists between France and its former colonial nations.

Diouana's idyllic image of France is highlighted at the beginning of the film when the camera assumes her subjective point of view as she travels from the port to her employer's home. Her car-window view of Antibes and the surrounding countryside is shot in colour in an otherwise black and white landscape, as if seen through rose-tinted spectacles.[9] As Diouana becomes increasingly alienated, trapped in a cycle of cleaning and cooking, the flashbacks to Dakar and the expectations she then had of life in France provide a harsh contrast with her present reality. In the Dakar scenes, Diouana admires the sophistication and comfort of all that is French, exemplified by her wonder at her employer's garden sprinkler, an image that in itself contrasts sharply with the preceding shots of her neighbourhood women fetching water from a public fountain. Other flashbacks show Diouana, with her boyfriend, flicking through *Elle* magazine, wearing a Westernised wig and dressed in her boss's second-hand clothes. Even in the early days of her stay in France, and despite her increasing disillusionment, Diouana still wishes that, 'Madame will take me to visit the town. We'll go to the pretty shops. I'll buy pretty dresses, shoes, silk underwear, and fine wigs, and I'll have my photo taken on the beach and send it to Dakar and the others will die of envy.' Whilst the France of her dreams is a glamorous world of pretty things, in reality it becomes the nightmare of the four walls of her bosses' flat. She comments, 'France here is the kitchen, the dining room, the bathroom

9 This colour sequence was cut from most copies of the film when Sembene registered *La Noire de...* at the French Centre National de la Cinématographie as a short film.

and the bedroom', or 'Is this black hole really France?', only able to wonder, 'What are the people like here? All the doors are shut day and night.' Diouana's disenchanting discovery of a reality that is so very far removed from the one she had imagined serves retrospectively to re-assess life in the previously undervalued African space, thereby positioning *La Noire de...* within Francophone African cinema's general aim to promote African cultures and mores.

Diouana undergoes a process of depersonalisation until she is effectively no more than 'la noire de ...', or somebody else's maid. This is symbolised shortly after Diouana arrives in France when she slowly wipes the bathroom mirror clean, thereby appearing at the same time to erase her own reflection and, by extension, herself. This image is con-firmed shortly afterwards when Madame forces Diouana to wear an apron so she looks more like a maid, and later orders her to take off her high-heel shoes reminding her, 'Don't forget you're a maid'. Her employer humiliates her even further by behaving as if she were no more than a purchasable commodity, reacting to her depression by merely offering her money.[10] Reinforcing her status, Diouana has no direct voice in France. Unlike her employers, who always speak directly, all of her thoughts are expressed in voice-over monologues. Her employers always speak for and about her, to the extent that they even decide to write a letter to her mother without asking her consent. During the letter writing sequence, Diouana is systematically framed alone, accentuating her distance from them and the letter. Diouana's alienation is heightened by the reactions of the only other French people she meets. Her employers invite their friends to lunch; one guest visibly offends her when he jumps up from the table to give her a kiss, declaring, 'I've never kissed a black woman before', and another female guest stares at Diouana as she serves the coffee, speaking to her employer about her as if she were not there and were incapable of understanding. These reactions make it clear that in their eyes, Diouana is an exotic curiosity, rather than a 'real' person.

Diouana rebels in the only way available to her – by defying her employer's authority. The first confrontation arises when Madame orders her to remove her shoes. Diouana obeys, but leaves the shoes lying where they are, the camera remaining focused on the 'incriminating' item as Diouana's bare feet walk out of the shot. When Madame decides to punish her maid by not feeding her, Diouana in turn retaliates by refusing to look after her boss's child. Later, when her employers write to her mother, the camera focuses on Diouana's hands as she slowly rips up the letter from her mother and walks away from the table, literally dissociating herself from the reply they have decided to write. Finally, Diouana takes back the mask she gave her employers in Dakar (the same mask that she 'addresses' in one of her moments of desperation and which symbolises her ties to Senegal), throws her maid's apron at Madame's feet, and gives Monsieur back his money. Diouana removes her Western clothing and wig, and plaits her hair in a traditional style, as if finally rejecting the accoutrements of a country that has disappointed

10 When Diouana's employer returns her belongings to her mother in Dakar at the end of the film, he also unsuc-cessfully tries to give the mother money as 'compensation' for her daughter's death.

Joseph Kumbela, Perle Noire, *1994. The end of an illusion: the harsh reality awaiting a young immigrant woman in Europe.*
(Courtesy of Joseph Kumbela)

her as she declares, 'I refuse to be a slave.' Even though suicide is the only way Diouana finds to escape, therefore, it is portrayed as much as an act of defiance as one of desperation.

Sembene's evocation of the question of exploitation brings to mind Joseph Kumbela's first short film *Perle Noire* (DCR-France, 1994), which can arguably be seen as a contemporary version of *La Noire de...*. Blandine, a young African woman who comes to France to marry Roland, finds herself trapped in a nightmarish situation, married to an abusive husband who forces her into prostitution. In the opening dream sequence, Blandine marvels at a chic dress in a shop window, dazzled by the glamorous image of France just like Diouana. The dream progressively turns into a nightmare from which she awakes into the nightmare of her real life, the camera tracking from her to her brutish snoring husband. Like Diouana, Blandine also becomes more of an object – a 'black pearl' – than a person. Roland tells Sonia, the woman in charge of the brothel where Blandine is sent to work, 'Break her in properly', as if Blandine were no more than an animal. This domination-subordination is visually symbolised when Blandine sits reading a letter from Africa next to an African statuette of a white man in a colonial-style pith helmet, placed obviously in the foreground. The outcome of the film is fundamentally different from that of *La Noire de...*, however. Whilst Blandine's initial defiance is met with punches and abuse, she finally finds the courage to leave Roland. The film also ends in drama, but here Blandine emerges as the survivor and the power relations are reversed.

Whilst a number of other Europe-based films similarly chart the destruction of their characters' illusions, none do so quite so uncompromisingly as Med Hondo's first radically political 'filmed essay', *Soleil O* (Mauritania-France, 1969).[11] Through a series of largely non-linear, digressional sequences that combine an unconventional mix of styles, ranging from politically committed documentary filmmaking to highly stylised enactments, *Soleil O* traces the growing disillusion and political awakening of an African accountant confronted with racial discrimination in France. At the same time, Hondo denounces immigrant conditions in France, documenting and analysing the facts, figures and historical reasons behind the situation. The opening animation sequences summarise how the West colonised Africa, setting up a relation of domination/subordination, as two white colonial figures 'befriend' an African chief whose traditional hat symbolically turns into a pith helmet. The following 'surreal' sequences similarly evoke the conquest of Africa by the cross and the gun, a point Hondo makes very clearly when the newly-baptised African converts march out of the church, turning their crucifixes round to become swords.

Through the experiences of Jean, the protagonist, Hondo explores many of the dilemmas facing immigrants in France. Firstly, Hondo points to the irony that 'assimilated' Africans taught to accept Western values and to identify with the colonial or neo-colonial powers, often find themselves stigmatised and rejected as immigrants in France. As Jean's voice-over states at the beginning of the film, 'One day, I started studying your graphics, reading your thoughts, speaking Shakespeare and Molière. Sweet France, your culture has whitened me, but I am still black'. Despite his optimism on arrival in France, Jean, a qualified accountant, is seen being repeatedly refused even the most menial jobs and accommodation. Turned away for the third time from a garage job – the boss simply looks him over and says, 'No, no', even though he affirms that the post is still vacant – Jean's optimism gives way to bitter irony. Sardonically, he highlights the emptiness of the traditional French claim to want to assimilate its former colonial subjects. When a racist concierge tries to bar him from the building where he goes to apply for an accountancy job, Jean finally reacts and answers back. Framed separately in a series of shot-counter-shots until then, Jean steps into the same frame with her in a confrontational manner, sending her scurrying back to the 'safety' of her lodge. When she tells him to go home, Jean is filmed from her low-angle point of view as he walks 'menacingly' forwards asking, 'Excuse me Madam, could you tell me where I am from, please?', a question she clearly cannot answer, and which exemplifies the dilemma facing many acculturated ex-colonial subjects.

11 The film's closing title, 'To be continued...', confers an openness on the film that suggests that Hondo sees it as part of a continuing debate, thereby confirming the idea that the film can be seen as a dialogic essay.

Filming the Immigrant Experience

Soleil O contains many such discriminatory scenes, and is undoubtedly the first Francophone African film to tackle the question of racism vehemently by focusing extensively on French reactions to the immigrant population.[12] The film is punctuated by extracts of an interview between Jean and a French sociologist in which the latter pontificates on the question of immigrant workers, articulating racist clichés. He expresses people's desire to find workers willing to accept, 'the toughest, most banal jobs that nationals no longer want to do', on the condition that they are, 'capable of understanding things the way we do', that they prove 'their ability to evolve', and that 'they keep a low profile, or live elsewhere'. 'Surreal' scenes that apparently reflect Jean's thoughts as he listens to, and sardonically interprets the sociologist's euphemisms follow many of the interview extracts. The sequence in which the sociologist discusses the need for workers capable of understanding and thinking 'like us' is followed, for example, by a classroom scene in which the sociologist teaches Jean and a class of immigrant pupils the names of a series of manual labour tools, which the pupils repeat in unison. The lesson, which can also be seen as a parody of the type of education dispensed in the colonial schools, ends as the teacher holds up three different types of broom, thus clearly alluding to the anticipated immigrant status. Elsewhere in the film, Hondo includes a number of short documentary-style scenes in which diverse characters from all social milieus, ranging from a couple of concierges to bourgeois men, talk directly to the camera, articulating racist views.

In addition to this outright hostility, *Soleil O* also evokes the equally punishing sense of indifference encountered by the immigrant community that hastens their erasure in French society. In one very powerful scene, Jean arrives home thoroughly isolated and depressed to hear music and voices coming from the open door of a neighbouring apartment. He knocks and enters hesitantly, where a couple is seen from his point of view, seated in front of two different TV sets watching different programmes. The form of an alcove window physically separates them, an image of the lack of communication and isolating individualism of the West. When Jean asks for their help, the man and the woman simply glance over their shoulders before turning back to their respective TVs as if he were not there. His invisibility and their indifference is repeated later in the film in a fleeting documentary-type scene in which an immigrant worker interviews an African street sweeper, asking him, 'Tell me what you think', to which the sweeper simply replies 'No one cares. The French don't care'.

Soleil O also focuses on the recurrent problem of immigrant housing. In one scene, Jean is seen suitcase in hand, entering first one, then another building. Both times, he disappears out of sight before being almost literally spat back out onto the street. As if to leave absolutely no ambiguity about the reasons for this (r)ejection, the camera cuts suddenly to a close-up shot of graffiti that reads, 'stop the NEGRO-ARAB invasion'. The housing situation is also evoked later in another scene in which the camera pans past a line of immigrant workers as they stare

12 Med Hondo himself stresses this aspect of his work, commenting, 'I cannot help but show the lot of Africans in Paris because it is a reality which hurts and torments me', and, 'People should be educated about ... the discrimination faced by immigrants in France.' Cited by Françoise Pfaff, *Twenty-five Black African Filmmakers*, pp 160 and 161.

incriminatingly at the camera, whilst what appears to be a real news report recounts the fate of eighty rent-paying immigrants lodged by an unscrupulous landlord in a dilapidated seven-room flat with one kitchen and one toilet.

Jean's growing disillusion and frustration is clearly shared by the other immigrants in the film. This tension is conveyed by the increasingly fast and tense rhythm of the montage, and by the high-angle of the many shots of Jean alone in his room or in the street, which give the impression that he is literally being crushed by the oppression. Jean's anguish develops with the film's persistent and oppressive dull percussive leitmotif and the 'nightmare' scenes in his room. During a meeting at Jean's flat, which illustrates the sense of solidarity in the community (shown in a number of films), the discussion turns to the problems of surviving in France. The different characters vent their frustration, one character insisting that they should think about going home rather than putting up with the hostile climate. This enables Hondo to introduce the question of whether or not it is better to leave France, an issue raised in a number of other films, as shall be seen in more detail later.

The accumulation of injustices finally breaks Jean's composure. In the last sequence, he is seen smashing up his room and fleeing down the street and along a railway track, echoing the station setting of the beginning of the film. This creates a circularity common in African narrative structures and suggests that Jean has been changed by his initiatory 'journey'.[13] Pursued by an anguished screaming that mirrors his own catharsis, Jean finally collapses in a clearing in the forest, surrounded by portraits of Malcolm X, Che Guevara, Patrice Lumumba, and Ben Barka, symbolising the radicalisation of his own political consciousness. The film, which ends openly on the words, 'To be continued...', suggests that the only possible recourse is to fight back.

Influenced by *Soleil O*'s political engagement, Sidney Sokhana's *Nationalité Immigré* (Mauritania-France, 1975) is, in a sense, the logical conclusion of Hondo's film.[14] Mixing documentary-style enactments, real documentary interviews, and Brechtian-style fictional scenes, the film sets out to explain the immigrant phenomenon, to trace the conditions in which immigrants come to France to work and, above all, to reconstruct the director's own involvement in a two-year immigrant workers' strike for better housing conditions in Paris. The film depicts the immigrants' evolution from passivity to activism.

The reconstruction of the hostel strike and its foregrounding of the terrible conditions in the decrepit, overcrowded, rat-infested hostel allows Sokhana to trace the political awakening of the immigrant workers whose very status makes them vulnerable to all forms of exploitation. When they decide to withhold their rent in protest, the hostel owner's representatives try to divide the African elders from the younger 'militant' hostel inhabitants, forcing them to end the strike by reminding them that, as immigrants, they 'can end up in big trouble'. Sidi, played by Sokhana himself, is later arrested by the police simply for taking part in a demonstration, and when the immigrant workers finally win their

13 In a short part of the nightmare sequence before Jean flees, Jean's silhouette is seen running along a hilltop with a dog. The extreme back-lighting and the undetermined setting recall the beginning of the film when Jean is seen in silhouette with his case. Unlike the opening shots in which Jean was seen to be smiling, however, here he slowly and jerkily raises his arm in a Black Power salute.

14 Sokhana makes a reference to Hondo's film when part of a *Soleil O* poster is seen on the wall of the immigrant workers' hostel.

Filming the Immigrant Experience

battle, the rules of the new hostel stipulate that 'any tenant who misbehaves will lose his resident's permit and risks being immediately deported from France'. Over the final long shot of Sidi entering the new hostel, however, his voice-over responds defiantly, 'To this the immigrants reply, we are not the well-behaved babies of the past anymore.' The film clearly marks a change in climate, and, as one of the last first wave productions, also marks the end of a certain vein of politically committed filmmaking that has only ever resurfaced in Med Hondo's *Watani: Un monde sans mal* (France, 1998). In it, Hondo indeed returns to the politically and stylistically militant fragmentary style of his earlier works to denounce the current wave of xenophobia in France, epitomised by the political successes of the National Front party and by the recent tightening of immigration controls that led to the eviction of the African *sans-papiers* from the St-Bernard church in Paris in 1996, live shots of which are included in the film. Tracing the downward spiral of a wealthy French businessman who loses his job and flat, Hondo portrays and denounces the way in which an 'average' Frenchman gets involved in the racist attacks committed by a group of extreme right-wing thugs.

It is interesting to note that, unlike *Watani*, the majority of second wave films are striking for their relative lack of preoccupation with questions of racism and discrimination, even though these remain very real issues in France. Both Carrie Tarr and Christian Bosséno highlight a parallel trend in the films made by North African and second-generation *beur* filmmakers in France in the same period, which also tend to explore multiculturalism and integration, rather than racism and exclusion.[15] The immigrant characters in the second wave of Francophone African Europe-based films are generally portrayed to be more comfortably off and their relations with the host country less fraught. Whilst tensions and difficulties do occasionally surface, they no longer tend to be the central focus of the narrative. Incidents of racism are still present – for example, when the old woman automatically takes Soriba to be a bag snatcher when he bumps into her in the metro in *Toubabi*, or when the airport official obtrusively questions Sobgui in *Clando* – but they are more isolated, and certainly more covert. A film like *Toubabi* even introduces a new kind of white archetype, namely the over-eager 'Africa lover' with plaited hair and African clothing who comes to try out her (incorrect) Wolof phrases on Soriba in a restaurant.

Jean-Marie Teno's *Clando* offers an interesting example of how second wave films differ in this respect. Whilst the experiences of the Cameroonian expatriate, Rigobert Chamba, are evocative of the spiralling sense of disillusionment common in the first wave films, *Clando* focuses on Sobgui's more positive experience of Germany. Sobgui has been sent to find Chamba after he breaks off all contact with his family back home.[16] When Sobgui finds the missing man, we gradually learn that, unlike the immigrant characters of the Seventies, Chamba had successfully integrated, was wealthy and had married a German woman before plummeting to his present impoverished condition. As the conversations of his Cameroonian acquaintances suggest, Chamba is at least partially

15 See Carrie Tarr, 'French Cinema and Post-Colonial Minorities', and Christian Bosséno, 'Immigrant Cinema: National Cinema. The case of beur film', in R. Dyer & G. Vincendeau (eds.), *Popular European Cinema* (London: Routledge, 1992), pp 47-58.

16 In Moussa Touré's film, *Toubabi* (1991), the main character Soriba is also entrusted with the mission of finding his childhood friend Issa, who has similarly broken off all contact with his family.

responsible for his present state, rather than simply being a victim as in the past. The two Cameroonians discuss the fact that Chamba's wife left him because he was unfaithful, one answering the other's remark that she reacted too harshly by saying, 'But he behaved like an idiot too ... When in Rome, do as the Romans. That's life.'

Chamba is disillusioned – he remarks as he arrives at the anniversary of the Cameroonian expatriate association he founded, 'Just when you begin to think that people accept you, they show their real feelings ... These people don't like us. Whatever you do, you'll always be a nigger to them'. He is also in a precarious position in Germany for he no longer has a residency permit but still hesitates to return to Cameroon, commenting that in Europe at least, 'No one judges me.'[17] Chamba's hesitation and the allegoric hunter tale periodically narrated in voice-over throughout the film raise the real dilemma facing many African immigrants who are under great pressure to succeed and help support their families back home. Such immigrant characters are often shown to prefer to suffer in silence than to face the humiliation of returning home 'empty-handed'.

A number of films explore this dilemma. Blandine is reluctant to leave Roland in Joseph Kumbela's short film *Perle Noire*, for example, because she has 'a family who depends on [her] financially. They think Europe is paradise'. In *Bouzié*, Jacques Trabi illustrates the tensions that arise in a middle-class immigrant family when both husband and wife are pressurised by their respective families to provide. Zébia's mother voices the traditional view of the immigrants' obligation to their families, stating, 'You only fell a tree in the woods if you mean to use it.' *Clando* is one of the rare films to challenge this situation, however. The film's allegoric tale describes the fate of a hunter who refuses to return home until he has caught something to feed his starving village. Lost and on the point of starvation himself, he unwittingly stumbles home, only to find that the village's fortune has improved in his absence, despite his efforts and sacrifice. The protagonist, Sobgui, finally manages to persuade Chamba to return to Cameroon by arguing, 'We often say that if you reach the point where you don't know where to go anymore, retrace your steps and start again. Come back to the source and grow', thereby re-qualifying return as a new departure rather than a defeat.

The question of return is central to the Ivoirian filmmaker Desiré Ecaré's *Concerto pour un exil* (France, 1968), which focuses on the lives of a group of African students in Paris. Its style brings to mind elements of the oral narrative structures and the influences of the French Sixties' *New Wave*. The film opens with a close-up freeze frame of two of the main characters, Hervé and his wife, in the street, looking perplexed. It is only when the same freeze frame is seen at the end of the film after the couple have been thrown out of their tiny apartment by their unfriendly concierge – again, the hostile French concierge archetype – that we realise that the film has come full circle. The whole film builds up to its inevitable conclusion, despite Hervé's efforts to convince himself that he really is doing something useful in France. The film avoids simplistically

17 The residency permit/deportation question arises in a number of second wave films. This suggests that, whilst second wave immigrant characters are generally more settled than before, they are always seen primarily as immigrants and thus remain in a precarious position in Europe.

Filming the Immigrant Experience

promoting the return home by also evoking the inverse experience of a recently graduated student who is seen heading home at the start of the film declaring, 'Now's the time to go home while there are still jobs going.' As the film closes, Hervé and his wife have finally resolved to leave, while the same student returns looking crestfallen, his 'triumphant' return having failed to go as planned. Like the opening and closing freeze-frame shot, the student's departure and return also echo the circularity of a narrative structure that seems to suggest that these migratory movements will continue in their unending cycle.

Moussa Touré's *Toubabi* and José (Zeka) Laplaine's short film *Le Clandestin* (France-DRC, 1996) also broach the question of return. Like in *Clando*, *Toubabi*'s main character Soriba is entrusted with the task of finding and bringing back his childhood friend Issa. He comes to France to take a film-editing course, and eventually locates Issa, who runs a sex shop. Whilst Issa's work brings him money and the respect he craves in his milieu, he prefers to hide the nature of his work from his family back home. Issa and Soriba clearly represent opposite poles and opposite reactions to being in France.[18] Issa, who appears to have abandoned all ties with Senegal and to have opted for a Westernised way of life epitomised by his work, clothing, and straightened hair, tells Soriba that he is physically and psychologically 'five thousand kilometres from Dakar', adding, 'You're wasting your time if you've come to play the ancestor because I've forgotten everything about Africa.' Despite his claims, however, at home he dons a *boubou* and is served by his two wives, suggesting that he is in fact not so far removed from his original Senegalese culture. Soriba, on the other hand, pleads with Issa to abandon his morally unhealthy, corrupt way of life and to come home to a simple lifestyle. This contrast between life in Senegal and France serves to promote African cultural values, as is characteristic in many of the region's films. Issa is forced to return to Senegal when he is deported, but the overriding message of the film is thus that this return is for his own good.

Shot in the style of a burlesque silent film, Laplaine's *Le Clandestin* alternates silent movie titles in the form of a letter that an illegal immigrant writes to the cousin he was trying to join in Europe. Images narrate the events that constitute his short stay in Lisbon. Even though the visual sequences of the film appear to take place in the present, the past tense of the letter lets us know that the illegal immigrant is already back in Africa. The 'moral' of the story is that it is better to stay in at home than to suffer the harsh lot of an illegal immigrant, or *clandestin*, in Europe. From the moment he arrives in Lisbon stowed away in a container, the hero is pursued by a burlesque, over-zealous policeman who repeatedly pops up out of nowhere every time the hero thinks he is safe.[19] The hero also loses his Angolan companion, who dies in a ship's container on arrival, and constantly finds himself in hostile situations. He is shown no compassion by the other African characters he meets (the construction workers stopped for lunch who just stare back at him as he stares longingly at their sandwiches; the two 'crooks' who run off with

18 This mirror structure, already discussed in Chapter 3, is a common oral narrative device in which two protagonists react in opposite ways to the same challenges. As Denise Paulme points out, although incarnated by two different characters, the positive and negative heroes in fact represent the opposing but complementary aspects of human nature, offering examples of two possible paths. (in *La mère dévorante: Essai sur la morphologie des contes africains* (Paris: Editions Gallimard, 1976), p 38).

19 The policeman played by Laplaine is a reference to the equally zealous and overweight policeman in Djibril Diop Mambety's *Badou Boy* (Senegal, 1970). Diop Mambety's policeman relentlessly pursues the protagonist, peeping his whistle like Laplaine's policeman, the close-ups of his face echoing those in *Badou Boy*.

José Zeka Laplaine, Le Clandestin, 1996. Europe's hostile environment: two unscrupulous African 'compatriots' rob a freshly disembarked illegal immigrant. (Courtesy of Zeka Laplaine)

his money when he turns to them for help), and even less from the white characters (the queue of people at the bus stop who look through him as if he were invisible when he greets them, and who turn to snarl when he is chased by the policeman; the market woman who nearly chops off his finger as he lingers near her stall; the driver who barks 'NEGRO!' at him when he runs him over). His spirit is finally broken when he realises the hopelessness of the situation. He comes across an elderly African woman living alone in a shack on a piece of scrubland. As these two people stare at one another, the emotion in the impoverished and isolated old lady's eyes speaks volumes, as does her silence. After this encounter, the hero gives himself up to the policeman who, ironically, seems to have given up chasing him. As the film ends with a long shot of the policeman accompanying the illegal immigrant back to the port, the end of the letter scrolls up on the screen: 'Cousin, he threw me out, but he was kind enough at heart. I've decided to stay at home for the time being and to try to make it here', thus once again opting for the return home.

The theme of departure is one of the central motors of Abderrahmane Sissako's lyrical, highly evocative *Octobre* (Russia-Mauritania, 1992) made when Sissako was himself a film student in Russia. The film centres on the difficult communication between Idriss, an African student about to leave Russia, and his Russian girlfriend Irina who, unknown to him, is pregnant with his child. The inevitability of his departure dictates the terms of their relationship and places Irina in a difficult position. The whole film is permeated with the crushing weight of this inability to communicate, with each character isolated in solitude. Very little is actually said, but the succession of non-linear sequences build up the impression of an engulfing, depersonalised society. Throughout most of the film, the characters are filmed in isolation, occasionally passing through each other's frames without ever really connecting. They are also rendered small and anonymous by the tall angular architecture and

Filming the Immigrant Experience

the series of long, bleak corridors accentuated by the film's vertical pans, high-angle shots, and the camera's interminable backward tracking movements. On two occasions (when Irina goes to the hospital to book an appointment for an abortion, and again when she arrives at work), the depth of focus of the tracking camera which keeps her in a fixed frame as she advances, with only her echoing footsteps breaking the crushing silence, gives the impression that her surroundings are bearing down on her, reflecting the psychological weight of her situation.

Later, in one of the rare scenes in which Irina and Idriss are seen together, the couple are filmed either in separate frames, or with one character always leaving the frame, as if they were physically fleeing one another. They hardly speak, and any moment of 'intimacy' is interrupted both by the cut-in shots of other isolated residents in the anonymous block of flats, or by the visit of the policeman who has been called by two fearful elderly neighbours, suspicious of Irina's African boyfriend.

In another scene, Sissako suggests the foreclosure of Idriss and Irina's relationship in a highly poignant flash-forward in time. Idriss, alone in the snow, is suddenly hit in the back by a snowball. A mixed-race child tramps into the shot out of nowhere, tenderly placing Idriss's hat on his head before stepping back to look at him. As Idriss reaches out to the child, asking his name and where he is from, the child just smiles back enigmatically. Suddenly, the camera focuses on a Russian woman trudging along by herself, who calls the child, breaking this fleeting (and rare) moment of intimacy. In the following three-shot (Idriss in the foreground, the woman far off in the distance), the child turns to look at his mother, then back at Idriss, as if torn between the two, before heading off and turning to look back at Idriss one last time. The child's attraction to Idriss somehow gives the impression that the child's African father is absent, as of course Idriss will be if Irina keeps their baby.

Absence is again emphasised at the end of the film when Lena, Irina's colleague, guesses that Irina has not told Idriss about the pregnancy, adding, 'He'll leave anyway'. Irina confirms his departure, as she turns and walks out of the shot, again 'fleeing' contact. Lena comfortingly puts her head on Irina's shoulder in what is probably the only physically intimate moment in the film, while the two woman stare silently at the grossly caricatured, 'devilish' blackface character dancing on the television, presumably evoking how blackness is seen in the (white) Russian environment. Even the snow seems to highlight Idriss's difference, reinforcing the impossible gulf between the couple. The film ends as it begins with a shot of Idriss in the airport, confirming Idriss's departure as we also finally understand that what seemed to be the present tense of the film was in fact a flashback.

It is interesting to consider what this emphasis on returning to Africa in both the first and second wave films says about the position of the immigrant community in France and the position of the filmmakers in question. Nearly all the films discussed here indeed show their characters, many of whom are students, to be simply 'passing through'. The immigrant community itself is portrayed on the margins of its host

Abderrahmane Sissako, Octobre, 1992. Irina: often filmed alone or physically isolated from one another in separate frames, the film highlights the characters' solitude and difficulty in communicating.
(Courtesy of Abderrahmane Sissako)

society, rather than as a permanent and integral part of it. This lack of roots is less surprising in the Europe-based films of the Sixties and Seventies, as the majority of those filmmakers did in fact return, or made their subsequent films in Africa.[20] Many of the younger generation of filmmakers based in France, including Gahité Fofana, Dany Kouyaté, Fanta Nacro, or Issa Serge Coelo, some of whom are mixed-race, also tend to return to Africa to make their films. Whilst this tendency may well be influenced by the sources of funding available to Francophone African filmmakers, which tend to prioritise works set in Africa, it suggests that these filmmakers tend to situate themselves primarily in an African, rather than European, cinematographic landscape.

Apart from Moussa Touré, the majority of the second wave directors discussed here are currently resident in Europe, which no doubt accounts for both the centrality and exteriority of *Toubabi*'s portrayal of the French – 'toubabi' itself meaning 'white people' in Wolof – which constitutes a humorous ethnographic gaze in reverse.[21] Most of their characters are nonetheless still on the verge of leaving (Idriss in Sissako's *Octobre*; Sobgui and Chamba in Teno's *Clando*), or being deported (Issa in *Toubabi*; the illegal immigrant in *Le Clandestin*; the groups of Africans in Med Hondo's *Lumière Noire* and *Watani*). The emergence of the latter theme in film is an interesting contemporary development that reflects the real fragility of immigrant status as Europe has begun to tighten its borders. Films such as Med Hondo's *Lumière Noire* (France, 1992) and *Watani*, provide critiques of the brutality of such deportation procedures. *Lumière Noire* contains a key deportation scene in which the Malian deportees are roughly handcuffed together, unequivocally recalling the chaining of African slaves. *Watani* also includes live footage of the brutal eviction of the *sans-papiers* from the Saint-Bernard church in Paris in 1996 and a

20 Only Med Hondo is still resident in France, and even he turned his cinematic gaze back to the African continent in a series of films before making his most recent works, *Lumière Noire* and *Watani*, in France in 1992 & 1998. In Ibrahima Signaté's book *Med Hondo: Un Cinéaste Rebelle*, Hondo, who also openly advocated returning to Africa in *Les Bicot-Nègres vos voisins* (France, 1974), explains that at that time most African immigrants did not expect to stay in France for a significant length of time, even if in reality many have now settled down with their own families.

21 When Soriba and the child, Idi, arrive in France, the camera often assumes Idi's point of view as he looks in amazement at what he discovers there. Via Idi's gaze, the film focuses on 'strange' European phenomena, like the old lady who talks to her little dog in the airport, or the punks with hair that reminds Idi of the plumage of President Diouf's exotic birds. Soriba's letter home to his family lists all the 'strange' things he discovers about the French, particularly their lack of communication. Conversely, Soriba, like the grandmother in *Bouzié*, often deliberately behaves in ways that seem out of place in France, accentuating his cultural difference in a number of good-humoured situations.

Filming the Immigrant Experience

theatrical re-enactment of the eviction of all the tenants from an immigrant hostel.

A few films made in more recent years have started to reflect the sociological reality of the settlement of the African community in France and the emergence of second-generation immigrants. Such films include Jean Odoutan's *Djib* (France-Benin, 2000) and *Mama Aloko* (2002), Zeka Laplaine's *(Paris : xy)* (DRC-France, 2001), Idrissa Ouedraogo's *Cri du Coeur* (France, 1994) and Jacques Trabi's short film *Bouzié* (1996).[22] In *Bouzié*, Trabi exposes a range of complex integration issues facing a young married couple who live in France but remain intrinsically linked to their homes and families in Côte d'Ivoire. Although their lifestyle is largely Western, Zébia and his wife Dian are shown to have achieved a synthesis between their original and adopted cultures as they also continue to embrace their African traditions. Zébia's mother, who is first clearly positioned in her close-knit home environment in Côte d'Ivoire, is a symbol and advocate of African traditions. When she comes to join the family in France, she upsets their bi-cultural equilibrium by pressurising the couple not to try to be 'like white people'.

In this 'confrontation' of values, the question of language becomes both the focus of cultural synthesis and integration issues. In scenes with the mother, Zébia and Dian speak Goro, but together, they speak French. Their young son Tizié, who has grown up in France and is more familiar with French culture, does not speak Goro, however, much to his grandmother's consternation. She repeatedly reproaches the parents for cutting the child off from his roots, adding, 'A piece of driftwood fallen in the water will never turn into a crocodile.' Other allusions to language are constantly made throughout the film, notably when the angry Dian curtly answers her mother-in-law in French, which shocks and offends her more than the tone of Dian's voice.

Through the child Tizié, Trabi also evokes the new generation of French-born children who have been strangely absent from Francophone African film until now. Although Tizié is a 'proper little French boy', to coin Rigobert Chamba's expression in *Clando*, he is also shown to be uninhibited and curious about his African origins. At the outset of the film, Tizié refuses his grandmother's traditions when she wants to wash him – an act that is repeatedly referred to in the film, and which apparently symbolises the union between the grandmother and her descendants. However, he is the one who asks her to dry him before she leaves, and also asks her to teach him Goro, thereby embracing the values and culture she represents. Despite the vast differences in their lifestyles, there is a complicity, an intimacy between them that is made clear when they dance together in the park in their respective traditional African and contemporary Western styles. Whilst Tizié's parents at times appear to be subjected to certain pressures vis-à-vis their bi-culturalism, Tizié, as a second-generation immigrant, seems to represent a more comfortable synthesis between the two cultures.

Idrissa Ouedraogo's *Cri du Coeur* centres on the child Moktar who was born in France and then spent five years living in West Africa with his

22 Although set in Africa, Franco-Guinean filmmaker Gahité Fofana's personalised documentary *Tanun* (France-Guinea, 1994) and fiction *Immatriculation Temporaire* (France-Guinea, 2000), also reflect the rooting of the African community in Europe. Both focus on mixed-race characters brought up in Europe who return to Guinea to find/discover their African families and roots.

mother before returning to France live with his parents. Moktar's cousin was also born in France, but, unlike Moktar, has never been to Africa. The film is notable for the way it debunks many of the preconceptions concerning immigrant families in France that are at times reinforced even by African filmmakers. In the opening shots of the film Moktar's father, Ibrahim, leaves his up-market apartment building and crosses paths with two white street-sweepers, placed in the foreground, giving an ironic twist to the 'typical' job roles. This move away from the image of the exploited immigrant worker is confirmed later in the film when we discover that Ibrahim owns his own garage (in one scene, it is he who shows his white employees how to do the job), just as his North African friend Moustapha is the boss of a building site.

Ibrahim's social status is also reflected in the family's comfortable apartment, which is uncharacteristically devoid of any African regalia, just as the family never wears African clothing, or eats African food. The family always speaks in French together, language again becoming a marker of their integration and bi-cultural identities. Moktar's own integration at school is equally clear. Not only is he seen to do well at school, but is immediately accepted by the other children. On his first day, he is positioned in the centre of the hub of children in the playground and also sits in the centre of the class, the spatial disposition thus emphasising his integration, rather than social exclusion. The only indication that Moktar still remains attached to his African home are his periodic sightings of a hyena, which is later understood to be an incarnation of his grandfather back in Africa. Ouedraogo deflates even the possible exotic connotations of this image, however, as his father remarks, 'what's funniest of all is that he's probably never even seen a hyena in Africa before'.

Despite this idyllic image of a perfectly integrated immigrant family, Ouedraogo does not completely avoid evoking their immigrant status. Angry about the attention Moktar's hyena story is drawing at school, Ibrahim warns Moktar, 'We are foreigners here. Don't you realise that we have to keep our heads down? Don't you realise that the slightest thing can get us into trouble', reminding us of the vulnerability of their position. Africa is also subtly present throughout the Lyon sequences. At one point, for instance, Moktar is seen sitting at his desk next to a globe which is turned so the African continent is visible. Later in the film, an African landscape is visible on the television as the family sit talking together. The photo of Moktar on his grandfather's shoulders similarly recalls the African setting of the opening of the film. Finally, the circularity of the narrative structure, and certain shots, such as recurrent images of sky, trees, and water, also strongly echo the stylistic characteristics of Francophone African film.

The rooting of the African community evoked in *Bouzié* and *Cri du Coeur* is also present in several other recent films that are difficult to define in terms of 'African' or 'French' cinema. In Med Hondo's *Watani*, a multi-ethnic group of second-generation immigrant youths crop up in the film, as if to affirm the cosmopolitan nature of contemporary France. The

Filming the Immigrant Experience

Idrissa Ouedraogo, Cri du Coeur, *1994. Debunking clichés about archetypal immigrant families. Ibrahim shows his uncharacteristically 'un-African' family around his own garage.*
(Courtesy of Idrissa Ouedraogo)

Idrissa Ouedraogo, Cri du Coeur, *1994. The timid emergence of 'second-generation' characters in African films set in Europe: Moktar, a thoroughly integrated French-born child.*
(Courtesy of Idrissa Ouedraogo)

words of the rap songs that accompany their sporadic appearances – rap symbolising a multiracial youth expression *par excellence* – also highlight their rejection of the kind of racism denounced throughout the film. The final freeze-frame images of each youth's face staring into the camera are a challenge to anyone not accepting their presence. The film ends on a powerful affirmative note that is confirmed by the closing image of a black and a white toddler playing together in a park.

On a completely different register, *Djib*, by the Paris-based filmmaker Jean Odoutan is set in Paris' multiracial suburbs where it follows the antics of the fourteen-year-old French-born youth, Djibril, who lives with his African grandmother. The film provides an up-beat, colourful portrayal of life on the economically deprived housing estates with all its joys and tensions as Djib struggles to earn enough money to take his girlfriend, who is of North African descent, on holiday. Playing on a range of genres and addressing a number of race-relations issues, the film captures contemporary France's cosmopolitan make-up and faithfully reproduces the urban youth's streams of destructured, hybrid language. Whilst Odoutan has shot other films in Africa – *Barbecu Pejo* (Benin, 1999); *La Valse des gros derrières* (forthcoming) – *Djib* is definitely more part of a multi-cultural contemporary French environment than an African one. Similarly, *Le 11e commandement* (France, 1997) by the Franco-Guinean filmmaker Mama Keita, the short film *Le Génie d'Abou* (France, 1997) by the young Paris-based Ivoirian director Isabelle Boni-Claverie, and Paris-based Zeka Laplaine's most recent film *(Paris : xy)* may also be classed as 'French' films. Whilst they each feature characters of African descent, they are completely Europeanised and the films do not refer to immigration as such. The multicultural nature of these works suggests that a new and still embryonic generation of films is beginning to reflect our increasingly globalized world. Med Hondo's adaptation of Didier Daeninckx's political thriller *Lumière Noire*, which Hondo himself has described as his first French film, is further evidence of this tendency. Whilst the theme of the book and film remains faithful to Hondo's own political engagement, *Lumière Noire* is not in itself a film about immigration. Hondo abandons his more typically experimental film-making style in order to adhere to the conventions of the French *polar*. One may argue that all of these films blur 'national' film boundaries, as is inevitable in a nomadic or migrant cinema.

Interracial relationships and immigrant communities

Amongst the themes frequently portrayed since Francophone African directors first started making films in Europe is that of interracial male/female relationships. As Carrie Tarr points out, such relationships are often allegories for the domination and subordination between the former coloniser and colonised.[23] One of the first films to explore the

23 Carrie Tarr, 'French Cinema and Post-Colonial Minorities', p 62.

Filming the Immigrant Experience

theme was Desiré Ecaré's *Concerto pour un exil*. Doudou, a would-be law student, who represents the 'African dandy' archetype, concentrates his energies on meeting women (when he is not with his 'steady' Swedish girlfriend). The ironic juxtaposition of their mock-idyllic imaginary wedding scene and the domestic scene in which Doudou's irate girlfriend throws eggs at him, plays up the fragility of their relationship. Whilst Doudou enjoys the Sixties' 'free love' climate in Paris, he is less at ease with the notion of equality at home, and even less keen on emotional commitment. When his friends joke later that he has found true love, he grumbles, 'Tell me about it! You mean I've found universal suffrage', suggesting that his interracial relationship will not last.

In his second film *A Nous Deux, France* (France, 1969), Ecaré develops the question of mixed-race relationships in more detail. Comprising a series of non-linear sequences that mix derision with pathos, the film follows the complicated relationships of a group of African and French characters. In the opening West African sequence, a woman's voice-over introduces the theme: 'Every time we send them to Europe, they come back with a white wife.' The statement is followed by images of an African man arriving in his village with his white wife and mixed-race children, whilst the young village women look on with a feigned disinterestedness that sets up the rivalry developed in the film.

The rest of the narrative set in Paris centres on two mixed-race couples connected by a mutual acquaintance, Magali. Like the group of other young African women seen sitting around waiting for the phone to ring, Magali has come to France to stop African men being 'snatched up'. In Paris, she bumps into two old friends – Tarzan, the ironically-named, impeccably dressed, but penniless, 'dandy' who is married and has a child with a French woman (equally ironically called France); and Myriam, always sporting a blonde wig, who mockingly describes herself as 'over adapted'. Myriam is the lover of the French 'intellectual' Bonaventure, who, as the pun on his name, which can roughly be translated as 'Goodtime', suggests, has been promising to divorce his wife and to marry his mistress for ten years.

Ecaré's scathing portrayal of these different characters offers a bleak presentation of the nature of both postcolonial and all human relationships. Magali, for example, is portrayed as a complete opportunist. On the one hand, she actively disapproves of African men frequenting French women and unscrupulously does all she can to woo Tarzan away from his wife as she launches her 'battle cry', 'Africa for the Africans!' On the other hand, she has no qualms in accepting Bonaventure's barely masked advances when he decides to launch her as a singer. Tarzan is clearly a development of the Doudou character in *Concerto pour un exil*. He too spends all of his time out strolling, fussing over his exaggeratedly impeccable appearance (paid for with his wife's scant earnings). He deceives his wife as he chases after Magali, and, like Doudou, flees the marital home as soon he is confronted. Bonaventure, the ageing 'intellectual', is clearly in search of exoticism, switching his attentions from Myriam to Magali, as if the two women were interchangeable.

Myriam, finally, is the only one to manifest a degree of self-knowledge. Whilst she has taken on all the accoutrements of Paris life, even jokingly saying to Bonaventure, 'I'm not a black woman anymore. I've been in Paris for ten years', she knows Bonaventure will never really leave his wife for her and immediately recognises Bonaventure's efforts to launch Magali for what they are. Anticipating what is about to happen, she takes the initiative and heads off alone, crossing paths with the character who dances his way through the whole film, creating a leitmotif. After asking him why he is always dancing – to which he answers that he is just fulfilling the role he has been given – she dances off after him, aware that she too has been playing a role. The two of them dance in the middle of the suburban slum, a far cry from the locations of the rest of the film, that hints at the existence of a different reality, when Myriam suddenly stops, pulling her coat around her and crying in a brutal awakening, 'No! I'm cold. I'm scared of the cold', the frame freezing, her voice continuing off, 'That's all France has given me'.

Med Hondo's uncompromising portrayal of a mixed-race relationship in *Soleil O* also raises the question of exoticism in a scene that starkly contrasts with *Afrique sur Seine's* evocations of interracial fraternity. In one sequence of the film, two young women are filmed laughing hysterically, titillated at the idea of sleeping with a black man. This objectification, which recalls the fantasies about black sexuality common in the colonial era, is also reminiscent of the scene in *La Noire de...* in which a guest jumps up to kiss Diouana on the pretext that he has never kissed a black woman before. In the following scene of *Soleil O*, one of the girls paces up and down in the street making eyes at Jean. When he eventually follows her, shots of the couple walking hand-in-hand are alternated with what seem to be real shots of disapproving, indignantly staring passers-by whilst a montage of squawking, clucking, snorting farm animals can be heard off-screen. The 'episode' ends with a shot of the woman and Jean in bed, the woman puffing angrily on her cigarette saying, 'I thought that in bed, Africans were supposed to be ... but ... pfft!' Her exotic fantasies have clearly been disappointed.

Ben Diogaye Beye's film *Les Princes Noirs de Saint-Germain-des-Près* (France-Senegal, 1975), portrays a handful of African students who also spend their time chasing gullible young French women, suggesting that the sexual fantasies concerning the 'other' can be mutual. Throughout the film, the medley of street scenes, most of which follow the legs of a young African man as he strolls along window-shopping, are inter-spersed with a number of short scenes in which the diverse couples interact. Two young African men wait at the top of a metro escalator, commenting on the passing women. When one of them admires a black woman, his friend replies off, 'Can't you see she's black. What's exciting about a black woman?', confirming that the exotic fantasising is a two-way thing (behind the girl's head, the metro sign reads 'INTERDIT' ['forbidden']).

Later, a young African 'artist' deceives an impressionable French woman in a bar with a story about the symbolic (read: exotic) nature of the mask he is carrying. Excusing himself as he goes to phone 'his embassy', he is seen calling to borrow a friend's flat, adding, 'The mask trick always does the job ... I told her I was an artist from the 16th arrondissement.' Shortly afterwards, another French girl is also filmed in a bar telling a friend that her new Senegalese boyfriend is a noble, heir to a throne, and the President's cousin or nephew. As she explains that he wears a unique bracelet, the camera films him shaking hands with another African man wearing exactly the same piece of jewellery. After the girl and the 'artist' are seen walking off arm in arm, and the 'prince' and the other girl are seen making love, a title makes the message plain: 'Fifteen years after independence ... the same fantasies'.

The first wave's relatively negative image of mixed-race relationships is less marked in the second period. Here, the majority of interracial relations portrayed tend to be less manipulative, fraught, and/or motivated by exotic fantasies, and thus move away somewhat from being symbolic projections of the former colonial power relations. In this respect, they no doubt reflect a certain evolution in both multicultural relations and the socio-cultural climate in Europe. This is the case in Joseph Kumbela's two short films, *Perle Noire* and *Taxcarte* (France-DRC, 1996), which, at first sight, appear to be more closely associated with the representations of the first wave. In *Perle Noire*, Blandine is forced into prostitution by her French husband, and, in the much more humorous *Taxcarte*, Touré, the smooth-talking African filmmaker, strings along two French girlfriends, Corrine and Josianne, not to mention his three wives back in Africa. Corrine, who wears a 'Black men love me' t-shirt, and who at the end of the film unhesitatingly heads off with Touré's friend Diallo, offers a humorous caricature of the French female characters of the earlier films who are more drawn to their partners' exotic otherness than to their personalities. Josianne is also reminiscent of the earlier gullible characters who believe everything they are told. Unlike in the first wave films, the exploitative and/or deceitful characters now get their comeuppance, or, as Diallo tells Touré, 'N'golo-ngolo with no ties? This isn't '68 anymore, brother!' Blandine finally resolves to leave Roland, and Diallo's web of lies collapses around him as his two girlfriends discover each other's existence and leave him.

Sobgui's relationship with Irene in Jean-Marie Teno's *Clando* is much more positive, despite the fact that Sobgui is married and has no intention of staying in Germany, which Irene knows and accepts. The parameters of the interracial relationships in Moussa Touré's *Toubabi*, and Abderrahmane Sissako's *Octobre* are also defined by the fact that the African partner will not be staying in Europe. Irene's own political commitment and the discussions she and Sobgui have about how to react in the face of oppression are very much the catalysts for Sobgui's decision to take action. In the final scene of the film, which cuts directly from Irene's flat where Sobgui is seen in bed beside the sleeping Irene, to the moving car in Cameroon which signals that he has gone back, the insect noises off in the flat foreshadow the transition to the African space. The couple's off-screen conversation indeed clearly indicates that Sobgui has

(Above) Joseph Kumbela, Taxcarte, 1996. Corrine, a caricature of the women drawn simply to African men's exotic otherness.
(Left) Joseph Kumbela, Taxcarte, 1996. Diallo's web of lies collapses when confronted by Josianne.
(Courtesy of Joseph Kumbela)

Jean-Marie Teno, Clando, 1996. Positive representations of interracial relationships: Irene and Sobgui's discussions help Sobgui to take action.
(Courtesy of Jean-Marie Teno)

Filming the Immigrant Experience

made a new resolution, suggesting that their relationship has helped him grow.

In *Toubabi*, Soriba's relationship with Hélène is equally devoid of exotic motivations. Soriba comes to Hélène's assistance when he finds her alone in the corridor of his hostel, his kindness to her forming the basis of their relationship. As in *Clando*, it is destined to be short-lived, but again Hélène is under no illusions about this, nor about the fact that Soriba has his own family ties back in Senegal. We can presume that Soriba might not be so open about her back in Senegal, however, as he stops her from taking a photo of them together in Paris, refusing a permanent trace of their relationship. Unlike *Clando*, the film offers a brief hint of the kind of hostile reactions mixed-race couples can still sometimes elicit, although this is far from the outright hostility expressed in Med Hondo's earlier *Soleil O*. When Hélène offers to pay for Soriba's entrance to a jazz club, a loutish youth remarks, 'They're so hot you want to pay for him', suggesting some old fantasies still abound.

Irrespective of the period in which they were made, the majority of these films clearly position their characters in relation to their respective immigrant communities. Representations of these communities contrast with those that focus exclusively on 'exotic' cultural differences in French films such as *Black micmac*. More often than not, these communities are characterised by their sense of solidarity. This counterbalances the solitude and difficulties confronting the immigrant characters in Europe, thus again promoting African community values in the same way that films from the continent do. The immigrant communities are frequently represented as a space in which the characters can perpetuate and affirm their African traditions and practices, thus enabling them to recreate the absent African space.

In the first wave of films, many of the characters find support and comfort from their fellow immigrant friends. In both *Soleil O* and *Nationalité Immigré*, the immigrants group together in their struggle for better conditions. *Concerto pour un exil* and *Nationalité Immigré* focus on the way in which the characters help each other out, either lending money or lodging newcomers. The rare moments of warmth in both *Soleil O* and *Octobre* involve the coming together of black characters. The bar scene in *Soleil O* is one of the rare times we see Jean laughing, and in *Octobre*, the only time Idriss appears to relax is during the 'surreal' scene in which he fleetingly meets and dances with a black woman in front of the amazed Russian on-lookers in the metro station.

In the second wave films, the community spirit not only involves a sense of solidarity, but also focuses on the perpetuation of African traditions. In *Clando*, Sobgui attends a *tontine* meeting in Germany just like the one he attends in Cameroon.[24] Both function on exactly the same principal, with the same call-and-response cries of 'Family! Unity! For better or for worse!', the only noticeable difference being that there is a woman present at the German meeting. The camera pans around the circle of participants in both spaces, emphasising the group. In the later party scene, many of the Cameroonians are dressed in traditional

24 A voice-over explains in the first documentary-style *tontine* scene that *tontines* are traditional mutual support groups. Members regularly meet to discuss important issues and also pay a contribution to a common fund from which members can borrow money.

clothing and Cameroonian food is served. Similarly, in *Bouzié* the party held in honour of Zébia's mother is organised along traditional lines with speeches, gifts, African food and dancing. As Zébia's mother welcomes the guests, she recognises and hugs one man whose grandfather came from the same village as her mother, again stressing the importance of family and community ties.

A couple of films nonetheless temper the commonly expressed theme of solidarity. Inoussa Ouesseini's *Paris, c'est jolie* (France-Niger, 1974), shows how this sense of solidarity can be abused when one African unscrupulously takes advantage of another newly-arrived African's inexperience, robbing him of his money and belongings. In Laplaine's more recent *Le Clandestin*, two Africans also rob an illegal immigrant. When he stares longingly at a group of black road workers on their lunch break, they also simply stare back at him. However, these two films are exceptional in this respect.

Like the works set on the African continent, these European-based films also explore questions of identity, as the filmmakers formulate alternative representations of immigrant characters that again posit an alternative African voice. They thereby challenge the silences and mis-representations of a European cinema that often, even if unconsciously, perpetuates the legacies of the West's racial and colonial discourses. Stylistically, these films represent a whole range of trends also found in the films set in Africa. The influences of orature are frequently discernible in their non-linear digression, circular structures, or the repetition of motifs and forms, for example. Some of these works' stylistic aspects also have their parallels in different contemporaneous European avant-garde filmmaking trends. They are frequently a synthesis of both African and European forms, as might well be expected given their directors' bi-cultural position and the environment in which they are set.

Whilst the examples discussed in this chapter suggest that there are certain continuities in Francophone African representations of immigration produced over the years, a closer look reveals that several funda-mental differences have also emerged that reflect the evolutions in Europe's multicultural social climates. One such example is the emergence of a cinema that has begun to portray the real rooting of the African community in France. Echoed in some recent French films and television series, such as Mathieu Kassovitz's *Métisse* (France, 1993) and *La Haine* (1995), this is likely to provoke a new debate as to whether or not such works are better seen as part of a 'Black French', rather than an 'African cinema', a term which does not yet have the same currency as 'Black British' cinema in the UK.

This kind of questioning inevitably raises the issue of how the European films made by Francophone African directors are received in France and what this says about the position they occupy in the French cinematographic landscape. It is interesting to note that Med Hondo had significant difficulties finishing *Lumière Noire* when the necessary authorisation to shoot the deportation scene was unexpectedly with-drawn at the last minute on the pretext that the scenes were detrimental

Filming the Immigrant Experience

to the image of Air France and the Aéroports de Paris. When the film was finally completed after a long battle, Hondo had great difficulty in finding a distributor and no television channel agreed to buy the film, despite the favourable critical reviews in France. Hondo's difficulties continued with *Watani*, when the Ministry of Culture initially recommended that the film carry a warning about its alleged violence, causing a number of the cinemas to refuse the film. Given the politically committed nature of both films and, in particular, their criticism of the French authorities' treatment of immigrants, one can only conclude that certain subjects remain taboo, especially when dealt with by African directors. Given certain funding clauses in France which stipulate that African films be set primarily in Africa, one may also legitimately wonder whether or not European producers, critics, and film audiences are more interested in seeing 'exotic' images of a far-off continent rather than images of the harsh realities of immigration at home. It is certainly no accident that films such as Cissé's *Yeelen* and Ouedraogo's *Yaaba* and *Tilaï*, all of which are set in 'timeless' rural African locations, were acclaimed by Western audiences and critics alike.

The critics' reception of Ouedraogo's *Cri du Coeur*, his first film set outside Burkina Faso's rural environments, would seem to confirm this argument. Whilst the film is not a masterpiece, it has its qualities and, above all, offers a refreshingly new representation of an immigrant family in France. What was particularly disturbing in the critics' reaction to the film, however, were the terms in which they articulated their attacks. *Le Monde de l'Education* considered that Ouedraogo would have done better not to 'quitter les paysages et les villages de son pays' ['leave the landscapes and villages of his homeland'] that were so 'charming' in his earlier films, and *Télérama* judged that Ouedraogo, 'dont les contes africains nous avaient éblouis, n'arrive pas à filmer les acteurs et les paysages français' ['who stunned us with his African tales, fails to film French actors and landscapes'].[25] This suggests that French critics and audiences, conditioned by a tradition of 'assimilationist' policies and an official anathema to the existence of communities, still have difficulty in accepting a critical African gaze in their own country.

25 C. Helffer, *Le Monde de l'Education*, mai, 1995. Cited by Olivier Barlet, *African Cinemas: Decolonizing the gaze*, p 211; and Philippe Piazzo, *Télérama*, 2360, 5 avril 1995, p 42.

6 African Women & Film
On screen & behind the camera

Given the way in which Francophone African films use art to explore fundamental social issues, it is hardly surprising that the role and status of women in Africa should emerge as a predominant theme. Spectators of Francophone African film will immediately notice the frequency with which issues concerning women are addressed, the wide range of female characters portrayed, and the generally progressive attitude expressed in the majority of these representations. Such films about women occupy a central position within the overall corpus of Francophone African film. Films by female and male directors alike often address and promote the issue of equal rights for women, and also highlight the central role played by women in African society.

Most of these women-centred films give their female characters a clear and central voice that contrasts radically with the silence and/or absence of African women characters in Western images of the continent. They challenge the misrepresentations, preconceptions and stereotypes that abound vis-à-vis the position and role of women in Africa. As they offer alternative representations of their own, these films constitute part of the vital process of self-definition and construction of identity through film. Before looking more closely at the diverse examples of these empowering representations and the issues they explore, it is important to situate these questions in the wider context of feminist film practices and theories that emerged in Europe and the States in the Sixties and Seventies. The contributions that black and non-Western women have made to such debates will help to inform readings of non-Western women's film.

The emergence of women's filmmaking has enabled women directors everywhere to deconstruct stereotypical representations of female characters that are generally filmed from a male point of view. Sixties' and Seventies' British and American feminist theorists, many of whom based their work on Freud and Lacan's psychoanalytical concepts of fundamental sexual difference and binary male-female opposition, began to analyse the ways in which classical Western film narratives construct female stereotypes. Feminists also considered how the ways in which female film characters were positioned reflected the fears and desires of the male characters and, by extension, those of male spectators, perpetrating society's dominant male/passive female paradigms.

By deconstructing the paradigms that confine women in society's

'J'aime filmer des femmes qui triomphent. Si je peux leur donner la parole pour une fois, je le fais'.
['I like to film women who triumph. If I can give them the opportunity to speak out for once, I do so'.]
Safi Faye[1]

1 Safi Faye. Speaking on the French television talk show, *Le Cercle* (France 2, 8 April 1998).

147

2 Teresa de Laurentis, 'Aesthetic and Feminist Theory: Rethinking Women's Cinema', in Raven, Langer & Frueh (eds.), *Feminist Art Criticism: An Anthology* (New York: First Icon, 1991), p 140.

3 See Chandra Talpade Mohanty, 'Feminist Scholarship, Colonial Discourses', in Ashcroft, Griffiths & Tiffin (eds.), *The Post-Colonial Studies Reader* (London & New York: Routledge, 1995), p 260.

4 Jane Gaines, 'White Privilege and Looking Relations: Race and Gender in Feminist Film Theory', *Screen*, vol 29, 4, 1988, pp 12-27.

5 Although African-American and African women's history and experiences of oppression are by no means identical, there are some interesting parallels between the oppression that grew out of slavery and that engendered by colonialism.

6 The African-American filmmaker Alile Sharon Larkin has argued that whilst African-American women have historically been abused by black men, black men have 'never held the kind of power that white women hold in this culture. Both historically and currently, white women participate in and reap the benefits of white supremacy.' See 'Black Women Filmmakers Defining Ourselves: Feminism in Our Own Voice'. Quoted by Sheila Petty in 'Black African Feminist Film-Making?', in Bakari & Cham (eds.), *African Experiences of Cinema* (London: BFI Publishing, 1996), p 189.

7 See Ella Shohat, 'Culture impériale et différence sexuelle: pour une ethnographie féministe du cinéma', *Ciném-Action*, 67, 1993, p 42.

oppressive structures, the new generation of women directors strove to make films that positioned them as subjects, rather than as mere objects of the 'male gaze'. Their use of film to voice their own concerns and perspectives clearly parallels the Francophone African filmmakers' quest to appropriate their own images and to challenge their objectification in Western films. Like the Francophone African directors, women filmmakers began to develop new, unfamiliar representations of women and men that centred women characters, making them more visible in the narrative. Their roles and formerly overlooked daily gestures and spaces were foregrounded as women filmmakers constructed 'other objects and subjects of vision' which challenged notions about what constitutes the filmic subject.[2]

Since the mid-Eighties, these early feminist debates have themselves been critiqued and broadened by the inclusion of previously marginalized voices. Increasingly prolific black and non-Western feminists have, for example, called for their own cultural and ethnic specificities to be recognised. At the same time, they have warned against the tendency to replace their former absence in mainstream feminist theory with monolithic and reductive 'Black' or 'Third World Woman' constructs.[3] Black and non-Western feminists have also attacked the continuing ethnocentrism of the allegedly 'universal' mainstream feminist discourse articulated in the West by predominantly white, middle-class feminists. Jane Gaines has rightly demonstrated how this ethnocentrism has often encouraged Western feminist film critics to identify Euro-American cinematic gender codes inaccurately in films from other regions and cultures whose own practices and models can be quite different.[4]

Other recent developments reveal that the dominant male/subjugated female psychoanalytical paradigm may inadequately describe or actually mask the oppression of women in other cultures whose condition is often equally affected by other factors, such as ethnic origin, class, sexual preference or history. Many African-American women, who historically articulate their identity as much in terms of ethnic origin as gender, legitimately argue that they are as likely to experience racial oppression as they are gender oppression, and that their oppressor is as likely to be a white woman as a man.[5]

White feminist discourse cannot simply assume that all women face identical forms of oppression and white feminists have to recognise that they may also find themselves in the role of the oppressor.[6] Ella Shohat insists that the position of the Western woman may be ambiguous when feminism is combined with colonial discourse.[7] Western women may be oppressed by the patriarchal structures of the West, but colonial discourse reveals that they may simultaneously find themselves in a dominant position vis-à-vis non-Western women and men. A range of films set in the colonial period illustrate the traditionally dominant role of white women compared to the 'subordinate' African male and female characters. This role is most commonly exemplified by the (usually desexualised) black male servant/white mistress paradigm. In *Out of Africa* (USA, 1985), the benevolent Karen Blixen (played by Meryl

Streep), is consistently portrayed in a dominant position vis-à-vis her faithful African servant. Similarly, in *Le Crime de Monsieur Stil* (France, 1995) discussed in Chapter 2, the white female characters dominate both the African male servants and the local African women.

Another fundamental divergence between black/non-Western and predominantly white, 'mainstream' feminist perspectives lies in what Jane Gaines describes as the 'black female identification with the black male' that has arisen from black people's common experience of racial oppression, making them 'equal by default'.[8] Radically opposed to the Freudian and Lacanian notions of an essential gender difference and antagonism that formed the basis of mainstream feminist theory, this identification has neither been understood by, nor accommodated in, mainstream Western feminist discourse. This male-female identification certainly finds its echo in Francophone African filmmaking, however, where a number of women directors have referred to African men and women's shared struggle simply to make films that revalue African subjects and highlight/counter structures that oppress *both* sexes. It is true that certain gender-specific issues have at times been deemed less urgent, or even detrimental to the 'national' postcolonial cause. In the name of African authenticity, some people continue to defend traditions identified by African women themselves as oppressive. Yet many other African men and women consider women's emancipation as the way forward, as will be seen in many of the films discussed here.

Works by black feminist writers show how differences can be determining. They need to be acknowledged if, as Sheila Petty argues, non-African critics are to avoid obfuscating the meaning and realities of African texts by systematically projecting their own values and agendas.[9] More importantly, non-African critics need to approach African film texts free from the West's clichéd assumptions about African women. Chandra Talpade Mohanty accuses Western women (whom she characterises as representing themselves as, 'educated, modern, as having control over their own bodies and sexualities, and the freedom to make their own decisions') of representing non-Western women as leading, 'an essentially truncated life based on [their] feminine gender (read: sexually constrained) and being 'third world' (read: ignorant, poor, uneducated, tradition-bound, domestic, family-oriented, victimised, etc.)'.[10]

Like all women in the world, African women have to contend with certain culturally specific, oppressive practices, but a closer look at their societal structures also indicates that these women are often empowered in ways different from those in the West. A better understanding of these societies reveals that many women always have been mobilised in the battle for their own emancipation, even if this participation has often been overlooked or minimised in 'official' (male-authored) historiographies. Traditions of political involvement and power sharing were reinforced in the past by the existence of matrilineal structures that gave women a significant societal role and status. In more recent years, this continuing political involvement has been characterised by women's active participation in resistance movements and various anti-dictatorial uprisings.

8 Jane Gaines, 'White Privilege and Looking Relations: Race and Gender in Feminist Film Theory', pp 16 & 22.

9 See Sheila Petty, 'Miseria: Towards and African Feminist Framework of Analysis', *iris*, 18, Spring 1995, p 138.

10 Chandra Talpade Mohanty, 'Feminist Scholarship, Colonial Discourses', p 261.

A number of scholars claim that female subordination in Africa is a relatively recent phenomenon, intensified when Islam and Christianity disrupted existing women-centred matrilineal systems by introducing more oppressive patrilineal structures. European colonisation helped develop this trend by imposing its capitalistic economic systems, which also fundamentally modified social structures and upset the complementary nature of male-female roles. The colonial authorities' exclusive dealings with members of the male population undermined women's authority, power, and position in African society.[11] Cultural factors of this kind must be considered when looking at the representations formulated in these societies. It is crucial, therefore, that Westerners *hear* what African women are saying as they define their own priorities, conceptions, and agendas, as in the highly enlightening films discussed in this chapter.[12]

Francophone African women filmmakers and empathetic, 'womanist' male directors, to borrow Alice Waker's term, are confronted with the double gender and racial misrepresentation of African women in the Western images of the continent.[13] Western film has either tended to ignore African women characters completely, or to portray them as the disposable, sexually voracious objects of (white) male desire. Western media reports and documentaries often portray African women as the passive victims of poverty and patriarchal oppression. This both perpetuates the West's conception of their status and denies them any active, participatory role in their own destinies.

Both male and female Francophone African filmmakers have used their films to revalue the real roles African women play, focusing on their concerns and quotidian experiences. The majority of these works also analyse oppressive traditions and practices, adopting the socially and morally responsible style found in all the Francophone African films that continue the traditionally pedagogical, committed role of art in the region. These women's and 'womanist' films give voice and substance to their hitherto silenced women characters. Moreover, the women filmmakers' directing of their own gaze and telling of their own stories radically disrupts and challenges the authority of the male point of view: they have a strong, central voice, despite their numerical minority.

As they construct new representations of women, many films also provide uncompromising critiques of patriarchal male characters who cling blindly to their male prerogatives. Other films, such as Safi Faye's docu-fiction *Selbe, et tant d'autres* (Senegal, 1982), focuses on the ways in which rural women cope in the real or moral absence of their menfolk, denying men their 'traditional' patriarchal power. They debunk the stereotypical image of the passive and subjugated African woman. Other films highlight African women's previously ignored role in spearheading resistance movements or pushing for social change. Malian filmmaker Cheick Oumar Sissoko, whose films often feature strong women characters, confirms this: 'Women have always been quick to react to social injustice ever since the colonial era', adding that it is important both 'to show the reality of our countries' and 'the acts of which our

11 See Achola O. Pala & Madina Ly, *La femme africaine dans la société précoloniale* (Paris: UNESCO, 1979).

12 The Cameroonian feminist writer Calixthe Beyala offers her own conception of an African feminism capable of incorporating her own socio-cultural sensibilities, which she describes as, 'très proche du féminisme mais divergente dans la mesure où elle ne prône pas l'egalité entre l'homme et la femme, mais la différence-égalitaire ... Il fallait un autre mot pour définir cette nouvelle femme qui veut les trois pouvoirs: carrière, maternité et vie affective'. ['very close to feminism, but divergent in that it advocates egalitarian difference rather than equality between men and women ... Another word was needed to define this new woman who wants all three powers, namely a career, motherhood, and a love life'.] Adama Drabo's film *Taafe Fanga* also advocates 'egalitarian difference'. (*Lettre d'une Africaine à ses sœurs occidentales* (Paris: Spengler, 1995), pp 20–21).

13 See Alice Walker, *In Search of Our Mothers' Gardens: Womanist Prose* (San Diego & New York: Harvest/HBJ, 1984).

women are capable'.[14] Such acts sometimes need to be situated in their own socio-cultural context to be fully appreciated, however. The village women's threat to bar their husbands from their beds in protest at Nanyuma's forced re-marriage in Cheick Oumar Sissoko's *Finzan* (Mali, 1989) may not immediately seem that significant in many Western circles, yet the knowledge that a Bambara man has absolute authority over his wife and her body reveals the seriousness of this act of protest in the Malian context.

The films discussed in this chapter all categorically denounce the structures and practices which oppress women. They address a range of issues relating specifically to women in Francophone Africa, namely polygamy, prostitution, forced marriage, power relations between men and women, and female circumcision. At times there is a tendency to portray women simply as the victims of such practices, but the majority of these films – and particularly those by the women directors – show their female characters to be resisters. They are women who 'take their destinies in hand through their own hard grind', as one character comments in Safi Faye's *Testito* (Senegal, 1989), even if some ultimately lose their individual battle against what are denounced as oppressive traditions. All of these works prioritise the female point of view.

Directing the female gaze: Safi Faye; Anne Laure Folly; Fanta Régina Nacro

The films made by the prominent Francophone African women filmmakers, Safi Faye (Senegal), Anne Laure Folly (Togo), and Fanta Régina Nacro (Burkina Faso), offer examples of the various ways in which women directors use their own distinctive styles to posit an alternative, female viewpoint in film. As they address issues concerning women and other marginalized members of the community and fore-ground their voices and concerns, their works above all deconstruct the image of the passive victim.

Safi Faye, one of West Africa's pioneering women filmmakers, began making films in 1972.[15] Her first feature film, *Kaddu Beykat* ('the Voice of the Peasant', Senegal, 1975), is set in her Serer family village in the Sine-Saloum region of southern Senegal. The film immediately brings the often unheeded voices and concerns of Senegal's rural populations to the fore, establishing Faye's distinctive blend of documentary and fiction already referred to in Chapter 4. Reflecting the generic blending often found in the region's oral tales, Faye's style is firmly rooted in the narrative traditions of the people she films, situating her work and gaze centrally within the communities whose voice she prioritises.

Faye comes from an ethnographic background and her early cinematic experiences were with the well-known French ethnographic filmmaker Jean Rouch, who first developed *cinéma-verité's* use of non-professional actors, improvisation, and non-interventionist camera work. These have marked her own approach to filmmaking. Unlike many other

14 Interview with the author. Ouaga-dougou, February 1995.

15 Thérèse Sita Bella (Cameroon), who made the documentary *Tam Tam à Paris* in 1963, was Africa's very first woman filmmaker. Sarah Maldoror (France-Guadeloupe), who is often classed amongst African filmmakers as several of her major works are set in Africa and are very closely related to the African liberation cause, made her first film, *Monangambee*, on the continent in 1970.

African Women & Film

151

ethnographic filmmakers, however, she does not attempt to establish an omniscient and ironic distance from her filmed subjects. She instead positions herself within the community, thereby foregrounding the predominantly community-based social structures and conception of the artist's role discussed in Chapter 3. Faye always stresses the collective nature of her feature films (*Kaddu Beykat, Fad'jal, Mossane*) and later shorter 'docu-fictions' (*Goob na nu*, 1979; *Les Ames au Soleil*, 1981; *Selbé et tant d'autres*, 1982; *Testito*, 1989), rather than insisting on her own authoritative position as film director. Her work thus disrupts the authoritative point of view and individualistic role of the artist assumed by many Western filmmakers, and continues existing social traditions.

The villagers' active participation in the construction of the films in which they appear is evident from the centrality of their voice in the narratives. Faye comments on this participation, explaining that, 'even though I may write a script, ... I basically leave the peasants free to express themselves in front of a camera and I listen. My films are collective works in which everybody takes an active part'.[16] Her minimal, voluntarily subjective explanatory voice-overs thus play a secondary role in the film, positioning Faye within, rather than above, the community. This is particularly clear from the way in which she simply introduces and concludes the film in the form of a personal letter that acknowledges and positions the spectator. Throughout the rest of the film, she allows the images and villagers to speak for themselves, intervening only very occasionally to provide information that contextualises elements of the villagers' lives. At the end of the film, she stresses the collective nature of the work as she 'signs off': 'I wrote this letter. All the rest is by my farming family. I thank them. This is the word of the peasant. Kaddu beykat'. This foregrounding of the frequently unheeded or marginalized 'voice of the peasant' positions *Kaddu Beykat* in both Francophone Africa and women's community-based filmmaking traditions.

The film itself provides a chronicle of day-to-day village life. The unobtrusive camera which films the villagers' diverse household and farming chores, communal life-style, or traditional medical practices, gives a strong sense of both the village's cyclical daily rhythms and the passing of time. The village's specific temporal rhythm is recreated by filming several motifs, including shots of people getting up in the family compound, the cock crowing, the shots of villagers on their way to and from the fields in the morning and evening, and Coumba watching her fiancé Ngor pass by her compound each day. This repetition is not dissimilar to that found in certain European films by women filmmakers, such as Margerite Duras's *Nathalie Granger* (France, 1973), or Chantal Ackerman's *Jeanne Dielman, 23 Quai de Commerce, 1080 Bruxelles* (Belgium, 1975), which also foreground their female characters' repeated daily gestures.

Like *Fad'jal*, (discussed in Chapter 4) which similarly faithfully depicts village life, quotidian chores are punctuated with semi-fictionalised narratives and/or real events, such as Coumba and Ngor's courting and marriage, Ngor's temporary migration to Dakar in search of work, or the

16 Françoise Pfaff, *Twenty-five Black African Filmmakers* (Westport, Connecticut: Greenwood Press, 1988), p 117. In the same interview, Faye also adds: 'I do not work single-handedly but rather through and with other people. I go to talk to the farmers in their village, we discuss their problems and I take notes.'

lengthy palaver scenes in which the menfolk discuss the hardships caused by both drought and the government's imposition of the groundnut monoculture and (low) fixed prices.[17] This technique draws the spectator into the story, encouraging him/her to identify directly with the film's characters and their concerns.

The film offers a realistic, unromantic portrait of village life and labour. The people are often filmed at work together in the fields, the camera moving with them to emphasise the dynamism and arduous nature of their gestures. Simultaneously, the film shows the villagers to be articulate, politically committed and well aware of the mechanisms of their (geographically and metaphorically) distant government. By letting them express their own concerns, the film dismisses the idea that Africa's rural populations are in some way ignorant and backward. The film's slow pace and lengthy shots not only convey the rhythm of village life – which is contrasted with the hustle and bustle of the film's Dakar sequences – but also allows the villagers' voices to develop and impose themselves. In the lengthy palaver sequences, Faye's camera tends to film the group and to emphasise the collective before focusing on individual speakers, remaining at a respectful, unobtrusive distance. Medium and long shots are similarly favoured throughout the film, and the camera remains relatively static so as not to detract from the villagers' words, conferring a centrality on their voices within the very structures of the film. The villagers also occasionally address the camera directly, acknowledging both its and Faye's presence. This draws the director and the spectator into the narrative of the film, again positioning Faye as an 'insider', rather than an observing 'outsider'.

Safi Faye's 'documentary' works, such as *Selbé et tant d'autres* and *Testito*, highlight the pivotal role women play in the rural communities, and pay homage to them.[18] Faye insists on giving women a voice in her films, a desire that is all the more radical in a context where women are rarely given a public voice, as can be seen from the exclusively male composition of the village palavers in Faye's films.[19] Here, however, they speak out, express their concerns, and even criticise their menfolk rather than resisting in silence.

As the title suggests, *Selbé et tant d'autres* depicts the daily life of one village woman who is representative of many others. The film follows the thirty-nine-year-old Selbé, mother of eight, in an endless round of domestic chores and farm work as she struggles to support her children in the absence of her husband who, like many of the other village men, has gone to the city to try to find work. As in Faye's other films, the camera unobtrusively captures Selbé and the other village women's arduous daily routines. Their crucial role in assuring their families' livelihood is highlighted in a series of medium and long takes that foreground their domestic space. Certain shots, like those of Selbé breast-feeding her youngest child as she sits cooking at the fire, are regularly repeated throughout the film, forming visual leitmotifs. Like those in the oral tales, they punctuate the rhythm of the narrative, conferring

17 This critique of the government's agricultural policy caused the film to be banned in Senegal.

18 As already mentioned above, Safi Faye's films tend to blur the boundaries between documentary and fiction, her fictions containing documentary moments and vice versa. Films such as *Selbé* can be described as predominantly documentary, with 'fictional'/enacted moments.

19 Speaking on *Le Cercle* (France 2, 8 April 1998). Faye has also explained her choice to make films as the desire to 'écrire quelque chose que ma mère pourrait lire en étant analphabète' ['to write something that my illiterate mother would be able to read'].

coherence on the structure of the film and marking the constant cycle of the women's chores in a society where the conception of time itself is often cyclical.

On several occasions in the film, Selbé, still at work, candidly discusses her condition and her relations with her absent husband with Safi Faye. Whilst Faye is never actually seen, both her off-screen presence and the film in the making are frequently acknowledged, binding Faye into the same 'mutual, non-hierarchical relation with her subject' already discovered in *Kaddu Beykat*.[20] Faye's own voice-over only very occasionally intervenes to furnish biographical details about Selbé, or to clarify certain details. The absence of an authorial voice highlights the centrality of Selbé's words. Throughout the film, Selbé and the other women's conversations are filmed in real time. The women are also always filmed in the same frontal frame, as if to emphasise the sense of physical closeness and emotional solidarity between them. The subjects of these diverse conversations, which revolve around the questions of infant mortality, the high birth rate, and education for women, evoke the women's concerns in a subtle and undogmatic manner.

The women's solidarity and constant activity contrast starkly with the behaviour of the men left in the village. They sit looking on as the women work, thereby substantiating the women's complaints about their lack of support. This is most apparent in one sequence in which a husband categorically refuses to help his tired wife unload her cartload of wood, protesting, 'I'm not moving ... I already helped you yesterday'. As the film draws to an end, Selbé is seen breast-feeding her child again, her song, 'Farm until you drop. God, why do you reserve me this lot in life? Promise a better future for my children', continuing in a loop over the final, demonstrative image of her hard at work in the fields. As the credits roll up over Selbé working, it is clear that whilst the film has ended, Selbé and the other women's labour will continue in its unending cycle. But although their lot is indubitably harsh, the film refuses to portray them as victims. It shows them to be survivors and celebrates their remarkable inner and physical strength in the face of adversity. It is this quality which clearly distinguishes Faye's gaze from that of so many other documentaries about rural African women.

Safi Faye's most recent film *Mossane* (1996) marks a continuation of the style of her earlier works and a departure from it. On the one hand, the film is more obviously a 'traditional' fiction. It is more aesthetically 'polished', its predominant yellow colours visually echoing the ochre earth of its vast, flat landscapes. On the other hand, *Mossane* shares some of the earlier films' documentary moments. The inclusion of lengthy sacrificial and traditional healing rituals recalls Faye's ethnographic background, even though, according to Faye, the actual ceremonies themselves are a fictional invention.[21] However, these documentary-style moments become an integral part of the rest of the narrative. They underline the place such rituals have in the characters' lives and echo the way in which orature traditionally shifts between registers and modes.

20 Julia Lesage, 'Political Aesthetics of the Feminist Documentary Film', in Charlotte Brunsdon (ed.), *Films For Women* (London: BFI Books, 1986), p 21.

21 See Olivier Barlet, 'Entretien avec Safi Faye', *Africultures*, 2, novembre 1997, p 11.

Like Faye's earlier works, *Mossane* is set in the rural Serer environment, depicting its lifestyle, rhythms, and beliefs. The slow sweeping pans across the vast landscapes constantly underline the communion between the people and their environment, and the film evokes the environmental problems facing the rural populations. Most striking is the way in which Faye's portrait of the young protagonist Mossane centres the female domain, relegating the male characters to a secondary role.

The film not only addresses the question of women's choice, but also celebrates the adolescent stage in a woman's life. Faye has commented on this latter aspect of the film, explaining, 'Je voulais mettre l'accent sur la beauté ephémère de l'adolescence, chanter cette période confuse où le corps change, où l'adolescent est perturbé ... Je voulais que la plus belle fille au monde soit une Africaine, et je l'ai chanté parce que je suis mère' ['I wanted to place the accent on the ephemeral beauty of adolescence, to sing this confusing time when the body changes and the teenager is unsure of him/herself ... I wanted the most beautiful girl in the world to be African, and I sung her praises because I am a mother'].[22] This poses a subtle but radical challenge to the way in which blackness, and in particular black femininity, have traditionally been denied and reviled in Western representation and thought. Mossane is a strikingly beautiful young woman, 'Moss' meaning beauty, purity, and virtue, in Serer. As is reiterated by different characters in the film, however, her beauty is the source of constant strife, leaving no one indifferent, from her own brother to the Pangool spirits of the ancestors. Rather than simply turning Mossane into a reified icon, however, Faye makes her absolutely human by also focusing on her revolt against her parents and the arranged marriage they have planned for her. This is emphasised by the way in which Faye's camera always remains close to and level with Mossane.

Throughout *Mossane*, Faye films the main female characters with a rare sensuality. The love scene between Dibor and her husband Daouda, and Dibor's later, unusually candid conversation with Mossane show Dibor to be fully in control of her own body and sexuality. This representation diverges from Western notions that African women are little more than the disposable objects of male desire. It is no accident that Dibor is literally and metaphorically 'on top' as the couple make love, and that it is she who determines when their lovemaking happens and ends. Again, the camera remains both level with Dibor and at a respectful distance. Daouda is also seen from Dibor's point of view, but not vice versa, disrupting the potentially objectifying male gaze. Men and the male gaze are also completely absent in the scenes in which Dibor and Mossane wash together playfully, and Mossane scrubs her mother's naked back, the camera lingering on the textures of her skin as the soapy water and filtered light play on her body. The importance and intimacy of Dibor and Mossane's friendship is stressed by their physical closeness, which is accentuated by the fact that they are always filmed together in the same frame.

Mossane's beauty is by no means equated with passivity in the film, and she is clearly portrayed as a fighter. When Mossane's parents decide

Safi Faye, Mossane, *1996.*
Emphasising black femininity and beauty.
(Courtesy of Safi Faye)

22 Speaking on *Le Cercle*, op. cit. Faye often stresses the importance of her position as both filmmaker and mother, stating: 'I have remained close to the traditional [African] role of mother, and this responsibility is not a burden to me ... I cannot be a filmmaker without being a mother. As an African woman filmmaker, the two are very much a part of me'. See Mark A. Reid, *Redefining Black Film* (Berkeley & Los Angeles: University of California Press, 1993), p 124.

to marry her off to the rich Diogaye, she staunchly refuses, declaring herself 'ready to disobey' in a society that uncompromisingly advocates respect for one's elders. Mossane repeatedly defies her parents and continues to see Fara, the penniless student. When her parents go ahead with the marriage anyway, Mossane's revolt culminates in an unprecedented confrontation during the wedding ceremony. Her psychological division from the older members of the community is symbolically evoked by the alternation of colourful shots of the wedding celebration and her joyful mother outside, with the frontal mid-shots of the mortified Mossane inside, veiled in a white cloth that is symbolically reminiscent of a funeral shroud. Mossane refuses to succumb, and boldly goes out to confront the assembled guests, denouncing the marriage. Mossane and her mother are filmed in alternate, confrontational separate frames destroying the closeness that until now was symbolised by shots of their physical proximity.

When Mossane's courageous plea goes unheeded, she flees at night, the film denouncing arranged marriages and clearly advocating women's choice. Mossane's rebellion ends in tragedy, however. Whilst many Westerners might be tempted to read this as a 'punishment' for her rebellion, Mossane's death can also be seen as an ultimate act of defiance, as she refuses to relinquish her right to choose. Her death is predicted right from the start of the film when the voice-over song informs that the Pangool spirits will eventually come to reclaim their 'chosen one', and must be situated in its mystical African context. Safi Faye indeed describes the death as, 'une bagarre entre les humains et les inhumains' ['a battle between humans and non-humans'].[23] It is thus part of a specifically African belief system whose myths evoke the existence of 'spirit children' torn between the worlds of the living and the dead fated to die young. As in all her works, Faye combines women's concerns and a powerful female voice with her own cultural sensibilities, creating a distinctive and highly personal style that reflects both her dual female and African perspectives.

In her various documentary films, Anne Laure Folly similarly focuses on issues concerning women and their condition. She foregrounds their voices, her filmed interviews creating a space in which they can clearly convey their points of view. *Femmes aux yeux ouverts* (Togo, 1993), Anne Laure Folly's highly committed second film, offers one such example. The film opens with a close-up shot of a young woman staring defiantly into the camera as she recites the following, apparently sardonic, poem by a woman from Burkina Faso, her eyes well and truly open:

> A good woman should obey her husband at all times,
> A good woman should not know how to read,
> A good woman's eyes should not be open.

The film then introduces a range of very different women from Burkina, Mali, Senegal and Benin who all have at least one thing in common – their open eyes.

23. Olivier Barlet, 'Entretien avec Safi Faye', p 11.

Anne Laure Folly, Femmes aux yeux ouvertes, *1993. Women and girls with 'open eyes'.*
(Courtesy of Anne Laure Folly)

Divided into seven sections entitled 'Clitoridectomy', 'Forced marriage', 'AIDS', 'Struggle', 'Survival', 'Economics', and 'Politics', the film identifies the structures that oppress women in West Africa. More strikingly still, it lets the women discuss the issues that concern them and shows how they organise themselves to resist and survive. Whilst the director's off-screen presence is at times tangible in certain interviews, she does not intervene directly in the film, preferring to focus on the women's own multiple voices.

The interviews clearly establish the women's often-paradoxical position in West Africa. Whilst responsible for their children's education and very often for their families' financial survival too, women are still frequently subjected to their families' and/or husbands' authority and officially given little right to speak or make choices for themselves. The film explores different examples of this oppression by focusing on the voices of women who resist such practices. In the first section on female circumcision, Folly interviews women who have undergone clitoridectomy and are now involved in combating the practice. As one woman puts it, the interviewees and the film thus radically 'break the silence' surrounding the issue.[24] Whilst Folly's own position on the matter is clear both from her emphasis on these critical perspectives and from the section's opening close-up of an explicit, anti-clitoridectomy logo, she also interviews an elderly woman who performs the operation without passing judgement, letting her explain the traditional beliefs behind the practice.

In the section on forced marriages, the footage of girls who have fled from such marriages to older men, and widows who have formed a support group, allows the women to discuss the different types of forced

24 The culturally sensitive question of female circumcision is very rarely raised in Francophone African film. The only other two examples to date are Cheick Oumar Sissoko's *Finzan*, which will be discussed later, and the Chadian female director Mahamet Zara Yacoub's docu-fiction *Dilèmme au Féminin* (1994). Yacoub's film alternates real and enacted footage of a circumcision ceremony with the points of view of health officials, members of women's groups, and Christian and Muslim religious leaders. Religious officials in Chad attacked the film for its stark, close-up images of a real clitoridectomy, pronouncing a *fatwa* against the director that was later retracted.

Anne Laure Folly, Les Oubliées,
*1996. Foregrounding the
testimonies of the Angolan war's
forgotten and ignored victims.*
(Courtesy of Anne Laure Folly)

25 Olivier Barlet, 'Entretien: Anne-
Laure Folly', *Africultures*, 2, novembre
1997, p 16.

marriage whilst at the same time providing examples of their resistance to them. Later in the film when a female journalist discusses the terrible risk many African women run of catching AIDS, Folly similarly films a women's group's AIDS awareness campaign in the market. All of these examples consistently support the ways in which women mobilise themselves and actively take their own health and well-being into their hands, even when this means defying social traditions.

The rest of the film highlights the pivotal role women play in both political struggles and simply the daily struggle to survive. One of the most characteristic examples of Folly's approach can be seen in the juxtaposition of the 'official' archive footage of the 1991 Malian women's courageous mass demonstration that helped to bring down the dictator Moussa Traoré and extracts of one woman's moving account of her own participation in the violently-repressed revolt. As is often the case in Folly's work, alongside that of other Francophone African filmmakers, the woman's personal story intermingles with the 'official' historical footage and completes it.

These women's multiple and often highly personal testimonies are a far cry from the dominant image of African women as passive victims of oppression. Whilst clearly highlighting and denouncing the very real oppression facing women in West Africa, Anne Laure Folly, like Safi Faye, focuses on women who, as one of the Beninese women concludes at the end of the film, are 'brave and intrepid' like their Amazonian warrior ancestors, never hesitating to resist and to fight back.

Women's voices are again prioritised in *Les Oubliées* (1996), which pieces together personalised accounts of Angola's little publicised thirty-year war via the even more rarely heard testimonies of the war's forgotten and ignored victims – the 'forgotten women' of the title. The film thus offers an unusual perspective that subverts official readings of the war and its justifications by focusing on the views of its victims.

Throughout the film, Folly's camera maintains an intimate proximity with the women interviewed, respectfully framing their faces in mid- and close-up shots as they speak directly to the camera. This aesthetic choice not only underlines the immediacy of the women's voices within the film, but also deliberately breaks with what Folly rightly describes as 'l'esthétique reconnue au Noir [qui] n'est pas celle du visage, du trait et du regard [mais celle] du corps, du physique, d'une beauté plastique' ['the aesthetic normally associated with Black people [which] is not that of the face, the trait or the gaze, [but that] of the body, physique, and plastic beauty'].[25] Folly uses this close-up technique to encourage the spectator literally to look the women in the eye in an attempt to reduce the distance between the subject and the director/spectator, and thus to lessen the divide. This quest for filmic proximity is reminiscent of Faye's work, and again disrupts the director's authoritative point of view. It is precisely this proximity and the way in which the film takes the time to listen to and to convey what the women have to say that distinguishes it from the distant, media-type reports which frequently silence their subjects or violate them in sensationalised versions of their predicament.

This closeness is accentuated in *Les Oubliées* by Anne Laure Folly's direct voice and actual presence in the film, which subsequently becomes the record of her own personal journey. The accounts of the women interviewed and Folly's voice-over are voluntarily subjective, and thus openly acknowledge, 'la fiction que représente le documentaire' ['the fiction that documentary represents'].[26] This deconstructs both the documentary format and its supposed objectivity. The opening images of the departure lounge of an European airport, filmed from a subjective camera point of view, acknowledge Folly's position as an outsider in Angola, 'pour ne pas tromper et ne pas prétendre' ['so as not to deceive or pretend'.][27] Folly similarly refuses to assume a position of authority vis-à-vis her subject, as she frankly states off-screen, 'I didn't know a thing about Angola. I had only seen *Sambizanga*, the film Sarah [Maldoror] made thirty years earlier about the war for independence.' The reference to *Sambizanga* is not innocent, of course. It not only pays homage to another pioneering woman filmmaker in Africa, but also evokes a film that similarly focuses more on the actions, reactions, and solidarity of its female characters than on the horrors of war itself. Furthermore, Folly's opening statement, 'I didn't go there to understand this war, but to meet its victims', also rejects the habitual documentary approach and again situates the women at the centre of her film.

Later in the film, this 'meeting' develops into a direct interaction as she lets a group of women in a demobilisation camp actually appropriate the cinematic gaze and momentarily determine what is shown. Explaining their hardship, they ask Folly to transmit their message to the world by filming a malnourished, screaming baby. As the camera pans slowly in close-up past the faces of the women as they stare into the camera, Folly evokes the way in which her filmed subjects thus become direct actors in the filmmaking process, commenting off-screen, 'They knew the power of the image and that was the only power they had that day. They wanted to show the child so that there would be a trace of their suffering, so that someone would hear and understand. They used the camera lens in exactly the same way as I do.'

Throughout the rest of the film, Folly pieces together details of a wide range of experiences of the war. The women describe their direct involvement in the war – a participation that is rarely acknowledged in official historiographies or on film[28] – and their struggle to survive in the combat zones as they contend with the loss of their homes and livelihoods, punitive rape, and the presence of landmines. Combined with Folly's own explanatory voice-overs, these individual accounts provide some of the 'historic' details behind the fighting at different stages of the war, and bring a highly divergent range of female perspectives to the screen.

More unusually still, *Les Oubliées* also examines the lasting economic, social, and psychological consequences of the war today. By testifying to the continuing suffering and hardship that is often overlooked once the actual fighting has stopped and the media have lost interest, Folly demonstrates the ways in which these women continue to cope and survive, often by pooling their forces and resources. Once again,

26 Idem, p 12.

27 Idem, p 14.

28 Ingrid Sinclair's *Flame* (Zimbabwe, 1996), and Flora Gomes's *Mortu Nega* (Guinea-Bissau, 1988) do exceptionally focus on the direct and combative role played by women in their countries' liberation struggles.

therefore, the film shows us women who refuse to give up hope, who are survivors. It is not by accident that the film closes positively with an interview with a group of young women who exteriorise their suffering and instability in a theatre group. In spite of everything, they maintain an optimistic sense of hope, insisting, 'Only hope keeps us going, nothing else. Only hope.'

Fanta Régina Nacro's short fiction films, which include *Puk Nini* (1995) and *Le truc de Konaté* (1997), differ considerably from the work of Faye and Folly in that they embrace the fictional form and opt for an upbeat, humorous register. At the same time, they also present powerful women characters and address a range of serious issues in a deceptively simple, sharp and efficient style.

Like many other Francophone African directors, Fanta Nacro embraces the pedagogical possibilities of cinema without ever being overly didactic, arguing that 'film can help establish real exchange and communication ... as film is the best means of educating the masses'.[29] This situates her work in the same vein as other Francophone African films, inspired by the functional role of the region's oral traditions. Stylistically, a number of orature's narrative codes and motifs can also be identified in Nacro's work. Her films can be seen as contemporary tales and similarly focus on day-to-day experiences. *Le truc de Konaté* is a particularly good example, adopting the circular structure of the 'quest tales' as Konaté sets out on a journey to cure himself of an imaginary impotency spell. Like many tales, the film adopts a comic mode to educate African audiences about using condoms to protect themselves from AIDS. When Diénéba comes back from the town where she has witnessed the ravages of the AIDS virus, she insists that she and her husband, a renowned womaniser, start using condoms. Their amorous reunion, in which the couple are filmed together in the same frame, turns sour when Konaté refuses to comply with Diénéba's request, demanding 'have you ever seen a man enter his own home wearing a hat?'! As the scene progresses and Diénéba staunchly refuses to give in to her husband, Nacro increasingly films the couple in separate frames to visually accentuate the mounting tension between them. When Konaté tells the other menfolk what has happened the next day, they form a united bloc, encouraging him to show Diénéba who is in charge. Their further insistence that the town is a bad influence on women and warning that Konaté will loose his virility if he agrees to wear a condom, thus portrays the men to be more conservative and resistant to change than the women.[30]

The next night, Diénéba still refuses to sleep with Konaté without a condom, defending herself from his forceful advances. When Konaté angrily storms off to join his other wife, insulting Diénéba as he goes, he meets with another refusal when his first wife turns the polygamy 'rule' that a husband must honour his wives' respective nights against him. As Konaté storms off again, he second wife is seen chuckling to herself, manifestly happy to have subverted this male institution. Both wives' refusal of their husband is more radical than Western audiences might at

29. Interview with the author. Ouagadougou, February 1995.

30 The Cameroonian novelist Calixthe Beyala confirms this view in her highly political pro-woman essay *Lettre d'une Africaine à ses soeurs occidentales* (pp 114–117).

Fanta Régina Nacro, Le truc de Konaté, *1997. The initial harmony between Diénéba and Konaté is upset when Diénéba insists on using a condom to protect herself from AIDS.*
(Courtesy of Fanta Nacro)

Fanta Régina Nacro, Le truc de Konaté, *1997. Konaté's vision of the 'condom tree' that he believes the diviner has instructed him to find.*
(Courtesy of Fanta Nacro)

first appreciate, since this is a culture where men are considered to have unlimited rights over their wives' bodies. These incidents thus subtly affirm the female characters' right to control their own sexuality.

As the fuming Konaté finally goes to take refuge in the arms of his lover Fati, Nacro also subtly debunks the frequently (male) espoused argument that polygamy does away with marital infidelity. An unusually candid scene with Fati shows her to fully assume her own sexuality, rather than simply being the passive object of Konaté's desire – even if Konaté's movement from one woman's bed to another seems to imply that he considers them to be more or less interchangeable. Much to Konaté's distress, his sexual prowess deserts him at the crucial moment, convincing him that Diénéba has put a spell on him with her condoms. When the village diviner tells Konaté that he must touch the tree he sees in his vision to be cured, Konaté thus sets out on his quest to find what he presumes must be the condom tree.

Konaté's journey takes him as far as the town where he visits an AIDS ward with a friend whose father has caught the virus. He also comes across a team carrying out an AIDS awareness campaign, which is filmed in its entirety, enabling the film to broadcast its message and inform viewers.[31] One of the campaigners finally takes Konaté to see the tree the diviner saw in his vision – the hevea tree that produces latex – on the condition that he promises to use condoms if he is cured. As Konaté returns to the village, echoing Diénéba's return at the beginning of the film, he, like the characters in the quest tales, has been enlightened by his journey. He shares this transformation with the other villagers and is reunited with his wife as he finally accepts her more enlightened stance. At the end of the day it is Diénéba who triumphs, therefore, rather than submitting to her husband's reactionary demands.

Finally, Fanta Nacro's second film *Puk Nini*, which in Moré means 'open your eyes', offers a subtly audacious portrayal of the question of prostitution and of a young, urban woman's unexpected reaction to her husband's infidelity. The film foregrounds the female characters' points of view, and unmercilessly but humorously ridicules the behaviour of its main male character.

At the beginning of the film, Nacro depicts what initially appears to be an idyllic, upwardly mobile, 'modern' couple's domestic bliss. Very rapidly, the cracks begin to show, as it soon becomes apparent that Isa is torn between meeting the demands of both daughter and husband. Each time she prioritises her maternal 'duties', her husband is seen to become increasingly alienated and frustrated. At this stage, most of the scenes are set exclusively in the confines of the family home, which confirms the impression that Isa is solely mother and wife, rather than an individual with her own desires and rights. This representation is reinforced by the images of Isa as a bride, which are constantly repeated as her daughter keeps replaying the video of her parents' wedding.

The tension in the couple is soon confirmed when Salif, fed up with not receiving enough attention from his wife, starts seeing a Senegalese prostitute who has just arrived in Ouagadougou. The initial images of Astou also define her as solely the object of male desire. In both the taxi from the station and in the bar where she first meets Salif, the majority of the shots of her are filmed from different men's points of view as they openly discuss their desire to possess her. The images of the beautiful and seductive Astou contrast completely with those of the homely and maternal (read: asexual) Isa, setting up a typical 'mirror' contrast in the film. As the film progresses, Nacro cleverly deconstructs both of these stereotypes by turning the filmic gaze around to portray the women's point of view. As the candid scenes between Salif and Astou progress, it is Astou who is shown to be very much in command, and Salif is the one who is increasingly filmed from his wife's often mocking viewpoint, turning him into the object of her gaze.

The film's unjudgemental portrayal of prostitution, which highlights the reasons why Astou sells herself rather than showing her to be a victim, has shocked some Western critics, but is not uncommon in

31 José (Zeka) Laplaine and Idrissa Ouedraogo film theatre troupe's AIDS awareness campaigns in *Macadam Tribu* (DRC, 1997) and *Afrique mon Afrique* (Burkina Faso, 1995). A number of other films deal with the AIDS question, for example Henri Duparc's *Joli-coeur* (Côte d'Ivoire, 1992) and *Rue Princess* (1993), Kita Touré's *Les gestes ou la vie* series (Côte d'Ivoire, 1993); Ghaité Fofana's *Tèmèdy* (Guinea 1995), and Bouna Medoune Seye's *Saï Saï By* (Senegal, 1995).

Francophone African film. Indeed, whilst Nacro does not actually condone prostitution, her portrait of Astou is ultimately more empowering than tragic. (At the end of the film, however, Astou is 'absolved' as we learn that she is now working in theatre, an ironic reference to the 'acting' involved in her relations with her clients). In the absence of a controlling or profiteering male character, Astou is shown to use her sexuality uninhibitedly to her own ends, rather than simply being a victim of male oppression. Her comment that she 'gets all she wants from men' reinforces the film's assertion that it is Astou who manipulates the easily flattered and slightly ridiculous male characters. Like in many other Francophone African films that deal with the question of prostitution, it is the economic hardship that forces women into prostitution in the first place that is denounced, rather than male oppression or prostitution itself.[32] The film also insists on the fact that Astou is a mother too, rather than reductively defining her in terms of her trade.

Isa initially appears to be the perfect passive victim when she first discovers her husband's infidelity, but her angry smashing of the wedding video symbolically marks her liberation from the confines of her marital role. Following her friend Ade's advice, Isa decides to 'open her eyes' and act. Ade, we also learn, is regularly beaten by her husband, the film thus touching on another facet of women's oppression and condemning it.

From this moment on, Isa is increasingly filmed outside the home, without her daughter and her husband, becoming more of an individual in her own right. Despite Ade's advice that she consult a diviner in order to free herself of her 'rival', Isa quickly sees the diviner for what he really is – another womaniser, and rejects this male support, preferring to take matters into her own hands. Although one woman in the market typically blames and attacks Astou for her husband's infidelity whilst an old woman looks on and chuckles, 'Whatever happened to female solidarity? What an era!' Isa decides to go to meet Astou to try to understand the situation. This different reaction sets up another 'mirror' contrast in the film. When Astou finds Isa awaiting her, she immediately expects a confrontation and the tension is accentuated by the rapid sequence of reverse-angles which position the women in a confrontational face to face. As Isa insists on the peaceful nature of her visit, however, the framing and angles of the shots increasingly position the two women together, thus reflecting their growing confidence and solidarity.

Astou's description of the art of seduction traditionally handed down from mother to daughter in Senegal as a means of rivalling one's co-wives, evokes the way in which women are in fact encouraged by traditional polygamy to compete. However, Isa and Astou radically choose solidarity. When the surprised Salif arrives and finds Isa with Astou, the women remain imposingly together in the foreground, whilst Salif is framed in the weaker, lower position in the background. Isa denies his authority by refusing to get in the car on Salif's orders, leaving him little other option than to drive off, clearly humiliated, whilst the women stay together laughing like two old accomplices.

32 Ousmane Sembene's *Guelwaar* (Senegal, 1991), which denounces African countries' dependence on Western aid programmes, stresses the point that it is the films' two prostitute characters who enable their families to survive. Whilst the priest in the film absolves Hélène, saying, 'You are not guilty', Guelwaar insists that he prefers his daughter to be a prostitute than to depend on handouts. Her brother states, 'No one wants to see their sister or daughter become a prostitute, but, on the other hand, we have no right to condemn her. There is no virtue in want and poverty'. Referring to Djibril Diop Mambety's *Hyènes* (Senegal, 1992), Sheila Petty insists in her essay, 'Whose Nation Is It Anyhow? The Politics of Reading African Cinema in the West', that Diop Mambety's camera never presents the ex-prostitute Ramatou as a victim by filming her in high-angle shots or situating her in the weak position of the frame, as would be expected in Hollywood film. On the contrary, Ramatou is constantly centre frame and filmed in domineering low-angles as she literally and symbolically towers over the inhabitants of Colobane. (In FEPACI (ed), *L'Afrique et le Centenaire du Cinéma* (Paris & Dakar: Présence Africaine, 1995), pp 188–193.)

Fanta Régina Nacro, Puk Nini, *1995. Isa and Astou are gradually positioned in the same frame as their complicity grows and Astou reveals the art of seduction traditionally handed down from mother to daughter.*

(Courtesy of Fanta Nacro)

In the final sequence of the film, Ade, Isa and Astou are shown together in the same frontal shot in a bar, joking about men and their failings, when Salif walks out of one of the side rooms with a white prostitute. The alternation of the three-shots of the women looking at him witheringly, and the shots of him alone, shoulders sinking as he finds himself once more in the weak position, looking ridiculous, reinforces the solidarity of the women. Ultimately, in spite of its humour, the film thus offers a serious, positive image of both women's solidarity and a crushing indictment of the weakness of men. Like the women in Faye and Folly's films, Nacro's female characters clearly take their destinies in hand, relying on their own resources and one another, liberating themselves from the image of the passive victim. All of these films illustrate that Francophone Africa's women directors have radically different perspectives and images of women to propose than those habitually seen either in the West and in male-authored films. Surprising parallels can be found in a number of what can be described as 'womanist' films by male directors, as the following section will show.

'Womanist' films

A number of Francophone African male directors have chosen to explore some of the themes portrayed in the films discussed above, notably the theme of women's emancipation. In the process, they too have produced some interesting and progressive representations of African women that are generally a far cry from the dominant Western images of women as the passive objects of male desire. Unlike mainstream Western film narratives, these overtly independent female characters are rarely 'punished' for their stance, nor robbed of their humane or 'feminine' characteristics. The most sympathetic representations tend to be made by filmmakers who genuinely consider that female emancipation is the way forward for Africa. Malian filmmaker Cheick Oumar Sissoko has commented:

> At nearly every occasion where there has been a mass and democratic movement, women have been at the forefront, very often bearing arms. But their role in developing our nations is not acknowledged. You can't have developed states if you don't grant power and authority to women.[33]

Such filmmakers regularly express this desire to bring attention to African women's essential daily and political role. Some of the most progressive and combatant female characters are found in the works of the Malian directors Adama Drabo and Cheick Oumar Sissoko, no doubt reflecting the determining contribution Malian women made to bringing down the country's dictator in 1991.[34] The majority of the films focus on courageous, resisting women who either fight to survive in the face of adversity or, more commonly, refuse to accept the traditions that oppress them. On the one hand, the films pay homage to their diverse combats and, on the other, demystify and denounce the oppressive structures that still exist in certain African societies. Adama Drabo's *Taafe Fanga* (Mali, 1997) – which tellingly translates as 'Skirt Power' – and Cheick Oumar Sissoko's second film, *Finzan* (Mali, 1989), are both particularly radical in this respect.[35]

Taking inspiration from an incident that arises when a woman defies the man who rudely forbids her to sit with the men at a contemporary, urban storytelling session, the griot in Adama Drabo's *Taafe Fanga* narrates an ancient Dogon legend about a time when the Dogon women took over power. Through the legend, the director develops a series of reflections on male-female relations in Mali that clearly apply to the present.

The opening sequence immediately sets up the disruption of 'male order' that is developed throughout the rest of the film. As the beautiful, proud stranger deliberately turns her back on the women to join the men, she knowingly upsets the order of the compound where the male-female segregation reproduces the division between men and women in society at large. Ordered by one man to join the 'skirt-wearers', she upsets the established order by defiantly answering him back in a culture that would expect her to show deference. The positioning of the couple evokes the mounting tension as they are quite literally filmed face to face in an alternation of confrontational frontal shots. Finally, when the man goes to slap her in punishment, the woman unexpectedly blocks his blow and wrestles him to the ground, before proudly challenging the men by

33 Esi Eshun, 'Sissoko on GUIMBA', *Black Film Bulletin*, vol 3, 2/3, Summer/Autumn 1995, p 18. See too the author's interviews with Adama Drabo and Cheick Oumar Sissoko in appendices 1 and 7.

34 It is interesting to note that the judge at Moussa Traoré's trial – which in itself was exceptional as it was one of the rare times that an African dictator has been brought to court – was a woman. Women now hold a number of key governmental posts in Mali, other than the traditional Ministry for Women-type positions.

35 Both films were huge popular successes in Mali where they generated intense debate amongst audiences. The term 'taafe fanga' was even humorously coined in Bamako to describe any situation in which a woman defied a man or asserted her rights.

sitting herself with them. Neither a victim, nor reified – the camera constantly films her in level, frontal shots – the stranger's act is condoned by the amazed on-lookers' laughter and applause and the griot's singing of her exploit. The man and his order are ridiculed, setting up a pattern that is echoed throughout the film.

As the tale in the Dogon village of the past unfolds, Drabo focuses on the ways in which the men oppress the women, highlighting the women's point of view and expressing their begrudging acceptance of this state of affairs and their feelings of frustration. This situation is established right from the very first images of the tale sequence in which the women are seen at work whilst the men remain seated in the shade of the palaver spot. Ambara, one of the village elders, is seen scolding his elderly wife Timbé for failing to fulfil her marital duties properly – his bath water is cold. The announcement of his second young bride's imminent arrival, which comes almost in the guise of a punishment, is accompanied by domineering, high-angled shots of Timbé whose lowered eyes and silent, passive reaction clearly reveal her pain. Drabo's camera moves with Timbé as she visits her friend Nanton and her niece Yayèmé. Timbé's suffering and the other women's disgust at Ambara's behaviour are highlighted, the proximity of the camera drawing the spectator into an identification with Timbé's emotions. The indictment of Ambara's behaviour is echoed in the women's words. Timbé simply states, 'I thought better of him', and also later tells her niece, 'never really trust a man'. At this point, the women remain helplessly passive. When Yayèmé's young daughter asks her great aunt why they must put up with such injustices, all Timbé can answer is, 'Aren't we women?' The film so far portrays the women as resigned to the inevitability of their oppression.

Ambara's selfishness is immediately echoed by that of Yayèmé's husband Agro. Having promised to gather firewood for his wife, he comes back empty-handed, claiming to be fed up with being teased by the other village men for being 'a woman's slave'. Yayèmé's defiant reaction and the alternation of confrontational frontal shots of the couple echo the male–female conflict at the beginning of the film. On both occasions, the men react by physically striking out, except that now Agro actually beats Yayèmé until his daughter's cry brings him to his senses. Once again, Kouni's and Timbé's reactions to Agro's violence strongly condemn him and underline the solidarity between the women. The second time Agro beats Yayèmé, Kouni again asks why. Her mother's answer, 'Aren't I a woman', echoes Timbé's earlier answer and again confirms the women's resignation. In the moving scene that follows, however, in which mother and daughter are filmed together in an intimacy that is never shared with the men, Yayèmé promises to change things for her daughter, refusing to perpetuate these oppressive conditions.

Playing on the villagers' fear of the sacred Albarga mask captured by Yayèmé, Timbé and her niece hatch a plan to subjugate the men by reversing their roles. This upsetting of the established order echoes the defiant actions of the woman at the outset of the film and challenges the

Adama Drabo, Taafa Fanga, *1997.
Challenging patriarchal order as the
women take over and reverse the
traditional male–female roles.*
(Courtesy of Adama Drabo)

patriarchal order. The high-angled and panning shots of the women's circle as they sing and dance together to celebrate their victory over the men, emphasise their communion. Their action is affirmed by the griotte's song, 'Being a woman isn't a weakness; it's believing so that is', and by the women's ripping of their 'intimate' wrapper skirts which they transform into men's tops in a joyful act of liberation similar to the Western feminists' 'bra-burning' of the Seventies.

In the hilarious role-reversal sequences that follow, the men are forced to don their wives' wrapper skirts and to carry out the women's chores. By encouraging the audience to laugh at the men, their inadequacies, and their bad faith, Drabo uses satire to highlight the arduous nature of women's work and to reflect more generally on the question of power.

Having taken over, most of the women are happy to strut around in the men's clothes and to exploit their husbands in the same way that they themselves were exploited before. Indeed, in two long, amusing sequences, Drabo gives the female characters the space to mock their men gleefully and to express their desire for revenge. Timbé, however, who emerges as a charismatic and imposing leader, promotes a more forward-looking vision. Arguing that, 'The hyena learns to run on three legs in case it has an accident. Let's imitate it. Let's take advantage of our power to restore equality and sharing', she recognises that, whilst infinitely gratifying, this simple reversal of roles does not disrupt the pattern of domination and subordination and will therefore not provide a permanent solution to the women's situation. When she accompanies Ambara to meet his fifteen-year-old bride, Timbé uses her new position of power to give the girl the choice of whether she marries Ambara or not. The sequence not only condemns the arranged marriage system and the men's habit of taking very young brides, but thus also promotes women's choice. In a later sequence, Timbé's more constructive approach is again highlighted as she defends the importance of unity and of giving the women's power an economic base, an argument that can also clearly be read as an allegory for the question of economic power in post-colonial Africa. Timbé's foresight is symbolised by her position in the scene as she strides ahead of Yayèmé who, limps along behind her, literally divided from the forward-thinking Timbé by the stream.

At the end of the film, the women ultimately lose control of the mask, and the men regain their power, as Timbé feared. When the menfolk head back to the village together, one can only wonder if Agro and his friend's earlier realisation that they used to behave 'like monsters' will be remembered. Drabo's choice to respect the real ending of the legend with its re-establishing of the status quo, is not the reactionary one it might at first seen. The message of the film goes beyond the simple restoration of male power to reflect upon the prospects for women in the present and future. Kouni's final words, 'Mother, thanks to you, an eternal flame has been lit. We will win not power, but an equality that respects our differences', indeed reflect the film's ultimate argument that there will always be losers as long as the structures of domination and submission remain unchallenged. It is no accident that the young female protagonist pronounces these words, given that children often symbolise the hope for the future in African narratives. Drabo emphasises this point, explaining, 'I see this story is a warning to women. Women had the opportunity of taking over power in the past and they lost it ... We have to make sure that history doesn't repeat itself ... Defeat can be turned into victory if we correct the errors of the past.'[36] In the final images of the film, the griotte is seen symbolically positioned up on a rock in the foreground, watching the men filing back into the village below, while she sings loudly and prophetically, 'We have tasted freedom and we won't ever forget it. So beware!' The film ends optimistically with the message that women must and will be emancipated in Africa, whilst also warning that this emancipation (unlike that in the film), needs to be founded on a lasting modification of power relations. *Taafe Fanga* introduces a vital debate on the question of power and affords an empowering and uplifting representation of its women, whose force and dynamism leaves the spectator in no doubt that they will ultimately triumph.

Focusing principally on Nanyuma's battle against her traditional remarriage to her dead husband's clownish younger brother Bala, Cheick Oumar Sissoko's second feature film *Finzan* also focuses on a number of issues relating to women, notably their struggle to have their own say in a society that traditionally silences them. The film integrates the rhythms and styles of orature and Mali's traditional Koteba theatre into a realist vein that at times borders on the documentary. Rather than being used in a naturalistic manner, the film's realism more radically offers 'the means of reflecting on and analysing the socially constructed world, in

36 Interview with the author. Ouaga-dougou, February 1997.

Cheik Oumar Sissoko, Finzan, 1989. Nanyuma sits apart from her grieving co-wives, not saddened by the death of a husband she was forced to marry.
(Courtesy of Cheik Oumar Sissoko)

order to produce an understanding of its constitutive forces and underlying contradictions'.[37]

The opening extract of a United Nations' report on the double gender and social oppression facing women around the world unambiguously delineates the position of the director and his film. As the narrative unfolds, Nanyuma's silent but firm refusal to go to see her sick, elderly husband immediately reveals the nature of her feelings towards him. When he dies, Nanyuma's lack of grief is contrasted with that of her co-wives, as she sits apart from the crying women and is isolated from them in her own frame. When even her mother reproaches her insensitivity, Nanyuma quietly but forcefully asks whether her mother needs reminding of the circumstances of her wedding, and of her eight years of marital hell. Nanyuma's attitude thus already contradicts her mother's traditional answer that, 'patience and resignation are our only options', and is confirmed throughout the film which promotes a different, more active position.

When Bala seeks permission to marry his brother's widow in accordance with the custom, two figures – Dugutigi, the village chief, and Nanyuma's father, who represent patriarchal order in the film – immediately comply without consulting Nanyuma, despite the fact that Bala is clearly a depraved clown.[38] Dugutigi's various discussions with his griot reveal the chief's reactionary stance *vis-à-vis* women, allowing Sissoko to explore traditional attitudes that oppress women. In answer to his griot's question of why women never hold power, Dugutigi declares, 'All power is based on knowledge and secrecy. Do you know any women with these qualities?' The chief is shown to rely without question on sweeping commonplaces to exclude the women from the decisions that concern them.

Nanyuma's mother reveals that she too has been excluded from the decision on the remarriage of her daughter, explaining that Nanyuma's father has merely informed her of it. When Nanyuma returns to her parents for support, her father immediately orders her to go back to join her new husband, preferring to uphold the patriarchal system than to stand by his own daughter. Nanyuma goes into hiding, refusing to comply with the tradition and the men's authority in an effort to preserve her 'dignity as a woman', as she explains to Bengali, the man she wants to marry. Her father retaliates by throwing Nanyuma's mother and daughter out of his house. The two women still refuse to divulge Nanyuma's whereabouts, preferring to sacrifice their own well-being in an act of solidarity that contrasts with the men's behaviour. Nanyuma's young daughter is the only one who dares to criticise the system, as she demands to know whether women are people or slaves, and admonishes her grandfather in an irreverent gesture that emphasises the old man's stubbornness.

Despite the villagers' efforts to track her down, Nanyuma manages to escape to the town where she goes to seek the support of her eldest brother-in-law. Like her father, this man also refuses to defy tradition and puts an end to her rebellion by having her tied up and escorted back to the village along with his own 'wayward' daughter Fili. Sissoko clearly

37 Christine Gledhill, 'Recent Developments in Feminist Criticism', in G. Mast & M. Cohen (eds.), *Film Theory and Criticism*, third edition (New York: Oxford University Press, 1985), p 824.

38 As Manthia Diawara writes, 'For spectators in West Africa, Bala's role is recognisable from the traditional Koteba theatre: he is a buffoon whose trademarks embody cowardice, jealousy and greed. In folktales, the hyena often occupies the same role. Furthermore, the name Bala signifies stupidity, crudeness, and greed in Bambara ... The acting of Bala (played by Oumar Namory Keita, an actor from the Koteba in Mali) is exaggerated in the film to underscore its links with theatre.' (Manthia Diawara, *African Cinema: politics and culture* (Bloomington & Indianapolis: Indiana University Press, 1992), p 145).

denounces the brutality of this treatment by focusing on the rope and on Nanyuma's crying face, juxtaposing these close-ups with shots of the tethered goat (seen also at the beginning of the film). The disapproval of the on-lookers on the train and in the lorry add to this denunciation; when the passengers on the train insist that Nanyuma be untied, they also condone her defiant slapping of one of her escorts.

Back in the village, Nanyuma increases her acts of resistance, despite the weight of the patriarchal system against her. In the scene in which Bala bribes a local government official to sign the marriage act against her will, for example, the men have to physically force her to put her fingerprint on the act. Nanyuma defiantly spits in the corrupt official's face in protest. When Bala later tries to possess Nanyuma, she forcibly rejects him, again refuting the traditional male right over his wife's body. This assertion of her own will is accentuated by Nanyuma's progressively central position in the frame. This domination is temporarily thwarted as Bala finally manages to pin her down on the bed, the low-angle shot making him appear all the more menacing, his body occupying most of the frame. Nanyuma's resistance to the male order is again reinforced by the shot composition, when she pulls a knife on Bala, sending him scuttling into the corner and restoring her in the dominant position.

Sissoko also courageously explores a second taboo – that of female circumcision. In once scene, one of the village girls realises that Fili, who has been sent to stay with her uncle's family, has not been circumcised. The news quickly spreads around the whole village, eliciting widespread astonishment and a range of reactions and comments that enable the filmmaker to explore the reasons behind the tradition, whilst at the same time highlighting its dangers and condemning the practice. The reaction of Fili's uncle reinforces the way in which the men silence the women even in matters of utmost and intimate concern. As Fili tries to explain the medical reasons why she was not circumcised, her uncle refuses to believe her, sending a messenger to check with her father who is 'obviously' a more reliable source of authority, threatening to beat her when she insists that she is happy as she is.

Fili's explanations divide the village women. Some support her, while others defend circumcision on traditional grounds, revealing that women are as capable of perpetuating oppressive practices as men. A significant number of women are galvanised by the marriage and circumcision questions, however, as is apparent when a group of them finally go to confront Dugutigi, protesting that they are tired of never being consulted, and effectively challenging his authority.

This lack of consultation was demonstrated earlier in the film when Dugutigi tells the women, who demand the right to attend and speak at a public meeting with the government officials, that they must return to their cooking. The psychological division between Dugutigi and the women in the second confrontation is demonstrated by the way in which they are systematically filmed in separate frames. Dugutigi clearly perceives the women's attempt to give him advice as a threat to his authority, and responds contemptuously, 'The dog really has grown

FINZAN
CHEICK OUMAR SISSOKO

horns! Have you gone mad or are you trying to teach me my duty!' Unmoved, the women insist that Nanyuma be free to choose her own husband. They also inform the chief that Fili's explanations have enlightened them about the consequences of female circumcision, leaving them divided on what attitude to take. Dugutigi angrily refuses to take their views into account, insisting that only the men's opinion matters. Faced with his intransigence, the women finally revolt, rejecting his authority. They are fed up with being treated as inferiors, and warn the shocked Dugutigi that if he refuses to rethink Fili's case and does not support Nanyuma, the menfolk will be 'banned from their beds', thereby wielding the little power they have. Their momentary domination is highlighted by the empowering low-angle shot of the women's group.

As the film draws to its conclusion, Fili's uncle decides to uphold tradition and have Fili circumcised, despite her father's refusal and her own vehement protests. Rejecting her uncle's authority, Fili turns to Nanyuma for support, knowing that she will understand her actions. Nanyuma herself is on the verge of leaving the village, determined to escape Bala once and for all, even if this means cutting herself off from her family. As in most African cultures, this is considered to be one of the worst things that can happen to someone. In the brutal scene that follows, filmed almost exclusively in crushingly oppressive high-angle shots, the pro-circumcision group of women grab Fili and carry out the operation by force, violating Fili's body and wishes. Utterly disgusted, Nanyuma can do no more than leave the village, paying no heed to Bala's flood of tears, and declaring as she goes, 'We women are like birds with no tree to rest on. We have lost all hope. All we can do now is stand up and hitch up our wrappers. Our societies' progress depends on our liberation.' The film ends on a freeze frame of her walking into the distance. At least she has won the battle and her closing words act as a rallying cry to all women that they must take matters into their own hands if their societies are to progress. The film clearly condones Nanyuma's radical behaviour and her battle to impose her own will, and condemns the oppressive violation of women's rights and the silencing of their voices.

A wide range of other films highlight their female characters' struggles against oppressive patriarchal traditions, foregrounding their dignity. Many explore the question of arranged marriages, a contemporary variation on the oral tradition's familiar 'difficult girl' theme. When Halimé's father accepts the elderly but wealthy Abdoulaye Béchir's request to take his daughter as his second wife, in Mahamat Saleh Haroun's short film *Maral Tanié* (Chad, 1994), the camera closely films Halimé's face as she objects. She continues to resist after the couple are married, by refusing to sleep with her husband. The film condones her action; in one scene, for example, the camera tracks slowly with her as she walks alone in the woods, prioritising her voice as she reflects, 'I have to break free from this man ... It's my body. I'll keep on making him so angry that he repudiates me, and then I'll be free'. Although Halimé's plan finally works, she only just escapes being raped by Abdoulaye and incurs the murderous wrath of her father, who again prefers to uphold the patriarchal status quo than to support his own daughter.

Other films, such as Jean-Pierre Dikongue-Pipa's *Muna Moto* (Cameroon, 1975), and Idrissa Ouedraogo's *Tilaï* (Burkina Faso, 1990) discussed in Chapter 3, also provide critiques of forced marriage, focusing on the way in which young couples are prevented from being together when the woman is married off to an older man. All of these films tend to end tragically, even if the long final close-up of Halimé staring defiantly and unflinchingly at her father/the camera in *Maral Tanié* powerfully conveys her refusal to submit to the father, condemning the exaggerated and unjustified nature of such behaviour. Unlike classical Western cinema and the traditional oral tales, which frequently punish female characters who defy the patriarchal structures, however, these films' tragic endings serve more to criticise the traditions, not their heroines' behaviour. This position in itself demands for change.

A number of other films, only a few of which can be discussed here, highlight the role their female characters play in diverse resistance struggles. Women's mobilisation often contrasts with male characters' passivity or capitulation, as shown in the discussion of the 'colonial confrontation' films discussed in Chapter 4. Such female characters frequently challenge the patriarchal authority of either their own fathers, or their oppressive and corrupt leaders.

Med Hondo's *Sarraounia* (Mauritania, 1986) tells how the Aznas princess Sarraounia successfully resists the onslaught of the French colonial invaders, contrasting her intransigence with the other chiefs' capitulation and connivance. Hondo's decision to focus on a woman warrior who leads her men and, more unusually, her women soldiers to victory, clearly moves away from the image of the passive, subjugated female and stresses the instrumental role of women in the resistance struggle.

Sarraounia's warrior qualities in no way rob her of her femininity. Much emphasis is placed on the absence of her dead mother in her infancy, however, and the way in which her uncle trains her as if she were a boy. Her uncle's words, 'You were fed on mare's milk, not woman's milk. You have not been raised by women', stress her difference from other women. This is developed by by his insistence that, 'man will obey you, not command you. He will give you brief pleasure, but he won't be an arrogant lord.' It would seem that Hondo's heroine only achieves her powerful warrior status by being exceptional, not like other women. Whilst she is unquestionably a strong female character, she tends to represent the fight against colonialism, rather than women's emancipation. In the film, she is more of a mythical icon than a flesh and blood person. The systematically low-angle shots of the grown-up Sarraounia, her face hidden by a mask, and they way in which her enemies' constant evocations give her a mythical presence even when she is absent from the screen, add to this reification.

Souleymane Cissé's *Waati* (Mali, 1995) also highlights the key role women have played in resisting oppression as it traces Nandi's initiatory journey from the horrors of apartheid South Africa to West Africa and back. The film focuses on Nandi's courage and is a homage to the strength of South African women. Nandi's grandmother, who represents a sort of ancestral, guiding matriarchal force, refers to this strength, telling Bra Solly, 'women will change this country'.[39] In the first part of the film, it is indeed Nandi who confronts the oppressive order represented by her father's brutal boss and the racist policeman on the beach as she asserts her rights in a country that refuses to recognise black people. Cissé frequently opts for close-up shots of Nandi's face and

39 Commenting on the research he carried out in South Africa for the film, Souleymane Cissé stated: 'Partout j'ai recueilli des témoignages unanimes ... sur le fait que la véritable résistance dans ce pays était due en grande partie aux femmes ... D'ailleurs les Afrikaners craignaient davantage les femmes noires que les hommes' ['Everywhere I went, I gathered unanimous accounts ... that said that the real resistance in this country came mainly from the women ... Moreover, the Afrikaners feared black women more than they did the men'], (in Gaillac-Morgue, 'Entretien avec Souleymane Cissé', le 21 avril 1995. Published in the press book of the film *Waati*).

eyes as she stares unflinchingly at her adversaries throughout the film, emphasising her combative inner strength and resolve.

In Cissé's earlier, politically committed film *Finyé* (Mali, 1982), Batrou, the military Governor's daughter, confronts the repressive patriarchal order her father represents both within the home and the country at large.[40] In the family space, Batrou defies her father's order that she stop seeing her student boyfriend Bâ. On a broader political level, she also ignores her father's warning that she must stay out of student agitation, which similarly represents a challenge to the authority of the military regime and, by extension, to him. When the army violently represses the students' revolt, two women come to Batrou's rescue, risking their own lives to defend her in a characteristic display of female solidarity and a rejection of oppression.

Imprisoned with the other students, Batrou eventually finds herself face to face with her father, who has come to press the students into submission. Bâ and Batrou's refusal to capitulate to the authorities positions Batrou in direct confrontation with her father, the private and public patriarchy combined in one figure. Defying him directly and in public, she uses his official title to show the psychological divide between them. She even questions the filial tie, declaring, 'Now that I see things clearly, our conceptions have diverged and I wonder if your blood really runs in my veins'. Batrou renounces her father's authority over her as his daughter and political subject, as she refuses to submit to his will and the domineering order of the regime.

Like Batrou, Rama in Ousmane Sembene's *Xala* (Senegal, 1974) confronts her father and the order he represents. Rama is a positive synthesis of the other principal female characters. Her mother Adja symbolises the archetypal proud, silently suffering African woman, at one extreme, dressed in traditional Senegalese clothing, consistently loyal to her often unworthy husband, and faithfully fulfilling her senior wife duties even when these are painful to her personally. At the other extreme, is her father's far more rapacious, jealous and inconsistent second wife Oumi, who dresses in a Western wig, sunglasses and clothing, and who represents the shallow new African bourgeoisie who revel in all things Western. Rama, who sometimes dresses in Western-style jeans, sometimes in a Senegalese *boubou*, is a young, progressive university student whose political engagement is symbolised by her posters of the liberation theorist and resistance fighter Amilcar Cabral, and of Samory, who fought against French colonialism in West Africa at the end of the nineteenth century. As her clothing suggests, Rama is capable of benefiting from the positive elements of Western culture whilst at the same time affirming her Senegalese identity.

Rama's combative spirit is evident as soon as she appears in the film, advising her mother to divorce her father (who is about to take a third wife) or at least not to attend the wedding as duty requires. She challenges her father and his values by pointedly answering his French greetings in Wolof, and later refuses to drink his imported French mineral water in a gesture of rejection of Senegal's neo-colonial ties with France.

40 At home, Batrou's polygamous father is an authoritarian who resorts to beating his defiant youngest wife into submission. Agna's unfaithfulness also represents a challenge to his patriarchal authority.

Her father's third marriage disgusts her, causing her to declare that all men are bastards, and to refuse to withdraw the insult. Instead of showing deference to her father as would be expected, Rama stands to face him, announcing, 'Polygamous men are liars'. As father and daughter are filmed face to face in an antagonistic close-up shot, she repeats her words, refusing to succumb to his menacing show of force and refusing to accept the patriarchal order represented by both her father and the male-instigated system of polygamy.

Xala's evocation of this question allows Sembene to highlight the suffering that polygamous marriages cause to women, and to denounce men's egotistical motivations for taking several wives. N'gone, El Hadj's beautiful young third bride, is simply a trophy attesting to his successful status. Sembene intentionally gives her no voice and no existence beyond her marital role in the film. N'gone's objectification is particularly clear when El Hadj is seen standing next to a clothes dummy wearing N'gone's wig, which is almost interchangeable with the young woman herself.

Xala's portrait of the tensions caused by polygamy finds an echo in a number of Francophone African films. Henri Duparc's bawdy comedy *Bal Poussière* (Côte d'Ivoire, 1988), adopts a light-hearted approach to the question. It ridicules the male protagonist Demi-Dieu, whose polygamous paradise is upset when he takes a strong-willed, 'liberated' sixth wife whom he cannot control. When Demi-Dieu first sets eyes on Binta, he is determined to possess her as if she were no more than an object. She immediately reveals her strong character when Demi-Dieu asks her father for her hand in marriage, sending back the answer that she is the one who will decide. On their first meeting, it is Demi-Dieu who is filmed seated slavishly at Binta's feet, and Binta only agrees to marry him on the condition that she can finish her studies. Once married, Binta controls all affairs, making life hell for Demi-Dieu by wreaking havoc in the once calm household and aggravating the rivalry between certain wives. When Binta's trumpeter boyfriend comes to the village, she promptly leaves with him, asserting her own freedom and will right to the end.

Finally, several films, like those of the women directors discussed here, focus on the pivotal role of women in the daily battle simply to survive and feed their families. Abdoulaye Ascofare's film *Faraw! Une Mère des Sables* (Mali, 1997), whose title, derived from Songhai word for 'fatigue', means 'situation d'impasse ou de blocage absolu' ['a dead-end or completely blocked situation'], narrates twenty-four hours in the life of Zamiatou as she struggles to provide for her three children and hopelessly sick husband.[41] Throughout the film, Zamiatou is filmed in an endless cycle of housework as she tries to control her demanding, squabbling sons whilst also tending to her husband. She is seen on the move, begging for credit at the store, or trying to find work. Only her teenage daughter Hareyrata helps her in a characteristic display of female solidarity which, at the same time, suggests that Hareyrata is being primed to step into the same role as her mother. Zamiatou is often harsh with her daughter, whilst at the same time being completely indulgent

41 Abdoulaye Ascofare. Press book of the film *Faraw*.

with her tiresome sons, a difference of treatment that undoubtedly reflects a traditional cultural attitude that prioritises male children and spares them from domestic work. This contrast is particularly evident in the opening sequence, with close-up shots of Hareyrata's tired face as she arrives home from fetching water cut against shots of her brothers playing football together. Hareyrata's repeated attempts to defend herself from their contemptuous insults constantly meet with her mother's disapproval, thus perpetuating the boys' sense of domination over women, and implicating women in its continuation.

Despite these difficult conditions, Zamiatou maintains a sense of dignity throughout the film. When her daughter asks to be allowed to go to work in the expatriate quarters outside the village to help support the family, Zamiatou refuses, knowing that this would mean Hareyrata becoming the sexual plaything of an expatriate boss. The film clearly illustrates how the single expatriate men take advantage of their local maids, thereby constituting a rare critique of how certain European men continue to treat African women.

Preferring to protect her daughter, Zamiatou sacrifices herself and sets off on foot across the vast open dunes to seek the help of the man she nearly married in the past, Marou. At the same time, she proudly refuses his attempts to revive their relationship, thus asserting her own independence. With Marou's help, however, Zamiatou begins the arduous task of gathering and selling spring water in the desert. The film ends with a frontal close-up of Zamiatou's happy face the following morning when she gets up to see the silhouette of Hareyrata heading off into the distance in her place, in another gesture of solidarity with her exhausted mother. Although the film does not actively promote a change in Zamiatou and Hareyrata's self-sacrificing condition in the way that many other films do, it provides a realistic portrait of the resolve of many African women and the active role they play in assuring their families' survival.

It is clear from the above that, like the filmmakers whose work has been discussed throughout this book, Francophone African female directors and male directors sympathetic to their cause use the medium to formulate a range of alternative, empowering representations of African women. In so doing, their work challenges the reductive stereotypes and lack of representation of women in Africa, and constructs new images that highlight the key roles that women play. By focusing on female characters, these films centre their perspectives and give women the space to articulate their own concerns.

Like all of the works examined here, these alternative representations can be seen as part of the overall effort to reconstruct and revalue Francophone Africa's disfigured identities in film. By focusing on women's issues, rights and roles, these directors continue African traditions of politically and morally committed artistic expression. The relatively new film medium is used to expose and analyse the ways in which the traditional structures and codes affect women, proposing change where these structures are deemed oppressive. Most striking, however, is the empowering nature of these images which systematically highlight the ways in which female characters instigate change and defend their own rights and choices, irrespective of family and/or traditional societal pressures. Ultimately, these films by women or about women offer a radically new perspective on their lives and concerns. By conveying their powerful and challenging viewpoints and centring their voices they counter commonly held male and/or Western preconceptions about Africa's women.

Conclusion

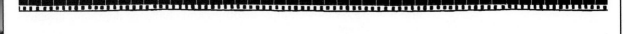

It clearly emerges from this study that filmmakers from the sub-Saharan Francophone African countries have produced a wide range of rich and challenging films in the forty or so years since African independence, despite the logistical, structural, and financial difficulties they face.

Whilst their themes and styles are varied and constantly evolving, all of the films discussed here reflect a continuing, almost obsessive desire to address the inescapable question of how to represent a continent that has been so categorically vilified by the dominant discourses and imagery of the West. This observation is born out by the filmmakers' own frequently reiterated comments. Cheick Oumar Sissoko has remarked, for example, that, 'we have things to show ... important things that need to be taken into account. We aren't what people have always shown us to be ... Africa has a wealth of very great cultures, of great civilisations, that ought to be respected.'[1] The prominent Burkinabè actor Rasmane Ouedraogo has stressed the importance of formulating positive images of African realities from an African point of view in order to challenge the hegemony of Western imagery and to counter the absence of African perspectives in the world. He comments that, 'up until now, the image people have had of us has not been explicit, clear, or objective. We have to make films that say who we are, and maybe then we will be able to understand one another.'[2] Western discourse proves to have been unwittingly instrumental in the development of Francophone African film, creating a polarity that African directors have urgently sought to deconstruct with alternative representations of their own, as Souleymane Cissé has made clear:

'La première tâche des cinéastes africains est d'affirmer que les gens d'ici sont des êtres humains, et de faire connaître celles de nos valeurs qui pourraient servir aux autres. La génération qui nous suivra s'ouvrira sur d'autres aspects du cinéma. Notre devoir à nous est de faire comprendre que les blancs ont menti par leurs images' ['African filmmakers' first task is to show that people here are human beings and to help people discover the African values that can be of service to others. The following generation will branch out into other aspects of film. Our duty is to make people understand that white people have lied through their images'][3]

In this particularly charged postcolonial context, filmmaking emerges as a radically political act – that of appropriating the right to represent oneself and one's concerns on the screen. These films can first and

1 Interview with the author. Ouagadougou, February 1995.

2 Interview with the author. Ouagadougou, February 1995.

3 Speaking in Rithy Panh's documentary *Souleymane Cissé* (Cambodia-France, 1991).

Conclusion

foremost be seen to offer an often-challenging, alternative African perspective as they give voice and presence to hitherto silenced or mis-represented African characters. Whether rearticulating history and memory from an African point of view, representing immigrant popula-tions in Europe, or focusing on women's rarely acknowledged pivotal role and struggles, all of the films discussed here thus create alternative, often empowering, and at times radical representations that explore, redefine and revalue Africa's multiple identities and challenge dominant absences and preconceptions.

This essentially committed style of filmmaking, which never excludes aesthetic pleasure or entertainment, reflects local conceptions of both the community-based role of the arts and artists and the dual aesthetic and functional nature of the arts, as has been shown in both the discussions of Francophone Africa's socio-cultural contexts and local oral traditions. Directors frequently use the cinema in a manner that is closer to local conceptions of the role of the arts and the artist than it is to Western understandings of film. As this book's focus on the relations between orature and film has demonstrated, the relatively recently imported film medium has been very much integrated into the existing cultural environment. Local narrative traditions and aesthetic codes have inspired or been adapted and integrated into the universal film medium to reflect African cultural sensibilities. This has given Franco-phone African film its specificity without limiting or confining its expressive possibilities.

The analysis of both the cultural context and the postcolonial political climate in which Francophone African filmmaking was born and has developed demonstrates the centrality of the cultural identity, representa-tion and voice questions. It has highlighted the many ways in which such questions inform both the agendas and the styles of a wide range of filmmakers in the region. But whilst Francophone African cinema is clearly deeply marked by the political and artistic concerns of the postcolonial climate in which it was born, filmmaking has continued to develop. After favouring an overtly committed social realist vein in the early years, cinematic themes and styles in the region have increasingly diversified. New genres have developed and filmmakers have begun to experiment with new forms in an effort to enhance the aesthetic quality and narrative pleasure of their works and, above all, better to reflect their ever-changing identities, realities, and concerns. Particularly striking in this respect has been the emergence of film forms that integrate and portray both the region's 'traditional' and 'hybrid' urban cultural codes and styles and, on a wider international level, that reflect the rooting of the African community in Europe.

Whilst the overwhelming concern with the question of representation and identity forms a common and unifying preoccupation, these works are characterised by their diversity and by their directors' individual, evolving styles. Many younger filmmakers continue to consider it important to impose their images and to explore African identities in film, as Abderrahmane Sissako confirms:

People have always done things in our place, they have always forced things on us … today, they are forcing images on us … It's another form of acculturation. If Africans can manage to make films and to fight back, if other images get made and screened, that's a victory.[4]

Such filmmakers tend to be less inhibited by a distorting Western gaze, and are thus perhaps freer in their choice of agendas and styles. As their often vibrant, hybrid and increasingly diverse cinematic works indicate, many of the younger directors more readily embrace both Western and African influences and cultural forms that exist side-by-side in contemporary African society. Whilst the question of representation clearly remains pertinent to contemporary Francophone African film, these more recent developments suggest that film is constantly evolving and increasingly polymorphous, as are the diverse and multiple identities articulated and explored in it. The diversity, inventiveness, aesthetic richness and evolution of film in the region contradicts the reductive Euro-American tendency to treat African film as a homogeneous and static entity.

The effort to contextualise Francophone African film throughout this work has highlighted the importance of taking the directors' own aims and agendas into account in order to understand filmmakers' creative choices. By focusing on the ways in which the cinema is perceived in Africa and on the kinds of cultural codes it reflects, this contextualisation has confirmed that the common tendency to apply Western critical paradigms to work from divergent cultural zones can be both misleading and reductive. At the same time, it has drawn on other pertinent paradigms, such as representation, feminist and postcolonial theory, to help develop a more flexible critical approach capable of encompassing divergent cultural references.

By analysing Francophone African film through what has been identified here as the fundamentally important prism of the representation question, Francophone West African film has therefore been shown to offer audiences a wealth of challenging perspectives that portray the African continent in a new light and develop a range of exciting new cinematic codes. This book situates Francophone African film in its rightful cinematic place and opens the way to a deeper understanding of the issues involved in postcolonial Francophone African film.

4 Interview with the author. Ouagadougou, February 1995.

Interview I
Adama Drabo director

Ougadougou, February 1997

The film *Taafe Fanga* is structured like a tale. What made you decide to take inspiration from the oral traditions? What role can orature play in African film?

I adopted the tale format because the film's story is taken from a legend that I heard on the radio one day about thirteen years ago. A professor was talking about Dogon cosmogony and mentioned in the passing a time in Dogon history when the women took over power using the first mask man possessed. I found that extraordinary. I thought it was a superb subject. The very next day, I went to the National Library and dug up everything I could get my hands on. I found the legend and, six months later, had written a play. When I decided to adapt it to the screen, I had a choice – to adapt it to the present, or to treat it in a more traditional manner, setting it further back in the past. The second option wouldn't have allowed me to raise the contemporary male-female question, so I decided to go for something more timeless that could have equally well taken place two centuries ago as in an African village the day after tomorrow. I then thought about how to handle the structure of the narrative. I decided that it would be better for a griot to take us back into the legend, rather than me, a contemporary man. Griots have deeply marked me. I already narrated my first film, *Ta Dona*, in the same way that a griot would have. I never said so explicitly, but this gave the film a certain form that people liked, but which not everyone understood. A lot of people didn't realise that I tried to put myself in the griot's shoes because I listened to griots' stories throughout my whole childhood, griots who show up, who start telling stories that they can decide to break off at any moment to address the listeners directly, to ask them questions, before taking off in another direction, controlling the digression before bringing it back to the original story. I tried to follow the same procedure in *Ta Dona*. You start the story off, head in one direction, you appear to stray, circle round, come back and take up the original story again. As few people understood that, I decided to show the griot this time, to make it much clearer, even if the film is more linear as a result.

People often say that African filmmakers are like modern griots. Do you think that your filmmaking role is similar to that of the griot?

Yes. I at times identify with the griot's way of telling stories. As the griot says at the start of my film, it's my duty to capture the past to prepare the present and the future. African filmmakers work in the same spirit, in the

Le film *Taafe Fanga* est présenté sous forme de conte. Pourquoi avez-vous choisi de vous vous référer aux traditions orales? Quel rôle peuvent-elles jouer dans le cinéma africain?

J'ai choisi la forme du conte parce que l'histoire du film est tirée d'une légende que j'ai entendue un jour à la radio, il y a à peu près treize ans. Un professeur parlait de la cosmogonie dogon et, au passage, il racontait qu'il y a eu un moment dans l'histoire des Dogons où les femmes ont pris le pouvoir à partir du premier masque possédé par l'homme. Je trouvais ça extraordinaire. Je me suis dit que c'était un sujet superbe et le lendemain je suis allé à la bibliothèque nationale où j'ai fouillé et lu tout ce qui me tombait sous la main. J'ai retrouvé la légende, et au bout de six mois, j'avais écrit une pièce de théâtre. Quand j'ai décidé de l'adapter au cinéma, j'avais un choix : l'adapter et en faire quelque chose d'actuel, ou la traiter de la façon la plus traditionnelle, la plus éloignée dans le temps. Or, cette deuxième solution ne me permettait pas de poser le problème contemporain de la femme et de l'homme. J'ai donc décidé de faire quelque chose d'intemporel, qui pouvait autant se passer il y a deux siècles, que dans un village africain après-demain. Ensuite, je me suis demandé comment j'allais aborder la forme du récit. Je me suis dit que pour rentrer dans la légende, il valait mieux que ça ne soit pas moi, un contemporain, qui la raconte, mais un griot qui nous entraînerait dans le récit. Je suis très marqué par le griot. J'avais déjà raconté mon premier film *Ta Dona* comme un griot l'aurait raconté. Je ne l'avais pas dit explicitement, mais cela a donné une forme particulière à ce film, que les gens ont aimé, mais que beaucoup n'ont pas compris. Ils n'avaient pas compris que je me suis mis à la place du griot parce que, pendant toute mon enfance, j'ai écouté des récits du griot, ce griot qui vient, qui commence une histoire qu'il peut interrompre à tout moment, qui va vers son auditoire pour lui poser des questions, pour partir dans une autre direction, mais qu'il contrôle et qu'il ramène à son histoire. Dans *Ta Dona*, j'ai essayé de suivre le même processus. On lance l'histoire, on prend un chemin, on a l'impression qu'on s'éloigne, on fait un tour, on revient, et on reprend l'histoire. Comme beaucoup n'ont pas compris cela, je me suis dit que cette fois-ci je montrerais le griot, pour que cela soit beaucoup plus clair, plus net, même si, du coup, le film est plus linéaire.

On dit souvent que les cinéastes africains sont en quelque sorte des griots modernes. Est-ce que vous avez l'impression que votre rôle de cinéaste est proche de celui du griot?

Oui. Dans la manière de raconter des histoires, je m'identifie à certains moments au griot. Comme dit le griot au début du film, mon devoir est d'emprisonner le passé pour préparer le présent

183

et l'avenir. Les cinéastes africains travaillent dans la même mouvance, dans le même but, même si chaque réalisateur a sa position, ses objectifs. Personnellement, je ne veux pas faire des films que pour la beauté, que pour l'esthétique. Je suis devant un peuple qui attend beaucoup de moi parce que c'est une chance exceptionnelle d'être derrière la caméra dans nos pays, et il faut en profiter chaque fois que c'est possible afin d'amener les gens à la réflexion, d'amener les gens à se poser des questions, à se surpasser, donc de participer à l'effort de reconstruction de nos pays. Je me donne cette mission en plus du rôle de conteur, de rapporteur de l'histoire africaine. En fin de compte, c'est la même mission que celle du griot qui, dans son temps, a fait la même chose. Les griots ont conseillé les empereurs, ils ont suivi la marche de leurs empires. C'est à peu près le même objectif. Nous voulons avoir un peu plus de présence dans la destinée de nos pays.

Vous estimez donc que le cinéaste a un rôle important à jouer dans sa société. Est-ce que vous êtes au courant des réactions de votre public ? Avez-vous l'impression que vous réussissez à faire réfléchir les gens grâce au cinéma ?
Oui, quand *Ta Dona* est sorti au Mali, en prédisant la chute du dictateur avant sa véritable chute, en prédisant que le pays entier allait brûler avant qu'il ne brûle, le public malien a compris le film comme un signe prémonitoire. Après vingt-trois ans de pouvoir militaire, dix tentatives de coup d'état, le peuple malien avait commencé à désespérer. Rien ne marchait plus, les gens se disaient que le dictateur allait rester toute sa vie à la tête du pays, ils commençaient à se décourager. Il n'avait plus que la jeunesse, les étudiants et les femmes qui gardaient l'espoir. Alors, quand le film est sorti et que l'on a compris le message, on disait que c'était peut-être un signe. Il y a eu des manifestations et, finalement, le dictateur est tombé. Beaucoup m'ont attribué sa fin, me disait que j'avais fait chuter le régime. Les gens me félicitent toujours pour *Ta Dona*, ils me disent souvent qu'ils me soutiennent, donc je ne peux pas être plus heureux. On m'a souvent dit que j'avais pris trop de risques, parce que le dictateur lui-même m'avait convoqué au palais pour lui projeter le film et, douze jours après, ce fut sa chute. Les gens me sont reconnaissants pour ce film. Seulement, maintenant, ils ont peur quand je dis 'Taafe Fanga', le pouvoir de la femme, parce qu'autant ils étaient d'accord avec le message de *Ta Dona*, autant, là, ils n'ont pas forcément envie de changer les choses !

Justement, *Taafe Fanga* traite du pouvoir de la femme. Quelle est la position de la femme dans la société malienne d'aujourd'hui et pourquoi avez-vous choisi cette thématique-là ?
Je marche avec le peuple malien. Je suis là, je vis les mêmes problèmes. Je suis ouvert, j'emmagasine, je ramasse des choses partout, et quand je suis rempli d'une impression, je l'exprime par un film. C'est ça ma manière de vivre. Après la chute de la dictature, je me suis dit que j'avais voulu sa chute et que c'était arrivé. La démocratie s'est installée au Mali. Nous avons une vingtaine de radios libres, trente titres de journaux. On peut aller à la radio critiquer le régime ; si l'on ne l'insulte pas, on n'est pas inquiété. Donc, même si elle n'est pas parfaite, il

same direction, even if each director has his or her position and objectives. Personally, I don't want to make films just for their beauty, just for the aesthetics. I am accountable to a people who expect a lot of me because you're incredibly lucky to find yourself behind a camera in our countries and you have to make the most of it every time you can to encourage people to think, to encourage people to ask themselves questions, to surpass themselves, and thus to participate in the effort to reconstruct our countries. That's the mission I give myself in addition to being a storyteller, to telling African history. At the end of the day, it's the same as the griot's mission, who, in his time, did the same thing. The griots advised emperors, accompanied the progress of their empires. This is pretty much the same objective. We want more say in our countries' destinies.

So you feel that filmmakers have an important role to play in their societies. How do your audiences react? Do you think that your films manage to make people think?
Yes. When *Ta Dona* came out in Mali predicting that the dictator would fall before he really did, predicting that the whole country would burn before it really did, Malian audiences saw the film as a premonition. After twenty-three years of military power and ten failed coup d'états, the Malians were getting desperate. Nothing worked anymore, people thought that the dictator was going to stay put at the head of the country forever. They had started to lose hope. Only the young people, students and women remained hopeful. So, when the film came out and they understood the message, people started saying that it was perhaps a sign. The demonstrations took place and the dictator finally fell. A lot of people attributed his end to me, telling me that I had brought the regime down. People still congratulate me for *Ta Dona*. They often tell me that they are behind me, so I could not be happier. They have often told me that I took too many risks because the dictator himself ordered me to come to his palace to show him the film and twelve days later he fell. People are grateful for such a film. Only now, they are afraid when I say 'taafe fanga' – 'women's power' – because although they agreed with the message of *Ta Dona*, they don't necessarily want things to change in this domain!

Taafe Fanga indeed addresses the question of women's power. What position do women hold in Mali today and why did you choose this theme?
I walk hand-in-hand with the Malian people. I live there, I experience the same problems. I am open, I gather and store things all the time and when an impression begins to overflow, I express it in a film. That's the way I live. After the dictator fell, I thought to myself, I wanted him to fall and it happened. Mali is now a democracy. We have twenty or so free radios, thirty different newspapers. We can speak on the radio and criticise the regime. As long as we don't insult it, there's no risk anymore. So, even if things aren't perfect, there is a semblance of democracy. There

is freedom. Mali is starting to live again. Things are on the move, things are changing very fast, which is great. So I wondered where to take my combat next. The event that made me decide to focus on women took place when the regime fell. I was standing at the roadside, the bridge was blocked, the students and army were fighting, and there was tear gas everywhere. I saw the women from the Mali district come out, about a hundred women, who tightened their belts and said to the youths, 'Stand aside! Let us take your place! The tanks will have to crush us first before getting you.' I said to myself that very day that that was the end of the regime. Anyone familiar with Malian history – and you can go back as far as the tenth century if you like – knows that every time Mali has been in trouble, its women have contributed the necessary drop of water. So, when I was wondering where to focus my attention once the dictatorship had ended, I said to myself, on women. First of all, let's pay homage to these women, to these Malian women who have always been there at the right moment. When I was thinking about how to express this homage, I thought about the play I had written thirteen years ago and decided to adapt it. I thought, here is an important group, perhaps the most important group given that women constitute 51% of the Malian population, an extraordinarily strong group but one which is nonetheless muzzled by the traditions. Tradition forbids women from doing many of the things of which they are capable. Today they are fighting back, they go to school, there are women ministers, journalists, women in all the professional fields – even the presiding judge in the court that judged the dictator was a woman – so I said to myself that sooner or later, they are going to get their rights. It's a long fight, but they are going to end up winning. What interested me, therefore, was the inferiority complex that the traditions perpetuate. I felt that my play was most fitting because it was women who brought men the first mask, but the irony of the story is that in all our societies today, the women have to hide when the mask comes out. It's unfair and this irony somehow has to be repaired. You are a woman, you are a filmmaker, I am a filmmaker, which means we have the same abilities, but if we went to a Malian village tonight and a mask came out, I'd be able to stay outside peacefully smoking my cigarette whilst you'd have to stay inside your hut. This sets up a complex in our egalitarian relationship. So I decided to leave the fight for women's rights to the women in order to challenge this complex. The film addresses a legend that many people have forgotten. They need to be reminded of this legend so that they can digest it, so that they can think, so that they can see that there is something that needs to be repaired vis-à-vis our women. I don't expect miracles, but I hope that by showing this legend, people will think, that the women too will hear the message and fight in this direction.

The men take back control of the mask at the end of the film. Some people might be happy that the women's attempt to take over power fails. Is that how you see the end of the film, or is the film's conciliatory message, its call for an 'equality that respects difference' more important?

y a un semblant de démocratie. Il y a une liberté, on commence à voir un Mali qui renaît. Ça bouge, ça change beaucoup et très vite, ce qui est agréable. Je me suis donc demandé où j'allais porter mon combat ensuite. L'événement qui m'a focalisé vers la femme s'est passé pendant la chute du régime. J'étais au bord de la route, le pont était bloqué, les étudiants et les militaires s'affrontaient, il y avait du gaz lacrymogène partout. J'ai vu les femmes du quartier Mali sortir, une centaine de femmes qui se serraient la ceinture en disant aux enfants, 'Laissez nous la place! Laissez nous passer devant! Les chars vont nous écraser avant de vous atteindre'. Dès ce jour, je me suis dit que c'en était fini ce régime. Pour qui connaît l'histoire du Mali – et on peut remonter jusqu'au dixième siècle si vous voulez – chaque fois que le Mali a franchi une étape difficile, les femmes ont amené la goutte d'eau nécessaire. Et donc, quand je me suis posé la question de savoir où porter mon regard après la fin de la dictature, je me suis dit : sur la femme. D'abord, rendons hommage à ces femmes, à la femme malienne qui a toujours été là au bon moment. Lorsque je me suis demandé comment exprimer cet hommage, j'ai pensé à cette pièce de théâtre que j'avais écrit, il y a treize ans, et je l'ai adaptée. Je me suis dit : voici une couche importante – peut-être la couche la plus importante de nos sociétés vu que la femme représente 51% de la population malienne – une couche qui a une force extraordinaire, mais qui est tout de même bâillonnée par les traditions. De par les traditions, les femmes n'ont pas le droit de faire beaucoup de choses dont elles sont capables. Elles se battent aujourd'hui, elles vont à l'école, il y a des femmes ministres, journalistes, des femmes dans tous les métiers – même le président du tribunal qui a jugé le dictateur était une femme – donc je me suis dit, tôt ou tard, elles vont finir par avoir leurs droits ; c'est une longue lutte mais elles vont finir par la gagner. Ce qui m'intéressait donc, c'était le complexe d'infériorité, perpétué par la tradition. Je pensais que ma pièce s'y prêtait bien, car c'est la femme qui a amené le premier masque à l'homme. Or, ironie de l'histoire : aujourd'hui dans toutes nos sociétés, quand le masque apparaît, la femme se cache. C'est une injustice et il faut quelque part une réparation de cette ironie-là. Vous êtes femme, vous êtes réalisatrice, moi je suis réalisateur, ce qui veut dire qu'on a les mêmes capacités ; mais si l'on va dans un village malien ce soir et le masque apparaît, moi je peux rester là tranquillement en train de fumer ma cigarette, mais vous, vous ne pourrait pas quitter votre case. Dans nos rapports d'égalité, c'est un complexe. Donc j'ai décidé de laisser aux femmes le combat pour leurs droits, afin de m'attaquer à ce complexe. Le film traite d'une légende que certains ont oubliée. Il faut leur rappeler cette légende afin qu'ils la digèrent, qu'ils réfléchissent, qu'ils voient qu'il y a quelque chose à réparer vis-à-vis de nos femmes. Je ne m'attends pas à des miracles, mais j'espère en montrant cette légende que les gens vont réfléchir, que les femmes elles-mêmes vont bien recevoir le message et se battre dans ce sens-là.

A la fin du film, les hommes reprennent le masque. Certains pourraient se réjouir du fait que la tentative des femmes de prendre le pouvoir échoue. Est-ce que vous voyez la fin du film sous cet angle, ou est-ce que son message de conciliation, 'd'égalité dans la différence', est plus important?
Je suis sûr que les Occidentaux vont dire que la

fin est trop didactique ; or je n'ai pas voulu faire un film didactique. S'il le devient un peu à la fin, j'ai mes raisons. Malheureusement, on ne me pose pas la question que vous venez de poser. Pour moi, je m'adresse aux femmes. Je m'adresse aussi aux hommes, mais le public n'a pas toujours le même niveau de compréhension. Certains ont été à l'école, ont appris à raisonner dans un certain sens, d'autres sont restés dans leur village et n'ont pas appris à réfléchir de la même manière ; et je ne voulais en aucune manière que le message ne soit pas perçu. Même si cela fait une fin un peu didactique, je préfère cela à l'idée que le message ne soit pas bien reçu. Cela est très important pour moi. Il ne s'agit pas d'un problème de pouvoir, que ça soit ici ou en Europe. Tout le monde prend le rapport homme-femme pour un problème de pouvoir. La question n'est pas de savoir si c'est l'homme ou la femme qui devrait avoir le pouvoir. Pour moi, il s'agit simplement d'égalité dans la différence. Un homme et une femme ne sont pas deux êtres identiques mais, pour moi, ils sont au même niveau et donc sont égaux. A partir du moment où l'on est à égalité, c'est important d'exploiter ses différences, de les mettre ensemble pour construire une vie meilleure. Ce n'est pas la peine de dire : 'les hommes ont eu le pouvoir et ils nous ont écrasées ; maintenant nous allons prendre le pouvoir et les écraser.' Ce n'est que le même problème inversé. C'est un jeu qui pourrait perdurer. La vie est tellement difficile, tellement courte pour nous tous, qu'il faut trouver une harmonie pour bien vivre avant de disparaître.

Est-ce que ce message est une proposition aux gens?
C'est effectivement une proposition. Cette histoire n'est pas censée dire que les femmes ont pris le pouvoir, mais qu'elles n'ont pas su l'utiliser et donc l'ont perdu. Je tiens à préciser que c'est une histoire qui existait déjà, qui est l'émanation de la culture Dogon, que je respecte beaucoup. Je ne voulais pas déformer leur histoire en aucune manière. Je ne pense pas que mon droit de metteur en scène, d'artiste me permet cela. J'ai tellement de respect pour cette culture, quelquefois je doute même que je l'aie réellement comprise, donc je n'ai pas voulu prendre le risque de détourner cette légende. Cette légende est claire : les femmes ont eu le masque, elles ont pris le pouvoir, et elles l'ont perdu. J'ai décidé de ne pas déformer la légende, même si cela semble être au détriment du film. Pour moi, cette histoire est à prendre comme un avertissement aux femmes. Les femmes ont eu à prendre le pouvoir pour cette culture, autrefois, et elles l'ont perdu. Si un jour elles le reprennent, elles se rappelleront certainement de *Taafe Fanga* et diront, attention, cela s'est déjà passé dans l'histoire, mais nous avons perdu. Pourquoi ? Il faut faire en sorte que l'histoire ne se répète pas. Ça c'est le premier message vis-à-vis des femmes. Pour moi, c'est un message positif parce que ce n'est qu'en perdant qu'on gagne. La défaite peut être transformée en victoire si l'on corrige les erreurs du passé dans l'avenir. Deuxièmement, le film est un avertissement aux hommes, en disant si vous continuez à opprimer les femmes, voilà ce qui va arriver. Comme le dit un des personnages dans le film, 'la femme est comme une abeille. Si vous la soignez, elle produit du miel, mais si vous la maltraitez, elle vous pique'. C'est l'avertissement que je donne aux hommes, car aujourd'hui, même en Occident, c'est les hommes qui détiennent le pouvoir. Il faut être réaliste. Mais je dis aux femmes ce n'est pas la peine d'essayer d'inverser simplement la vapeur, parce qu'après les hommes vont essayer d'en faire autant, et ainsi de suite éternellement. Il faut plutôt viser l'égalité dans la

I am sure that Westerners will say that the end is too didactic, but I didn't want to make a didactic film. If the ending is a bit didactic, I have my reasons. Unfortunately, people don't ask me the question you just asked. As I see it, I am addressing women. I am addressing men too, but the audience doesn't always have the same level of understanding. Some have been to school and have learnt to think in a certain way. Others have stayed in their villages and have not learnt to reason like this, and I didn't want the message to be missed in any way. Even if that makes the ending a bit didactic, I preferred that to the idea that the message be missed. That is vital for me. It's not a problem of power, whether here or in Europe. Everybody sees male-female relationships as a question of power. The question isn't whether the men or women should be in control. For me, it is simply a question of being equal irrespective of our differences. Men and women are not identical beings but, for me, they are at the same level and are thus equal. As long as we are equal, it is important to use our differences, to put them together to build a better life. There's no point in saying, 'the men had power and they oppressed us so we are going to take power now and oppress them'. That simply inverts the problem. That game could go on forever. Life is so hard, so short for us all, that we need to find harmony to live happily before dying.

Is this message a proposal?
It is indeed a proposal. This story doesn't mean women took power, but they didn't know how to take advantage of it and so they lost it. I must insist that this story already existed. It is an emanation of Dogon culture, which I respect a great deal. I didn't want to deform their legend in any way. I don't think that my right as a director, as an artist, gave me the right to do that. I respect this culture so much – I sometimes doubt even that I have really understood it – that I didn't want to risk subverting this legend. The legend is clear. The women had the mask, they took over power, and they lost it. I decided not to deform the legend, even if that might seem detrimental to the film. I see this story as a warning to women. Women had the opportunity of taking over power in the past and they lost it. If they manage to take over power again one day, they will certainly remember *Taafe Fanga* and think, 'Let's be careful, this has already happened in the past, but we lost power. Why? We have to make sure that history doesn't repeat itself.' That is the first message to women. I see this as a positive message, because losing helps us win in the end. Defeat can be turned into victory if we correct the errors of the past. Secondly, the film is a warning to men. It says that this is what will happen if you continue to oppress women. As one of the film characters says, 'Women are like bees. If you treat them well, they produce honey, but if you treat them badly they sting.' That is my warning to men, because today, even in the West, men still hold power. We have to be realistic. But I say to women that it isn't worth simply inverting the situation, because afterwards men will try to do the same, and so on forever. We need to aim for equality in respect of our differences. That is what I propose to both men and women.

The character Sidy in *Ta Dona* is a blend of traditional and modern culture and in *Taafe Fanga* you advocate male-female equality. Does this vision reflect your conception of society?

This is my general conception of life. I see all life as duality. It's not that I want to sound religious by saying that there is good and bad in life, but somewhere it's true that life is made up of good and bad, that it is really contradictory. Life is full of contradictions and we have to find harmony in these contradictions. That's how I see the world. My culture, my research makes me perceive everything as double. We need to bring these dualities together, to live with them. Life is never just pleasure. There is pain, failure, success, illness, health. As I've already said, the whole of life is contradictory, and we have to find a balance to live happily.

Taafe Fanga criticises power abuses, just as Ta Dona criticised political corruption. Is film an appropriate vehicle for such criticism? Can it really trigger social change?

We mustn't kid ourselves that films can perform miracles. A director is an auteur, not a prophet. But having said that, the power of the image enables us to focus people's attention on a given problem, to make them think, to help make things advance. The past shows us that every time there has been a sudden upheaval, a revolution, it has never really changed things. Things only change little by little, from one generation to the next. That brings me back to the Dogon conception of disorder. They say that life is order and disorder. They see life as an assortment of identical elements that turn in a spiral, improving and improving life. But there comes a time when man's actions, cupidity and thirst for domination stop the spiral from turning properly. Its movement regresses, almost stagnating, and life stops improving, which is when their God intervenes to send a new power. This provokes disorder, because it is disorder that generates a new order. Once the new order is established, life starts again and improves. Let's take an example closer to Europe, the example of the Second World War. Life was getting better in Europe, but because of men, because of their desire for domination, the Second World War broke out. The spiral stopped turning at this time, life regressed, monstrosities were committed, and lives were destroyed. When peace came, installing a new power, the spiral began to turn again and Europe is now highly developed. I am certain that the order Europe is currently experiencing will be blocked again one day and a new power will intervene to enable it to continue. I agree with this Dogon conception. It is wonderful, because it helps us to understand that a country, a nation's wealth can be compromised at a given moment in history, but that one mustn't give up because the spiral can always start to turn again. You have to fight to work towards a new order. The same thing applies to individuals. If we accept that everything is order and disorder, we know that if we fall one day, we can always pick ourselves up again, fight back and start back out again rather than giving up. That is the lesson I try to get over in my films. I set the ball rolling – even if people don't understand everything, because

différence. C'est la proposition que je fais et aux hommes, et aux femmes.

Dans *Ta Dona* le personnage de Sidy est une synthèse entre la culture traditionnelle et la culture moderne, et dans *Taafe Fanga* vous prônez l'égalité entre l'homme et la femme. Est-ce que cette vision reflète votre conception de la société?

C'est ma conception générale de la vie. Pour moi, toute vie est une dualité. Ce n'est pas que je veuille rejoindre la religion pour dire que dans la vie il y a le bien et le mal, mais quelque part c'est vrai que la vie est composée du bien et du mal, qu'elle est réellement contradiction. C'est la contradiction qui fait la vie, et il faut trouver l'harmonie dans cette contradiction. C'est comme cela que je conçois le monde. D'après ma culture, d'après mes recherches, je perçois que tout est double. Il faut pouvoir mettre ces dualités ensemble, il faut pouvoir vivre avec. La vie n'est jamais que joie. Il y a la douleur, l'échec, la réussite, la maladie, la santé. Comme j'ai déjà dit, toute la vie est contradiction, et donc il faut trouver l'équilibre pour bien vivre.

Taafe Fanga critique l'abus du pouvoir, tout comme Ta Dona critique des hommes politiques corrompus. Est-ce que le cinéma est un bon support pour la critique? Est-ce qu'il peut réellement entamer des changements sociaux?

Un film ne peut pas faire des miracles, il ne faut pas se leurrer. Un réalisateur est un auteur, il n'est pas un prophète. Mais tout de même, la puissance des images permet de focaliser les gens sur un problème donné, de les faire réfléchir, de faire avancer les choses. Le passé nous montre que chaque fois qu'il y a eu un changement brusque, une révolution, cela n'a finalement jamais rien changé. Les choses changent petit à petit, de génération en génération. Cela me ramène à la conception du désordre chez les Dogons, car d'après eux, la vie est ordre et désordre. Ils conçoivent la vie comme un assemblage d'éléments identiques qui tournent en spirale en s'améliorant, en améliorant la vie. Or, il arrive un moment où, de par les actions des hommes, de par leur cupidité, leur soif de domination, cette spirale est freinée. Le mouvement régresse, stagne presque, et la vie ne s'améliore plus. C'est à ce moment-là que leur Dieu intervient afin d'envoyer un nouveau pouvoir, qui provoque le désordre, car c'est le désordre qui amènera un ordre nouveau. Une fois que l'on arrive à l'ordre nouveau, la vie reprend et s'améliore. Prenons un exemple plus proche de l'Europe, l'exemple de la guerre de '39-'45. La vie en Europe était en train de s'améliorer, mais à cause des hommes, à cause de leur désir de domination, il y a eu la Deuxième Guerre Mondiale. Pendant cette période, la spirale s'est arrêtée de tourner, la vie a régressé, il y a eu des monstruosités, des vies ont été détruites. Avec la venue de la paix, et son nouveau pouvoir, la spirale s'est remise à tourner, et aujourd'hui l'Europe est très développée. J'en suis sûr que l'ordre que vit actuellement l'Europe sera de nouveau bloqué un jour, et un autre pouvoir interviendra, et ça va continuer. Je suis d'accord avec cette conception dogon. Elle est merveilleuse car elle nous aide à comprendre que la prospérité d'un pays, d'une nation peut être compromise à un certain moment de l'histoire, mais qu'il ne faille pas pour autant en démordre parce que la spirale peut toujours reprendre. Il faut toujours se battre pour repartir vers un nouvel ordre. Cela de même pour l'individu. Si l'on accepte que tout soit ordre et désordre, on sait que si un jour on tombe, qu'au lieu de se baisser les bras, on peut toujours se relever, lutter et repartir. C'est ça l'enseignement que j'essaye de faire passer dans mes films. Je lance la balle – même si les gens ne comprennent pas tout, parce que finalement je ne suis pas là pour tout expliquer – en espérant que la curiosité intellectuelle des gens leur pousse à poser des questions, à comprendre. Donc, pour en revenir à la question, je ne fais pas des films pour faire des révolutions, mais pour lancer des idées aux gens, pour les faire comprendre.

Vos deux films, et surtout *Taafe Fanga*, mettent en scène le peuple dogon. Qu'est-ce qui vous attire chez ce peuple? Est-ce qu'on peut tirer des enseignements de la culture dogon?
Ils ont énormément de choses à nous apprendre. J'ai déjà parlé de leur conception de l'ordre et du désordre. D'après l'histoire, le peuple dogon était une branche de la famille royale mandingue qui est parti de l'empire en condamnant les guerres. Il s'est séparé du noyau central et a erré pendant quelques siècles avant de s'installer au pays dogon. C'est un peuple qui s'est installé sur les falaises pour éviter la guerre, qui est arrivé à concevoir une architecture originale qui se fond complètement dans les rochers. Le peuple dogon est très épris de paix, ils ont banni la guerre, ils n'ont jamais pris les armes une fois qu'ils avaient chassé les Tellems qui vivaient là auparavant et avec qui ils n'arrivaient pas à vivre en harmonie. Ils ont donc une manière spéciale et très forte de concevoir la paix, la vie. Quand on étudie ces gens, on se rend compte qu'ils ont toujours connu la science des étoiles, par exemple. Leur cosmogonie est extraordinaire. Depuis des siècles ils connaissaient l'existence de l'étoile du Sirrus, or ce n'est qu'en 1924 que les savants occidentaux ont découvert cette étoile. Leur formule simple 'la vie est mouvement', la vie part de la plus petite des choses et se forme par adjonction d'éléments identiques, c'est presque la formule de l'atome. Cette cosmogonie est extraordinaire, tellement distillé, tellement terre-à-terre, elle s'est néanmoins transporté à des concepts scientifiques. La pensée dogon peut nous permettre d'avoir une autre conception de la vie qui va dans le sens de la paix et du progrès.

Taafe Fanga *se focalise sur le masque, et *Ta Dona* laisse aussi une place importante aux rituels. Pourquoi choisissez-vous de mettre l'accent sur cet aspect magique dans vos films?
Je suis d'une société qui vit avec la magie, mais pas forcément la magie au sens européen du terme. Dans notre culture, tout est interprétation. Dans *Ta Dona*, tout le village s'assemble au soleil pour conjurer la pluie. Ils pensent tous ensemble à la même chose en même temps pendant des heures, et il finit par pleuvoir. Les gens se disent forcément qu'il s'agit de la magie ; or, pour moi, la pensée c'est de l'énergie. Ces gens pensent ensemble et créent de l'énergie. Vu qu'il y a de l'énergie dans le cosmos, pourquoi ces deux énergies ne seraient-elles pas capables de se rencontrer et faire tomber la pluie? Pour moi ce n'est pas magique, cela peut avoir des explications scientifiques mais personne ne s'est penché sur ce domaine. Si vous donnez à quelqu'un qui n'a pas vécu dans notre monde un téléphone, il va pouvoir entendre une autre voix, mais il ne saura pas comment ça se fait, il pensera sûrement que c'est de la magie. Or, si vous lui expliquez le système téléphonique, il va comprendre, et la magie sera finie. L'Afrique est pleine de choses comme ça. On explique souvent

at the end of the day I'm not here to explain everything – hoping that people's intellectual curiosity will encourage them to ask questions, to understand. So, coming back to the question, I don't make films to start revolutions, but to give people ideas, to help them understand.

Both your films, and particularly *Taafe Fanga*, depict the Dogon people. What is it about the Dogon that attracts you? What can we learn from Dogon culture?
They have loads of things to teach us. I have already mentioned their conception of order and disorder. History tells us that the Dogon were a branch of the Manding royal family who left the empire because they denounced war. They broke away from the core group and wandered for several centuries before settling in the Dogon country. This is a people that settled on the escarpments to avoid war, who managed to come up with an original architecture that blends perfectly into the rocks. The Dogon are very passionate about peace. They have banished war. They have never taken up arms again since they chased away the Tellem who used to live there first, with whom they couldn't manage to live harmoniously. They thus have a special, very strong way of conceiving of peace, of life. When you study these people, you realise that they have always known the science of the stars, for example. Their cosmogony is extraordinary. They have known about the existence of the Sirrus star for centuries, whereas Western scientists only discovered it in 1924. Their simple formula 'life is movement', that life comes from the smallest of things and is constituted through the adjunction of identical elements, is almost the formula of the atom. Their cosmogony is extraordinary. It is so distilled, so down-to-earth, but nonetheless articulates scientific concepts. Dogon thought can offer us another conception of life that works towards peace and progress.

Taafe Fanga *focuses on the mask, and *Ta Dona* gives a lot of space to rituals. Why do you choose to foreground this magical aspect in your films?
I come from a society that lives with magic – not necessarily magic in the European sense of the word. Everything comes down to interpretation in our culture. In *Ta Dona*, the whole village gathers in the sun to conjure the rain. They all concentrate on the same thing at the same time for hours and it ends up raining. People obviously think that this is magic, but for me, thought is energy. These people think together and create energy. As there is energy in the cosmos, why shouldn't these two energies be able to meet and make it rain? I don't see this as magic. There may well be a scientific explanation, but no one has ever researched into this domain. If you give someone who hasn't lived in our world a telephone, they will be able to hear a voice, but they won't know how. They will no doubt think that this is magic. But if you explain the phone system to them, they will understand and that will be the end of the magic. Africa if full of things like that. We often explain these phenomena

as magic because we don't have any rational explanations. We are steeped in this atmosphere all our lives, so it seems completely normal to me that my films, which really come from the heart, from my whole culture, inevitably be tinged with this knowledge that people call magic, but which I don't consider magic. The magic will be over the day we give these phenomena a rational explanation. But, I also feel that there is really magic in all things. It's up to us to know how to capture, to know how to interpret the magic that the world gives off. Our power is to perceive the magic. It is up to man to show this sensitivity. Not everyone is capable.

Do you try to find a specifically African film style that is distinct from Western styles when you write a film? Do you think it's important for African filmmakers to find their own film style?

I can't stand imitating. I hate it. I'm lucky not to have been to film school. In film school you learn to follow a predetermined path, you position yourself in relation to what you learn. I was fortunate enough to have picked the trade up on shoots, which taught me to understand the technical side of film and film language, and I am very happy today to be able to express myself freely, rather than to have a master, a guiding line. Your question is interesting, because it's a problem that faces African film. A lot of other filmmakers before me were tempted to make images for Europe, to satisfy Europe, but they soon realised their mistake. I do not try to make images for Europe. I come from a given society and I make films to help advance things, not just for art's sake. I refuse to use the term 'commitment' because the word has lost its meaning, but I make films so that my society can apprehend, cope, and advance. I try to be open in this approach, to open up my culture to other cultures. I give people the keys to enter my culture. The best thing that can happen to a film is that gets shown and is accepted and understood by everyone, whether in Europe or Asia. This is both very difficult and very easy – easy in the sense that you can take a theme that is pertinent to people from all horizons and express it the best you can, giving people as much emotion and pleasure as possible. It might be hard, but it's not impossible. This approach is better than saying I'm going to target such and such an audience. That is dangerous. I will not make films for a given audience. I start out from my home. I have a culture. I have to express my culture to be a part of universal culture. If you've got to be selfish, you've got to be selfish. Do the French or the Americans think of Malian audiences when they make their films? Of course not. They express their own cultures and it's up to me to make an effort to enter their culture. I don't always understand everything in Western films, but that doesn't mean that they aren't good films. I would love all those people who take an interest in African film to watch our films in the same frame of mind, instead of always telling us we should have done it like this or that. I hate that attitude, their habit of saying, 'You didn't do it right, that's not how we would have done it.' Sadly, that's what happens most of the time. When our directors follow these instructions, they tend to come a cropper. We

ces phénomènes par la magie parce que nous n'avons pas l'explication rationnelle de la chose. Nous baignons dans cette ambiance toute notre vie, donc il me semble normal que mes films, qui me sortent vraiment des tripes, de toute ma culture, soient forcément teintés de ces connaissances qu'on appelle magie, mais qui ne sont pas magie pour moi. La magie finira le jour où l'on donnera une explication rationnelle à un phénomène. Mais, je dis aussi que dans toute chose, il y a réellement une magie. Maintenant c'est à moi de savoir capter, de savoir interpréter la magie qui se dégage de ce monde. Notre pouvoir est de percevoir la magie. C'est à l'homme d'avoir cette sensibilité. Pas tout le monde en est capable.

Lorsque vous écrivez un film, est-ce que vous essayez de trouver une cinématographie spécifiquement africaine, distincte de celle que l'on trouve en Occident? Pensez-vous qu'il soit important que les cinéastes africains trouvent une expression cinématographique qui leur est propre?

Ce dont j'ai horreur, c'est d'imiter. J'ai horreur de ça. J'ai la chance de ne pas avoir fait d'école de cinéma. Quand on fait une école, on apprend à suivre une ligne construite, on se repère par rapport à ce qu'on a reçu. J'ai eu la chance de faire des stages qui m'ont permis de comprendre la technique et le langage cinématographique, et je suis très heureux, aujourd'hui, de pouvoir m'exprimer librement, de ne pas avoir de maître, de ligne directrice. Votre question est intéressante parce que c'est un problème qui se pose au niveau du cinéma africain. Beaucoup d'autres cinéastes avant moi ont été tentés de faire des images pour l'Europe, pour contenter l'Europe, et ils se sont vite rendus compte qu'ils se sont trompés. Moi, je ne cherche pas à faire des images pour l'Europe. Je viens d'une société donnée, et je fais des films pour faire avancer les choses, pas simplement pour faire de l'art. Je ne veux même pas parler de militantisme parce que c'est un mot qui a perdu son sens, mais je fais des films pour que ma société puisse appréhender, s'en sortir, avancer. Dans cette démarche, j'essaye de m'ouvrir, d'ouvrir ma culture aux autres cultures. Je donne des clés pour que les gens viennent à ma culture. L'idéal pour un film c'est qu'il soit vu, accepté et compris par tous, que ça soit en Europe ou en Asie. C'est à la fois très difficile et très facile, facile dans le sens qu'on prend un thème qui est pertinent aux gens de tout horizon, on l'exprime de la meilleure manière possible, en donnant le plus d'émotion, de plaisir aux gens, cela est peut-être difficile, mais c'est possible. Il vaut mieux cette approche que de dire que je vais à la conquête de tel ou tel public. Ça c'est un danger. Je ne ferai pas de films pour un public donné. Je pars de chez moi, j'ai une culture, je dois participer à la culture universelle en exprimant ma culture. S'il faut être égoïste, il faut être égoïste. Quand un Français ou un Américain fait un film, est-ce qu'il pense au public malien? Evidement que non, il exprime sa propre culture et c'est à moi de faire l'effort de rentrer dans sa culture. Parfois je ne comprends pas tous les films occidentaux, mais cela ne veut pas dire que ce ne sont pas des films réussis. Je voudrais que tous ceux qui s'intéressent au cinéma africain voient nos films dans le même esprit, au lieu de toujours nous dire, vous auriez dû faire comme ci ou comme ça. Je déteste cette attitude, cette habitude de dire vous n'avez pas bien fait, nous nous ne le voyons pas comme ça. Malheureusement c'est ce qui se passe la plupart du temps. Lorsque nos réalisateurs suivent ces consignes, ils ont tendance à se casser les dents. Il faut rester soi-même, trouver les moyens de mettre à la disposition du monde sa culture, son originalité. Chaque peuple du chaque coin du monde a sa culture et il faut l'apporter aux autres. C'est tellement un plaisir quand je vois un bon film français, américain, asiatique où le réalisateur est arrivé à me faire rentrer dans son histoire. Je sais que c'est un monde différent du mien, mais je rentre dans le film, je découvre, je fais la comparaison avec ma culture. Il faut qu'on permette aux cinéastes africains d'en faire autant. Malheureusement parce que le cinéma est presque à cent pour cent financé par l'Europe, il arrive qu'on pousse les gens à aller dans un sens qui n'est pas forcément le bon. Si cela continue, ça va tellement gangrener le cinéma africain qu'on va perdre notre identité. Cela sera dommage pour tout le monde parce qu'on ne leur apportera que la copie pâle de ce qu'ils sont. Les gens n'en prennent pas conscience, mais c'est très grave. Je suis catégorique là-dessus : je ne ferai pas de films dans ce sens. J'ai mes objectifs, j'ai ma culture à proposer aux gens. J'essaye de travailler de la façon la plus ouverte possible, en donnant des clés aux gens, mais après c'est à eux de faire l'effort.

Est-ce que vous estimez important que le public africain voie des images tournées par les réalisateurs africains?

C'est essentiel, mais malheureusement nous n'arrivons toujours pas à assurer une distribution pour nos films. Ce problème revient toujours, mais je pense que de plus en plus, on va y arriver. Il faut voir l'engouement du public africain pour nos films. Ils s'y reconnaissent, ils savent que ce sont leurs histoires. Malheureusement, on n'a toujours pas les infrastructures, il y a toujours des problèmes du côté économique. C'est une chose qui fait vraiment mal de voir la population là en attente. Je me rappelle qu'à la sortie de *Nyamanton*, j'étais avec Cheick Oumar [Sissoko] à l'entrée de la salle. Les gens étaient tellement impatients qu'ils nous ont bousculés, ils nous ont poussés dans la salle, ils nous ont piétinés en disant 'allez contrôler les billets ailleurs, nous avons nos billets et nous voulons rentrer!' C'était extraordinaire. Les gens parlent, ils viennent voir nos films vingt fois, tous les soirs à la même place, mais, on n'arrive toujours pas à en profiter parce qu'il y a encore des pressions extérieures, les compagnies étrangères qui ont le monopole de nos cinémas, qui nous envoient que des films de karaté, hindous, ou des navets. On n'a pas encore réussi à sortir de cet étau, mais je pense que les cinéastes africains ont compris. Il faut faire de plus en plus de films parce que le jour où on arrivera à bloquer l'arrivée massive de ces films de mauvaise qualité, il va falloir pouvoir les remplacer par autre chose. Si l'on se décourage parce que nos films ne sortent pas, que donnerons-nous aux gens quand la situation aura changé? Il faut continuer à faire des films, à se battre, à les faire voir autant que possible. C'est très important pour moi.

Comment expliquez vous le manque de distribution des films africains en Europe? Comment se fait-il qu'un film comme *Guimba* de Cheick Oumar Sissoko, le lauréat du FESPACO '95, n'est toujours pas sorti en France, par exemple?

Nous-mêmes nous n'avons pas compris. *Guimba* n'était même pas sélectionné à Cannes. Qu'est-ce qui s'est passé? Un film qui a été primé à Ouagadougou, un prix que personne n'a contesté, un film qui était l'expression filmique la plus aboutie

have to be ourselves, to find the way to offer the world our culture, our originality. People all over the world have their own cultures and need to offer them to others. It's such a pleasure to see a good French, American, or Asian film in which the director succeeds in engaging me in his or her story. I know it's different to my world, but I enter the film, I discover, I compare it to my culture. African filmmakers have to be allowed to do the same thing. Unfortunately, as film is almost entirely financed by Europe, people are sometimes encouraged to go down a certain route that is not necessarily the best path. If this goes on much longer, it will corrupt African film so much that we will lose our identity. That will be a shame for everyone because we will only offer people the pale copy of what they already are. People don't realise, but this is very serious. I am quite categorical about this. I refuse to make films in this way. I have my own objectives. I have my culture to offer people. I try to work in the most open manner possible, giving people the keys, but it's then up to them to make an effort.

Do you think it's important for African audiences to see images made by African directors?

It's essential, but unfortunately we don't always manage to get our films distributed. It's an on-going problem, but I think that we will manage more and more. You have to see the African public's enthusiasm for our films. They recognise themselves in them; they know that they are their stories. Unfortunately, we don't always have the infrastructures. There are always economic hitches. It really hurts to see the population there, waiting. I remember when *Nyamanton* was released. I was with Cheick Oumar [Sissoko] at the entrance of the cinema. People were so impatient that they shoved us aside, they pushed us into the cinema, they trampled us saying 'Go and check the tickets elsewhere! We've got our tickets and we want to go in!' It was incredible. People talk, they come to see our films twenty times, every night in the same place, but we can't always make the most of this because there are still outside pressures, foreign companies who monopolise our screens, who send us karate, Bollywood, or low-quality films. We haven't managed to break this stranglehold yet, but African filmmakers have understood. We need to make more and more films, because the day we manage to stop the massive influx of low-quality films, we will need to replace them with something else. If we get despondent because our films aren't released, what will we offer people when the situation changes? We have to carry on making films, to carry on fighting, to get them screened as much as possible. That is very important to me.

How do you explain the fact that African films are so badly distributed in Europe? Why was a film like Cheick Oumar Sissoko's *Guimba*, which won the last FESPACO, never released in France, for example?

We don't understand ourselves. *Guimba* wasn't even selected at Cannes. What happened? A film that won the main prize at Ouagadougou – a prize that no one contested – a film that was the most polished filmic expression of the 1995 FESPACO, received no recognition in Europe? Is there anything to understand? There are a lot of things that go on behind the scenes, things that are controlled. I personally think that Europe is not in a good way, that there is a feeling of unease, which maybe explains all that.

Interview II
Anne Laure Folly director

Ouagadougou. February 1995

We have just seen your film *Femmes aux yeux ouverts*. Why did you choose to tackle the question of African women in this film?
I simply wanted to show African women's ability to reach the end of the twentieth century and to enter the twenty-first century positively, that is, by articulating a set of problems, questions, and answers that contribute to world development. I wanted to show that they participate fully in the questions that concern all women.

Was it easy to deal with all the subjects addressed in the film, such as female circumcision, for example?
It was very easy to film, but I was amazed that some women in African intellectual circles told me that you have to let the traditions be, or that I shouldn't have entered into this type of problematic because it isn't so much a question of saying no to female circumcision as of giving all women the choice of practicing female circumcision if they want to. I thought everyone agreed in the highly privileged African circles with giving women their freedom.

Perhaps this is reaction against what is perceived as outside Western pressure?
That's effectively the right word. But even if it's a reaction, it needs to be overcome because it's not a question of attacking traditions, but of individual rights and respecting bodily integrity above all.

Did you get the impression that the women wanted to give their views, to speak about this kind of subject when you were making the film?
Yes. Women have a great sense of female solidarity in Africa. We can

du dernier FESPACO, n'a pas été reconnu là-bas. Qu'est-ce qu'on peut comprendre? Il y a beaucoup de choses qui se passent qui sont cachées, qui sont dirigées. Personnellement, j'ai le sentiment que l'Europe se trouve très mal, qu'il y a un sentiment de malaise, ce qui explique peut-être cela.

Nous venons de voir votre film *Femmes aux yeux ouverts*. Pourquoi avez-vous choisi d'aborder le sujet des femmes africaines dans ce film?
Je voulais simplement montrer la capacité des femmes d'Afrique à accéder à la fin du XX siècle, et à aborder le XXI siècle de façon positive, c'est-à-dire, en ayant une problématique, une interrogation, et des réponses qui participent au développement du monde. Je voulais montrer qu'elles participent pleinement aux interrogations qui concernent toutes les femmes.

Est-ce qu'il était facile d'aborder tous les sujets dont le film parle, l'excision, par exemple?
C'était très facile à filmer, mais j'étais étonnée que dans le milieu intellectuel africain, certaines femmes me disent qu'il faut laisser la tradition se faire, ou qu'il ne fallait pas rentrer dans ce type de problématique, parce que le problème n'est pas tant de refuser l'excision, que de donner le choix à n'importe quelle femme de pratiquer l'excision si elle le veut. Je pensais que tout le monde était d'accord, dans les milieux très privilégiés africains, pour donner leur liberté aux femmes.

C'est peut-être une réaction contre ce qu'elles ressentent comme une pression de la part des Occidentaux?
Je crois que c'est le mot. Mais, même si c'est une réaction, elle doit être maîtrisée car ce n'est pas une question d'atteinte à la tradition, mais tout d'abord du droit de l'individu, du respect de l'intégrité du corps.

Lorsque vous avez réalisé le film, est-ce que vous aviez l'impression que les femmes avaient envie de s'exprimer, de parler de ce genre de sujet?
Oui. Les femmes sont très solidaires en Afrique. C'est un monde de solidarité féminine dont on n'a pas idée ailleurs. On ne peut exister que si

l'on a des amies. Quand vous avez un problème, vous en parlez avec vos amies, vous le résolvez ensemble. Toute la structure sociale est régie par des réseaux féminins.

hardly even imagine the world of female solidarity that exists. You can only exist if you have women friends. If you have a problem, you talk to your friends about it, you resolve it together. Female networks govern the whole social structure.

Comment est-ce que ces femmes ont réagi lorsqu'elles se sont vues dans le film?
Certaines des femmes qui avaient dit des choses fortes ont eu des réticences après, lorsqu'elles ont compris qu'elles allaient être vues par leurs paires, et par la société. La pression sociale est telle en Afrique qu'il y a une timidité, une pudeur. C'est cette pression excessive qui fait que les changements sont très lents, car on demande toujours à l'individu de participer à la pensée majoritaire, à la reproduire, et dès qu'il y a un discours féminin, qui est dissident par définition, parce que normalement il ne doit même pas exister en tant que discours féminin, c'est gênant.

How did these women react when they saw themselves in the film?
Some of the women who spoke out strongly were reticent afterwards when they understood that they were going to be seen by their peers and by society. Social pressure is such in Africa that people are very timid, or modest. It's this excessive pressure that makes change so slow because the individual is always expected to participate in and to reproduce the way the majority thinks. A female discourse, which is dissident by definition because it shouldn't normally exist as a female discourse, is automatically problematic.

Le film est très militant, et les femmes qui y figurent également. . .
Oui. Oui, toutes les associations sont des associations militantes. Le drame est que cette politique est diffuse. Quand vous avez un ennemi politique qui contrecarre de façon théorique votre argumentation, il est visible ; tandis que ce qu'elles ont à combattre, c'est la tradition, ce sont les usages, c'est une forme invisible de pression, ce qui est beaucoup plus difficile.

The film is extremely militant, the women in it too...
Yes. All the women's groups are militant associations. The tragedy is that these politics are diffuse. When you are up against a political enemy who counters your position in a theoretical way, the enemy is visible. What these women have to fight, however, is tradition, customs, an invisible form of pressure, which is much more difficult.

Est-il important que les femmes font des films en Afrique?
Je crois qu'il est important qu'il y ait une voix de femme quel que soit l'espace dans lequel on vit. Une femme m'a dit en visionnant les rushes, 'vous vivez et vous nous apportez une démocratie qui est masculine'. Je n'avais jamais réalisé avant qu'on puisse concevoir la démocratie de cette façon ; mais effectivement, plus j'y pense, plus je crois qu'on vit dans un monde qui est éminemment masculin, dans lequel je suis éduquée, et je crois qu'il y pense, mon mode d'agir sont également dans cette optique. Je suis, moi, le produit d'une société masculine. Je crois qu'on vit dans une culture de guerre dans le monde, une culture d'affrontement, et que cette culture est biologiquement masculine. Les femmes, par contre, du fait qu'elles produisent des êtres qui vivent au-delà d'elles-mêmes, sont, à mon sens, plus conservateur et projeté dans le futur du fait qu'on produit pour l'avenir, on ne veut rien détruire. De ce fait, je crois que les femmes, qu'elles le veuillent ou non, vivent une culture qui est beaucoup plus pacifique. Je crois qu'on est donc capable de produire des termes de pensée et d'action, des produits sociaux, qui soient totalement différents.

Is it important for women to make films in Africa?
For me it's important that a female voice exists in whichever region you live. One woman said to me when watching the rushes, 'You live in and are bringing us a masculine democracy.' I had never realised before that it was possible to see democracy in this way, but the more I think about it now, the more I believe that we live and that I have been educated in an eminently masculine world, that my way of thinking and acting are guided by this. I am the product of a masculine society. I think that we are living in a culture of war in the world, a culture of confrontation, and that this culture is biologically masculine. As women produce beings that live beyond themselves, they, on the other hand, are, to my mind, more interested in preserving. As women are conservationists and are projected into the future given that we produce for the future, we don't want to destroy things. As a result, women live a culture that is much more pacifistic, whether intentionally or not. I think that we are thus capable of producing totally different modes of thought and action, or social products.

On entend souvent dire que l'avenir de l'Afrique passera par les femmes.
Oui, et l'avenir du monde en général. Il est, en effet, important qu'on équilibre la primauté de l'action, de l'action violente, par un autre regard, un regard plus préservateur.

People often say that the future of Africa lies in its women.
Yes, and the future of the world in general. It is indeed vital that we balance the primacy of action, of violent action, with another viewpoint, a more preventative viewpoint.

Le cinéma est-il un bon moyen de porter cet autre regard?
Je crois que le seul discours moderne de la fin du

Is film a good way of conveying this other viewpoint?
I feel that visual discourse is the only modern discourse possible at the

end of this century. All discourses, even aggressive discourses, are conveyed by images. So, if I have a different discourse, I can convey it in images too. Images are the only vector possible at the end of this century. That's terrifying because I get the impression that people think less and less, so audiovisual and visual discourse are responsible for conveying societal discourse. You can make society think anything you like – all you have to do is show it in images. That can lead to incredible perversions.

Can film play an educational role?

I think that images are a pedagogical product for the masses. Every time you show something, you give profiles and examples for living. You create a possible and future societal model. All negative or reductive images, or images that despise any individual are completely regrettable.

Is it important for audiences to see African films?

Absolutely, so that Africa's own way of thinking can emerge, so that an African culture that affirms itself as such, that has its specificities and differences, can emerge. I'm interested in identity, in living at a time when a mass of people who represent one fifth of mankind are asserting a culture that is different and alive.

Interview III
Dani Kouyaté director

Ouagadougou. February 1995

Why did you choose a traditional epic tale as the subject of your film *Keïta*?

Epic tales, stories, all African folklore constitute a real thematic storehouse for African film. These fictions are fabulous stories that absolutely have to be filmed. That's what I was interested in doing above all, but I also wanted to ring the alarm bells to say to Africans: 'You've got stories to tell right on your doorsteps, so don't go looking there where they don't exist.'

The film appears to warn Africans about straying too far from their roots...

The problem doesn't only concern Africa. Mankind is straying from its humane roots. That's the problem. Man in general has roots and

siècle, c'est le discours de l'image. Tous les discours, mêmes agressifs, sont portés par l'image ; donc si l'on en a un autre, on peut aussi le porter par l'image. L'image est l'unique vecteur de la fin du siècle, et je dirai même que c'est effrayant parce que j'ai l'impression que les gens pensent moins, et donc c'est le discours de l'audiovisuel et du visuel qui porte le discours de la société. On peut faire penser à la société n'importe quoi : il suffit de le montrer par l'image, ce qui aboutit à des perversions incroyables.

Le cinéma peut-il jouer un rôle éducatif?
Je crois que l'image est un produit pédagogique pour les masses. A chaque fois qu'on montre quelque chose, on donne des profils et on donne des exemples à vivre. On crée un modèle de société possible et future. Toutes les images qui sont néfastes ou minimalistes, ou qui méprisent l'individu quel qu'il soit, sont donc tout à fait regrettables.

Est-il est important que le public puisse voir des films africains?
Tout à fait, pour qu'on puisse voir émerger une pensée africaine qui s'exprime par elle-même, une culture africaine qui se revendique comme telle, qui a ses spécificités et ses différences. C'est l'identité qui m'intéresse, c'est de vivre dans un moment où une masse des gens qui représentent un cinquième de l'humanité revendique une culture qui est différente et vivante.

Pourquoi avez-vous choisi de mettre en scène une épopée traditionnelle dans votre film *Keïta*?
Les épopées, les contes, tout le folklore africain, sont une mine pour la thématique du cinéma africain. En tant que fictions, ce sont des histoires fabuleuses, qui sont à filmer absolument. C'est d'abord ce qui m'a intéressé, mais j'ai aussi voulu tirer la sonnette d'alarme pour dire aux Africains : 'Vous avez à côté de vous des histoires à raconter, n'allez pas chercher là où il n'y a pas d'histoires'.

Dans le film, vous semblez vouloir mettre en garde les Africains qui s'éloignent de leurs racines...
Le problème ne se limite pas à l'Afrique. L'Homme s'éloigne de ses racines humaines. Le problème est là. L'Homme, d'une façon générale, a des racines, des préoccupations humaines qui

sont parfois nobles, essentielles et fondamentales, mais on s'éloigne de cela par la force du système. L'économique tue l'humain. Je pense que mon film se situe dans un contexte universel pour dire à l'homme: 'Attention! Faisons marche arrière pour réfléchir sur notre histoire; a-t-on pris la bonne direction?'

humane preoccupations that are at times noble, essential and fundamental. However, the power of the system distances us from them. Economics kill the human. I see my film in a universal context, saying to people: 'Watch out! Let's go back a bit and think about our history. Have we taken the right path?'

Un des personnages principaux est un griot. En tant que cinéaste, estimez-vous être 'un griot moderne'?

Absolument. En tout cas, j'essaye d'être griot, vu que dans la société traditionnelle, le griot avait une fonction assez complexe. Il était la mémoire du peuple, le conseiller du roi. Son rôle était de recueillir l'histoire, de la transmettre; donc on ne peut pas simplement prétendre être un griot moderne, il faut assumer, il faut prouver aussi. Pour moi, le griot est un homme de communication qui est en perte de vitesse. Aujourd'hui, les moyens de communication l'ont dépassé. Il y a toute sorte de médias qui pénètrent directement chez les gens, et le griot ne peut pas suivre cela. Il va donc falloir qu'il passe par ces mêmes médias pour se faire entendre. Il me semble donc qu'aujourd'hui, le cinéma soit un moyen fabuleux pour reconquérir mon public; et cela vaut pour tous les griots. Si tous les griots avaient le cinéma comme moyen de communication, ils auraient repris la parole. En effet, aujourd'hui le griot n'a plus la parole, et c'est ça le problème. On dit qu'aujourd'hui, c'est plus facile de parler que d'écouter, que l'homme a perdu l'écoute, l'écoute est devenue une performance. Or le griot a besoin d'être écouté. A travers le cinéma, le griot peut aujourd'hui reprendre la parole.

One of the main characters is a griot. Do you see yourself, as a filmmaker, as a 'modern griot'?

Absolutely. In any case, I try to be a griot, given that griots fulfilled quite a complex function in traditional society. They were the people's memory and advisors to the king. It was their role to record and to pass on history. So, you can't just claim to be a modern griot; you have to be up to it and to prove your worth. I personally see the griot as a communicator who is losing his touch. He has been left behind by modern modes of communication. There are all kinds of media that directly penetrate people's own homes and the griot can't keep up. It is therefore necessary to use these same media to be heard. I thus see the cinema as a fabulous means for re-conquering my audience today – and that goes for all griots. If all griots had access to film to communicate, they would be able to reappropriate the word. The griot finds it hard to speak out nowadays, and that's the problem. Today, people say that it's easier to speak than to listen, that man has lost the ability to listen, that listening itself is now an achievement. But the griot needs to be listened to. Today, griots can use film to reappropriate the word.

Est-il important que le public en Afrique et en Occident voie des images réalisées par les cinéastes africains?

Tout dépend des images. Il y en a beaucoup qui desservent l'Afrique mais, heureusement, on en voit de moins en moins. De toutes façons, comme les politiciens aiment dire d'une manière souvent démagogique: nous sommes dans un village planétaire aujourd'hui. C'est une réalité. De ce point de vue-là, l'homme n'a pas le choix: la communication s'impose, le brassage s'impose. Personne ne peut rien contre ça. Le système qu'on nous a imposé, l'impose. Aujourd'hui les Occidentaux ont bombardé le ciel de satellites, on voit des images partout. Nous suivons à la seconde près ce qui se passe à Paris, sans parfois savoir ce qui se passe à côté de nous. Néanmoins, quand on arrive à projeter nos propres films, on se rend compte que le public ici a soif de nos images; on voit les gens qui courent pour voir nos films. Quant à la projection de nos films en Occident, tout ce qui peut concourir à un meilleur dialogue, à une meilleure compréhension entre les gens, est positif. Les phénomènes de racisme sont en effet très souvent liés à l'ignorance, à la peur de l'inconnu, à la peur de l'autre, à la peur du vrai visage de l'autre. Et quand, à travers le cinéma, la radio, la presse écrite, j'arrive à montrer à mon alter ego qui je suis, ça peut l'amener à avoir moins peur de moi. C'est pour ça qu'il est fondamental, pour nous, de montrer notre image ailleurs et de la montrer dans ses valeurs, parce que tout n'est pas bon, tout n'est jamais bon. Mais il faut montrer les bonnes choses, il faut reconnaître ce qui est mauvais, il faut le dénoncer. La performance consiste à prendre

Is it important for African and Western audiences to see images made by African directors?

It all depends on the images. There are a lot of images that do Africa a disservice but, fortunately, we see less and less of them. Come what may, as the politicians often demagogically like to say, we are living in a global village today. That's a fact. In that respect, people don't have a choice. We are forced to communicate and to intermingle. No one can change that. The system that was forced on us forces us to. Westerners have now bombarded the sky with satellites. We are surrounded by images. We follow what is going on in Paris practically in real time without always knowing what is happening over here. And yet, when we manage to screen our own films, we soon realise that audiences here are thirsty for our images. We see people flocking to see our films. As for showing our films in the West, anything that contributes to a better dialogue, a better understanding between people is positive. Racist phenomena are very often caused by ignorance, by the fear of the unknown, by the fear of the other, by the fear of the other's real face. When I manage to show my alter ego who I really am in my films, on the radio, in the press, that can help him or her to be less afraid of me. That is why it's crucial to show our image elsewhere and to show this image in all its real value, because not everything is good. Nothing can always be good. But we need to show the good things, we need to recognise what's bad and denounce it. It's an achievement if we can draw on the good in everyone. I'd say that

that more or less sums up my approach as an artist, as a griot. I'm not a purist. I'm not a traditionalist. I am just an African who is culturally hybrid, who thinks in French, who has African impulses, and I want all that to come over in my work. That's why I show a young boy in my film who finds himself caught between his teacher and the elder, and who says he wants both, that he doesn't want to have to choose.

Are the oral traditions a good source of thematic and stylistic inspiration?

Absolutely. That's my whole approach. Griots have techniques for expressing themselves. They tell stories all night long to a whole crowd of people. That's a technical feat. They have techniques to stop the audience from getting bored. If we apply the griot's techniques to film, I believe that we can manage to capture our audiences. In my film, I try to make sure that the audience has no time to catch its breath. That's a traditional griot technique. Griots, like films, are above all about play. Griots play with things without belittling them. They address everyone. They take fateful, fundamental stories and turn them into amusing legends. All those with experience, who are perspicacious, who read between the lines, will understand their meaning. That too is a technique, an achievement that can be of service to film. We ought to try to understand the griot's techniques and adapt them to the new media.

What state is African film in today?

You can't diagnose African film in isolation from film in general. Cinema is in difficulty in general. Film is in difficulty, and African film is in difficulty with film. It just so happens that all over the world, certain major production and distribution companies have a monopoly and when you're not part of the system, you're dead. Thanks to international funding, I, as an African filmmaker, can manage to make films. But it has to be said that these grants don't necessarily help us in terms of profitability, in professional terms. The problem is that we sometimes lack professional reflexes because we are subsidised. When you haven't invested any money in a product, you don't need to earn any back. You don't have the reflex to sell; there are no stakes involved. That's the flip side of the coin. So there are a lot of interesting films that don't get seen simply because they aren't distributed because there is no one behind them who wants to recoup his or her investment. If we one day manage to find producers who take risks, who invest, we might be able to develop a real industry with commercial stakes. But you also need to place things in an international context. We are part of a worldwide economic system where the big sharks devour the little fish. We African filmmakers have to find our bearings all the same and go for it. We have been making films for thirty years, whereas the cinema is a hundred years old. We are still young, therefore, we have the future before us. I am completely optimistic, especially as we have seen some major African films these last few years, which are mature, which are complete.

chez chacun ce qu'il a de bien. Je pense que c'est un peu ma démarche en tant qu'artiste, en tant que griot. Je ne suis pas un puriste, je ne suis pas un traditionaliste, je suis juste un Africain qui est un métisse culturel, qui réfléchit en français, qui a des impulsions africaines et j'ai envie que tout ça ressorte dans mon travail. C'est pour ça que, dans mon film, j'ai montré un petit garçon qui se trouve pris entre son instituteur et un vieux, et qui dit qu'il veut tous les deux, qu'il ne veut pas choisir.

Les traditions orales sont-elles une bonne source d'inspiration à la fois au niveau thématique et au niveau du langage cinématographique?
Complètement. D'ailleurs c'est toute ma démarche. Le griot a une technique d'expression, c'est quelqu'un qui raconte des histoires pendant toute la nuit à toute une assistance. C'est de la performance technique. Il a des astuces pour ne pas ennuyer. Quand on arrive à suivre cette technique du griot à travers le cinéma, je pense qu'on peut capter le public. Dans mon film, j'ai essayé de faire en sorte qu'à aucun moment on ne respire, et ça c'est une technique traditionnelle du griot. Le griot, comme le cinéma, c'est avant tout le jeu, il joue avec les choses sans les détériorer, il s'adresse à tout le monde, il prend des histoires fatidiques, fondamentales et en fait des légendes amusantes. Tous ceux qui sont avertis, qui ont l'esprit perspicace, qui lisent au second degré, vont trouver leur grain là-dedans, et ça aussi c'est de la technique, c'est la performance, qui peut servir au cinéma. On devrait essayer de comprendre les techniques du griot et de les adapter à nos nouveaux médias.

Dans quel état se trouve le cinéma africain aujourd'hui?
On ne peut pas faire le diagnostic du cinéma africain hors du cinéma en général. Le cinéma, en général, est en difficulté. Le cinéma est en difficulté, et le cinéma africain est en difficulté avec le cinéma. Il se trouve que partout dans le monde, il y a un monopole de certaines grandes sociétés de production, de distribution, etc., et quand on n'est pas dedans, on est mort. Grâce aux aides internationales, j'arrive, en tant que jeune cinéaste africain, à faire des films. Mais du point de vue de la rentabilité, d'un point de vue professionnel, il faut dire que ces subventions ne nous aident pas forcément. Notre problème est parfois d'avoir un manque de réflexe professionnel parce qu'on est subventionné. Quand on n'a pas investi d'argent dans un produit, on n'a pas besoin d'en récupérer, on n'a pas le réflexe de la vente, il n'y a pas d'enjeu. C'est le revers de la médaille. Il y a donc beaucoup de films qui sont intéressants, mais qui ne sont pas vus tout simplement parce qu'ils ne sont pas distribués, puisqu'il n'y a personne derrière qui ait envie de récupérer son investissement. Si un jour on arrive à avoir des producteurs qui prennent des risques, qui investissent, on pourra peut-être développer une véritable industrie, avec des enjeux commerciaux. Mais il faut aussi voir tout cela à l'échelle mondiale. On est dans un système économique mondial où les plus grands mangent les plus petits. Là-dedans, nous, réalisateurs africains, devons trouver nos marques et foncer. On a trente ans d'existence, tandis que le cinéma a cent ans ; donc on est jeune. Nos aînés, les premiers qui ont fait des films en Afrique, sont encore jeunes, donc on a l'avenir devant nous. Je suis complètement optimiste, d'autant que ces dernières années, on a vu des films africains majeurs, qui sont mûrs, qui sont complets.

Interview IV
Fanta Régina Nacro director   Ouagadougou. February 1995

Comment se porte le cinéma africain aujourd'hui?
Il est à l'agonie, à cause de la dévaluation, et du fait que les états africains n'ont plus d'argent à investir dans le cinéma. D'autre part, en France on réduit l'aide au cinéma africain. La mode est aujourd'hui plutôt au cinéma d'Asie qu'au cinéma africain.

Qu'est-ce qui pourrait améliorer cette situation?
D'abord, il faut essayer de trouver un public pour nos cinémas et de rentabiliser les films africains sur nos territoires, parce qu'on a un grand public potentiel. Si l'on arrive à développer un réseau d'exploitation à la fois dans les villes et dans le milieu rural, on pourra rentabiliser nos productions. C'est la seule façon, d'après moi, de sauver le cinéma africain.

Est-ce que vous arrivez aujourd'hui à atteindre ce public africain?
Le public africain existe. Lorsqu'on a récemment passé le film *Keita! L'Héritage du Griot* au Cinéma Burkina à Ouagadougou, la salle était comble. Le public s'est déplacé. Pendant trois jours, c'était impossible d'accueillir tout le monde, et on a dû programmer le film dans d'autres salles. Le problème au Burkina Faso, c'est que les films passent seulement en milieu urbain. Ils n'atteignent donc qu'un faible pourcentage de la population. Si l'on arrivait à atteindre la majorité de la population, qui habite en zone rurale, on pourrait commencer à rentabiliser nos films.

Estimez-vous qu'il est important que le public africain voie des images réalisées par des cinéastes africains?
Tout à fait. Quand nous faisons des films, on pense d'abord à notre public africain, aux histoires qui leur plaisent. Ensuite, on pense à internationaliser le public.

Est-ce qu'il est également important que le public occidental voie les films africains?
Oui. Moi, je suis pour l'échange des idées, l'échange culturel. Nous recevons bien des films européens. On fait la part des choses, on retient ce qui est positif de la culture occidentale, et on rejette ce qui est négatif, donc il n'y a pas de raison que le public occidental soit privé des images africaines. D'ailleurs, je pense que plus le public occidental verra des films africains, plus la notion de racisme disparaîtra, car plus on connaît quelqu'un, mieux on comprend ses aspirations, son comportement. A travers le cinéma, qui me semble le moyen le plus adéquat d'éduquer les masses, je pense qu'on peut réussir à établir un échange et une communication véritables entre différentes nations.

What state is African film in today?
It's in dire straits, thanks to devaluation and the fact that the African states have no more money to invest in film. France is reducing its African film funding too. People are more into Asiatic film than African film today.

What might improve the situation?
Firstly, we have to try to find an audience for our films and make returns on African films in our countries because we have large potential audiences here. If we can develop an exploitation network both in the towns and rural areas, we will be able to make our productions cost-effective. I think that that's the only way to save African film.

Do you manage to reach an African audience today?
An African audience exists. When the film *Keita! L'Héritage du Griot* was recently shown at the Cinéma Burkina in Ouagadougou, the place was packed. People came. For three days running, they had to turn people away and ended up having to put the film on in other cinemas. The problem in Burkina Faso is that films are only shown in the urban centres, so they only reach a small percentage of the population. If we could reach the majority of the population who live in rural areas, we'd be able to make our films cost-effective.

Do you think it's important for the African public to see images shot by African directors?
Of course. We have primarily our African audiences and the stories they like in mind when we make our films. Then we think about internationalising the audience.

Is it also important for Western audiences to see African films?
Yes. I believe in exchanging ideas, in cultural exchange. We watch European films. We make allowances, retain what is positive in Western culture and reject the negative, so I don't see why Western audiences shouldn't see African images. Furthermore, the more Western audiences see African films, the more racist preconceptions will be challenged because the more you know someone, the better you understand his or her aspirations and behaviour. I believe that film can help to establish real exchange and communication between different nations, as film is the best means of educating the masses.

Is it possible to identify certain trends in African film today?

There are a lot. I get the impression that some directors are beginning to make films destined for mass audiences. We have understood that people mainly go to the cinema to enjoy themselves. But our films still have an educational aspect, so we necessarily convey messages. In the past, we used, as Sembene put it, to use film as night schools to educate the population and to raise societal questions. That was good, but we need to move on to something different today.

Is it more difficult to make films as a woman director?

I don't know if it's any more difficult. I have to say that I come up against exactly the same problems as a man to shoot. But it's true that there is a certain veiled mentality, a refusal to finance women because they are women, because people imagine that they don't have the necessary talent. Women have to work very hard to make their mark. However, as soon as you do manage to make that mark, to produce proper work, people forget your gender. Having said that, if a woman makes a poor film, people immediately say that that's to be expected because the filmmaker was a woman! So it's up to us to fight back, to propose good products, to prove our talents. It's a shame that we have to convince people that we can produce good work in this way, that we aren't automatically considered to be on an equal footing with other young filmmakers.

Interview V
Idrissa Ouedraogo director

Ouagadougou. February 1995

After having shot several films in rural African environments, why did you choose to set your latest film, *Cri du Coeur*, in a French town?

Quite simply because I wanted to. It's important to be able to shoot wherever we want, wherever we feel is right. The world should be open to film.

Do you think that audiences readily accept African filmmakers changing their settings and styles in this way?

There are prejudices about what African directors should or shouldn't do, but it must be said that these prejudices exist on both sides. Certain

Certains Africains pensent sûrement qu'un Africain ne devrait pas tourner en Europe, qu'il y perd quelque chose, qu'en Europe on n'est plus Africain du tout. Personnellement, j'ai pris tellement de distance par rapport à ce qui est communément appelé 'le cinéma africain' que cela ne me fait plus rien. Petit à petit, je pense que les gens seront d'accord pour admettre qu'il ne faut pas s'enfermer. Même si au départ on est mal compris, même si les gens me disent que mon personnage ne ressemble pas à un immigré de base, dans quelques années ils verront peut-être les choses différemment.

Est-ce que vous essayer de cibler un certain public avec vos films?
Quand on fait quelque chose, on espère que tous les publics pourront le voir. Même quand quelqu'un s'enferme dans sa case pour faire quelque chose, il le fait d'abord pour lui-même, et ensuite il a envie que les autres le voient. Personne ne fait quelque chose pour un public délimité, précis. Je pense que la fonction de l'art c'est d'aller vers d'autres horizons, d'autres cieux, malgré le fait que les gens n'ont souvent pas les mêmes cultures, les mêmes ouvertures sur le monde.

Vous avez produit le film *Guimba* de Cheick Oumar Sissoko. Est-ce que cette complicité reflète une certaine solidarité entre les cinéastes africains?
Je ne peux pas en parler en dehors de mon expérience personnelle. Les cinéastes africains ne se ressemblent pas, ils n'ont pas les mêmes goûts, les mêmes envies. Ce n'est pas parce qu'on est tous cinéastes africains qu'on partage la même vision du monde. Tout ça nous met toujours dans le ghetto, on ne se ressemble pas, on ne pense pas la même chose, on n'a pas les mêmes envies. C'est normal, c'est la diversité d'idées, d'opinions qui mettra un jour sur pied un véritable cinéma national d'une part, et peut-être des cinémas africains forts d'autre part.

Les cinéastes africains arrivent-ils à s'imposer dans le paysage cinématographique mondial?
Cela va arriver. Le cinéma est encore dans sa phase de balbutiements, de recherche de voie, et c'est sûr que, quand nous retrouverons notre voie en nous disant que ce n'est peut-être pas nécessaire de produire dans les mêmes conditions que les Européens, qu'il y a peut-être une autre voie, on aura trouvé la vraie solution à nos problèmes. Le cinéma, après tout, c'est aussi économique, c'est de l'argent, or on n'en a pas beaucoup, donc il faut réinventer le cinéma autrement. C'est ça qui devrait être notre réflexion maintenant.

Est-ce que vous avez l'impression qu'on voit assez d'images issues d'autres cultures dans le monde?
Non. Les pays occidentaux refusent cette complémentarité des cinémas d'outre mer, ce qui est dommage. J'espère que ça changera un jour, vraiment, dans l'intérêt du cinéma mondial. On arrive tous à un certain type d'expression qu'on ne peut plus renouveler parce que toutes les grandes histoires ont été faites et dites. On ne peut les renouveler qu'en tenant compte de l'apport de toutes les cultures.

Africans unquestionably think that an African shouldn't shoot in Europe, that you lose something, that you're not truly African in Europe. Personally, I have distanced myself so far from what is commonly referred to as 'African cinema' that it doesn't bother me anymore. I think that people will gradually accept that we shouldn't restrict ourselves. Even if you're initially misunderstood, even if people tell me that my character doesn't resemble your average immigrant, in a few years time they might see things differently.

Do you try to reach a certain type of audience in your films?
When you make something, you hope that all kinds of audiences will see it. Even when a person shuts himself up in his hut to make something, he might do so for himself first of all, but then wants others to see it too. No one makes things for a specific, determined audience. I believe that the function of art is to reach out to other horizons, other skies, even though people rarely have the same cultures or the same visions of the world.

You produced Cheick Oumar Sissoko's film *Guimba*. Does this collaboration reflect a certain solidarity between African filmmakers?
I can only speak about my own personal experience. African filmmakers are not all alike. They don't have the same tastes, the same desires. We don't all share the same vision of the world just because we're all African filmmakers. All that always puts us in a ghetto. We aren't alike, we don't think the same things, and we don't have the same desires. That's normal. It's the diversity of ideas, of opinions that will lead to the creation of a real national cinema one day, and perhaps to thriving African cinemas too.

Do African filmmakers make enough of a mark in international film circles?
They will eventually. Our cinema is still in its early stages. It is still seeking its path and it is certain that when we do find it by accepting that we maybe don't have to produce in the same conditions as the Europeans, that there may be another way, we will have found the real solution to our problems. Film is economic too, after all; it involves money. But we don't have much, so we have to reinvent the cinema differently. That's what we should be thinking about now.

Do you think that we get to see enough images made by people of different cultures?
No. Western countries reject the complementarity of overseas films, which is a real shame. I hope that that will change one day, I really do, in the interest of world film. We have all reached a certain type of expression that is impossible to renew anymore because all the big stories have been said and done. They can only be given a new lease of life by taking all cultures' contributions into account.

Does film reflect the culture it is from?

What's marvellous in film is that all peoples share major universal emotions such as joy, fear, violence, and hatred. So there is already something fundamentally open in what we call the world's major emotions. These emotions are an integral part of film.

Le cinéma peut donc refléter la culture dont il est issu?
Ce qui est beau dans le cinéma, c'est que les grandes émotions universelles - la joie, la peur, la violence, la haine - sont partagées par tous les peuples ; donc il y a déjà quelque chose de fondamentalement ouvert dans ce qu'on appelle les grandes émotions du monde. Ce sont ces émotions qui font partis du cinéma.

Interview VI
Abderrahmane Sissako director

Ouagadougou. February 1995

What made you chose film as a form of expression?

Film is much more universal as it uses images. It's not a language that belongs to a given country. It is thus somehow easier to appropriate film than to write in French, for example – a language I don't completely master, that isn't my language – or to write in my own language which, due to acculturation in Africa, is neither written nor very widespread. Film thus struck me as the most adequate means of expression.

Can African filmmakers reappropriate the image of Africa by making films?

If there are a lot of African filmmakers, there will be a lot of African images made by African filmmakers, but I don't think that that should be a priority in itself. I believe that life, the image, the continent belongs to everyone. People are free to go wherever they want to do the things they feel strongly about. It is good that Africans make films here that they feel strongly about, that Europeans come here to make films that they feel strongly about too. I see it as a personal matter every time. But, having said that, Africans are maybe in a better position to touch on, to speak about their childhood, as that's what film is about too. You speak about things you know, your culture, whether consciously or not.

Do you think it's important for African audiences to see films made by Africans?

Of course. It's vital, even, because people have always done things in our place, they have always forced things on us. They forced us to grow cotton, they forced us to grow coffee, they forced us to grow peanuts, they imposed such and such a product, and today, they are forcing images on us. We are being invaded once again. It's another form of acculturation. If Africans can manage to make films and to fight back, if other images get made and screened, that's a victory. People can be

Pourquoi avez-vous choisi le cinéma comme moyen d'expression?
Le cinéma est beaucoup plus universel du fait qu'il s'agit de l'image. Ce n'est pas une langue qui appartient à tel ou tel pays, donc il est en quelque sorte plus facile de se l'approprier, que d'écrire en français par exemple, une langue que je ne maîtrise pas, qui n'est pas ma langue, ou que d'écrire dans ma propre langue qui, à cause de l'acculturation en Afrique, n'est ni écrite ni véritablement répandu. Le cinéma me semblait donc le moyen le plus adéquat.

Est-ce qu'en faisant des films, les cinéastes africains peuvent réapproprier l'image de l'Afrique?
S'il y a beaucoup de cinéastes africains, il y aura beaucoup d'images africaines faites par les cinéastes africains, mais je ne pense pas que cela doit être une priorité en soi. Je crois que la vie, l'image, le continent n'est pas une appartenance, chaque personne peut aller là où il le sent pour faire les choses qui le touchent. Que les Africains fassent des films ici qui les touchent est une bonne chose. Que les Européens viennent ici faire des films qui les touchent, je crois que c'est une question personnelle à chaque fois. Mais, ceci dit, les Africains sont mieux placés peut-être pour toucher, pour parler de leur enfance, car le cinéma c'est cela aussi. On parle de choses qu'on connaît, de sa culture, inconsciemment ou sciemment.

Est-ce que vous pensez que c'est important que le public africain voie des films tournés par les Africains?
Forcément. C'est même vital, parce qu'on a toujours fait les choses à notre place, on nous a toujours imposé des choses. On nous a imposé de cultiver le coton, on a imposé à certains de cultiver le café, on a imposé à d'autres de cultiver l'arachide, on a imposé telle ou telle chose, tel produit, et aujourd'hui on nous impose les images. On est donc envahi, encore une fois. C'est une autre forme d'acculturation. Si les Africains arrivent à faire des films et à se battre, s'il y a d'autres images à côté de cela, qui se font, qui se montrent, cela est une victoire.

199

On peut ainsi former les gens, on peut former une jeunesse, et les gens prendront plus conscience. Je crois que ce problème existe également en Europe, où l'on impose à des enfants depuis le bas âge des images, un certain cinéma américain. C'est un danger. Mais la solution n'est pas l'interdiction de ces images-là. Il ne faut pas qu'on dise qu'il y a trop de films américains ou chinois ici, qu'il faut les taxer, qu'il faut les interdire, non. Cela ne résoudrait jamais la question. Il faut encourager son propre cinéma pour qu'il y ait plus d'images.

Justement, est-ce qu'il existe des moyens d'aide en Afrique?
Non, mais ça va venir. Il y a de plus en plus de films, et malgré les difficultés de production, les films se font. Il ne faut pas non plus chercher à misérabiliser la production africaine. C'est aussi très difficile pour les Européens. Il faut être conscient de ces difficultés, mais il ne faut pas toujours pleurer dessus. Il faut tenir et faire ce qu'on a envie de faire.

Vous sentez-vous concerné par le fait qu'on fête aujourd'hui le centenaire du cinéma?
Le centenaire du cinéma nous a donné ici au Fespaco l'occasion de faire une rétrospective des films coloniaux, qui ont presque cent ans aujourd'hui. Cela nous a permis de voir comment l'Afrique a été filmée, il y a presque cent ans. C'est une chose très importante pour moi. Je savais l'existence de ces images là, mais en les revoyant, j'ai vu comme on a de différentes façons de violer les gens. Le regard d'un Pygmée devant la caméra qui ne comprend pas ce qui se passe est un viol. Il faut le dire, c'est vrai. Peut-être que ces gens là avaient des intentions positives, mais il y a eu viol, il y a toujours eu viol, et les images sont là pour prouver ce viol permanent. Sans essayer d'être péjoratif, je dirai que le blanc a vécu trois mille ans le privilège de voir les autres sans qu'on le voie lui-même, et aujourd'hui les Africains font des films, ils peuvent porter leur regard ailleurs, au-delà de leur continent. Cela est une priorité pour moi.

Pensez-vous que les Occidentaux sont prêts à s'ouvrir aux images venues du continent africain?
Je pense qu'ils ne sont pas prêts à refuser. C'est une question de longue haleine. Il faut connaître – on n'accepte pas facilement ce qu'on ne connaît pas. Plus il y aura d'images, plus il y aura des gens qui sont intéressés par ces images. Mais la priorité doit d'abord être l'Afrique. Il y aura toujours de bons et de mauvais films. Il ne faut pas exiger que tous les films soient bons, ici ou ailleurs. Mais il faut qu'il y ait une amélioration des films, de plus en plus d'exigences, que nous soyons beaucoup plus attentifs à ce qu'on fait dans la forme, que nous comprenions que le problème le plus fondamental n'est pas la production, c'est l'apprentissage de la profession.

trained in this way, we can form a generation, and people will become more aware. I think that the same problem exists in Europe too, where images, where a certain type of American cinema, are forced on children at a very young age. That's dangerous. But the answer isn't to ban these images. We shouldn't say there are too many American or Chinese films here, that we must tax them or ban them, no. That would never resolve the problem. We have to encourage our own cinema so that there are more images.

Are there any film subsidies in Africa?
No, but they'll come. There are more and more films. Despite the production difficulties, films do get made. We mustn't try to pauperise African production. It's very difficult for Europeans too. We need to be aware of these difficulties, but we shouldn't spend all our time carrying on about them. We have to hang on in there and do what we want to do.

Do you feel concerned by the fact that it's the centenary of cinema this year?
The centenary of cinema has given us the opportunity here at the FESPACO to put on a retrospective of colonial films that are nearly a hundred years old today. This retrospective has shown us how Africa was filmed almost a hundred years ago. That has been very important for me. I knew that these images existed, but seeing them again, I realised how we have different ways of violating people. A Pygmy's gaze before a camera who doesn't know what is going on is a violation. We have to say so. It's true. Maybe those people had positive intentions, but there were a lot of violations, there have always been, and the images are there to prove this constant violation. Without wanting to be pejorative, I would say that white people have had the privilege of seeing others without being seen for three thousand years. Today, Africans are making films, they can project their gaze elsewhere, outside their continent. I consider that a priority.

Do you think that Westerners are ready to accept images made on the African continent?
I don't think they are ready to refuse. It's an on-going question. You have to be familiar with things. People don't easily accept what they don't know. The more images there are, the more people there will be who are interested in these images. But Africa initially needs to be the priority. There will always be good and bad films. You can't expect all films to be good, here or elsewhere. But films need to improve, we need to be more and more demanding, much more attentive to what we do in terms of form, we need to understand that the most fundamental problem isn't production, it's learning the trade.

Interview VII
Cheick Oumar Sissoko director

Ouagadougou. February 1995

Guimba represents a clear change of style compared to your first two overtly political films. Is it still a politically committed film all the same?

Yes. I think that if you look at the film closely, it still poses the problem of African societies and Malian society in particular. The film questions the aspects that hinder society's development. Even if we use a tale, a legend, the film oscillates between the tale and reality. The reality is that of the continent today, which is at a turning point between the days of the tyrant, which are not completely over, and the days of democracy, of the demands of a nation that wants to take its destiny in hand. We are looking at a question here that will impede our society's harmonious development towards social progress if it is not resolved. The question is what man should make of the continent's cultural, human and spiritual heritage. Up until now, it has been supremely ignored. It has never been allowed to blossom. Are Africa's currently emerging cultural and political horizons going to ignore this cultural, human and spiritual heritage, which is indispensable if initiatives are to flourish, if we really want to tackle our problems?

Is there a risk that the film's symbolic aspect might cloud its message?

We insisted on the style of the film because audiences are often uncomfortable when a film tries to be very political in the banner-waving sense of the term. I think that the message can be got over better when a work is made artistically. Of course, people who are not of Manding culture will sometimes find it hard to understand all the messages. The film is also in an African language that is so metaphoric, so vivid, so full of verve that it's difficult to capture all its subtleties in the subtitles. That's another aspect that can make it difficult to understand.

Do you think that the film can help audiences, and especially Western audiences, to understand Manding culture better?

What I'd like most of all is that Westerners get to see the film, that they understand that we have things to show, that we have important things that need to be taken into account. We aren't what people have always shown us to be. But I'm not the first, and I won't be the last, to show this kind of image, images that try to show that Africa has a wealth of very great cultures, of great civilisations, that ought to be respected. People should even immerse themselves in these civilisations' values, as they can help enrich other cultures.

Guimba marque un net changement de style par rapport à vos deux premiers films qui étaient très ouvertement politiques. Reste-t-il cependant un film engagé?

Oui. Je pense que si l'on regarde le fond de ce film, il pose toujours le problème des sociétés africaines, et en particulier la société malienne. Le film s'interroge sur les aspects qui entrave le développement d'une société. Même si nous utilisons un conte, une légende, le film varie entre conte et réalité. La réalité c'est celle du continent aujourd'hui qui se trouve à une charnière entre l'époque du tyran, qui n'est pas révolue, et l'époque de la démocratie, des exigences de nos peuples qui veulent se prendre en charge. Et là, nous posons une question qui, si elle n'est pas résolue, constitue une entrave au développement harmonieux de notre société vers le progrès social. C'est la question de ce que l'homme doit faire de l'héritage culturel, humain et spirituel du continent. Jusque-là, celui-ci a été superbement ignoré, il n'a jamais pu s'épanouir. Alors, est-ce que le nouvel horizon qui est en train de se développer en Afrique, que l'on peut qualifier de culturel et de politique, va ignorer cet héritage culturel, humain et spirituel qui est indispensable à l'éclosion des initiatives, à la prise en charge véritable de nos problèmes?

Avez-vous l'impression que l'aspect symbolique de ce film risque d'obscurcir son message?

Nous avons insisté sur l'écriture cinématographique parce que très souvent, le public est fort embarrassé quand le film essaie d'être très politique dans le sens slogan. Je pense que, quand l'œuvre est faite artistiquement, le message peut passer beaucoup plus sûrement. Evidemment, les gens qui ne sont pas de culture mandingue vont avoir quelques difficultés à comprendre tous ses messages. En outre, le film est dans une langue africaine tellement métaphorique, tellement imagée, tellement vive qu'on arrive difficilement à tout mettre dans les sous-titres. Ça c'est un autre aspect de difficulté de compréhension.

Justement, pensez-vous que ce film peut aider le public, et surtout le public occidental, à mieux comprendre la culture mandingue?

Ce que je souhaiterais surtout, c'est que le film puisse être vu par les Occidentaux, qu'ils comprennent que nous avons des choses à montrer, que nous avons des choses importantes dont il faut tenir compte. Nous ne sommes pas ceux que l'on a toujours dépeint. Mais je n'ai pas été le premier, et je ne serai pas le dernier, à avoir montré des images de ce genre, des images qui essaient de montrer que l'Afrique est riche de très grandes cultures, de très grandes civilisations, et qu'à ce titre, elle doit être respectée. On doit rechercher même à s'imprégner des valeurs de ces civilisations parce qu'elles ne peuvent qu'enrichir les autres cultures.

Il y a, depuis quelque temps, une tendance chez certains réalisateurs africains à se tourner vers les sujets historiques ou traditionnels. Pour quelle raison y a-t-il ce retour vers le passé? Est-ce que c'est un moyen de mieux contempler l'avenir?

Je crois qu'auparavant, les sujets historiques étaient focalisés uniquement sur le passé sans essayer de poser le regard sur la situation actuelle. On pensait qu'il fallait nécessairement, et c'est très juste, montrer que l'Afrique a eu ses grandes civilisations, a une histoire. Elle n'a pas été écrite, ou quand elle a été écrite, c'était avec le regard d'autres personnes qui l'ont écrite à leur avantage, donc elle a été plus ou moins falsifiée. Dans mon film, au contraire, nous parlons d'un passé, mais en se référant à ce qui est en train de se passer aujourd'hui, et c'est ça l'utilisation, disons politique, de ce passé. L'héritage du passé est certes important, mais on ne peut pas l'embrasser complètement. Il faut faire la part des choses ; et ce qui est intéressant, c'est que nous sommes justement en train d'entamer l'époque de la démocratie, l'époque des exigences pour aller vers le progrès social ; et ceci demande non pas un ressourcement, mais une utilisation judicieuse de cet héritage.

Est-ce que vous estimez qu'il est important pour le public africain de voir des images tournées par les réalisateurs africains?

Absolument, sinon nous n'aurons que des références venues d'ailleurs, c'est-à-dire d'autres valeurs culturelles, des films, des images qui vont devenir nos repères ; et ceci amène au mimétisme, à l'acculturation. Dans une Afrique où il y a un grand pourcentage d'analphabètes, les images et le son peuvent être d'un apport formidable, ils peuvent permettre aux gens de comprendre les choses, de comprendre leur continent, de comprendre le monde. Je crois que ceci doit nous amener à nous battre pour que nos films soient vus.

Est-ce que vous arrivez à savoir comment le public africain réagit à vos films?

Nous, cinéastes africains, avons la chance que le public africain ait soif d'images de l'Afrique, soif d'images des cinéastes africains. Il est curieux de lire entre les images, de se reconnaître dedans, de voir son pays, et de voir un pays africain dans le mouvement, parce que jusqu'à là on n'a vu que les images des autres.

Votre précédent film Finzan adresse la question de l'oppression des femmes. Comment a-t-il été accueilli?

D'une façon générale, Finzan a été très bien accueilli. Il faut dire aussi que les femmes au Mali sont suffisamment mobilisées pour défendre leurs droits. Une des questions traitées dans le film a été l'objet de beaucoup de discussions, néanmoins, c'est la question de l'excision. Dans les débats, on a senti que les gens lient la question de l'excision à l'Islam, alors que l'excision est tout à fait facultative dans cette religion. Cela montre cependant que ce genre de film est tout à fait nécessaire pour engager les débats.

Comme dans vos précédents films, dans Guimba vous peignez le portrait des femmes qui résistent à la volonté des hommes. Pour quelle raison choisissez-vous toujours de représenter ces femmes puissantes?

Several African directors have started exploring historical or traditional subjects in recent years. What has prompted this revisiting of the past? Is it a way of better contemplating the future?

Previously, historical subjects focused solely on the past without trying to make people consider the current situation. We used – quite rightly – to think that we had to show that Africa has had its major civilisations, that it has its own history. This history wasn't written, or when it was, it was written from the point of view of people who wrote it to their own advantage, which means that it was more or less falsified. In my film, however, we address the past by referring to what is happening today. That is what you could call a 'political' use of this past. The heritage of the past is obviously important, but we cannot embrace it entirely. We have to weigh things up. What's interesting is that we are precisely just entering the democratic era, an era of greater demands for social progress. This means that we have to use this heritage judiciously, rather than simply returning to the roots.

Do you think it is important for African audiences to see images shot by African directors?

Absolutely, otherwise we will end up with only foreign references. Other cultural values, films, and images will become our markers, leading to mimesis and acculturation. In an Africa where there are a large percentage of illiterate people, images and sound can be of massive value. They can help people to understand things, to understand their continent, to understand the world. I think that that alone should make us fight to make sure our films get shown.

How do African audiences tend to react to your films?

We African filmmakers are lucky that the African public is thirsty for images of Africa, thirsty for images by African filmmakers. Our public is willing to read between the images, wants to recognise itself in them, to see its own country, to see African countries on the move, because up until now, it has only seen other people's images.

Your previous film, *Finzan*, addressed the issue of female oppression. How did audiences react to this?

Finzan was generally given a very good reception. It has to be said that Malian women are sufficiently mobilised to defend their rights. However, one of the issues addressed in the film caused a lot of debate – the question of female circumcision. We could tell from the debates that people link the question of female circumcision to Islam, when it is in fact totally optional in this religion. This showed, however, that this kind of film was very necessary for launching the debate.

As in your previous films, you paint the portrait of women who resist their menfolk's will in *Guimba*. Why do you always choose to represent such powerful women?

Firstly, to show the reality of our countries. Women have always been quick to react to social injustice ever since the colonial era. They are very sensitive to other people's problems. Secondly, it is part of a political approach that insists on the necessary emancipation of women. This has to be part of all social progress in our societies. We have to show the acts of which our women are capable.

Guimba adopts a tale format. Why did you choose to take inspiration from the oral traditions?

We are totally immersed in these oral traditions. Any African could have told the story I tell in the film – or at least any Manding – because our ears have heard so many things from our mothers, our grandmothers, our sisters, from the griot storytellers. There are thousands of fabulous tales. We can adapt them. There is above all an oral style of narration that, if used wisely, can help us to bring something to film.

Can oral narrative structures help constitute a specifically African film language?

This narrative style has enabled me to blend fiction and documentary in each of my films. When the narrator, the storyteller, the griot tells a story, he becomes an actor in the story at a given moment. He sometimes reinforces the story with a second tale that is related to the first one. This enables filmmakers who take inspiration from these techniques to introduce images that are closer to documentary and which confirm or reinforce the narrator's words, or which demonstrate that it's not just an isolated event.

Do you, as a filmmaker, consider yourself a modern griot?

Even if we aren't griots – it's difficult to replace the griot – we can at least play part of the griot's role in Africa today. We can certainly be compared to the griot, but 'modern griot' is such a heavy name to bear because the griot was the storehouse of all a country or a family's knowledge. He was the one who had to transmit the principals of social and family life and it was his job to assist and educate new kings.

African films often play an educational role. Does this reflect the role the oral traditions play in African society?

I believe that there is always a moral in all films. It is true that in African film, in an Africa that has huge problems to resolve, we have a duty to use our images to generate a movement, a dynamic of understanding our problems, so that this can then engender a dynamic of change. That's vital.

Do you think that African film will end up imposing its voice on the international cinematic stage?

I'm truly convinced so because we have many stories to tell, we have new approaches to offer in film, which will increasingly interest audiences.

D'abord pour montrer une réalité des faits que connaissent nos pays. Depuis la période coloniale, ce sont les femmes qui sont promptes à réagir devant l'injustice sociale. Elles sont très sensibles aux problèmes des autres. Et puis, ensuite, cela procède d'une démarche politique qui insiste sur la nécessaire émancipation de la femme qui doit accompagner tout progrès social dans nos sociétés. Il faut montrer les actes dont sont capables nos femmes.

Guimba se présente sous forme de conte. Pourquoi avez-vous choisi de vous inspirer des traditions orales?

On est imprégné de cette tradition orale. L'histoire que je raconte dans le film aurait pu être racontée par n'importe quel Africain, en tout cas de la société mandingue ; parce que nos oreilles ont beaucoup entendu de nos mères, de nos grandes-mères, de nos sœurs, des conteurs, des griots. Des histoires fabuleuses, il y en a des milliers. Nous avons la possibilité de faire des adaptations. Il y a surtout un style de narration de cette tradition orale qui peut nous permettre, si nous arrivons à l'utiliser à bon escient, d'apporter quelque chose au cinéma.

Est-ce que les structures narratives des traditions orales peuvent enrichir un langage cinématographique proprement africain?

Ce style de narration m'a permis d'allier fiction et documentaire dans chacun des mes films. Quand le narrateur, le conteur, le griot, raconte une histoire, il devient, à un moment donné, un acteur de cette histoire. Parfois, il renforce également son histoire par une deuxième histoire, qui est liée à la première. Cela permet aux cinéastes qui s'inspirent de ces techniques, d'introduire des images, qui ont plus l'aspect du reportage, et qui confirment ou renforcent les propos du narrateur, ou qui montrent qu'il ne s'agit pas d'un fait isolé.

Est-ce que vous avez l'impression en tant que cinéaste d'être un griot moderne?

Même si nous ne sommes pas des griots, car il est difficile de remplacer le griot, nous avons en tout cas une partie du rôle du griot à jouer dans l'Afrique d'aujourd'hui. On peut sûrement nous assimiler à cela, mais c'est un nom tellement lourd à porter 'griot moderne', parce que le griot était détenteur de tout le savoir d'un pays ou d'une famille ; c'est lui qui devait transmettre les principes de la vie sociale et familiale, et quand il avait un nouveau roi, c'était à lui de le former, de l'éduquer.

Les films africains jouent souvent un rôle éducatif. Est-ce que cela est un reflet du rôle que jouent les traditions orales dans les sociétés africaines?

Je crois qu'il y a toujours une morale dans tous les films. Dans les films africains nous avons le devoir, c'est vrai, dans une Afrique qui a d'immenses problèmes à résoudre, d'utiliser nos images pour entraîner un mouvement, une dynamique de compréhension des problèmes pour ensuite entraîner une dynamique de changement. C'est capital.

Pensez-vous que le cinéma africain finira par imposer sa voix sur la scène cinématographique mondiale?

J'en suis vraiment convaincu parce que nous avons beaucoup de choses à raconter, nous avons des démarches nouvelles à proposer par le cinéma qui vont intéresser de plus en plus le public.

Interview VIII
Jean-Marie Teno director

Paris, August 1997

Vos propres films sont plutôt engagés. Estimez-vous donc que le cinéaste a une responsabilité vis-à-vis de sa société?
Toute personne qui s'exprime, qui compose de la musique, qui écrit, qui peint a une responsabilité vis-à-vis du monde qui l'entoure. Moi, j'ai choisi le cinéma pour exprimer ma frustration face à l'injustice. C'est un choix personnel. Il y a des gens qui peuvent vivre dans l'injustice et tout à fait s'en accommoder. Ce n'est pas une vocation de cinéaste. Chacun choisit le moyen qui lui est propre pour exprimer sa frustration ou son refus d'une forme d'injustice, donc je ne dirai pas que c'est le cinéaste qui a une responsabilité. Chaque individu a cette responsabilité.

Pourquoi avez-vous choisi de vous exprimer par l'image?
Pour moi c'était tout un concours de circonstances. Je n'ai pas réfléchi en me disant 'c'est du cinéma que je veux faire'. Je suis né dans un pays où il y avait une très forte censure quand j'étais petit, et où il y avait, où il y a toujours, une injustice très grande. L'écrit était tellement censuré que c'était presque impossible d'écrire. Je voyais des journalistes, des écrivains qui avaient beaucoup de problèmes, comme Mongo Beti, par exemple, qui était un des plus grands écrivains camerounais. Je voyais comment les journalistes étaient régulièrement soumis à la censure. Je me suis donc dit que les images seraient totalement incontestables. Je voyais comment de les manipuler. En plus, j'avais remarqué en 1974 quand Daniel Kamwa avait fait *Pousse-Pousse*, à quel point la fascination des gens pour l'image pouvait être utilisée pour éventuellement leur passer des messages autres que le message officiel. J'aimais beaucoup aller au cinéma aussi, j'aimais beaucoup les films indiens qui étaient les seuls films disponibles dans la petite ville d'où je venais. Donc toutes ces choses ont fait que j'ai choisi le cinéma.

Est-ce qu'il y a une censure au niveau des images? Est-ce que vous pouvez montrer vos films librement au Cameroun?
J'ai toujours voulu toucher le plus grand nombre de gens avec mes films, et donc la télévision était le premier lieu où je voulais que mes documentaires, mes courts-métrages et, enfin, mon premier film de fiction soient montrés pour qu'ils puissent toucher les gens vraiment et complètement chez eux. Or, mes films sont totalement inaccessibles à la télévision camerounaise parce qu'il y a une censure de fait qui a fait dire au directeur de la télévision que, de son vivant, il ne passerait pas mes films. Une réelle censure s'exerce donc à l'encontre de mon travail sauf quand il est imposé de l'extérieur par les gens avec qui je travaille et qui décident que ce film doit passer à la télévision. C'est tout. Je pourrais montrer mes films dans les salles, mais je ne

Your films are highly committed. Do you think that filmmakers have a responsibility vis-à-vis their societies?
Any person who expresses themselves, who composes music, who writes, who paints, has a responsibility to the world around him or her. I personally chose film to express my frustration in the face of injustice. It's a personal choice. There are people who can live in injustice and adapt to it no problem. It's not a question of having a vocation as a filmmaker. Everyone chooses their own means to express their frustration or their refusal of a form of injustice, so I wouldn't say that it's the filmmaker who has a responsibility. Every individual has that responsibility.

Why did you choose film as a form of expression?
Due to a whole combination of circumstances. I never sat down and thought, 'I want to make films'. I was born in a country where there was very strict censorship when I was little and where there was – and still is – a great deal of injustice. Writing was so censored that it was almost impossible to write. I saw journalists, writers who had a lot of problems, like Mongo Beti, for example, who was one of Cameroon's best writers. I saw how journalists were regularly censored. So I said to myself that images would be totally incontestable, that they would be difficult to manipulate. Moreover, in 1974 when Daniel Kamwa made *Pousse-Pousse*, I saw the extent to which people's fascination with images could be used to get messages over that were different to the official one. I used to love going to the cinema too. I loved the Indian films that were the only films you could see in the little town I was from. So, all these things made me choose film.

Are images censored? Are you free to show your work in Cameroon?
I have always wanted to reach the widest audience possible with my films, so I wanted my documentaries, my shorts, and my first fiction film to be shown on television first of all so that they could truly and completely reach people in their own homes. My films are totally inaccessible on Cameroonian television, however, because there is a *de facto* censorship. The chairman of the television company once told me that he would never show my films in his lifetime. My work is effectively censored, therefore, except when it is imposed from the outside by the people I work with and who decide that a film has to be shown on TV. That's all. I could show my films in the cinemas, but I don't think that

that's the right place, or the right audience. For the time being, I don't make films that are intended for the cinemas.

Not even *Clando*?
Even *Clando* started out as a television drama. It was initially meant to be shown on TV.

What do you consider the role of film to be in Africa? Your own films are highly committed. Can film change things?
Film is both entertainment and also a great means of raising people's awareness. I mean, for example, Italian neo-realism and all the films that marked me, that have contributed to forging my culture. I think that film is part of culture and it is perhaps culture that can encourage people to change, to question themselves. It's great if film can serve that purpose alone. Entertainment film also exists and independent cinema has its place here too. I don't think film is any different in Africa from elsewhere. There are always independent filmmakers trying to survive the onslaught of dominant thought.

Can it be said that there are only 'independent' filmmakers in Africa today?
Yes, you could say that, but at the same time, they are so due to circumstances. Not everyone has really chosen independent film. Their films are often independent simply because budgets are small and they don't have the adequate means. I consider that we are in a transition period. Industries will get set up and, with digital video, there will maybe be more and more low-budget mainstream films made.

Is it important for African filmmakers to produce other images than those that come from elsewhere? Is it important that African audiences see these images?
Of course it's important. All over the world people are fighting for their images to exist, to express their own realities. It is obviously important for people to be able to speak about themselves, so that they don't just become objects or settings in which other people come to tell their stories. It is important for individuals to be able to identify with people who are like them, to be able to see their reality on the screen, so that they feel that they exist, especially for people who have been colonised, because colonisation amounts to reducing the other to a non-being. From the moment people come and try to annihilate your whole culture, it is vital that artists resist through themselves, through what they do, through their art, because everything possible is done on an economic level to stop you from existing.

Do you think it's important for African directors to find a specifically 'African' film style? Is it important to distinguish from other film cultures?
There is an automatic distinction that comes from the fact that it's an

crois pas que ce soit ni le bon endroit, ni le bon public. Pour le moment je n'ai pas fait de films destinés à être montrés en salle.

Même *Clando*?
Clando reste quand même un téléfilm au départ. Sa première vocation était de passer à la télévision.

Quelle place accordez-vous au cinéma en Afrique? Vos propres films sont très politisés. Est-ce que le cinéma peut faire changer les choses?
Le cinéma est à la fois un divertissement, mais aussi un formidable moyen de 'conscientisation' des gens. Je pense au néo-réalisme italien, à tous ces films qui m'ont marqué, qui ont fait aussi ma culture. Je crois que le cinéma est un élément de la culture, et c'est peut-être la culture qui amène les gens à changer, à réfléchir sur eux-mêmes. Si le cinéma pouvait ne servir qu'à ça, ça serait bien. De l'autre côté il y a aussi le cinéma de divertissement. Je crois que la place du cinéma indépendant est là aussi. Je ne pense pas que le cinéma en Afrique soit différent d'ailleurs. Il y a toujours des indépendants qui essayent de se battre pour exister au milieu de la pensée unique.

Peut-on dire qu'il n'y a que des cinéastes 'indépendants' en Afrique actuellement?
Oui, on peut dire ça, mais à la fois ils le sont certainement parce que c'est dans la conjoncture. Ce ne sont pas tous des gens qui ont réellement fait le choix d'un cinéma indépendant. Leur cinéma est souvent indépendant simplement parce que les budgets sont petits et qu'il n'y a pas de moyens. Je crois qu'on est dans une période de transition. Des industries vont se mettre en place et, avec la vidéo numérique, peut-être y aura-t-il de plus en plus de films grand public qui seront faits avec peu de moyens.

Est-il est important que les cinéastes africains produisent d'autres images que celles qui viennent d'ailleurs? Est-il important que le public africain voie ces images?
Evidemment c'est important. Partout dans le monde les gens se battent pour que leurs images existent, pour exprimer eux-mêmes leur réalité. Il est évident que c'est important que les gens puissent parler d'eux-mêmes, qu'ils ne soient pas juste des objets ou alors des décors, pour qu'on vienne raconter leurs histoires. C'est important pour les individus de pouvoir s'identifier à des gens qui sont comme eux, de pouvoir voir leur réalité sur l'écran pour avoir le sentiment d'exister, surtout pour des peuples qui ont été colonisés, car la colonisation, c'est la négation de l'un par l'autre. A partir du moment où l'on vient essayer de faire disparaître toute votre culture, il est important que des artistes résistent par eux-mêmes, par ce qu'ils font, par leur art, parce qu'économiquement, tout est fait pour qu'on n'existe pas.

Considérez-vous qu'il soit important que les réalisateurs africains trouvent un style cinématographique proprement 'africain'? Est-ce qu'important de se distinguer des autres cultures cinématographiques?
La distinction se fait dès lors que c'est un Africain qui fait un film de toute façon. Qu'on le

veuille ou non, un Africain n'écrira pas son histoire de la même façon qu'un Européen. Même s'il veut imiter, plagier, il n'y arrivera pas forcément. Donc, je crois que cela fait partie des choses qu'on fait, qui sont là, donc on n'a même pas besoin de se glorifier parce qu'on ne peut pas faire autrement. Je parle comme je parle. Je ne saurai parler d'une autre façon.

Est-ce que vous cherchez sciemment à dépasser les définitions habituelles imposées au documentaire et à la fiction dans vos films?
Je dirai que c'est ma démarche, mais la part de ce que je fais d'une manière consciente ou inconsciente est difficile à déterminer. Toujours est-il que, quand je commence à réfléchir sur un sujet, il y a des choses que je peux trouver sur le terrain, et d'autres qui n'existent pas ; donc je m'exprime par l'écrit, par la fiction, par l'envie de raconter une histoire, mais qui s'incruste vraiment dans la réalité des gens. C'est vrai qu'on a du mal à me classer dans le documentaire, mais à la limite, est-ce que c'est important? L'important, c'est de regarder un film, de se laisser transporter par une émotion, une réflexion. Je crois que cela est quand même plus important que d'essayer de savoir si une scène est jouée ou pas. Je n'ai pas envie de faire un travail soit d'ethnologue, soit d'anthropologue. Je fais juste des films parce que j'ai envie d'exprimer une frustration, j'ai envie d'exprimer le désarroi des gens, j'ai envie de voir comment démonter un système qui enferme les gens dans quelque chose qu'ils refusent.

Comment concevez-vous le rapport entre les textes et les images dans vos films?
Moi, on m'a toujours dit que le cinéma c'était l'image. C'est en quelque sorte la dictature de l'image. Quelque part, j'avais du mal, il fallait que j'apprenne à lire les images pour arriver à faire les images qui disent ce que je voulais dire. Parfois je n'arrivais jamais à les avoir. Je me suis dis qu'après tout, si je n'arrivais pas à avoir les images qui expriment complètement ce que je voulais, il fallait utiliser des mots. Et puis, après tout, il y a une force, une beauté, une poésie dans les mots. Derrière les images quotidiennes, il y a des mots, des mots d'une grande dureté, parce que chez moi on vit dans des situations qu'on n'arrive même plus à identifier. Quand je vais au Cameroun, je ressens beaucoup de violence, d'oppression dans les choses que je vois. Je me suis dit que ça serait bien de me servir de tous ces mots, de toute cette poésie aussi.

Les textes sont souvent un contre-point aux images...
Oui, parce qu'il y a toujours beaucoup de niveaux de lecture par rapport aux choses qui se passent autour de nous. Il y a des gens qui te parlent, qui te regardent, qui te racontent une histoire ; mais quand tu les regardes, tu te rends bien compte que ce qu'ils disent n'est pas ce qu'ils sont en train de penser. Il y a toujours une distance entre ce que les gens disent, et ce qu'ils sont réellement. Si je mets du son et des images, je ne voudrais pas qu'ils disent les même choses. Les sons et les images doivent s'enrichir, se compléter, s'entrechoquer et tout ça tend vers quelque chose, vers l'émotion. C'est ça qui me guide. Si j'arrive à toucher les gens, à les énerver, à les agresser, ou à leur tirer une larme par moment, c'est bien. Il ne faudrait pas que les gens sortent d'un film sans avoir changé ne fût-ce qu'à un instant donné.

African making the film. Africans don't write their stories in the same ways as Europeans, whether intentionally or not. Even if they want to imitate, to plagiarise, they won't necessarily manage to. So, I think that this is just part of the things we do, that are given, so there's no point in glorifying ourselves, because we can't do things any other way. I speak the way I speak. I don't know how to speak any other way.

Do you consciously try to break down the habitual boundaries between documentary and fiction in your films?
That's my intention, but it's difficult to say to what degree this is conscious or not. When I begin to think about a subject, there are things I can find on the ground and others that don't exist. So I express myself through writing, through fiction, through the desire to tell a story that is really couched in peoples' realities. It's true that it's hard to class me in the documentary vein, but does it really matter? What matters most is to watch the film, to let oneself be transported by an emotion, a line of thought. I see that as more important than trying to work out which scene is enacted or not. I don't want to make ethnological or anthropological works. I simply make films because I want to express a frustration, I want to express people's disarray, I want to see how to dismantle a system that locks people into things they don't want.

How do you see the relationship between the texts and images in your films?
People have always told me that film is about images. It's a kind of visual dictatorship. Deep down that bothered me. I had to learn to read images to manage to make images that say what I want them to say. I sometimes never managed to capture the right image, so I decided that, after all, if I couldn't manage to get the images that expressed what I wanted properly, I had to use words. After all, there is a power, a beauty, a poetry in words. Behind the day-to-day images are words, very harsh words, because we live situations we can no longer even identify in my country. When I go to Cameroon, I sense a great deal of violence, of oppression in the things I see. I thought it was a good idea to make use of these words, of all the poetry too.

The texts often counter the images...
Yes, because the things that happen around us can always be read on several levels. There are people who speak to you, who look you in the eye, who talk to you about things, but when you look at them, you realise that what they are not saying what they think. There is always a distance between what people say and what they really are. If I use sound and image, I don't want them to say the same things. The sounds and images should enrich and complete one another, or clash, and all that works towards something, towards emotion. That's my guide. If I manage to move people, to irritate them, to put their backs up or to draw a tear at times, that's good. I don't want people to leave a film without having changed, even if only for a moment.

Are people sometimes irritated by your work?

Yes, especially my first films. *Bikutsi Water Blues* irritated a lot of people. I watched it again the other day and it's true that I'd edit it differently today. But, at the same time, I understood what I was trying to say at the time. If people have found some of my films irritating, maybe it's because they are unbearable, insupportable, because they contain a reality they don't want to see. I remember people saying on the radio when these films were showing, 'but there are so many fine things in this country, why don't you show them, why bring us more filth, why show us things we don't want to see, why show us the things that hurt?'

How do you go about constructing a film?

I start out from an idea first of all, and then I try to see if I can weave a subject around it. During the shoot, I try to note phrases that come to mind. As things advance bit by bit, there are things I want to say about the subject, so I try to see how to introduce them. The subject takes me through several stages. After the shoot, I start nearly everything all over again because I find myself before an editor who has seen none of the images, who doesn't know the story, and I see if the images can tell the same story. I start working from there. I start writing the commentary.

You write the commentary afterwards?

Yes, I always write the text and the framework of the film at the editing stage. That's when I determine the film's construction.

One indeed gets the impression that the editing plays a fundamental role in your work, especially in a film like *Afrique, je te plumerai*.

Yes, it plays an important role. The editing of *Afrique, je te plumerai* was very long and difficult. I had so much material that I had to find a way to organise it, to give it meaning.

Do you always intentionally opt for a non-linear construction?

Yes, it's a choice, mainly because I am dealing with things that aren't simple stories. Life is so complicated.

What role does music play in your films?

Music is one of the everyday sounds and noises. At the same time, my work has gradually progressed and I get the impression that I have more or less said what I wanted to say, editing my films in this way. If people haven't understood, I'm not going to waste my breath. At the same time, sounds and images are also the fabric of life. Film remains a representation of life. Music is a part of the way in which I feel a certain number of things. The music chosen can characterise the protagonists. If I choose a given music for a film, it's because there's something that I want to convey.

There are pieces of music that repeatedly crop up like a leitmotif in certain films.

Est-ce qu'il est arrivé que des gens soient énervés par vos films?
Oui, surtout mes premiers films. Un film comme *Bikutsi Water Blues* a énervé beaucoup de gens. Je l'ai encore regardé il y a quelques jours, et c'est vrai qu'aujourd'hui je le monterai différemment ; mais en même temps, je me suis bien rendu compte de ce que je voulais dire à ce moment-là. Si des gens ont été énervés par certains de mes films c'est peut-être parce qu'ils sont insoutenables, insupportables, qu'il y a une réalité qu'ils ne veulent pas voir. Je me rappelle à la radio, quand on montrait ces films, les gens disaient, 'mais il y a tellement de belles choses dans ce pays, pourquoi ne pas les montrer, pourquoi nous ramener encore des ordures, pourquoi nous montrer ces choses qu'on ne veut pas voir, pourquoi montrer ce qui nous fait mal?'.

Par quelle procédure construisez-vous un film?
D'abord je pars d'une idée et, après, j'essaye de voir s'il peut avoir un sujet. Ensuite, pendant le tournage, j'essaie de noter des phrases qui me viennent. A fur et à mesure qu'on avance, il y a des choses que j'ai envie de dire sur le sujet ; donc j'essaie de voir comment les amener. Il y a des étapes par lesquelles le sujet me fait passer. Après le tournage, je recommence presque tout à zéro, parce qu'il y a en face de moi un monteur qui n'a rien vu des images, qui ne connaît pas l'histoire, et je vois si les images peuvent raconter la même histoire. A partir de là je commence le travail, je commence à écrire un texte.

Le texte s'écrit après?
Oui, le texte et la trame du film s'écrivent toujours pendant le montage. C'est à ce moment-là que je fais la construction du film.

On a l'impression que le montage joue un rôle fondamental dans vos films, et surtout dans un film comme *Afrique, je te plumerai*.
Oui, il a un rôle important. Le montage d'*Afrique, je te plumerai* a été très long et difficile. J'avais tellement de matériel qu'il fallait trouver comment l'organiser, comment lui donner du sens.

Est-ce une décision consciente que de toujours opter pour une construction non-linéaire?
Oui, c'est un choix, d'abord parce que j'aborde des choses qui ne sont pas des histoires simples. La vie est tellement compliquée.

Quel rôle accordez-vous à la musique dans vos films?
La musique fait partie des sons, du bruit de tous les jours. En même temps mon travail a évolué progressivement, et j'ai le sentiment d'avoir dit un peu ce que je voulais dire, d'avoir essayé de monter des films de cette structure-là. Si les gens n'ont pas compris, je ne vais pas me casser ma voix. Donc, en même temps, les images et les sons c'est aussi ce qui fait la vie. Le cinéma reste une représentation de la vie. La musique ça fait partie de la façon dont je ressens un certain nombre de choses. La musique choisie peut caractériser les personnages. Si je choisis une musique pour un film c'est parce que je veux faire passer des choses.

Dans certains de vos films, il y a des morceaux de musique qui reviennent comme un leitmotiv.

Oui, dans un film comme *Clando* la musique est censée fonctionner avec l'état psychologique du personnage.

Les contes et les proverbes ont toujours une place importante dans vos films. A quel point les traditions orales influencent-elles votre travail?
Elles influencent mon travail d'une manière inconsciente. Quand j'écris des textes, il y en a des proverbes qui sortent comme ça. Quant aux contes, ils font partie de mon enfance ; donc ça fait partie des choses qui sont totalement inconscientes dans le travail. J'ai envie de comprendre quelle dramaturgie les gens utilisent pour raconter des histoires. Les contes font partie d'une dramaturgie dans un espace donné que je connais, où j'ai grandi ; alors pourquoi pas les utiliser quelque part?

Est-ce que les traditions orales ont aussi une influence sur les structures de vos films?
Certainement. C'était dans *Bitkusi Water Blues* que j'avais le plus exploré ça. Dans le film, il y avait quelqu'un qui commençait une histoire en voix off, et dans l'histoire, il y avait une autre voix off qui racontait une autre histoire, et ainsi de suite avec plusieurs niveaux d'histoire. Tout le monde n'a pas suivi cette démarche parce qu'on n'est pas habitué à ce qu'il y ait une voix off dans la voix off, un flash-back dans le flash-back.

Il y a souvent plusieurs niveaux d'histoire dans les traditions orales?
Oui, il y a tellement d'histoires où quelqu'un raconte une histoire et dans son histoire, il y a une autre personne qui raconte une autre histoire. On peut arriver à deux, trois niveaux qui se superposent sans que ça pose de problème. C'est marrant parce que c'est souvent les Européens qui n'arrivent pas à rentrer là-dedans. Les Africains suivent sans aucun problème.

Certains thèmes reviennent de film en film. Est-ce que vous voyez votre travail comme un ensemble?
C'est vrai qu'il y a eu, pendant tout une période, des questionnements dans mon travail qui ont fait que ces thèmes, quoique je fasse, reviennent toujours. En regardant *Bitkusi Water Blues* que j'ai fait il y a dix ans, on peut retrouver le même thématique que dans *Clando*. Si l'on a le sentiment d'avoir ne pas avoir été jusqu'au bout de quelque chose, quand on recommence, c'est finalement les mêmes choses qui reviennent. C'est un peu comme si quand il y avait quelque chose qui gratte, on a toujours envie de se gratter, qu'on le veuille ou non. Pour le moment, ça fait des choses qui m'ont empêché de faire ce que j'ai le plus envie de faire. C'est vrai que le cinéma, pour moi, c'était d'abord l'envie de raconter des histoires drôles ; mais je me suis laissé entraîner dans ces histoires dures.

A travers le personnage de Rigoberto Chamba dans *Clando*, vous peignez un portrait assez pessimiste de l'expérience de l'immigré en Europe et le film semble prôner le retour au pays. Est-ce votre conviction personnelle?
Je crois que dans la vie, il y a des personnes qui réussissent et d'autres qui ne réussissent pas. J'ai choisi de parler d'un personnage qui ne réussit pas ses entreprises, ce qui ne veut pas dire qu'il devient complètement symbolique de quelque chose. On peut aussi prendre l'exemple du personnage de la femme de Sobgui, qui ne comprend pas son engagement, tandis qu'il y a

Yes. In a film like *Clando*, the music is meant to function with the character's psychological state.

Tales and proverbs always play an important role in your films. To what extent do the oral traditions influence you work?
They influence my work unconsciously. When I write a commentary, certain proverbs just come out. As for the tales, they are a part of my childhood and thus are amongst the things that are totally unconscious in my work. I try to understand the dramatic art people use to tell stories. Tales belong to the dramatic art in a given space that I know, in which I grew up, so why not use them?

Do the oral traditions influence the structures of your films too?
Undoubtedly. I explored this most extensively in *Bitkusi Water Blues*. A person starts the story in voice-over, and in the story, there is another voice-over that tells another story, and so on, with several layers of story. Some people were lost by this approach because people aren't used to there being a voice-over within the voice-over, a flashback within a flashback.

Are there often several layers of story in the oral traditions?
Yes, there are so many tales in which someone tells a story, and in that story there is another character who tells another story. You can end up with two or three superimposed layers without that causing a problem. It's funny because it's often the Europeans who can't keep up with this. Africans follow easily.

Certain themes crop up from film to film. Do you see your work as an ensemble?
It's true that over a whole period, there were questions in my work that repeatedly brought these themes up, whatever I did. When you watch *Bitkusi Water Blues*, which I made ten years ago, you can find the same themes as in *Clando*. If you feel that you didn't go right to the end of something, the same things end up surfacing when you start again. It's a bit like not being able to help scratching an itch. For the moment, it is one of the things that have stopped me from doing what I want to do most of all. It's true that I originally wanted to use film to tell funny stories, but I let myself get dragged into these harsh tales.

The character Rigobert Chamba in *Clando* offers quite a pessimistic portrait of the immigrant experience in Europe and the film seems to advocate returning home. Is that a view you personally share?
I think that in life, there are people who succeed and others who don't. I chose to speak about a character who doesn't succeed what he undertakes, which doesn't mean that he becomes completely symbolic of something. You could also take the example of Sobgui's wife, who doesn't understand his commitment when there are many African women who

understand commitment and who are very active; so you can't take one character as a general example. Each is a specific character with a specific past, and each gives his or her answer to the question 'to shoot or not to shoot?' Having said that, I have often heard of or seen examples of Chamba's experience.

What role does memory play in your work?

We can't live without remembering, especially in the combative phase in which things have to be made to change. We can try to learn from the past, to learn something to bring about change. Memory, souvenirs, seeing the errors of the past, understanding why things happened like they did, learning, learning from other people's experiences are vital. Memory is also a way of gaining experience, the confirmation that things go together.

beaucoup de femmes africaines qui comprennent leur engagement et qui sont très militantes ; donc on ne peut pas prendre un personnage et faire un cas général. Ce sont des personnages particuliers, qui ont des histoires particulières, qui donneront chacun leur réponse à la question 'tirer ou ne pas tirer?' Par contre, l'histoire de Chamba est une histoire que j'ai souvent entendue ou vue.

Quelle est l'importance de la mémoire dans votre travail?

On ne peut pas vivre sans s'en souvenir, surtout dans une phase de combat, où il faut faire changer les choses. On peut essayer d'apprendre du passé, apprendre quelque chose pour apporter des changements. C'est primordial, la mémoire, le souvenir, de voir les erreurs qui ont été commises, de comprendre pourquoi les choses se sont passées comme elles se sont passées, d'apprendre, d'apprendre de l'expérience des autres. Et puis la mémoire, c'est en même temps l'apprentissage, la confirmation que les choses vont ensemble.

Bibliography

Note on related reading

It is both surprising and no doubt significant that relatively little literature has yet been published specifically concerning Francophone African film. This situation appears to reflect the persistent tendency to ignore the African voices that challenge and disrupt Western preconceptions and/or the legacy of Western cultural and economic imperialism in Africa. The scope, diversity, and manifest interest of the films discussed in this book clearly indicate, however, that Francophone African film deserves critical attention. As Western scholarship increasingly recognises and incorporates formerly marginalized perspectives, it is important to heed the filmic viewpoints of directors who are at last able to portray their own realities and concerns.

The majority of existing works dealing with African film tend to provide general surveys of film production throughout the whole continent. Olivier Barlet's *Les cinémas d'Afrique noire: le regard en question* (1996)/*African Cinemas: Decolonizing the gaze* (2000), for example, provides a very useful introduction to the subject, highlighting many of the key thematic, stylistic, cultural and political issues at play, and offering some pertinent and sensitive insights. Nwachukwu Frank Ukadike's *Black African Cinema* (1994) also offers a comprehensive chronological approach to both Francophone and Anglophone sub-Saharan filmmaking from its origins to the early Nineties, again highlighting the general cultural and political contexts in which the works are set and identifying its major trends. Roy Armes' book, *Arab & African Film Making* (1991), co-authored by Lizbeth Malkmus, positions sub-Saharan filmmaking in relation to North African film and other art forms in the colonial and postcolonial periods as it explores some of the key characteristics of African film. His other book, *Third World Film Making and the West* (1987) relates African films to other 'Third World' cinemas and their social, cultural, economic and theoretical contexts. Finally, Manthia Diawara's *African Cinema: politics and culture* (1992) focuses on the conditions of production and the political context of African film, whilst also highlighting general characteristics of African film.

To date, only a handful of works specialising in specific areas of

Francophone African film have been published. André Gardies' book *Cinéma d'Afrique Noire Francophone: L'Espace Miroir* (1989), for example, provides a fascinating analysis of the aesthetic and metaphorical use of space in Francophone African film, highlighting how this differs from Western spatial concepts. Françoise Pfaff's *The Cinema of Ousmane Sembene, A Pioneer of African Film* (1984) provides a thorough and detailed analysis of Sembene's films, and considers both his stylistic and thematic approaches to filmmaking, providing extracts of reviews of Sembene's work. Her other book, *Twenty-five Black African Filmmakers: A Critical Study with Filmography and Bio-Bibliography* (1988) gives a useful analytical and chronological presentation of the work and styles of selection of filmmakers, thereby highlighting the continuities in individual directors' bodies of work. Other publications on individual filmmakers include Sheila Petty's edited collection of essays *A Call to Action: The films of Ousmane Sembene* (1996), which provides additional insights into diverse aspects of this pioneering filmmaker's work, including Sembene's representation of women and approach to film language; David Murphy's *Sembene: Imagining Alternatives in Film and Fiction* (2000) and Samba Gadjigo, Ralph Faulkingham, Thomas Cassirer, and Reinhard Sander's collection of articles and transcriptions of debates and interviews in *Ousmane Sembène: Dialogues with Critics and Writers* (1993), which again explores different facets of the director's works. Finally, Ibrahima Signaté has published the fascinating book *Med Hondo: Un Cinéaste Rebelle* (1994) based on a series of interviews with the director that deals with both his filmic preoccupations and a range of issues concerning the African continent.

Several other publications, such as *Symbolic Narratives/African Cinema: Audiences, Theory and the Moving Image* (2000) edited by June Givinni, *African Experiences of Cinema* (1996) edited by Imruh Bakari and Mbye Cham, *L'Afrique et le Centenaire du Cinéma* (1995) edited by the FEPACI, the special issues of *CinémAction* ('Cinémas noirs d'Afrique', 1981), *CinémAction* ('Cinémas africains, une oasis dans le desert?', 106, 2003), *iris* ('New Discourses of African Cinema', 1995) and *Positif* ('Regards sur les cinémas d'Afrique noire', 1993), and specialist journals including *Ecrans d'Afrique/African Screen*, *Le Film Africain*, and *Africultures*, provide compilations of essays and interviews on diverse aspects of Francophone African film. Many of these, for example Sheila Petty's various articles on women in African film, or Manthia Diawara's essays on oral narrative and film, to cite but a few, offer excellent insights into given aspects of this film work.

Related film and intellectual theory

Andrew, Dudley, *Concepts in Film Theory* (New York: Oxford University Press, 1984).

Arvon, Henri, *L'Esthétique marxiste* (Vendôme: Presses Universitares de France, 1970).

Brunsdon, Charlotte (ed.), *Films For Women* (London: BFI Books, 1986).

CinémAction ('20 ans de théories feministes sur le cinéma'), 67, 1993.

Clifford, James, *The Predicament of Culture: Twentieth-Century Ethnography, Literature, and Art* (Cambridge, Massachusetts & London: Harvard University Press, 1988).

Everett, Wendy (ed.), *European Identity in Cinema* (London: Intellect, 1996).

Foucault, Michel, *Language, Counter-Memory, Practice: Selected Essays and Interviews*, translated by D. F. Bouchard & S. Simon (New York: Ithaca, Cornell University Press, 1977).

Huyssen, Andreas, *After the Great Divide: Modernism, Mass Culture, Postmodernism* (Bloomington & Indianapolis: Indiana University Press, 1986).

Issari, M. Ali & Paul, Doris A, *What is Cinéma Vérité?* (London: The Scarecrow Press, 1979).

Mast, Gerald & Cohen, Marshall (eds.), *Film Theory and Criticism*, 3rd edition (New York: Oxford University Press, 1985).

Monaco, James, *How To Read A Film*, revised edition (New York: Oxford University Press, 1981).

Raven, Arlene, Langer, Cassandra & Frueh, Joanna (eds.), *Feminist Art Criticism: An Anthology* (New York: First Icon, 1991).

Wollen, Peter, *Signs and Meaning in the Cinema*, 3rd edition (London: Secker & Warburg, 1972).

Walker, Alice, *In Search of Our Mothers' Gardens: Womanist Prose* (San Diego & New York: Harvest/HBJ, 1984).

Works on other black and Third World cinemas

Armes, Roy, *Third World Film Making and the West* (Berkeley & Los Angeles: University of California Press, 1987).

Bogle, Donald, *Toms, Coons, Mulattoes, Mamies and Bucks: An Interpretive History of Blacks in American Films* (New York: A Frederick Ungar Book, Continuum: 1990).

Bosséno, Christian, 'Immigrant Cinema: National Cinema. The case of beur film', in R. Dyer & G. Vincendeau (eds.), *Popular European Cinema* (London: Routledge, 1992), pp 47-58.

Diawara, Manthia (ed.), *Black American Cinema* (New York: Rouledge, 1993).

Downing, John D.H (ed.), *Film and Politics in the Third World* (New York: Praeger, 1987).

Gabriel, Teshome, 'Third Cinema as Guardian of Popular Memory: Towards a Third Aesthetics', in Jim Pines & Paul Willemen (eds.), *Questions of Third Cinema* (London: BFI, 1989), pp 53-64.

Gabriel, Teshome, *Third Cinema in the Third World: The Dynamics of Style and Ideology* (Ann Arbor, Michigan: U.M.I Dissertation Services, 1979).

Gabriel, Teshome, 'Thoughts on Nomadic Aesthetics and The Black Independent Cinema: Traces of a Journey', in Cham, Mbye B. & Andrade-Watkins, Claire (eds.), *Blackframes: Critical Perspectives on Black Independent Cinema* (Cambridge, Massachusetts: The MIT Press, 1988), p 62-79.

Gabriel, Teshome, 'Towards a Critical Theory of Third World Films', in Jim Pines & Paul Willemen (eds.), *Questions of Third Cinema* (London: BFI, 1989), pp 30-52.

Mercer, Kobena (ed.), *Black Film British Cinema* (London: ICA Documents 7, 1988).

Pines, Jim & Willemen, Paul (eds.), *Questions of Third Cinema* (London: BFI, 1989).

Reid, Marc A., *Redefining Black Film* (Berkeley & Los Angeles: University of California Press, 1993).

Tarr, Carrie, 'French Cinema and Post-Colonial Minorities', in Alec Hargreaves & Mark McKinney (eds.),

Post-Colonial Cultures in France (London & New York: Routledge, 1997), pp 59-83.

Tompson, Felix, 'Metaphors of space: polarization, dualism and Third World cinema', *Screen*, vol 34, 1, Spring 1993, pp 38-53.

Yearwood, Gladstone (ed.), *Black Cinema Aesthetics* (Athens: Ohio University Centre for Afro-American Studies, 1982).

Liberation, post-colonial and representation theory

Appiah, Kwame Anthony, *In My Father's House: Africa in the Philosophy of Culture* (New York & Oxford: Oxford University Press, 1992).

Ashcroft, Bill, Griffiths, Gareth & Tiffin, Helen (eds.), *The Post-Colonial Studies Reader* (London & New York: Routledge, 1995).

Bhabha, Homi K., 'The Other Question ... Homi K Bhabha Reconsiders The Stereotype and Colonial Discourse', *Screen*, vol 24, 6, 1983, pp 18-36.

Cabral, Amilcar, *Unité et lutte I: l'arme de la théorie* (Paris: François Maspero, 1975).

Cameron, Kenneth M., *Africa on Film: Beyond Black and White* (New York: Continuum, 1994).

Césaire, Aimé, *Discours sur le colonialisme*, réedition (Paris & Dakar: Présence Africaine, 1955).

Cham, Mbye B. & Andrade-Watkins, Claire (eds.), *Blackframes: Critical Perspectives on Black Independent Cinema* (Cambridge, Massachusetts: The MIT Press, 1988).

Fanon, Frantz, *Les damnés de la terre* (Paris: Editions Gallimard, 1991, 1st edition 1961)/*The Damned*, translated by Constance Farrington (Paris: Présence Africaine, 1963).

Fanon, Frantz, *Peau noire, masques blancs* (Paris: Editions du Seuil, 1952).

Ferguson, Russell, Gever, Martha, Trinh, T. Minh-ha & West, Cornel (eds.), *Out There: Marginalization and Contemporary Cultures* (New York & Massachusetts: The New Museum of Contemporary Art & The MIT Press, 1990).

Gabriel, Teshome, 'Colonialism And "Law And Order" Criticism', *Screen*, vol. 27, 3-4, May/August 1986, pp140-145.

Gaines, Jane, 'White Privilege and Looking Relations: Race and Gender in Film Theory', *Screen*, vol 29, 4, 1988, pp 12-26.

Gates, Henry Louis, Jr. 'Authority, (White) Power and the (Black) Critic; or, it's all Greek to me', *Cutural Critique*, 7, Fall 1987, pp 324-346.

Hall, Stuart, 'Cultural Identity and Cinematic Representation', *Framework*, 36, 1989, pp 68-81.

Hargreaves, Alec & McKinney, Mark (eds.), *Post-Colonial Cultures in France* (London & New York: Routledge, 1997).

Hommes & Migrations ('Imaginaire colonial, Figures de l'immigré'), 1207, Mai-Juin 1997.

hooks, bell, *Black Looks: Race and Representation.*(Boston, MA: South End Press, 1992).

hooks, bell, *Reel to Real: Race, sex, and class at the movies* (New York & London: Routledge, 1996).

hooks, bell, *Talking Back: thinking feminist, thinking black* (Boston, MA: South End Press, 1989).

Mazrui, Ali A., *The African Condition: A Political Diagnosis* (Heinemann: London, 1980).

Mazrui, Ali A., *World Culture and the Black Experience* (Seattle & London: University of Washington Press, 1974).

Mercer, Kobena, *Welcome to the Jungle: New Positions in Black Cultural Studies* (New York & London: Routledge, 1994).

Nkrumah, Kwame, *Towards Colonial Freedom* (London: Panaf Books, 1973, 1st edition 1945).

Nkrumah, Kwame, *Consciencism: Philosophy and Ideology for De-Colonization* (London: Panaf Books, 1964).

Owens, Craig. 'The Discourses of Others: Feminists and Postmodernism', in Hal Foster (ed.), *The Anti-Aesthetic: Essays on Postmodern Culture* (Washington: Bay Press, 1983), pp 57-77.

Said, Edward W., *Orientalism.*(London: Penguin Books, 1995, 1st edition 1978).

Screen ('Other Cinemas, Other Criticisms'), vol 26, 3-4, 1985.

Screen ('The Last "Special Issue" on Race?'), vol 29, 4, 1988.

Shohat, Ella, 'Notes on the "Post-Colonial"', *Social Text*, 31/31, 1992.

Taylor, Clyde, 'Black Cinema in the Post-aesthetic Era', in Jim Pines & Paul Willemen (eds.), *Questions of Third Cinema* (London: BFI, 1989), pp 90-110.

Taylor, Clyde, 'Eurocentrics vs New Thought', *Framework*, 34, 1987, pp 140-148.

Taylor, Clyde, 'We Don't Need Another Hero: Anti-Thesis on Aesthetics', in Cham,

Mbye B. & Andrade-Watkins, Claire (eds.), *Blackframes: Critical Perspectives on Black Independent Cinema* (Cambridge, Massachusetts: The MIT Press, 1988), pp 80-85.

Trinh, T. Minh-ha, *Women, Native, Other: Writing Postcoloniality and Feminism* (Bloomington & Indianapolis: Indiana University Press, 1989).

UNESCO (ed.), *L'affirmation de l'identité culturelle et la formation de la conscience nationale dans l'Afrique contemporaine* (Paris: UNESCO, 1981).

The socio-cultural context of Francophone African film.

Ayisi, Eric O., *An Introduction to the Study of African Culture*, 2nd edition (London: Heinemann, 1979).

Bâ, Amadou Hampaté, *Amkoullel, l'Enfant Peul* (Paris: Babel, 1991).

Bâ, Amadou Hampaté, *Aspects de la civilisation africaine* (Paris & Dakar: Présence Africaine, 1972).

Bâ, Amadou Hampaté, *Contes initiatiques peuls* (Paris: Editions Stock, 1994).

Bâ, Amadou Hampaté, 'The Living Tradition', in Joseph Ki-Zerbo (ed.), *General History of Africa vol I* (Paris: UNESCO, 1981), pp 166-203.

Banham, Martin & Wake, Clive, *African Theatre Today* (London: Pitman Publishing, 1976).

Davidson, Basil, *The Story of Africa* (London: Mitchell Beazley/Channel 4 Books, 1984).

Beyala, Calixthe, *Lettre d'une Africaine à ses soeurs occidentales* (Paris: Spengler, 1995).

Camara, Sory, *Gens de la Parole: Essai sur la condition et le rôle des griots dans la société malinké* (Paris/Conakry: ACCT, Karthala, SAEC, 1992, 1st edition 1975).

Camara, Sory, *Paroles très anciennes, ou le mythe de l'accomplissement de l'homme* (Grenoble: La Pensée Sauvage, 1982).

Cauvin, Jean, *La Parole traditionnelle* (Paris: Les classiques africains, 1980).

Chernoff, John Miller, *African Rhythm and African Sensibility: Aesthetics and Social Action in African Musical Idioms* (Chicago & London: University of Chicago Press, 1979).

Chevrier, Jacques, *L'Arbre à Palabres: essai sur les contes et récits traditionnels d'Afrique noire* (Paris: Hatier, 1986).

Eno Belinga, S.-M., *La littérature orale africaine* (Issy les Moulineaux: Les classiques africains, 1985, 1st edition 1978).

Etherton, Micheal, *The Development of African Drama* (London: Hutchinson, 1983).

Gaudio, Attilio, *Le Mali* (Paris: Editions Karthala, 1988).

Gordon, David C., *The French Language and National Identity* (The Hague: Mouton Publishers, 1978).

Görög, Veronika, *Contes bambara du Mali* (Paris: INLACO, 1979).

Griaule, Marcel, *Dieu d'Eau : Entretiens avec Ogotemmêli* (Paris: Fayard, 1966).

Irele, Abiola, *The African Experience in Literature and Ideology*. Bloomington and Indianapolis: Indiana University Press, 1981.

Jahn, Janheinz, *Muntu: African Culture and the Western World*, translated by Marjorie Grene, (New York: Grove Weidenfeld, 1961).

Killam, G. D. (ed.), *African Writers on African Writing* (London: Heinemann, 1973).

Kesteloot, Lilyan, *Anthologie Négro-Africaine* (Vanves: EDICEF, 1992).

Mbiti, John S., *Introduction to African Religion* (London: Heinemann, 1975).

Mbiti, John S., 'African Cosmology', in *Festac '77* (London & Lagos: Africa Journal Limited & The

International Festival Committee, 1977), pp 40-49.

Meyer, Gérard, *Contes du pays mandingue* (Paris: CILF & EDICEF, 1988).

Miller, Christopher L., *Theories of Africans: Francophone Literature and Anthropology in Africa* (Chicago: University of Chicago Press, 1990).

Minces, Juliette, *La femme Voilée: L'Islam au féminin* (Paris: Calmann-Lévy, 1990).

Mouralis, Bernard, *Les contres-littératures* (Vendôme: Presses Universitaries de France, 1975).

Mouralis, Bernard, *Littérature et développement* (Paris: Editions Silex/ ACCT, 1984).

Mudimbe, V.Y., *The Invention of Africa: Gnosis, Philosophy and the Order of Knowledge* (Bloomington & Indianapolis: Indiana University Press, 1988).

Ngugi, wa Thiong'o, *Decolonising the Mind: The Politics of Language in African Literature* (London & Nairobi: James Currey/Heinemann, 1986).

Niane, D.T., *Soundjata, ou l'épopée Manding* (Paris & Dakar: Présence Africaine, 1971).

Obiechina, Emmanuel, *Culture, Tradition and Society in the West African Novel* (Cambridge: Cambridge University Press, 1975).

Obiechina, Emmanuel, *Language and Theme: Essays on African Literature* (Washington DC: Howard University Press, 1990).

Okpewho, Isidore, *African Oral Literature: Backgrounds, Character, and Continuity* (Bloomington & Indianapolis: Indiana University Press, 1992).

Pala, Achola O. & Ly, Madina, *La femme africaine dans la société précoloniale* (Paris: UNESCO, 1979).

Paulme, Denise, *La mère dévorante: Essai sur la morphologie des contes africains* (Paris: Editions Gallimard, 1976).

Soyinka, Wole, *Myth, Literature and the African World* (Cambridge: Canto/Cambridge University Press, 1976).

Thiam, Awa, *La Parole Aux Negresses* (Paris: Editions Denoël/Gonthier, 1978).

Traoré, Bakary, *Le théâtre Négro-Africain et ses fonctions sociales* (Paris & Dakar: Présence Africaine, 1958).

Wauthier, Claude, *The Literature and Thought of Modern Africa* (Washington DC: Three Contintents Press, Inc., 1979).

Webster & Boahen, *The Growth of African Civilisation: West Africa Since 1800* (London: Longmans, 1967).

Books, articles and unpublished papers on Francophone African film

Armes, Roy & Malkmus, Lizbeth, *Arab & African Film Making* (London & New Jersey: Zed Books, 1991).

Association des Trois Mondes. *Dictionnaire du cinéma africain*. Tome 1 (Paris: Editions Karthala, 1991).

Aufderheide, Pat, 'Interview with Cheick Oumar Sissoko', *Black Film Review*, vol 6, 2, 1990, pp 4-5.

Bakari, Imruh & Cham, Mbye (eds.), *African Experiences of Cinema* (London: BFI Publishing, 1996).

Barlet, Olivier, 'Entretien: Anne-Laure Folly', *Africultures*, 2, novembre 1997, pp 12-15.

Barlet, Olivier, 'Entretien: Safi Faye', *Africultures*, 2, novembre 1997, pp 9-11.

Barlet, Olivier, *Les cinémas d'Afrique noire: le regard en question* (Paris: L'Harmattan, 1996)/*African Cinemas: Decolonizing the gaze*, translated by Chris Turner (London, Zed Books Ltd, 2000).

Barlet, Olivier, 'La critique occidentale des images d'Afrique', *Africultures*, 1, octobre 1997, pp 5-11 .

Boughedir, Férid, *Le Cinéma Africain de A à Z* (Brussels: OCIC, 1987).

Boughedir, Férid, 'African Cinema and Ideology: Tendencies and Evolutions' (unpublished paper, BFI *Screen Griots Conference*, London 9-10 September 1995).

CESCA (ed.), *Caméra Nigra, Le Discours du Film Africain* (Brussels & Paris: OCIC/L'Harmattan, 1985).

Cham, Mbye Baboucar, 'Film Production in West Africa 1975-1981', *Présence Africaine*, 124, 1982, pp 168-190.

Diawara, Manthia, *African Cinema: politics and culture* (Bloomington & Indianapolis: Indiana University Press, 1992).

Diawara, Manthia, 'African Cinema Today', *Framework*, 37, 1989, pp 110-128.

Diawara, Manthia, 'The Iconography of African Cinema: What is it and how is it identified?' (paper given at BFI *Screen Griots Conference*, London 9-10 September 1995).

Diawara, Manthia, 'Oral Literature and African Film: Narratology in *Wend Kuuni*', in Jim Pines & Paul Willemen (eds.), *Questions of Third Cinema* (London: BFI, 1989), pp 199-211.

Diawara, Manthia, 'Souleymane Cissé's Light on Africa', *Black Film Review*, vol 4, 4, Fall 1988, pp 12-15.

Downing, John D.H., 'Post-Tricolour African Cinema', in Sherzer, Dina (ed.), *Cinema, Colonialism, Postcolonialism: Perspectives from the French and Francophone Worlds* (Austin: University of Texas Press, 1996), pp 188-228.

Eshun, Esi, 'Sissoko on GUIMBA', *Black Film Bulletin*, vol 3, 2/3, Summer/Autumn 1995, pp 18-19.

FEPACI, 'La Charte d'Alger du cinéma africain', *Afrique Artistique et Littéraire*, 35, 1975, pp 100-101.

FEPACI (ed.), *L'Afrique et le Centenaire du Cinéma* (Paris & Dakar: Présence Africaine, 1995).

Gabriel, Teshome, 'The Intolerable Gift' (paper given at BFI *Screen Griots Conference*, London 9-10 September 1995).

Gabriel, Teshome, *Third Cinema in Third World: The Dynamics of Style and Ideology* (Ann Arbor, Michigan: U.M.I Dissertation Services, 1979).

Gadjigo, Samba, Faulkingham, Ralph H., Cassirer, Thomas & Sander, Reinhard (eds.), *Ousmane Sembène: Dialogues with Critics and Writers* (Amherst: University of Massachusetts Press, 1993).

Gardies, André, *Cinéma d'Afrique Noire Francophone: L'Espace Miroir.* (Paris: L'Harmattan, 1989).

Gardies, A. & Haffner, P., *Regards sur le Cinéma Négro-Africain* (Bruxelles: Editions OCIC, 1987).

Givanni, June, *African Conversations* (published in conjunction with the *Screen Griots Conference*, London: BFI, 1995).

Givanni, June (ed.), *Symbolic Narratives/African Cinema: Audiences, Theory and the Moving Image* (London: BFI, 2000).

Haffner, Pierre, *Essai sur les Fondaments du Cinéma Africain* (Abidjan: Les Nouvelles Editions Africaines, 1978).

Kaboré, Gaston, 'L'image de Soi, Un Besoin Vital', in FEPACI (ed.), *L'Afrique et le Centenaire du Cinéma* (Paris & Dakar: Présence Africaine, 1995), pp 21-23.

Lalanne, Jean-Marc, 'Terre et mère', *Cahiers du Cinéma*, 492, juin 1995, pp 50-53.

Lalanne, Jean-Marc & Strauss, Frédéric, 'Entretien avec Souleymane Cissé', *Les Cahiers du Cinéma*, 492, juin 1995, pp 54-58.

Mahoso, Tafataona, 'Unwinding the African Dream on African Grounds: Audiences and the Critical Appreciation of Cinema in Africa' (paper given at BFI *Screen Griots Conference*, London 9-10 September 1995).

Martin, Angela (ed.), *African Films, the Context of Production* (London: BFI Dossier n° 6, 1982).

Petty, Sheila (ed.), *A Call To Action. The Films of Ousmane Sembene* (Trowbridge: Flick Books, 1996).

Petty, Sheila, 'Miseria: Towards an African Feminist Framework of Analysis', *iris*, 18, Spring 1995, pp 137-145.

Petty, Sheila, 'Whose nation is it anyhow? The politics of reading African cinema in the West', in FEPACI (ed), *L'Afrique et le Centenaire du Cinéma* (Paris & Dakar: Présence Africaine, 1995), pp 188-193.

Pffaf, Françoise, *The Cinema of Ousmane Sembene, A Pioneer of African Film* (Westport, Connecticut: Greenwood Press, 1984).

Pffaf, Françoise, *Twenty-five Black African Filmmakers: A Critical Study with Filmography and Bio-Bibliograpy* (Westport, Connecticut: Greenwood Press, 1988).

Pommier, Pierre, *Cinéma et Développement en Afrique Noire Francophone* (Paris: Editions A. Pedone, 1974).

Présence Africaine ('Séminaire sur le rôle du Cinéaste africain dans l'éveil d'une conscience de civilisation noire'), 90, 1974, pp 3-202.

Sembene, Ousmane, *Man is Culture* (Bloomington: African Studies Program, Indiana University, 1979).

Sembene, Ousmane, 'Filmmakers and African Culture', *Africa*, 71, 1977, p 80.

Sherzer, Dina (ed.), *Cinema, Colonialism, Postcolonialism: Perspectives from the French and Francophone Worlds* (Austin: University of Texas Press, 1996).

Signaté, Ibrahima, *Med Hondo: Un Cinéaste Rebelle* (Paris & Dakar: Présence Africaine, 1994).

Taylor, Clyde, 'Searching for the Post-Modern in African Cinema' (unpublished paper, BFI *Screen Griots Conference*, London 9-10 September 1995).

Teno, Jean-Marie, 'Liberté, le pouvoir de dire non', in FEPACI (ed.), *L'Afrique et le Centenaire du Cinéma* (Paris & Dakar: Présence Africaine, 1995), pp 375-378.

Thackway, Melissa, 'Interview: Cheick Oumar Sissoko', *Jeune Afrique*, 1787, 6-12 avril 1995, p 47.

Thackway, Melissa, 'Les Africaines à Créteil: la voix en images', *Africultures*, 9, juin 1998.

Thackway, Melissa, 'Secondary Orality: Oral Narrative Techniques in Adama Drabo's *Taafe Fanga*' ASCALF *Bulletin*, 20, Spring/Summer 2000, pp 38-52.

Thackway, Melissa, 'Future Past: Integrating Orality into Francophone West African Film', in Döring, Tobias (ed.), *African Cultures, Visual Arts and the Museum*, Matatu 25-26 (Amsterdam/New York: Editions Rodopi B.V., 2002) pp 229-242.

Thackway, Melissa, 'Images d'immigrés', *CinémAction*, 106, 2003, pp 50-55.

Tomaselli, Keyan & Eke, Maureen, 'Secondary Orality in South African Film', *iris*, 18, Spring 1995, pp 61-71.

Ukadike, Nwachukwu Frank, *Black African Cinema* (Berkeley/Los Angeles: University of California Press, 1994).

Ukadike, Nwachukwu Frank, 'The Other Voices of Documentary: *Allah Tantou* and *Afrique, je te plumerai*', *iris*, 18, Spring 1995, pp 81-94.

Vieyra, Paulin Soumanou, *Le Cinéma Africain des origines à 1973* (Paris & Dakar: Présence Africaine, 1975).

Vokouma, François, 'Produire Nos Propres Images. . . Malgré l'Etat de l'Afrique', in FEPACI (ed.), *L'Afrique et le Centenaire du Cinéma* (Paris & Dakar: Présence Africaine, 1995), pp 269-275.

Wamby, Onyekachi, 'Decolonizing Film: Interview with Haile Gerima', *Black Film Bulletin*, vol 3, 2/3, Summer/Autumn 1995, pp 14-17.

Wynter, Sylvia, 'Africa, the West and the Analogy of Culture: the Cinematic Text After Man' (paper given at BFI *Screen Griots Conference*, London 9-10 September 1995).

Specialist journals

Africultures,1-49, octobre 1997-juin 2002.

Black Film Bulletin ('African Cinema Double Issue'), vol 3, 2/3, Summer/Autumn, 1995.

CinémAction ('Cinémas noirs d'Afrique'), 26, 1981; (Cinémas africains, une oasis dans le désert?) 106, 2000.

Ecrans d'Afrique/African Screen, 1-22, 1991-1998.

iris ('New Discourses of African Cinema'), 18, Spring, 1995.

Jump Cut ('Third World Film'), 27, 1982.

Le Film Africain, 1-31, fevrier 1991-mai 1999.

Positif ('Regards sur les cinémas d'Afrique noire'), 385, Mars 1993.

Documentary films on Francophone African cinema

Férid Boughedir. *Caméra d'Afrique : 20 ans de cinéma africain.* (France-Tunisia, 1983, 99 min).

Samba Félix N'Diaye, G. Debroise, S. Interlegator, O. Lichen. *Cinés d'Afrique.* (France-Senegal, 1993, 59 min).

Rithy Panh. *Souleymane Cissé.* (Cambodia-France, 1991, 53 min).

Melissa Thackway, Xavier Tutein, Laurent Yé. *Cinéma en Plein Air: Parole aux Cinéastes Africains.* (France, 1995, 26 min).

Filmography

This filmography provides a select list of the principal films made by the directors cited in this book, and thus does not aim to provide an exhaustive directory of either their work or the films made in Francophone Africa since the Sixties. A more complete filmography of African film can be found in the *Dictionnaire du Cinéma Africain*, Tome 1, compiled by the Association des Trois Mondes (Tome 2 forthcoming).

The conventional academic filmographic criteria used are: 'c' for colour, 'b/w' for black and white, 'r' for running time, and, where known, 'p' for producer/s and the country/countries of production. The official French subtitle is given where possible. Directors have been classed in alphabetical order.

David Achkar (Guinea)
Allah Tantou
1990, 16 mm, c, documentary, r. 52 min, p. Archibald Films (France).

Kiti: Justice en Guinée
1996, video, c, documentary, r. 58 min.

Abdoulaye Ascofare (Mali)
Faraw! (Une Mère des Sables)
1997, 35 mm, c, fiction, r. 90 min, p. Les Films de la Dune Rose/CNCP (Mali).

Bassek Ba Kobhio (Cameroon).
Sango Malo (Le Maître du Canton).
1990, 35 mm, c, fiction, r. 98 min, p. Les Films Terre Africaine (Cameroon).

Le Grand blanc de Lambaréné.
1994, 35 mm, c, fiction, r. 100 min, p. Les Films Terre Africaine/ACCT/L.N. Production/ CENACI/Chrysalide Films (Cameroon/France).

Balufu Bakupa-Kanyinda
(DRC)
Thomas Sankara
1991, 16 mm, c, documentary, r. 21 min, p. Scolopendra (France).

Le Damier: Papa National Oyé!
1996, 35 mm, b/w, fiction, r. 40 min, p. Diapanda Yo!/Centre National du Cinéma du Gabon/ Central Productions/Myriapodus (DRC/Gabon/France).

Article 15 bis
1999, 35 mm, c, fiction, r. 15 min, p. Akangbé Productions (DRC/France)

Jean-Pierre Bekolo (Cameroon)
Quartier Mozart
1992, super-16 mm, c, fiction, r. 80 min, p. Kola Cases (France).

Le Complot d'Aristotle
1997, 35 mm, c, fiction, r. 70 min, p. JBA Production/British Film Institute/Framework International (France/GB/Zimbabwe).

Ben Diogaye Beye (Senegal)
Les Princes Noirs de Saint-Germain-des-Près
1975, 16 mm, c, fiction, r. 16 min, p. Société Nationale de Cinéma/ Consortium Audio-Visuel International (Senegal/France).

Sey Seyeti (Un Homme, Des Femmes)
1980, 16 mm, c, fiction, r. 73 min, p. Ben Diogaye Beye (Senegal).

Moytuleen
1996, 35 mm, c, fiction, r. 13 min, p. B.D.B Productions (Senegal).

Isabelle Boni-Claverie
(Côte d'Ivoire)
Le Génie d'Abou
1997, Beta, c, fiction, r. 9 min, p. FEMIS (France).

Souleymane Cissé (Mali)
Cinq Jours d'une Vie
1973, 35 mm, b/w, fiction, r. 50 min, p. SCINFOMA (Senegal).

Den Muso (La Jeune Fille)
1975, 16 mm, c, fiction, r. 90 min.

Baara (Le Travail)
1977, 16 mm, c, fiction, r. 90 min, p. Les Films Cissé (Mali).

Finyé (Le Vent)
1982, 35 mm, c, fiction, r. 100 min, p. Les Films Cissé (Mali).

Yeelen (La Lumière)
1987, 35 mm, c, fiction, r. 105 min, p. Les Films Cissé (Mali).

Waati (Le Temps)
1995, 35 mm, c, fiction, r. 142 min, p. Les Films Cissé/Erato Films/Renn Production/Carthago Films/La Sept (Mali/France).

Issa Serge Coelo (Chad)
Un taxi pour Aouzou
1994, 35 mm, c, fiction, r. 23 min, p. Movimento Productions (France).
Daresalam
2000, 35 mm, c, fiction, r. 90 min, p. Parenthèse Films/ARTE (Chad/France)

Clarence Delgado (Senegal)
Niwaam
1991, 35 mm, c, fiction, r. 80 min, p. Yves Diange/Emmanuel Films/Les Ateliers de l'Arche/Société Nouvelle Pathé Cinéma (Senegal/France).

Ahmadou Diallo (Senegal)
Le Symbole
1994, 16 mm, c, fiction, r. 8 min, p. Ahmadou Diallo (Senegal).

Amet Diallo (Senegal)
Boxulmaleen!! (L'An Fer City)
1991, 35 mm, c, fiction, r. 30 min, p. Les Ateliers de l'Arche (France).

Jean-Pierre Dikongue-Pipa (Cameroon)
Muna Moto (L'Enfant de l'Autre)
1975, 35 mm, b/w, fiction, r. 90 min, p. Avant Garde Africaine (Cameroon).
Le Prix de la Liberté
1978, 35 mm, c, fiction, r. 98 min, p. Cameroun Spectacles (Cameroon).

Djibril Diop Mambety (Senegal)
Contras-City
1968, 16 mm, c, fiction, r. 16 min.
Badou Boy
1970, 16 mm, c, fiction, r. 60 min, p. Myriam Smadja/Films Kankourama (Senegal/France).
Touki Bouki (Le Voyage de l'Hyène)
1973, 35 mm, c, fiction, r. 110 min, p. Cinégrit (Senegal).

Parlons Grand-Mère
1989, 16 mm, c, documentary, r. 34 min, p. Maag Daan (Senegal).
Hyènes
1991, 35 mm, c, fiction, r. 113 min, p. Maag Daan/Thelma Films AG/ADR Productions (Senegal/Switzerland/ France).
Le Franc
1994, 35 mm, c, fiction, r. 36 min, p. p. Maag Daan/Waka Films AG/Scolopendra Productions (Senegal/Switzerland/France).
La Petite Vendeuses de Soleil
1999, 35 mm, c, fiction, r. 35 min, p. Maag Daan/Waka Films AG/Cephéide Productions (Senegal/Switzerland/ France).

Adama Drabo (Mali)
Ta Dona
1991, 35 mm, c, fiction, r. 105 min, p. Kora Films (Mali).
Taafe Fanga (Le Pouvoir du Pagne)
1997, 35 mm, c, fiction, r. 100 min, p. Taare Films/CNCP/ZDF (Mali/ Germany).

Henri Duparc (Côte d'Ivoire)
Abusuan (La Famille)
1972, 35 mm, c, fiction, r. 95 min, p. Société Ivoirienne de Cinéma (Côte d'Ivoire).
Bal Poussière
1988, 35 mm, c, fiction, r. 91 min, p. Focale 13 (Côte d'Ivoire).
Rue Princess
1993, 35 mm, c, fiction, r. 88 min, p. Focale 13/Blue Films/DIPROCI/Canal + (Côte d'Ivoire/Burkina Faso/France).
Une Couleur Café
1997, 35 mm, c, fiction, r. 105 min, p. Focale 13 (Côte d'Ivoire).

Desiré Ecaré (Côte d'Ivoire)
Concerto pour un exil
1968, 16 mm, b/w, fiction,

r. 42 min, p. Myriam Smadja/Argos Films (France).
A nous deux, France
1969, 16mm, b/w, fiction, r. 60 min, p. Films de la Lagune/Argos Films (Côte d'Ivoire/France).
Visages de Femmes
1985, 16 mm, c, fiction, r. 105 min, p. Films de la Lagune (Côte d'Ivoire).

Safi Faye (Senegal)
La Passante
1972, 16 mm, b/w, fiction, r. 10 min.
Kaddu Beykat (Lettre Paysanne)
1975, 16 mm, b/w, docu-fiction, r. 98 min, p. Safi Films (Senegal).
Fad'jal (Grand-Père Raconte)
1979, 16 mm, c, docu-fiction, r. 108 min, p. Safi Films/Ministère des Rélations Extérieurs/INA (Senegal/France).
Selbé et Tant d'Autres
1982, 16 mm, c, documentary, r. 30 min, p. Safi Films/Faust Films (Senegal/Germany).
Testito
1989, video, c, documenatry, r. 27 min, p.Comité Français Contre La Faim et Pour Le Développement (France).
Mossane
1990-1996, 35 mm, c, fiction, r. 100 min, p. Muss Cinématographie (Senegal/France).

Gahité Fofana (Guinea)
Tanun
1994, 35 mm, c, documentary, r. 54 min, p. Bafila Films/ONACIG (Guinea)
Temedy
1996, 35 mm, c, fiction, r. 10, p. FGF/Revue Noire Productions (Guinea/France)
Immatriculation temporaire
2000, 35 mm, c, fiction, r. 77 min, p. Arte France/Léo & Cie/FGF (France/Guinea).

Anne Laure Folly (Togo)

Femmes aux yeux ouverts
1993, video, c, documentary, r. 51 min,
p. Amanou Production (France).

Les Oubliées
1996, video, c, documentary, r. 53 min,
p. Amanou Production (France).

Sarah Maldoror, La Nostalgie de l'Utopie
1998, 16 mm, c, documentary, r. 26 min.

Oumarou Ganda (Niger)

Cabascabo
1968, 16 mm, b/w, fiction, r. 45 min,
p. Argos Films (France).

Le Wazzou Polygame
1970, 16 mm, c, fiction, r. 50 min,
p. Argos Films (France).

Saitane
1972, 35 mm, c, fiction, r. 55 min,
p. Oumarou Ganda (Niger).

L'Exilé
1980, 16 mm, c, fiction, r. 90 min,
p. Oumarou Ganda/Cabas Film (Niger).

Mahamat Saleh Haroun (Chad)

Maral Tanié
1994,16 mm, c, fiction, r. 25 min,
p. Sahelis/Les Productions de la
Lanterne (Burkina Faso/France).

Goï-Goï (Le Nain)
 1995, 35 mm, c, fiction, r. 15 min,
p. Sahelis/Les Productions de la Lanterne
(Burkina Faso/France).

Bye Bye Africa
1999, 35 mm, c, fiction, r. 60 min,
p. Les Productions de la Lanterne
(France).

Abouna
2002, 35 mm, c, fiction, r. 81 min,
p. Duo Films/Goï-Goï Productions
(Chad/France)

Med Hondo (Mauritania)

Soleil O
1969, 35 mm, b/w, fiction, r. 98 min,
p. Films Soleil O (France).

Le Bicots Nègres Vos Voisins
1974, 35 mm, c, fiction, r. 190 min,
p. Films Soleil O (France).

West Indies, Les Nègres Marrons de la Liberté
1979, 35 mm, c, fiction, r. 110 min,
p. Films Soleil O/Yanek (France/
Mauritania).

Sarraounia
1986, 35 mm, c, fiction, r. 120 min,
p. Films Soleil O (France).

Lumière Noire
1992, 35 mm, c, fiction, r. 105 min,
p. M.H. Films (France).

Watani, un monde sans mal
1998, 35 mm, c, fiction, r. 78 min,
p. M.H. Films (France).

Gaston J-M Kaboré

(Burkina Faso)

Wend Kuuni (Le Don de Dieu)
1982, 35 mm, c, fiction, r. 75 min,
p. Direction du Cinéma (Burkina Faso).

Zan Boko
1988, 35 mm, c, fiction, r. 95 min,
p. Gaston Kaboré/Bras de Fer (Burkina
Faso).

Rabi
1992, 35 mm, c, fiction, r. 63 min,
p. Cinécom Production/BBC/TVE One
World Group of Broadcasters (Burkina
Faso/G.B).

Buud Yam
1997, 35 mm, c, fiction, r. 97 min,
p. Cinécom Production/Caroline
Production/France Production/Canal +
(Burkina Faso/France).

Dani Kouyaté (Burkina Faso)

Bilakoro
1989, 16 mm, c, fiction, r. 15 min,
p. Arcadia Films (France).
co-directed by Issa de Brahima Traore
and Sekou Traore.

Tobbere Kosam
1990, 16 mm, c, fiction, r. 25 min,
p. Les Productions de la
Lanterne/Tracoutra (France).
co-directed by Philippe Baque (France).

Keïta! l'Héritage du Griot
1995, 35 mm, c, fiction, r. 94 min,
p. Afix Productions/Sahélis/Les
Productions de la Lanterne (Burkina
Faso/France).

Sia, le rêve du python
2001, 35 mm, c, fiction, r. 96 min,
p. Sahélis/Les Productions de la Lanterne
(Burkina Faso/France)

Joseph Kumbela (DRC)

Perle Noire
1994, 35 mm, c, fiction, r. 27 min,
p. 17 Films Productions (Switzerland).

Taxcarte
1996, 35 mm, c, fiction, r. 8 min,
p. 17 Films Productions (Switzerland).

Feizhou Laowai (L'Etranger venu d'Afrique)
1998, 35 mm, c, fiction, r. 13 min,
p. 17 Films Productions/Les Productions
de la Lanterne (Switzerland/France).

Fadika Kramo Lancine

(Côte d'Ivoire)

Djeli (Un conte d'aujourd'hui)
1980, 16 mm, c, fiction, r. 90 min,
p. Ministère de l'Information
(Côte d'Ivoire).

Wariko (Le Gros lot)
1993, 35 mm, c, fiction, r. 95 min,
p. Kramo-Lanciné Production (Côte
d'Ivoire).

Zeka Laplaine (DRC)

Macadam Tribu
1996, 35 mm, c, fiction, r. 90 min,
p. Bakia Films/CNCP/Flamingo
Films/Animatografo
(DRC/Mali/France/Portugal).

Le Clandestin
1996, 35 mm, b/w, fiction, r. 15 min,
 p. Bakia Films/Flamingo Films
(DRC/France).

(Paris : xy)
2002, 35 mm, c and b/w, fiction, r. 80
min, p. Les Histoires Weba (France)

Gnoan Roger M'Bala
(Côte d'Ivoire)

Amanié (Quelles sont les nouvelles?)
1972, 16 mm, b/w, fiction, r. 32 min,
p. Radio Télévision Ivoirienne (Côte
d'Ivoire).

Ablakon
1984, 35 mm, c, fiction, r. 90 min,
p. Films du Koundoun (Côte d'Ivoire).

Au nom du Christ
1992, 35 mm, c, fiction, r. 90 min,
p. Abyssa Films/Amka Films Production
(Côte d'Ivoire/Switzerland).

Adanggaman
2000, 35 mm, c, fiction, r. 90 min,
p. Amka Films (Switzerland).

Bouna Medoune Seye (Senegal)

Bandit Cinéma
1993, 35 mm, c, fiction, r. 24 min,
p. Kus/La Huit Production (Senegal/
France).

Saï Saï By
1995, video, c, fiction, r. 11 min, p.
Revue Noire Production (France).

Fanta Régina Nacro
(Burkina Faso)

Un certain matin
1991, 16 mm, c, fiction, r. 16 min,
p. Les Films du Défi/Atriascop (Burkina
Faso/France).

Puuk Nini (Ouvre les yeux)
1995, 35 mm, c, fiction, r. 30 min,
p. Les Films du Défi/Atriascop (Burkina
Faso/France).

Le Truc de Konate
1997, 35 mm, c, fiction, r. 26 min,
p. Les Films du Défi/Atriascop (Burkina
Faso/France).

Bintou
2001, 35 mm, c, fiction, r. 31 min,
p. Zimmedia (South Africa).

Jean Odoutan (Benin)

Barbecu-Pejo
1999, 35 mm, c, fiction, r. 90 min,
p. 45 rdlc (France/Benin)

Djib
2000, 35 mm, c, fiction, r. 90 min,
p. 45 rdlc (France/Benin).

Mama Aloko
2002, 35 mm, c, fiction, r. 90 min,
p. 45 rdlc/Tabou-Tabac Films
(France/Benin).

Idrissa Ouedraogo
(Burkina Faso)

Yam Daabo (Le Choix)
1987, 16 mm, c, fiction, r. 80 min,
p. Films de l'Avenir (Burkina Faso).

Yaaba (Grand-mère)
1987, 35 mm, c, fiction, r. 90 min,
p. Films de l'Avenir/Thelma Film
(Burkina Faso/Switzerland).

Tilaï (Le loi)
1990, 35 mm, c, fiction, r. 81 min,
p. Les Films de l'Avenir/Waka Films
AG/Rhea Film (Burkina
Faso/Switzerland/France).

A Karim na Sala
1990, 35 mm, c, fiction, 96 min,
p. Les Films du Crépuscule/Arcadia
Films/Thelma Films/FR3/ZDF (Burkina
Faso/Switzerland/France/Germany).

Samba Traore
1993, 35 mm, c, fiction, r. 85 min,
p. Les Films de la Plaine/Waka Films
SA/Les Films de l'Avenir (Burkina
Faso/Switzerland/France).

Afrique mon Afrique
1994, 35 mm, c, fiction, r. 53 min,
p. Noé Productions/Polygram
Audiovisuel/La Sept-ARTE (France).

Cri du Coeur
1994, 35 mm, c, fiction, r. 85 min,
p. Les Films de la Plaine/Les Films de
l'Avenir/Le Centre Européen
Cinématographique Rhône-Alpes
(Burkina Faso/France).

Kini et Adams
1997, 35 mm, c, fiction, r. 93 min,
p. Les Films de la Plaine/Noé
Productions/Les Films de l'Avenir/Polar
Prod. Ltd/Framework international
(Burkina Faso/France/Zimbabwe).

Ababacar Samb Makharam
(Senegal)

Et la neige n'était plus
1965, 16 mm, b/w, fiction, 22 min,
p. Groupe Africain de Cinéma/Baobab
Films (Senegal).

Kodou
1971, 16 mm, b/w, fiction, 90 min,
p. Baobab Films (Senegal).

Jom (L'Histoire d'un Peuple)
1981, 16 mm, c, fiction, 80 min,
p. Baobab Films/ZDF Mainz
(Senegal/Germany).

Ousmane Sembene (Senegal)

Borom Sarret
1962, 16 mm, b/w, fiction, r. 22 min,
p. Filmi Domireew/Actualités Française
(Senegal/France).

Niaye
1964, 35 mm, b/w, fiction, r. 35 min,
p. Filmi Domireew/Actualités Française
(Senegal/France).

La Noire de...
1966, 35 mm, b/w, fiction, r. 65 min,
p. Filmi Domireew/Actualités Française
(Senegal/France).

Mandabi (Le Mandat)
1968, 35 mm, c, fiction, r. 90 min,
p. Filmi Domireew/Comptoir Français du
Film (Senegal/France).

Taw
1970, 16 mm, c, fiction, r. 24 min,
p. Broadcasting Film Commission
National Council of the Church of Christ
(USA).

Emitaï (Dieu du Tonnerre)
1971, 35 mm, c, fiction, r. 95 min,
p. Filmi Domireew/Myriam Smadja
(Senegal/France).

Xala
1974, 35 mm, c, fiction, r. 128 min,
p. Filmi Domireew/Société Nationale de
Cinéma (Senegal).

Ceddo
1976, 35 mm, c, fiction, r. 120 min,
p. Filmi Domireew (Senegal).

Camp de Thiaroye
1988, 35 mm, c, fiction, r. 90 min,
p. SNPC/SATPEC/ENAPROC

(Senegal/Tunisia/Algeria).
co-directed by Thierno Faty Sow.

Guelwaar
1992, 35 mm, c, fiction, r. 113 min,
p. Filmi Domireew/Galatée Films/FR3
Prod (Senegal/France).

Faat Kine
2001, 35 mm, c, fiction, r. 120 min,
p. Filmi Domireew (Senegal).

Moussa Sene Absa (Senegal)

Ken Bugal
1990, 16 mm, c, fiction, r. 80 min,
p. KUS Production/KE EMTAAN Film
(Senegal).

Yalla Yaana (Pressés de voir le Bon Dieu)
1994, 16 mm, c, fiction, r. 48 min,
p. MSA Production/INA/HBF/COE
(Senegal/France/Netherlands/Italy).

Tableau Ferraille
1997, 35 mm, c, fiction, r. 90 min,
p. ADR Productions/La Sept
Cinéma/MSA/Canal Horizons (France).

Abderrahmane Sissako
(Mauritania)

Le Jeu
1988, 35 mm, b/w, fiction, r. 23 min,
p. State Film Institute (Russia).

Octobre
1992, 35 mm, b/w, fiction, r. 38 min,
p. EJVA/La Sept/Atriascop
(Russia/France).

Sabriya
1997, 35 mm, c, fiction, r. 25 min,
p. Nomadis/SABC/ARTE (Tunisia/South
Africa/France).

Rostov-Luanda
1997, video, c, documentary, r. 60 min,
p. Movimento Productions (France).

La Vie sur Terre
1998, super-16 mm, c, fiction, r. 61
min, p. Haut et Court/C. Scotta/C.
Beno/S. Arnal/La Sept-ARTE/Pierre
Chevalier (France).

Heremakono, En attendant le bonheur
2002, 35 mm, c, fiction, r. 95 min,
p. Duo Films/ARTE-France (France)

Cheick Oumar Sissoko (Mali)

Nyamanton (La Leçon des ordures)
1986, 16 mm, c, fiction, r. 94 min,
p. CNPC (Mali).

Finzan
1989, 16 mm, c, fiction, r. 113 min, p.
Kora Films/CNPC/ZDF (Mali/Germany).

Etre jeune à Bamako
1992, video, c, documentary, r. 28 min.

Guimba, un tyran, une époque
1995, 35 mm, c, fiction, r. 94 min,
p. Kora Films/CNPC/DIPROCI/INDR
(Mali/Burkina Faso).

La Genèse
1999, 35 mm, c, fiction, r. 100 min,
p. Kora Films/CNCP/Cinéma Public Films
(Mali/France).

Battu
2000, 35 mm, c, fiction, r. 105 min,
p. Emet Films (France).

Sidney Sokhana (Mauritania)

Nationalité Immigré
1975, 16 mm, b/w, fiction, r. 85 min.

Safrana, Le Droit à la Parole
1978, 16 mm, c, fiction, r. 110 min.

Jean-Marie Teno (Cameroon)

Hommage
1985, 16 mm, c, docu-fiction, r. 13 min.

Bikutsi Water Blues
1988, 35 mm, c, docu-fiction, r. 93 min,
p. Films du Raphia (Cameroon).

Afrique, je te plumerai
1991, 16 mm, c, docu-fiction, r. 92 min,
p. Films du Raphia (France).

La Tête dans les Nuages
1994, 35 mm, c, docu-fiction, r. 35 min,
p. Films du Raphia/WDR/ARTE
(France).

Clando
1996, 35 mm, c, fiction, r. 98 min,
p. Films du Raphia/ARTE/ZDF
(France/Germany).

Chef!
1999, video, c, documentary, r. 61 min,
p. Films du Raphia (France).

Vacances au pays
2000, video and 35 mm, c, documentary, r. 75 min, p. Films du Raphia,
(France).

Drissa Touré (Burkina Faso).

Laada
1990, 35 mm, c, fiction, r. 84 min,
p. DIPROCI/Lolo Films (Burkina Faso).

Haramuya (Les Proscrits)
1995, 35 mm, c, fiction, r. 87 min,
p. Lolo Films/3B Productions (Burkina
Faso/France).

Moussa Touré (Senegal)

Toubabi
1991, 35 mm, c, fiction, r. 100 min,
p.Valprod (France).

TGV
1997, 35 mm, c, fiction, r. 90 min,
p. Flach Films/J.F. Lepetit/Les Films de la
Saga/Bernard Giraudeau/Les Films du
Crocodile/Moussa Touré
(Senegal/France).

Jacques Trabi (Côte d'Ivoire)

Bouzié (A ma mère)
1996, 35 mm, c, fiction, r. 27 min,
p. Parenthèses Films (France).

Paulin Soumarou Vieyra
(Senegal)

Afrique sur Seine
1955, 16 mm, b/w, fiction, r. 21 min,
p. Ministère de la Coopération (France).
co-directed by Mamadou Sarr and the
Groupe Africain du Cinéma

Lamb
1963, 16 mm, c, documentary, r. 18
min.

Mol
1966, 16 mm, c, fiction, r. 27 min,
p. Groupe Africain du Cinéma/Ministère
de la Coopération (Senegal/France).

L'Envers du Décor
1981, 16 mm, c, documentary, r. 25
min.

En Résidence Surveillée
1981, 16 mm, c, fiction, r. 100 min,
p. Présence Africaine (Senegal).

Mansour Sora Wade (Senegal)
Fary l'Anesse
1987, 16 mm, c, fiction, r. 20 min,
p. MPA Productions/Les Films du Baobab
(Senegal).

Taal Peex
1991, 35 mm, c, fiction, r. 26 min,
p. Ministère de la Coopération (France).

Aïda Souka
1992, 16 mm, c, fiction, r. 16 min, p.
Les Films Kaany/Sesame (Sengal/France).

Picc Mi
1992, 35 mm, c, fiction, r. 16 min,
p. Kaany Productions (Senegal).

Le Prix du pardon
2001, 35 mm, c, fiction, r. 90 min,
p. Films du Safran/Kaany Productions
(Senegal/France).

François Woukoache
(Cameroon).
Asientos
1995, 35 mm, c, docu-fiction, r. 52 min,
p. PBC. Pictures (Belgium).

Fragments de vie
2000, 35 mm, c, fiction, r. 87 min,
p. PBC Pictures/Zala'men
(Belgium/Cameroon)

Pierre Yameogo (Burkina Faso).
Laafi (Tout Va Bien)
1990, 16 mm, c, fiction, r. 98 min, p.
Les Films de l'Espoir/Thelma Film
(Burkina Faso/Switzerland).

Wendemi (L'enfant du Bon Dieu)
1992, 35 mm, c, fiction, r. 98 min,
 p. Laafi Productions/Les Films de
l'Espoir/Thelma Film (Burkina
Faso/Switzerland).

Silimande (Tourbillon)
1998, 35 mm, c, fiction, r. 85 min,
p. Afix
Productions/DIPROCI/ACCT/Thelma
Film (Burkina Faso/France/Switzerland).

Principle distribution outlets/organisations

Below are the addresses of several principal distribution outlets and/or organisations that may be useful in locating copies of Francophone African films:

British Film Institute, 21 Stephen Street, London W1P 2LN; phone: 0207 255 1444; www.bfi.org.uk

California Newsreel, 500 Third Street, Suite 500, San Francisco, CA 94107; phone: 415.284.7800; fax: 415.284.7801; www.newsreel.org; contact@newsreel.org

ADPF Cinémathèque Afrique, 6 rue Ferrus, 75683 Paris cedex 14; phone: 01 43 13 11 15; fax: 01 43 13 11 16; www.adpf.asso.fr; cinematheque@adpf.assso.fr

La Médiathèque des trois Mondes, 63 bis rue du Cardinal Lemoine, 75005 Paris; phone 01 42 34 99 00; fax: 01 42 34 99 01; www.cine3mondes.com; groupe3mondes@wanadoo.fr

La Guilde Africaine des Réalisateurs et Producteurs, www.cinemasdafrique.com

Index

Index